AF328923

NOTICE.

Of the many collections which have been offered for sale in this country of late years, none, it is believed, have presented greater attractions to the general lover of literature than the present. An examination of the following Catalogue will show that the Library formed by Mr. Holliday is distinguished for the breadth of the selection, covering the most important departments of liberal inquiry and research in Science, Philosophy, History, Biography, Criticism, and the Fine Arts. It is seldom, indeed, that a private library is got together on so comprehensive a plan. Its solid character, too, is eminently supported by the excellence of the editions, the best copies of standard authors having been procured without regard to expense. The Catalogue includes not only a great number of books of universal interest, but a variety of others in the less familiar walks of literature, which will well repay the attention of the curious collector. The main features of the Library have been, perhaps, sufficiently indicated in the enumeration on the title-page; but we may make particular reference to the specialties of several of the departments. The collection of Galleries of Engravings, and the illustrated works of the Fine Arts, will be found to include many of rare merit seldom now to be met with. There are also a number of choice selections of Extra Illustrated Works, with inserted portraits, views, etc., worthy of special attention. The illustrated works of Natural History are also of peculiar value and interest. The volumes of Autograph Manuscript of Cotton Mather, William Godwin, the novelist Cooper, the poet Halleck, and Charles Dickens, are, of course, unique. In Books relating to America, including the extraordinary collection of MS. Orderly Books of the Revolution, and the exceedingly fine copy of the Harvard "Pietas et Gratulatis;' in Privately Printed Books; in Society and Club Publications; in the higher class of Periodical Literature; in Bibliography and Literary History, the collection will be found to be particularly well furnished. In conclusion, what is of no little importance to purchasers at a distance, unable personally to examine the library, assurance may be confidently given that the books will be found in the best possible condition.

J. W. Bouton.

New York, Sept. 1st, 1870.

CATALOGUE

OF THE

EXTENSIVE AND VALUABLE

LIBRARY

FORMED BY THE

Hon. GEORGE H. HOLLIDAY,

OF

Carlinville, Ill.

LEAVITT, STREBEIGH & CO., Auctioneers,

CLINTON HALL, NEW YORK.

Monday, October 10, and following days.

NEW YORK:

THE TROW & SMITH BOOK MANUFACTURING CO.,

205 to 213 East Twelfth Street.

1870.

CATALOGUE

OF THE

Extensive and Valuable Library,

FORMED BY THE

HON. GEORGE H. HOLLIDAY,

OF CARLINVILLE, ILL.

COMPRISING THE BEST EDITIONS OF STANDARD AUTHORS IN EVERY
DEPARTMENT OF LITERATURE;

INCLUDING AN UNUSUAL ASSEMBLAGE OF

Fine-Art and Illustrated Works,

AMONGST WHICH WILL BE FOUND

KINGSBOROUGH'S MEXICAN ANTIQUITIES, *with* COLORED *plates*; AUDUBON'S BIRDS AND QUAD-
RUPEDS OF AMERICA, *folio edition*; MUSÉE FRANCAIS, 4 *vols.*; FLORENCE, PITTI, ORLEANS,
DRESDEN, MUNICH, DUSSELDORF. AGUADO, STAFFORD, ROYAL, SHAKESPEARE, AND OTHER
GALLERIES; MUSÉE NAPOLEON; GALERIE DES PEINTURES, 12 vols. 4to.; MUSEUM FLOREN-
TINUM, RAPHAEL'S LOGGIES OF THE VATICAN, *elephant fol.*; THE WORKS OF HOGARTH,
GILLRAY, OTTLEY, WYATT, OWEN JONES, STRUTT, GILPIN, HUMPHREYS, LA CROIX, LA
BARTE, &C. *Extensive series of* BIBLE PRINTS, PORTRAITS, ETCHINGS, ENGRAVINGS, &C. &C.

Original Manuscripts,

Including an unpublished MS. BY COTTON MATHER, addressed to his son, (255 pp. 8vo.);
CHARLES DICKENS' "HUNTED DOWN," FITZ-GREENE HALLECK'S "YOUNG AMERICA,"
GEORGE H. BOKER'S "PODESTA'S DAUGHTER," WM. GODWIN'S "CLOUDSLEY," A Novel,
The complete MSS.; FENIMORE COOPER'S "LIFE OF CAPT. RICHARD SOMMERS;" MARY COW-
DEN CLARKE'S "CONCORDANCE" (*a large portion of the* ORIGINAL MSS.); BERANGER'S "CHAN-
SONS," *the author's copy, with the suppressed Chansons in his autograph,* and numerous others.

Illuminated Missals on Vellum, and Specimens of Early Typography.

EXTRA ILLUSTRATED BOOKS,

Prominent among which are BRYAN'S DICTIONARY OF PAINTERS (*with* 1000 *extra plates*),
CHALMERS' BIOGRAPHICAL DICTIONARY, *upwards of* 1500 *extra plates*; CROMWELLIANA;
MATTHIAS' PURSUITS OF LITERATURE; BRAYLEY'S TOWER OF LONDON, 2 VOLS.; WAL-
POLE'S CORRESPONDENCE; PEPY'S MEMOIRS; WALTON'S LIVES; LA CROIX' ARTS OF THE
MIDDLE AGES, 2 VOLS.; KEYSLER'S TRAVELS, *extended to* 8 *vols. folio*; LIFE OF MORLAND,
&C. &C. &C.

BOOKS RELATING TO AMERICA.

AN UNRIVALLED SERIES OF

MS. ORDERLY BOOKS OF THE REVOLUTION,

THE MOST COMPLETE EVER OFFERED FOR SALE.

COMPLETE SETS OF THE PUBLICATIONS OF THE SHAKESPEARE, HAKLUYT, EARLY ENGLISH
TEXT, AND BALLAD SOCIETIES, SPALDING CLUB, &C., &C.

PUBLICATIONS OF THE ENGLISH RECORD COMMISSION.

BOOKS PRINTED ON VELLUM, SATIN, AND INDIA PAPER.

PRIVATELY PRINTED BOOKS, FROM THE STRAWBERRY-HILL, HAFOD, LEE PRIORY, *and other*
Private Presses.

Encyclopedias and Works of Reference.

PERIODICAL LITERATURE,

Including sets of the North American, Edinburgh, Quarterly, North British and Foreign Quar-
terlies, Blackwood, Dodsley's Annual Register, Niles' Register, Harper's Magazine and
Weekly, Putnam's Monthly, London Society, Anti-Jacobin and Retrospective Reviews, London Magazine, Hunt's Merchants' Magazine, Dublin University, Notes and Queries, &c., &c.
All in fine condition, including many that are bound by the best English and French binders.

The whole will be sold by Auction, Monday, October 10th, and the following days, by

LEAVITT, STREBEIGH & CO., Auctioneers,

CLINTON HALL, NEW YORK.

Sale will be commenced at 4 o'clock each day, and will be adjourned one hour for dinner.

CATALOGUE

COMPILED BY

J. W. BOUTON,

Bookseller and Importer,

706 BROADWAY,

NEW YORK.

NOTICE.

Of the many collections which have been offered for sale in this country of late years, none, it is believed, have presented greater attractions to the general lover of literature than the present. An examination of the following Catalogue will show that the Library formed by Mr. Holliday is distinguished for the breadth of the selection, covering the most important departments of liberal inquiry and research in Science, Philosophy, History, Biography, Criticism, and the Fine Arts. It is seldom, indeed, that a private library is got together on so comprehensive a plan. Its solid character, too, is eminently supported by the excellence of the editions, the best copies of standard authors having been procured without regard to expense. The Catalogue includes not only a great number of books of universal interest, but a variety of others in the less familiar walks of literature, which will well repay the attention of the curious collector. The main features of the Library have been, perhaps, sufficiently indicated in the enumeration on the title-page; but we may make particular reference to the specialties of several of the departments. The collection of Galleries of Engravings, and the illustrated works of the Fine Arts, will be found to include many of rare merit seldom now to be met with. There are also a number of choice selections of Extra Illustrated Works, with inserted portraits, views, etc., worthy of special attention. The illustrated works of Natural History are also of peculiar value and interest. The volumes of Autograph Manuscript of Cotton Mather, William Godwin, the novelist Cooper, the poet Halleck, and Charles Dickens, are, of course, unique. In Books relating to America, including the extraordinary collection of MS. Orderly Books of the Revolution, and the exceedingly fine copy of the Harvard " Pietas et Gratulatis; ' in Privately Printed Books; in Society and Club Publications; in the higher class of Periodical Literature; in Bibliography and Literary History, the collection will be found to be particularly well furnished. In conclusion, what is of no little importance to purchasers at a distance, unable personally to examine the library, assurance may be confidently given that the books will be found in the best possible condition.

J. W. Bouton.

New York, Sept. 1st, 1870.

CATALOGUE.

1 A CALL FROM DEATH TO LIFE, being An Account of the Sufferings of Marmaduke Stevenson, William Robinson and Mary Dyer, in New England, in the year 1659. *4to. hf. crim. morocco, gilt top.* *(London, 1660.)*
Reprinted, Providence, 1845.

Only 100 copies printed.

2 ACCOUNT of an EXISTING CORRESPONDENCE now carrying on between the Inhabitants of the Moon and the Natives of this Country, &c. *8vo. pp. 37, uncut.* *London, 1800, Cincinnati, 1868.*

125 copies.

3 ——— Another copy, *4to. uncut.* LARGE PAPER (*25 copies*).
Cincinnati, 1868.

4 ACKERMANN'S WESTMINSTER ABBEY; its History, Antiquities, and Monuments, *with 70 finely* COLORED *engravings from Drawings by Pugin, Mackenzie, &c.* 2 vols. impl. 4to. *hf. russia, uncut edges,* (pub. £15.) *London, 1812.*

5 ADAM, WILLIAM. An INQUIRY into the THEORIES of HISTORY, with special reference to the Principles of the Positive Philosophy. *2d Edition. 8vo. new cloth.* *London, 1864.*

6 ADAM'S RUINS OF THE PALACE OF THE EMPEROR DIOCLETIAN, at Spalatro, in Dalmatia, *with 61 fine engravings, some very large, by* BARTOLOZZI *and others, impl. folio, new hf. morocco gilt.*
London, 1764.

FINE EARLY COPY, *scarce.*
Sir G. Wilkinson in his "Dalmatia" observes, "If I have confined my description of the Palace of Spalatro to a narrower compass than the importance of that monument deserves, it is from its having been so amply described by Adam."

7 ADAMS, JOHN. The Works, with Life of the Author. Notes and Illustrations by his Grandson, Charles Francis Adams. *Portrait.* 10 *vols. imperial 8vo. new cloth, uncut.* *Boston, 1856.*
LARGE PAPER: *uniform in size with the large paper editions of Bancroft, Franklin, Washington, Webster, and Everett.*

8 ADAMSON, JOHN. MEMOIRS of the Life and Writings of LUIS DE CAMOENS. *Numerous fine portraits.* 2 vols. royal 8vo. *handsomely bound in blue morocco extra, gilt leaves.* *London, 1820.* LARGE PAPER. *Very scarce in this size.*

An elegant and elaborate performance, for which the Author was elected an honorary member of the Royal Academy of Portugal.

FINE SPECIMEN OF PRINTING ON SATIN.

9 ADDRESS of the MAGISTRATES and CITIZENS OF GÖTTINGEN to their Royal Highnesses Ernest August, Duke of Cumberland, Augustus Frederick, Duke of Sussex, and Adolph Frederick, Duke of Cambridge, on the 50th Anniversary of their matriculation at the University of Göttingen. *Bound in maroon morocco, roy. 4to.* *Göttingen, N. D.*

UNIQUE. *From the Library of the Duke of Sussex,* one of Princes addressed.

10 ADVENTURE OF THE HUNCH-BACK, and the stories connected with it, (from the Arabian Night's Entertainments.) ILLUSTRATED EDITION, *with the celebrated series of engravings by Daniell, after designs by* ROBERT SMIRKE, R. A. PROOFS ON INDIA PAPER. Atlas 4to. *russia extra.* *London,* 1814.

LARGEST PAPER.

11 ADVICE TO OFFICERS OF THE BRITISH ARMY, A Fac Simile reprint of the Sixth London Edition. With an Introduction and Notes. *8vo. new cloth, uncut.*

New York: Agathynian Club, 1867.

120 COPIES PRINTED. "Written in imitation of Swift's ' Advice to Servants,' perhaps by Captain Grose."

12 ———— Another copy. *Roy. 8vo. maroon morocco, extra, gilt top, uncut.* *New York,* 1867.

ONE OF 5 COPIES *on Drawing Paper.*

13 𝕬𝕰𝕹𝕰𝕬𝕾 𝕾𝕴𝕷𝕭𝕴𝕾. (𝕻𝖎𝖈𝖈𝖔𝖑𝖔𝖒𝖎𝖓𝖎). 𝕰𝖕𝖎𝖘𝖙𝖔𝖑𝖆 𝕰𝖓𝖊𝖊 𝕾𝖎𝖑𝖓𝖎𝖎 𝖕𝖔𝖊𝖙𝖊 𝖑𝖆𝖚𝖗𝖊𝖆𝖙𝖎. (sive Pii Pape secūdi, &c.) Colophon.—Pii ii pontificis maximi cui ante summum episcopatus primum quidem imperiali secretario; tandem epō ēinde cardinali senen. Eneas silius nomen erat. familiares epistolæ ad diversos, &c., &c. *Impensis* ANTHONII KOBERGER nuremberge impresse, finuit xvi. klo augusti Anno salutis Christiane, &c. *MCCCCLXXXVI,* 1486.

Small 4to. printed in an early German character, original oak boards, backed with hogskin.

A fine specimen from the press of Anthony Koberger, printer of the celebrated "Nuremberg Chronicle," 1492.

14 ÆSOP'S FABLES. PHÆDRI, AUG. LIBERTI FABULARUM ÆSOPIARUM Librum V. notis illustrairt in usum serenissimi principis Nassauü. *Numerous beautiful vignettes on copper and full-page plates, comprising many examples, by* DAVID HOOGSTRATANUS. 4to. fine copy, hf. morocco extra. *Amsterdam,* 1701.

"Edition fort soignee sous le rapport de la metrique est contenant un bon choix de notes, mais de que la reccommande particulierement, ce sont les belles gravures dont il est ornée."—BRUNET.

15 ÆSOP'S FABLES, with Life of the Author. *One hundred and eleven fine engravings on wood from designs by* HERRICK. *Post 8vo. hf. rox. mor. uncut.* *Riverside Edn., New York,* 1865.

15* AGASSIZ, LOUIS. CONTRIBUTIONS TO THE NATURAL HISTORY OF THE UNITED STATES OF AMERICA, comprising, 1ST MONOGRAPH, I. Essay on Classification. II. North American Testudinata. III. Embryology of the Turtle, *with* 34 *plates, some colored.* 2D MONOGRAPH, I. Acalephs in General.

II. Ctenophoræ. III. Discophoræ. IV. Hydroidæ. V. Homologies of the Radiata, *with 46 plates; together 4 vols. roy. 4to. cloth.* *Boston*, 1860.

Published by subscription, *scarce*.

16 Agassiz, Louis. The Structure of Animal Life. Six lectures delivered at the Brooklyn Academy of Music in January and February, 1862. *Illustrations, 8vo. new cloth.*
New York, 1866.

17 Agassiz, L. Geological Sketches, *portrait, 12mo. new cloth.*
Boston, 1866.

18 AGRIPPA, Henrie Cornelius. Of the Vanitie and Uncertaintie of Artes and Sciences; Englished by Ja(mes) San(ford) Gent. 𝕭𝕷𝕬𝕮𝕶 𝕷𝕰𝕿𝕿𝕰𝕽. 12mo. (4to.) *hf. morocco*, (margins very closely trimmed.) Imprinted at London, by *Henrie Bynnemann*. Anno 1575.

See an interesting article on this work in the Retrospective Review, Vol. XIV. pp. 181–246.

19 Aiken, Lucy. Memoirs of the Court of King Charles I. 2 vols., 8vo. boards, *uncut*. *London*, 1833.

20 Ainsworth, W. Harrison. Novels and Romances. *New Edition.* 8 vols. thick 12mo. *new cloth*. *London*, 1867.

21 A Kempis. De Imitatione Christi. Libri quatuor. Elegantly printed with ornamental borders, in imitation of the early books of Hours, with Initial Letters, &c. 12mo. *vellum cloth, gilt*.
London, 1867.

22 Albin, Eleazer. History of Esculent Fish, and an Essay on Breeding of Fish, and Construction of Fish-Ponds, by the Hon. Roger North, *with a fine series of plates colored by the Author*. Roy. 4to. *hf. cf. extra*. *London*, 1794.

An Interesting Volume. Inserted in the present copy are the exquisite series of plates of fish, by Wood, *colored*, and an original drawing in water-colors, and in pencil, also numerous fine old views, &c.

23 Alcock, Sir R. The Capital of the Tycoon. A narrative of three years' residence in Japan. *Maps and Illustrations*, 2 vols. post 8vo. *new hf. cf. neat*. *New York*, 1863.

24 Aleman, Life and Adventures *of Guzman D'Alfrache*, or, the Spanish Rogue, translated from the French version of Le Sage by Jno. Henry Brady. 3 vols. post 8vo. hf. mor. *uncut. Best English Edition.* *London*, 1823.

25 Alexander, Dr. History of Women among all Nations, from the Earliest Antiquity, 2 vols. 4to. *calf, neat.* *London*, 1779.

26 Alison, Archibald. Essays on the Nature and Principles of Taste. 2 *vols. 8vo. hf. red morocco.* *Edinburgh*, 1811.

27 ALISON, ARCHIBALD. HISTORY OF EUROPE. Both Series *complete*, with Atlas. Large Type, Library Edition. 24 vols. 8vo. and oblong 4to. *uniformly bound in new hf. calf extra, marbled edges.* *Edinburgh*, 1860, &c.

Fine Copy.

28 Alison, Archibald. History of Europe. Both Series. 8 *vols. roy. 8vo. hf. cf. antique.* *New York*, 1860.

29 ALTAR SERVICE BOOKS of the Church of England.
Elegantly Printed on ribbed paper, by Whittingham, in red and black, with woodcut Initials, Rubrics and Music; in the same style as Pickering's splendid reprint of the folio Prayer Books, comprising Altar Service Book, folio, Book of the Gospels, 4*to. and Book of the Epistles, 2 vols. 4to. and 1 vol. folio, red morocco.* London, 1867.

These sumptuous volumes were edited by Dr. Lee, author of the " Directorum Anglicanum."
*** Each volume of the above set is bound in a different style ; the Altar Service in heavy gros-grained levant, with heavy brass corners, in which are inserted marbles, serving as bosses, and a very heavy cross in the centre field. The 4to. volumes are ornamented with elaborate tooling of a Grolier pattern, with broad inside borders, &c.
This fine set was imported by the owner at a cost of £18. 18s.

30 Allan, George. Life of Sir Walter Scott, with critical notices of his writings. 8*vo. hf. mor.* *Philadelphia*, 1835.

31 Allan, John. A Catalogue of the Books, Autographs, Engravings, Coins, and Medals, Articles of Vertu, and Miscellaneous Articles belonging to the Estate of the late John Allan. *Portrait. Imperial 8vo. boards, uncut.* *New York*, 1864.
Large Paper : *only* 100 *copies printed.*

32 Allan, John. Memorial of, by E. A. Duyckinck. *India Proof Portrait. Impl. 8vo. uncut.* *Bradford Club, New York,* 1864.

33 Amadis of Gaul, by Vasco Lobeira; from the Spanish version of Garciordonez de Montalvo, translated by Robert Southey. 4 *vols.* 12*mo. new hf. cf. extra. Very scarce.* London, 1803.
The best translation.

34 Ambrose, D. L. History of the Seventh Regiment of Illinois Volunteer Infantry, 1861–'65. 12*mo. cloth.*
Springfield, Ill., 1868.

35 America. The Substance of a Council held at Lancaster, August the 28th, 1764, by a committee of Presbyterian ministers, deputed from all parts of Pennsylvania, &c., &c.

> When Gospel Trumpeter surrounded
> With long-ear'd rout, to Battle sounded,
> And pulpit Drum ecclesiastic,
> Was beat by Fist instead of a Stick,
> Such Priests deserve to have their A—s kick'd.

12mo. pp. 19, *hf. cf. neat.* Printed in the year 1764.

36 America. The Annual Register of the Baptist Denomination in North America, to Nov. 1st, 1790, containing an account of their churches, constitutions, ministers, members, associations, &c., by John Asplund. 4to. (pp. 70), *hf. mor. totally uncut.*
S. L. et A. (1791).

37 AMERICA. Siege of Penobscot by the Rebels; containing a Journal of the Proceedings of his majestie's forces under Brig. Gen. Francis McLean and three of his majesty's sloops of war, when beseiged by Three Thousand Rebel land forces under command of Brig. Gen. Solomon Lovell, with an Appendix, &c., by J. C., Esq., a Volunteer. *Very large folding chart, 8vo.* pp. 44, *hf. morocco, edges untrimmed.* London, 1781.
Very Scarce.

38 AMERICAN HISTORICAL AND LITERARY CURIOSITIES. Containing Fac-similes of some Plates, &c., relating to Columbus, and Original Documents of the Revolution, &c., &c. Edited and arranged by John Jay Smith. *First Series. Roy. 4to, cloth.*
Philadelphia, 1861.

39 AMERICAN INSTRUCTOR; or YOUNG MAN'S BEST COMPANION, to which is added The Poor Planters' Physician, also advice to Young Tradesmen and Dealers, by George Fisher. 12mo. old cf.
Philadelphia; Printed by B. FRANKLIN and D. Hall, 1748.

40 AMERICAN STATE PAPERS. Documents, Legislative and Executive, of the Congress of the United States, from 1789 to 1833. Selected and Edited, under the Authority of Congress, by Walter Lowrie and M. S. Clarke. 21 vols. fol. hf. russ.
Wash. 1833–4.

41 AMES'S TYPOGRAPHICAL ANTIQUITIES, or History of Printing in Great Britain and Ireland, with Memoirs of Printers, and Register of Books, enlarged by HERBERT, *portraits and engravings,* 3 vols. 4to. *hf. morocco, gilt tops.* London, 1785–90.
" A very valuable and accurate work."—CLARKE.

42 AMOS, ANDREW. The OYER OF POISONING; the Trial of the Earl of Somerset for the poisoning of Sir Thomas Overbury, in the Tower of London. *Portrait. 8vo. hf. cf. extra.* London, 1846.

43 ANACREONTIS ODARIA, ad textus barnesiani fidem emendata; accedunt Variæ lectionis cura Evardi Forster. *Elegant edition, with charming vignettes in Stothard's manner,* 12mo. *hf. olive morocco.* Londini. 1812

44 ANALYSIS OF THE HUNTING FIELD; being a Series of Sk principal characters that compose one. The whole forming a slight souvenir of the season of 1845–46. *Frontispiece and six* LARGE COLORED PLATES, by H. ALKEN, also, *numerous wood cuts.* 8vo. *new cloth, uncut.* London, 1846.

45 ANCIENT AND MODERN UNIVERSAL HISTORY. *Second edition.* From the earliest account of Time. Complete, (Ancient, 18 vols.— Modern, 42 vols.), *numerous engravings and maps.* 60 *vols.* 8vo. old cf. neat. London, 1779—84.
" I generally consult the Universal History, a work of great merit, and perhaps not sufficiently valued."—*Butler's Horæ Biblicæ.*

46 ANDERSEN, HANS CHRISTIAN. DANISH FAIRY LEGENDS AND TALES. Translated, with a Memoir of the Author. *Upwards of 100 engravings. 2d edition,* 12mo. calf extra. London, 1861.

47 ANDERSSON, CHAS. J. The Okavango River; a narrative of Travel, Exploration and Adventure, *portrait, &c.* 8vo. *cloth.*
New York, 1861.

48 ANDERSON, WILLIAM. THE SCOTTISH NATION; or the Surnames Families, Literature, Honors, and Biographical History of the People of Scotland. *Profusely Illustrated with 25 large and finely engraved portraits on steel, Genealogical tables, and several hundred engravings on wood. 3 thick vols. imp. 8vo. new hf. morocco, gilt edges.* *Edinburgh,* 1866.

49 ANDRÉ, MAJ. Minutes of a Court of Inquiry, upon the case of Major John André, with Accompanying Documents, and An Appendix containing copies of the papers found upon Major André when arrested. *Fine portrait. 4to. boards, uncut.*
Munsell, Albany, 1865.

LARGE PAPER, only 10 *copies.*

50 ANDRÉANA : Containing the Trial, Execution and Various matters connected with the History of Major John André, Adjutant General of the British Army in America, 1780. *With 12 fine portraits, &c., folio, cloth, uncut.* *Philadelphia*, 1865.
LARGEST PAPER.

51 ANDRÉ. Vindication of the Capture of Major André, by Egbert Benson. *Royal 8vo. new hf. morocco, uncut.* *New York*, 1865.
Only 60 *copies.*

52 ANDRÉ, MAJOR. Vindication of the Capture of, by Egbert Benson. Impl. 8vo. *uncut.* *New York*, 1817, *reprinted* 1865.
LARGE PAPER, 50 *copies.* Sabin's Reprints, No. 3.

ANGERSTEIN GALLERY. See Gallery.

53 ANGLER, THE. A POEM. By PISCATOR [T. P. Lathy], with proper instructions in the Art, rules to choose Fishing Rods, Lines, Hooks, &c., and to make Artificial Flies, &c. &c. *Frontispiece by Scott.* ARTIST PROOF, *and numerous vignettes on wood by Nesbitt.* Small 4to. *maroon morocco, gilt, the sides emblematically embossed, gilt edges.* *London*, 1819.
LARGE AND THICK PAPER, *only* 20 *copies printed.*

54 ANGLING. Maxims and Hints to Anglers, *with humorous engravings.* 16mo. *new cloth.* *Philadelphia*, 1855.

OF THE ARMY OF THE CUMBERLAND : comprising Biographical Sketches, Description of Departments, Accounts of Expeditions, Battles, &c. &c. By an Officer. *Portraits, Maps, and woodcuts.* 8vo. *new cloth.* *Philadelphia*, 1863.

56 ANNUAL REGISTER, or View of History, Politics and Literature, from its commencement in 1758 to 1852. Vols. I-XCIV, with the General Index. Annual Register, 1853-1861, being Vols. XCV-CIII, 9 vols. in boards—together 105 vols. 8vo. polished calf, extra, and *vols. uncut.* *London*, 1758–62.
A SUPERB COPY *from the Library of Baron Dimsdale.*
Entirely of the genuine edition, and having the scarce General Index published in 1826, thus forming a most desirable set.
This valuable publication originated with Robert Dodsley, at the suggestion of Edmund Burke, who for some years was the principal contributor. It contains many most powerful and valuable articles from his pen ; and forms our most valuable record of historical and political events during the last hundred years.
An inferior set is priced by a Boston firm at $550.

57 ANNUAL OF SCIENTIFIC DISCOVERY, complete from its commencement in 1851 to and including the vol. for 1868. *Fine portraits, &c.* 18 vols. post 8vo. *new cloth.* *Boston*, 1851–69.

58 ANSTED, DAVID T. PHYSICAL GEOGRAPHY. 3d Edition, revised and enlarged. Thick 12mo. *new cloth.* *London*, 1868.

59 ANTHON, CHARLES. Dictionary of Greek and Roman Antiquities (Smith's Dic.). Thick impl. 8vo. *sheep.* *New York*, 1845.

60 Anthon, Charles. Classical Dictionary, containing an account of
the principal Proper Names mentioned in Ancient Authors.
Thick royal 8vo. sheep. *New York*, 1848.

61 ANTE-NICENE CHRISTIAN LIBRARY. A collection of all
the works of the Fathers of the Christian Church, prior to
the Council of Nicæa. Edited by the Rev. Alexander Roberts
and James Donaldson. Together 15 vols. 8vo. *new cloth, red
edges.* *Edinburgh*, 1867, &c.
Comprising: Clement of Alexandria, 2 vols.; Cyprian, 2 vols.; Irenæus and
Hippolytus, 4 vols. in 3; Justin Martyr and Athenagoras, 1 vol.; Tertullian
against Marcion, 1 vol.; Methodius, 1 vol.; Tatian, Theophilus and Clemen-
tine Recognitions, 1 vol.; Apostolic Fathers, 1 vol.; Tertullian, 1 vol.; and
Origen, 1 vol.

62 Anthropological Society. Memoirs Read before the Society, 1863,
'64, '65, & '66, 2 vols.; Waitz, Introduction to Anthropo-
logy, 1 vol.; Broca, on the Phenomena of Hybridity, 1 vol.;
Pouchet, Plurality of the Human Race, 1 vol.; Gastaldi,
Lake Inhabitants and Pre-Historic Remains, &c., 1 vol.;
Lectures on Man; his Place in Creation, by Dr. Vogt, 1 vol.;
Blumenbach's Anthropological Treatises, 1 vol. *Together
8 vols. 8vo. new cloth. Numerous Illus.* *London*, 1863–66.

63 ANTI-JACOBIN REVIEW and Magazine; or Monthly Political
and Literary Censor. From its commencement in July 1798
to and including Vol. 55 (for 1819), (except Vol. 54); the first
10 *volumes contain numerous large folding caricatures, by Gillray, Rowlandson, &c. Together 54 vols. 8vo. uniformly bound
in hf. cf., neat.* *London*, 1798–1819.
Complete sets are of rare occurrence.
Among the contributors to the earlier volumes were Gifford, Frere and Canning.

64 Antiquarian Repertory, by Grose, Astle, and other eminent Antiquaries, *with upwards of 200 fine and scarce portraits and engravings.* 4 vols. 4to. *bright calf, gilt.* *London*, 1798.
A most interesting assemblage of Topography, History, Biography, Customs,
and Manners, intended to illustrate and preserve several valuable Remains of
Old Times.

65 Antiquarian and Topographical Cabinet, *with upwards of 500
elegant engravings,* proofs. 6 vols. royal 8vo. *newly bound, hf.
russia, extra, fine copy.* *London*, 1817.
Large Paper.
This is one of the very few copies printed entirely on plate paper, *on one side
only,* with the engravings placed on the top of the pages.

66 ANTIQUITIES of ATHENS, (STUART and REVETT.) *The
Original splendid Edition, with fine impressions of the numerous large
and beautiful engravings,* with the Supplement. 5 vols. impl. folio,
new hf. russia gilt, 5th vol. in sheets folded. *London*, 1762–1830.
This fine and complete copy contains the supplement on the Antiquities of
Athens, Greece, Sicily, &c. by Cockerell, Kinnard, Donaldson, &c.

67 Antiquités D'Herculanum, ou les plus belles Peintures Antiques
et les Marbres, Bronzes, Meubles, &c. &c., trouvés dans les
excavations d'Herculanum, Stabia, et Pompeia. Gravée par F.
A. David, avec leur explications par Maréchal, *several hundred
fine engravings on copper, comprising several thousand examples.* 11
vols. 8vo. calf, neat. *Paris*, 1781, &c.

68 Aphrodisiacs and Anti-Aphrodisiacs. Three Essays on the Powers of Reproduction; with some account of the Judicial "Congress" as practised in France during the Seventeenth Century. By John Davenport. With eight full-page illustrations. Small 4to. half morocco, gilt top. *London*, 1869.

Beautifully printed on toned paper, *and Only One Hundred Copies,* for private distribution.

"The reproductive powers of Nature were regarded by the Nations of remote antiquity with an awe and reverence so great, as to form an object of worship, under a symbol of all others the most significant,—the *Phallus;* and thus was founded a religion, of which traces exist to this day not in Asia alone, but even in Europe itself."

69 Apocryphal New Testament, being all the Gospels, Epistles, and other pieces now extant, attributed to Jesus Christ, his Apostles, and their companions, and not included in the New Testament. *8vo. new cloth, uncut.* *London*, 1820.

70 Appeal to the Public on behalf of Cameria. (1781). 4to, uncut. *Cincinnati*, 1868.

Large Paper, 25 Copies.

71 ———— Another copy. 8vo. uncut. *Cincinnati*, 1868.

72 (Apperley, Chas. James.) "Nimrod" Hunting Reminiscences; comprising Memoirs of Masters of Hounds; notices of Crack Riders, &c. *Numerous fine plates by Wildrake, Henderson, and Alken. Impl. 8vo. new cloth.* *London*, 1843.

73 𝕬𝖕𝖚𝖑𝖊𝖎𝖎 𝕷𝖚𝖈𝖎𝖎. 𝕻𝖍𝖎𝖑𝖔𝖘𝖔𝖕𝖍𝖎 𝕻𝖑𝖆𝖙𝖔𝖓𝖎𝖈𝖎. 𝕸𝖊𝖙𝖆𝖒𝖔𝖗𝖕𝖍𝖔𝖘𝖊𝖔𝖘 𝖘𝖎𝖛𝖊 𝕬𝖘𝖎𝖓𝖔 𝕬𝖚𝖗𝖊𝖔. *A beautiful copy, with Illuminated Initial Letters, and a charming vignette in colors at the end. Folio, handsomely bound in blue crimped morocco, embossed sides, gilt edges.* Vicentia, per Henricum de Sacto Urso, 1488.

Scarce. A very fine copy from the Library of the Duke of Sussex, with his book plate.

74 ARABIAN NIGHTS' ENTERTAINMENTS. Knight's Pictorial Edition. Translated with Copious Notes by E. W. Lane. Many hundred beautiful engravings by Williams, Jackson, Landells, etc. From designs by William Harvey. *3 vols. royal 8vo. beautifully bound in dark green levant morocco, super-extra, gilt leaves, etc.* C. Knight, *London*, 1841.

A Fine Copy. *With the most brilliant impressions of the cuts.*

"The Notes of Mr. Lane throw more light upon the mystery of Arab Life than perhaps all other works in the language."—Athenæum.

75 ARBER, Edward. EARLY ENGLISH REPRINTS, carefully edited with Prefaces, Notes, &c., by Edward Arber, *handsomely printed on toned paper. 12 vols. small 4to. uncut.*

Large Paper. *Complete as far as published.* *London*, 1869–70.

1. John Milton, Areopagitica. 1644. 2. Bishop Latimer, the Ploughers. 1549. 3. Gosson's Schoole of Abuse. 1579. 4. Sir P. Sidney. Apologie for Poetrie. 1595. 5. Edw. Webbe's Wonderful Trauailles. 1590. 6. Seldon's Table Talk. 1689. 7. Roger Ascham's Toxophilus. 1545. 8. Addison's Criticism on Paradise Lost. 1711. 9. Euphues, by John Lyly. 1597. 10. Buckingham, The Rehearsal. 1671. 11. Earle, Microcosmogony. 1628. 12. Gascoigne, The Steele Glass, &c.

76 Archæologia Americana. Transactions, Collections and Catalogue of the Library of the American Antiquarian Society. 5 vols. 8vo. *sheets folded.* Engravings and Maps. 1820–1860.

*** The Rice copy brought $21 00.

77 ARCHÆOLOGY. INTERNATIONAL CONGRESS OF PREHISTORIC ARCHÆ-
OLOGY. Transactions of the 2d Session held in London,
August 1868. Roy. 8vo. *new cloth, uncut.* *London*, 1869.

78 ARCHAICA AND HELICONIA, containing REPRINTS OF RARE OLD
ENGLISH PIECES OF PROSE and POETRY, edited by Park, Sir
Egerton Brydges, and Haselwood. 5 vols. roy. 4to. *elegantly
bound in green crushed levant morocco, super-extra, gilt edges.*
London, 1814–15.

BEAUTIFUL COPY. *Only 250 copies printed.* (Pub. at £25 3s. unbound.)

Contents. ARCHAICA, Vol I. Greene's Philomela; Greene's Arcadia;
Southwell's Triumph over Death; Breton's Characters, and his Good and the
Bad; Nash's Christ's Tears over Jerusalem.

Vol. II. Harvey's Four Letters and Sonnets touching R. Greene; Harvey's
Pierce's Supererogation; Harvey's New Letter of Notable Contents; Braithwaite's Essays upon the Five Senses.

HELICONIA, Vol. I. Breton's Small Handful of Fragrant Flowers; Proctor's
Gorgeous Gallery of Gallant Inventions; Breton's Flourish upon Fancie.

Vol. II. Handefull of Pleasant Delites, edited by C. Robinson; Whitstone's
Life and Death of Francis, Earle of Bedford; Phœnix Nest, edited by R. S.;
Barnes' Spirituall Sonnets; Spirituall Sonnets, by H. C.; Churchyard's
Funeral of Sir F. Knowles; Storer's Life and Death of Cardinal Wolsey.

Vol. III. England's Parnassus's, edited by Robert Abbott; Churchyard's
Goodwill; Sad and Heavy Verses for the Loss of Archbishop Whitgift, by
Churchyard.

79 ARGYLL, DUKE OF. Primeval Man. An examination of some recent
speculations. *Front. 12mo. new cloth.* 1869.

80 ARIOSTO, LUDOVICO. ORLANDO FURIOSO; translated from the Italian,
with notes, &c. by John Hoole. *Illustrated with a fine series of
engravings on copper, also an additional series from an Italian
Edition. 5 vols. 8vo. new hf. cf. extra, marbled edges.*
London, 1799.

FINE COPY.

81 ARIOSTO. Orlando Furioso, BASKERVILLE'S BEAUTIFUL EDITION, *printed
with large type, with* 48 *engravings by Bartolozzi, &c. from the
designs by Cipriani.* 4 vols. royal 8vo. *red morocco extra, gilt
leaves, fine copy, bound by Walther.* *Birm.* 1773.

ELEGANT COPY, SCARCE.

One of the most elegantly printed books issued from the Press of the
famous Baskerville.

82 ARIOSTO'S ORLANDO FURIOSO, translated into English verse by W.
Stewart Rose, 8 vols. post 8vo. *new cloth.* *London,* 1823–31.

"Never was such a close, scrupulous fidelity of rendering associated with
such light-dancing elegance of language. This indeed will be an addition to
the Standard Literature of our country, and will rank with Dryden's Virgil,
Pope's Homer, and Cary's Dante."—BLACKWOOD.

83 ARIOSTO (PANIZZI A.) BIBLIOGRAPHICAL NOTICES of some early
editions of the Orlando Inamorato and Furioso. *Portrait on India
paper. 12mo. bds. uncut.* *Pickering, London,* 1831.

VERY SCARCE.

ONLY 24 COPIES PRINTED. Presentation copy to Mr. Foss, (Payne & Foss),
by Mr. Panizzi.

84 ARISTOTLE. Dissertation on the Philosophy of Aristotle, in four
books, by THOMAS TAYLOR. *Roy. 4to. hf. vellum, gilt top.*
For the Author, London, 1812.

85 ARISTOTLE. METAPHYSICS, translated from the Greek, with copious

notes, to which is added a Dissertation on Nulities and Diverg-ing Series, by Thomas Taylor. *Roy. 4to. hf. vellum, gilt top.*
For the Author, London, 1801.

86 Aristotle. Organon; or, Logical Treatises, translated from the Greek, with copious notes by Thomas Taylor. *Roy. 4to. hf. vellum, gilt top.* *For the Author, London, 1807.*

87 Aristotle. Commentary, Illustrating the Poetic of Aristotle, to which is prefixed a new translation of the Poetic, by Henry James Pye. *Roy. 4to. hf. vellum, gilt top.* *London, 1792.*

The above four lots are uniformly bound.

88 Armin, Robert. The Italian Taylor and his Boy. *Curious wood-cuts, 4to. hf. cf.* *London, 1609, (1810).*

A reprint in facsimile, *only* 100 *copies.*

89 Army Lists of the Roundheads and Cavaliers in the Civil War: Giving the names of all the Officers in the Royal and Parliamentary Armies of 1642. Reprinted from the compara-tively unknown originals. Edited with notes by Edward Peacock. *Beautifully printed by Whittingham. Small 4to. half morocco, uncut.* *London, 1863.*

These most curious *Lists* show on which side the gentlemen of England were to be found during the great conflict between the King and the Parliament. As illustrations of County History, they are exceedingly interesting. The literary antiquary and the genealogist will find much new and out-of-the-way matter in them; and there are but few families in England who cannot claim a relationship to one or other of the names mentioned in the Royalist or Round-head list. Only a very few copies reprinted.

90 Arnasson, Jón. Icelandic Legends, translated by George E. J. Powell. *Profusely illustrated. Crown 8vo. new cloth.*
London, 1864.

91 Arnaud, Henri. The Glorious Recovery of the Vaudois of their Valleys, translated, with a compendious History of that people, previous and subsequent to that event. *Map, and numerous beautiful engravings on steel, by E. Finden. 8vo. mottled calf, extra, yellow edges.* *London, 1828.*

92 Arnold, Matthew. Popular Education in France, with notices of that of Holland and Switzerland. *8vo. new cloth.*
London, 1861.

93 Arnold. Proceedings of a General Court Martial for the Trial of Major General Arnold, with an Introduction, Notes and Index. *Portrait on India paper. 4to. uncut.* *New York, 1865.*

Large Paper Copy; *privately printed; scarce. Thirty-five copies printed in this size.*

94 ARNOLD, Dr. T. (*of Rugby.*) WORKS, the best large type library editions. Comprises: History of Rome, *both series,* the Early History, and the later Commonwealth, 5 vols. Lectures on Modern History. Sermons, 3 vols. Interpretation of Scripture, Christian Life, 2 vols. The Church. Life and Correspond-ence by A. P. Stanley. Miscellaneous Works. 16 vols. *8vo. new tree calf, super-extra, fine uniform set.*
London, 1840, &c.

A Superb Copy.

95 Art of Real Pleasure. That new pleasure, for which an imperial reward was offered. *Vignettes*, 16mo. *cloth.*
Blanchard, New York, 1864.

96 Arthur of Little Britain. History of that Valiant Knight Arthur of Little Britain. A Romance of Chivalry. Translated by Lord Berners. *With a series of plates in fac-simile of illuminated drawings from an ancient MS.* 4to. *new hf. calf, gilt.* *Reprinted, London,* 1814.
Only 175 copies printed. *Scarce.*
The work was edited from the extremely rare original edition by E. V. Utterson, who uses extraordinary diligence in tracing out the name of the original writer of the Romance, the time of its composition, and other much-wished-ed for particulars.

97 Arundel, Thomas. Reminiscences of the City of London and its Livery Companies. Thick 8vo. *new cloth, uncut.*
London, 1869.

98 ARUNDEL SOCIETY. Maynard, F. W. Descriptive Notice of the Drawings and Publications of the Arundel Society from 1849 to 1868 inclusive. *Illustrated by Photographs (nearly 500) of all the Publications, one fifth their original size, arranged in the order of their issue,* with descriptive text; *folio, new cloth, gilt.* *London,* 1869.

An Elegant Volume.

99 Ascham, Roger. English Works. *Post 8vo. morocco, antique, gilt edges. Very scarce.* *London,* 1815.
Only 250 Copies Printed.
In this edition, there are some additional letters of Ascham from the originals in the British Museum.
"As only 250 copies were printed, I conjure the young philological enthusiast to leave neither shop nor stall unvisited until he procures it."—*Dibdin.*

100 Ascham, Roger. Whole Works, with life by the Rev. Dr. Gilles. 4 vols. *post 8vo. new cloth.*
Large Paper. *Russell Smith, London,* 1865.

101 ASIATIC RESEARCHES; or, Transactions of the Society Instituted in Bengal for inquiring into the History and Antiquities, the Arts, Sciences, and Literature of Asia. *English Reprint.* 1806—11. 10 *vols. 8vo. cf. neat.*
London, 1806—11.
Contains the Learned Essays by Colebrook, Sir William Jones, Carey, Strachey, Dr. Walich, &c.
"They are full of the most curious and valuable intelligence in every possible form and on every possible subject."—*Dibdin.*

102 Astrology. The Spirit of Partridge; or, the Astrologer's Pocket Companion, and General Magazine, &c. &c. *Post 8vo. boards, uncut.* *London Astrological Society,* 1825.

103 Atkinson, Thomas W. Oriental and Western Siberia, a Narrative of seven years' Explorations and Adventures in Siberia, Mongolia, Chinese Tartary, &c. *Illustrated. Post 8vo. cloth.*
Philadelphia, 1859.

104 Aubrey, John. Letters Written by Eminent Persons in the XVIIth and XVIIIth centuries; to which are added, Hearne

Journeys to Reading and to Whaddon Hall; also lives of
Eminent Men. 3 *vols. 8vo. hf. cf. neat.* *London,* 1813.
Robert Southey's copy with his autograph on the title.

This work contains the only edition of John Aubrey's "Lives of Eminent
Men" of the Elizabethan Era, so constantly quoted in illustration of the
Literature of the time. See vol. 2, p. 197.

105 AUDUBON, J. J. BIRDS OF AMERICA. 100 of these
Magnificent Colored Engravings, *executed on the largest
scale, giving the Birds in their* FULL NATURAL SIZE, *and in most
instances the male and female birds, their young, prey, nests, &c.,*
with descriptive text, revised by J. W. Audubon. 7 *vols. in 5
impl. 8vo. and one vol. elephant folio, neatly and substantially
bound in half russia, gilt.* *New York,* 1858.
Without exception the finest series of ornithological plates ever published.

106 AUDUBON AND BACHMAN'S VIVIPAROUS QUADRU-
PEDS of North America complete, *with* 150 VERY LARGE AND
MOST BEAUTIFULLY COLORED ENGRAVINGS of Quadrupeds, chiefly
of their *full natural sizes,* 2 *vols. imperial folio and descriptive
text, in* 3 *vols. impl. 8vo. uniformly bound in new hf. russia extra.*
New York, 1845–8.

One of the most magnificent works on Natural History ever published, the
very large and beautiful engravings exhibiting in most instances two or more
figures (male and female) in the most life-like attitudes, with their Young,
Prey, &c., the entire plate colored with views of their favorite haunts and
localities.

107 AUGUSTINE. DE CIVITATE DEI. Printed by Nicholas
Jenson. Folio, vellum, gilt, *fine perfect copy.*

𝕬urelii 𝕬ugustinii opus de civitate dei feliciter explicit; confectu3 venetiis ab egregio deligeti magis-
tro Nicolao ienson: Petro mo3enicho principe; 𝕬nno
a natiuctate domine milesimo quadringetesimo sep-
tuagesimo quinto; sexto nonas octobres.
Venice, 1475.

A BEAUTIFUL SPECIMEN in the small gothic type of Jenson, double columns,
without numerals, signatures, or catchwords.

108 Ausonius. D. Ausonii Peonii Burdegalensis Poetæ: Opera dili-
gentius iterū castigata, and in meliorem ordinē per quinqe Tomos restituta. *Printer's device representing the printing press,
compositors, &c., and numerous beautiful initial letters.* 8vo.
calf, gilt.
Impressus in chalcographia Ascencsiana ad eidus, Julias, Anno
MDXVII.

109 Austin, John. Lectures on Jurisprudence; or, the Philosophy of
Positive Law. Edited by Robert Campbell. 2 *vols. thick 8vo.
new cloth.* *London,* 1869.

110 AYA SOFIA. Constantinople, as recently restored by the Sultan
Abdul Medid. From the original drawings by Chevalier Gaspard Fossati. Lithographed by Louis Haghe. 25 *large and
beautifully executed plates in chromo-lithography, tinted to resemble water-color drawings. Impl. folio, hf. mor. neat.*
Colnaghi, London, 1852.

111 AYRES, PHILIP. EMBLEMATA AMATORIA. Emblems of Love in four Languages, (Latin, English, Italian, and French). *Dedicated to the Ladys.* 44 *fine copperplates, engraved by Nicholls.* 12mo. new crimson morocco, gilt edges, *fine copy.*
London, 1683.

112 BACON, FRANCIS. WORKS, Collected and Edited by James Spedding, Robert Leslie Ellis, and Douglas Denon Heath, with PERSONAL HISTORY. *Portraits on India paper. The Arms of Bacon in gold and colors on each title.* 16 *vols.* 8vo. *Half morocco, extra, uncut, by Matthews.*
LARGE PAPER : *only 100 copies printed. Very scarce in this size. The finest production of this celebrated Press, and the most beautiful example of American typography.*
Riverside Press, Cambridge, 1863.

112* —— Another copy. Small paper. 15 vols. fcap. 8vo. *new cloth.*
Boston, 1861.

THE BEST EDITION of Bacon's Works, it being a reprint of the best London edition, with corrections and some additions by the senior editor, Mr. Spedding. The Indexes are also much more copious.

113 BACON, FRANCIS. *Not the Author of "The Christian Paradoxes,"* being a reprint of " Memorials of Godliness and Christianity," by Herbert Palmer. With Introduction, Memoir, and Notes by the Rev. Alexander Grosart. *Facsimile portrait.* 8vo. *hf. morocco, uncut.* *Printed for private circulation, London, 1865.* ONLY 250 COPIES.

114 BAKER, SAMUEL W. The ALBERT NYANZA, great Basin of the Nile, and explorations of the Nile sources. *Maps, Portraits, &c.* 8vo. *new cloth.* *London, 1866.*

115 BALDWIN's REPRINTS, *comprising* QUARLES' ENCHIRIDION, WARWICK'S SPARE MINUTES, JENYNS' (Soame) DISQUISITIONS on several subjects, and MARIE MAGDALEN'S FUNERALL TEARS for the death of our Saviour, by Southwell. *Beautifully printed on heavy paper, and illustrated with portraits, fac-similes, &c.* ; together, 4 vols. *square* 12mo. *uniformly bound in sprinkled, calf extra, marbled edges.* *C. Baldwin, London, 1823, &c.*

A COMPLETE SET, *scarce.*

116 BALLAD SOCIETY. BALLADS from MSS. Vol. I. pt. I, BALLADS ON THE CONDITION of ENGLAND in Henry VIII. and Edward VI.'s Reigns, (including the State of the Clergy, Monks, and Friars), on Woolsey and Anne Boleyn. Vol. II. pt. I, THE POOR MAN'S PENITENCE, by Richard Williams. Edited by F. J. Furnivall, on Whatman's ribbed paper, *uncut.* 2 vols. r. 8vo.
Ballad Society, London, 1868.
LARGE PAPER, few printed.

117 BALLADS. The PEDLAR'S PACK of Ballads and Songs, with Illustrative Notes, by W. H. Logan. *Fac-simile wood-cuts.* Crown 8vo. *new cloth, uncut.* *Edinburgh, 1869.*
Limited Edition.

118 BALLADS OF IRELAND, collected and edited by E. Hayes. 2 vols. 12mo. *new cloth.* *Edinburgh, (1868).*
Ballads—See Percy, Utterson, Ellis, Ritson, &c., &c,

119 BANCROFT, GEORGE. HISTORY OF THE UNITED STATES, from the discovery of the American Continent. *Portraits on India Paper.* 8 *vols. imperial 8vo. cloth, uncut.* *Boston*, 1861.

VERY SCARCE. LARGE PAPER. 50 *copies printed*, 2 *of which were destroyed by the fire at C. B. Richardson's store, in New York, September,* 1864. Duplicate titles inserted.

120 BANCROFT, GEORGE. History of the United States. *Portraits, &c.* 8 vols. 8vo. *new cloth.* *Boston*, 1864.

121 BANKS, JOHN. VERTUE BETRAY'D; or Anna Bullen. Small 4*to.* *pp.* 80, *hf. vellum.* *London*, 1684.
Title and last leaf in MS.

122 BARBAULD, ANN LÆTITIA. WORKS, with a memoir by Lucy Aiken. ONLY LIBRARY EDITION. *Silhouette Portrait.* 2 *vols. 8vo. hf. morocco, uncut.* *London*, 1825.
LARGE PAPER, *very scarce.*

123 BARCLAI JOANNIS. SATYRICON. Thick 32mo. *vellum.*
Amstelodami, 1627.

124 BARCLAY, ROBERT. Apology for the true Christian Divinity, as the same is held forth, and preached by the people, called, in scorn, Quakers, &c. *Small 4to. dark sprinkled calf extra, gilt edges,* by PRATT. Printed in the year 1678.
ORIGINAL EDITION, *very scarce.*

125 BARKER, W. B. LARES AND PENATES, or Cilicia and its Governors, from the Earliest Times to the Present Day, *map and numerous engravings.* 8vo. *cloth.* *London*, 1853.
This interesting volume includes a description of some Household Gods of the Ancient Cilicians, broken up by them on their conversion to Christianity.

126 BARLOW, STEPHEN. HISTORY OF IRELAND, from the earliest period to the present time; with a statistical and geographical account of that Kingdom. 2 vols. 8vo. hf. cf. gilt. *London*, 1804.

127 BARNABEE'S JOURNAL: *Barnabee Itinerarium*, or Seventh Edition, with an account of the author (Richard Braithwaite), a Bibliographical History of former editions of the works, &c.; *fac-simile front. by Marshall, and numerous etchings.* 12mo. *new hf. morocco extra, gilt top, uncut edges.* *London*, 1818.
Choice Copy. See also Braithwaite.

128 BARR, CAPT. JAMES. Correct and Authentic Narrative of the Indian War in Florida; Major Dade's Massacre, &c. 16*mo.* *pp.* 32, *bds.* *New York*, 1836.

129 BARRETT, FRANCIS. THE MAGUS, or Celestial Intelligence; being a complete system of Occult Philosophy, in three books. *Portrait and numerous colored plates.* Roy. 4to. hf. green calf, gilt. *Very scarce.* *London*, 1801.

130 BARREUL, THE ABBE. Memoirs, illustrating the History of Jacobinism. 4 vols. 8vo. hf. russia, *neat.* *London*, 1797.
An account of the "Illuminati," Free Masons, and Secret Societies that brought about the French Revolution.

131 BARRY, SIR CHARLES, (*the celebrated architect*). LIFE AND WORKS OF, by the Rev. Alfred Barry. *Portrait, and numerous engravings on steel and wood, folding maps, &c.* Thick 8vo. new cloth, *uncut.* *London*, 1867.

132 BARRY, P. Wealth and Poverty considered. 12*mo. bds.*
London, 1870.

133 BARTH, HENRY. TRAVELS AND DISCOVERIES IN NORTH AND CENTRAL
AFRICA. 1849–55. *Several hundred illustrations.* 3 vols.
thick 8vo. cloth. *New York*, 1857.

134 BARTLE, REV. GEORGE. The Scriptural Doctrine of Hades. 12mo.
new cloth. *London*, 1869.

135 BARTLETT'S AMERICAN SCENERY, with Descriptions by N. P. Wil-
lis, and 120 *highly finished engravings, of the most beautiful
Land, Lake, and River Scenery.* 2 vols. 4to *hf. morocco.*
London, 1840.

136 BARTLETT'S CANADIAN SCENERY, with Descriptions by N. P. Willis,
and 120 *highly finished engravings from Drawings by Bartlett.*
2 vols. 4to. *hf. morocco extra.* *London*, 1842.

137 BARTLETT, JOHN RUSSELL. History of the Destruction of His Bri-
tannic Majesty's Schooner Gaspee in Narragansett Bay, on the
10th of June, 1772, with the Official Journal of the Proceedings of the Commission of Inquiry. *Imperial 8vo. boards.*
Providence, 1861.
PRIVATELY PRINTED ; 125 *copies.*

138 BARTLETT. MEMOIRS OF RHODE ISLAND OFFICERS who were engaged in the Service of their Country during the great Rebellion of the South. *Illustrated with* 34 *Portraits.* 4to. *boards,
uncut.* *Providence*, 1867.
50 copies printed.

139 BAUDII, DOMINICI. Epistolæ ; accedunt orationes et libellus de fœ-
nore. *Engraved front.* 16*mo. vellum.*
Amstelodami, *Ludovici Elzevirii*, 1654.

140 BAXLEY, H. WILLIS. What I saw on the West Coast of South and
North America, and at the Hawaiian Islands. *Profusely illustrated. Roy. 8vo. new cloth.* *New York*, 1865.

141 BAXTER, R. DUDLEY. The Taxation of the United Kingdom. 8*vo.
new limp cloth.* *London*, 1869.

142 BAYLE'S HISTORICAL AND CRITICAL DICTIONARY. Translated, with
Life, by Des Maizeaux. *Fine Portrait.* BEST EDITION. 5
vols. folio, calf, gilt. *London*, 1734–8.
A remarkably clean and perfect copy.

143 BAYLEY'S, JOHN, HISTORY AND ANTIQUITIES OF THE
TOWER OF LONDON, with Memoirs of Royal and Distinguished Persons, deduced from Records, State-Papers, and
Manuscripts, and from other Original and Authentic sources.
EXTENDED and ILLUSTRATED *by the insertion of nearly Three
Hundred extra plates, comprising an extraordinary assemblage
of Views of the Tower,* many of which are of *great rarity: also*
two ORIGINAL PENCIL DRAWINGS, *all in the finest condition, and
a large portion beautifully inlaid, numerous portraits, &c., &c.*
2 thick vols. royal 4to. polished calf extra, gilt leaves, &c., by
MACKENZIE. *London*, 1821.
EXTRA ILLUSTRATED COPY.
A beautiful work, exhibiting the best taste in the illustrator, who has evidently spared neither time nor expense in selecting his materials.

144 BAYLEY, RT. REV. BP. MEMOIR OF THE RIGHT REVEREND SIMON WM. GABRIEL BRUTÉ, D.D., first Bishop of Vincennes, with sketches describing his recollections of scenes connected with the French Revolution, and Extracts from his Journal. *Fine portrait on India paper, and cuts. Royal 4to. uncut.*
New York, J. G. Shea, 1860.

LARGE PAPER. *Only five copies printed.*
A note on the fly-leaf, by W. E. Woodward, Esq., states that he purchased this copy of the publisher for $50.00.

145 ANOTHER COPY. *Small paper. Small 4to. new hf. morocco, gilt top, by Bradstreet.* New York, 1860.
Only 50 copies.

146 BAYLIES, FRANCIS. Historical Memoir of New Plymouth, from the flight of the Pilgrims into Holland, in 1608, to the union of that Colony with Massachusetts, in 1692. *Plates.* 2 vols. 8vo. *new cloth, uncut edges.* Boston, 1866.

147 BEAL, SAMUEL. TRAVELS OF FAH-HIAN and Sung-yun, Buddist Pilgrims from China to India. (400 A. D. and 518 A. D.) Map. 12mo. *new cloth.* London, 1869.

148 BEALE, LIONEL S. Protoplasm; or, Life Force, and Matter. *Profusely illustrated, with colored plates.* 12mo. *new cloth.*
London, 1870.

149 BEARDSLEY, REV. E. E. History of the Episcopal Church in Connecticut, from the settlement of the Colony to the Death of Bp. Seabury. *Front.* 2 vols. 8vo. *hf. mor. uncut.*
New York, 1865.

150 BEATTIE's SCOTLAND Illustrated in a Series of Views, by Allom, Bartlett, &c., with Descriptions, *upwards of* 120 *highly finished engravings*, EARLY IMPRESSIONS, 2 vols. 4to. *hf. calf, gilt.*
London, 1838.

151 BEATTIE. THE DANUBE ILLUSTRATED, its History, Scenery, and Topography, *with nearly* 120 *highly finished engravings from drawings by Bartlett, and numerous beautiful woodcuts, fine early impressions,* thick 4to. *morocco, extra, gilt edges.*
London, 1844.

152 BEAUMONT and FLETCHER; DRAMATIC WORKS. Edited with the notes of George Coleman. *Portraits.* 3 vols. roy. 8vo. hf. cf. extra. London, 1811.

153 BEAUTIES OF ENGLAND AND WALES, by Britton and Brayley, with Introduction by Brewer, complete, *with upwards of* 700 *engravings of Mansions, Views, &c. by Storer and Greig, and woodcuts by Bewick.* 26 vols. 8vo. hf. cf. gilt. London, 1801-23.

A valuable and interesting work, the only one illustrating *all* the Counties of England and Wales.

154 BECK, DR. JOHN R. ELEMENTS OF MEDICAL Jurisprudence. 12th Edition, with revisions by Dr. C. R. Gilman. 2 *thick vols.* 8vo. *sheep.* Philadelphia, 1863.

155 BECKER, Prof. W. A. CHARICLES; or, illustrations of the Private Life of the Ancient Greeks. With Notes, &c. Tran. by the Rev. F. Metcalf. *Crown 8vo. new cloth.* London, 1866.

156 BECKER, Prof. GALLUS; or, Roman Scenes of the Time of Augus-

tus, with Notes, &c., translated by the Rev. F. Metcalf. *Crown 8vo. new cloth.* *London,* 1866.

157 BEETHOVEN'S LETTERS, translated by Lady Wallis. *Portrait.* 2 *vols. 12mo. hf. cf. extra.* *New York,* 1867.

158 "BEGGYNHOF;" or, the City of the Single. *12mo. new cloth.* *London,* 1869.

159 BEHMEN, JACOB. Works; to which is prefixed the Life of the Author, with Figures left by the Rev. William Law, *with the very curious series of movable plates, explanatory of his principles.* 3 *vols. roy. 4to. new hf. morocco, neat.* *London,* 1764, &c. SCARCE.

160 BEHN, MRS. APHRA. NOVELS, complete, with a History of the Life and Memoirs of Mrs. Behn, never before printed, with pleasant Love Letters, &c., &c. *3d Edition*, with additions. *Fine portrait.* 2 vols. *sml. 8vo. hf. calf, neat.* *London,* 1698–1700. VERY SCARCE.

161 BEHN, MRS. APHRA. DRAMATIC WORKS. Portrait by R. White. 3d Edition. 4 *vols. 12mo. hf. calf, antique.* *London,* 1724. BEST EDITION. VERY SCARCE.

Lowndes says, "In this edition the Prologues and Epilogues are omitted." This statement is incorrect; none of them are lacking. The character that Mrs. Behn has acquired for gross and licentious writing, is a blot on her reputation for judgment and ability, which was so great that Charles II. thought fit to entrust her with the conduct of some political affairs in Holland.

162 BEHN, MRS. APHRA. The Emperor of the Moon ; a Farce, as it is acted by their majesties' servants, at the Queen's Theatre. *Portrait inserted. 4to. pp. 56, hf. mor. neat.* *London,* 1688.

163 BEHN, MRS. APHRA. SIR PATIENT FANCY ; a Comedy, as it is acted at the Duke's Theatre. Sml. 4to. pp. 92, *hf. morocco, red edges.* *London,* 1678. *Original Edition.* Fine copy.

164 BEHN, MRS. APHRA. The FORC'D MARRIAGE, or the Jealous Bridegroom, a Tragi-Comedy. 4to. pp. 70, *hf. morocco, neat.* ORIG. EDITION. *London,* 1688.

Langbain supposes this play to have been the first of Mrs. Behn's productions.

165 BELOE, W. Sexagenarian, or The Recollections of a Literary Life. 2 *vols. 8vo. half calf extra.* *London,* 1818.

166 BENZONI, G. NARRATIVE OF THE OPERATIONS and RECENT DISCOVERIES within the Pyramids, Temples, Tombs, and Excavations in Egypt and Nubia. *Map, &c.* 2 vols. 8vo. *hf. cf. neat.* *London,* 1822. *Scarce.*

167 BENEDICT, GEN. LEWIS. MEMORIAL OF (killed in Battle at Pleasant Hill, La., 1864.) *8vo. hf. morocco, gilt top,* by *Bradstreet.* *Munsell, Albany,* 1866. *One of 5 copies* on INDIA PAPER.

168 BENGELS, JOHN A. GNOMON OF THE NEW TESTAMENT, pointing out from the natural force of the Words, the Simplicity, Depth, Harmony, and Saving Power of its divine thoughts; translated

3

by C. T. Lewis and M. R. Vincent. 2 thick vols. roy. 8vo. new hf. *morocco.* *Philadelphia,* 1864.

169 BENGER, MISS. Memoirs of the Life of Anne Boleyn, Queen of Henry VIIIth. *Portrait.* 2 *vols. 8vo. cf.* *London,* 1821.

170 BENGER, MISS. Memoirs of the Life of Mary Queen of Scots. 2 vols. 8vo. *hf. green cf. gilt.* *London,* 1823.

171 BENTHAM, JEREMY. COMPLETE WORKS, with his Memoirs and Correspondence, edited by Sir J. BOWRING, *fine portrait,* 11 large vols. imp. 8vo. *newly bound, half calf extra,* (pub. in bds. £9 18s.) *Edinburgh,* 1843.

"In Jeremy Bentham (says a great critic), the world has lost the great eacher and patriot of his time; the man who has exercised and is exercising over the fortunes of mankind the widest and most durable influence." "A knowledge of Bentham's works (says another) is a key which unlocks all the mysteries of social and political government." Sir James Mackintosh, Lord Jeffrey, Lord Brougham, Mr. Mill, and other great authorities, are equally emphatic in their appreciation of his labors.

"Dr. Parr considered Bentham as the wisest man of his time, whose powerful mind had anticipated the improvements of coming ages."—FIELD'S LIFE OF PARR.

172 BENTIVOGLIO, CARDINAL. COLLECTION OF LETTERS OF, during the time he was nuncio in France and Flanders, translated from the Italian. 8vo. *hf. red morocco, uncut.*

For the Author. London, 1753.

173 BENTON, NATHANIEL S. History of Herkimer County, including the Upper Mohawk Valley. *Maps, &c. Roy. 8vo. bds. uncut.*

Munsell, Albany, 1856.

174 BENTON, THOMAS H. Abridgment of the Debates of Congress from 1789 to 1856. 16 vols. thick roy. 8vo. *new cloth.*

New York, 1857–'61.

175 BENTON, THOMAS H. THIRTY YEARS IN THE UNITED STATES SENATE. *Engravings,* 2 *thick vols. 8vo. cloth.* *New York,* 1858.

176 BEOWULF. ANGLO-SAXON POEMS. The Scôp or Gleeman's Tale, and The Fight at Finnesburgh, with translation, Notes, Glossary, &c., by Benjamin Thorpe. *Post 8vo. hf. morocco.*

Oxford, 1855.

177 BERANGER, P. J. DE. CHANSONS, précédés d'une notice sur l'auteur et d'un essai sur les Poésies par M. P. F. Tissot. BEST EDITION. *Most profusely illustrated with beautiful engravings on steel after designs by Tony Johannot, Grenier, Granville, etc., etc.* FINE IMPRESSIONS. 6 *vols.* in 3, 12mo. *bound in morocco, ornamented with a gothic design, inlaid with morocco of various colors, full gilt.* By THOUVENIN. UNIQUE. *Paris,* 1829.

BERANGER'S OWN COPY, CONTAINING NUMEROUS SUPPLEMENTARY CHANSONS AND CORRECTIONS TO THE PREVIOUS EDITION IN THE HANDWRITING OF THE AUTHOR.

Appended to the 3d vol. will be found the music to the Chansons, entitled "*Nouveau Recueil contenant tous les Airs des Chansons de Beranger, dont le plus joli sont avec accompagnement de Piano ou Guitare,*" which is very scarce.

178 BERJEAU, J. PH. EARLY DUTCH, GERMAN, AND ENGLISH PRINTERS' MARKS. 100 *fac-simile plates, with indexes, &c. Roy. 8vo. cloth.* Scarce. *London,* 1866.

ONLY 250 COPIES PRINTED.

179 BERKELEY, *Bishop.* WORKS, with an account of his Life. *Fine portrait.* 2 vols. roy. 4to. cf. *neat.* *London,* 1784.

180 BERNARD, MME. L. LES MYTHOLOGIES de tous les peuples, racontées a la jeunesse, *numerous fine plates.* 12mo. hf. mor. gilt.
Paris, 1843.

181 BERNARD, SIR THOMAS. THE COMFORTS OF OLD AGE, with Biographical Illustrations. *Beautifully printed within ornamental borders.* Small 4to. morocco antique, *gilt edges.*
London, 1846.
PRIVATELY PRINTED. *Rare.*
The Author was the son of Sir Francis Bernard, Governor of Massachusetts, and a graduate of Harvard College.
The above work was edited by Chas. P. Cooper, Esq., Secretary of the Record Commission.

182 BERRY, MISS. Extracts of the JOURNALS and CORRESPONDENCE of, from the year 1783 to 1852. Edited by Lady Theresa Lewis. *Portraits, &c.* 3 vols. 8vo. *polished calf, extra.*
London, 1865.

183 BERTRAND DU GUESCLIN, The Life and Times of. A History of the Fourteenth Century, by D. F. Jamison, of South Carolina. *Portrait and beautiful head-pieces to each chapter. A very fine specimen of Typography.* 2 vols. 8vo. *cloth.*
Charleston, (London,) 1864.

184 BETHAM, Sir W. ETRURIA-CELTICA; ETRUSCAN LITERATURE and ANTIQUITIES Investigated, or the Language of that ancient People compared and identified with the Ibero-Celtic, *numerous plates of Etruscan and British Coins, Antiquities, the Round Towers, &c.* 2 vols. 8vo. *new cloth.* *Dublin,* 1842.
" A valuable treatise."

185 BETHAM, Sir WILLIAM. The GAEL and CYMBRI; or an Inquiry into the Origin and History of the Irish Scoti, Britons, and Gauls, &c. 8vo. *cloth. Scarce.* *Dublin,* 1834.

186 BETHAM, Sir WILLIAM. DIGNITIES, Feudal and Parliamentary and the Constitutional Legislature of the United Kingdom. Vol. I. (*all published*), 8vo. cloth, *uncut. Scarce.*
Dublin, 1830.

187 BETON, NICHOLAS. The LONGING of a BLESSED HEART; which, Loathing the World, doth Long to be with Christ; edited by Sir Egerton Brydges. *Roy. 4to. hf. morocco, uncut.*
Lee Priory Press, Kent, 1814.
PRIVATELY PRINTED, 100 *copies.*

188 BEYARD, COL. N. Journal of the Late Actions of the French at Canada. *Small 4to. bds. uncut.*
J. Sabin, New York, 1868.

189 —— Another copy. *Roy. 4to. bds. uncut.* *New York,* 1868.
LARGE PAPER, *only* 25 *copies.*

190 BIBLE. THE HOLY BIBLE, *an exact reprint page for page of the authorized version published in the year* 1611, thick 4to. *hf. morocco, uncut. Scarce.* *Oxford,* 1833.
This reprint is so exact as to agree with the original edition page for page, and letter for letter; retaining throughout the ancient mode of spelling and punctuation, and even the most manifest errors of the Press.

191 Bible. An Illustrated History of the Holy Bible, being a connected account of the Remarkable events and Distinguished Characters contained in the Old and New Testaments, by Jno. Kitto, &c. *Upwards of 100 maps and engravings, 8vo. hf. morocco, gilt.* *Norwich, Conn.,* 1868.

192 Bible in Every Land. A History of the Sacred Scriptures in every Language and Dialect into which translations have been made. *Illustrated by specimen portions in native characters, Series of Alphabets, Maps, &c., thick 4to. hf. mor.*
Bagster, London, 1850.

193 Bible Portraits, &c., Gajo, Barthol. Epitome Historico-Chronologica Gestorum, omnium patriarchum, Ducum, Judicum, Regum, et Pontificum Populi Hebraici. (113 *Plates*) also Series Ptolemæorum regum Ægypti. 31 *plates* and Portraits des Rois de France, depuis Pharamond jusqu'a Roy Louis XIV. 66 *plates, inlaid, together 210 fine portraits, thick folio, russia, gilt.* *Romæ, &c.,* 1751.
From the Library of Lord Farnham with his book-plate.

194 BIBLE PRINTS. (Blome's) Royaumont's History of the Old and New Testament, *with upwards of two hundred and forty large engravings on copper, after the best artists,* fine early impressions. Royal *folio, handsomely bound in old crimson morocco, full gilt sides, back, and gilt edges.* *London,* 1701.
A very large and fine copy, and a fine specimen of binding.

195 Bible Prints. Gallery of Scripture Engravings, Historical, and Engravings with Descriptions, Historical, Geographical and Pictorial, by the Rev. Jno. Kitto, *upwards of 200 large and finely executed engravings from drawings by celebrated artists.* 3 vols. 4to. morocco, gilt edges. *London, N. D.*

196 Bible Prints. Historiæ Celebriores Novi Testamenti Iconibus repræsentatæ, &c., à Christophoro Weigelio. 100 *large and fine copper plates after Luykens, Meloni, &c., engraved by Weigel,* early impressions, folio, old cf. gilt.
Nuremburg, N. D.
With Latin and German verses. This famous series of engravings illustrates the grandest events in the Old and New Testaments.

197 Bible Prints. Holbein's Bible cuts. Icones Veteris Testamenti ; *illustrations of the Old Testament, engraved on wood from designs by Hans Holbein.* Crown 8vo. hf. vox. morocco, uncut.
Pickering, London, 1830.

198 Bible Prints. Landscape Illustrations of the Bible, consisting of Views of the most remarkable places mentioned in the Old and New Testaments, with descriptions by the Rev. Thomas Hartwell Horne. 100 *beautifully engraved plates from Original Drawings made on the spot* by W. & E. Finden. 2 *vols.* roy. 4to. new, hf. morocco, extra, gilt edges. *London,* 1836.
Large Paper. *Proofs on India Paper.*

199 Bible Prints. Luikens, Johannes. De Schriftuurlyke Geschiedenissen en Gelykenissen van het Oude en Nieuwe Verbond. 336 *engravings on copper, representing the prominent scenes in the*

Old and New Testaments. Good impressions. 2 vols. small 4to. *vellum.* *Amsterdam,* 1712.

Fine copy from the Library of Lord Farnham.

200 BIBLE PRINTS. THEATRUM BIBLICUM, hoc est historiæ sacræ V. et N. Testamenti, tabulis ænis expressæ, opus in lucem editum, per N. S. Piscatorem. 496 *ptates, illustrating all the prominent events of the Old and New Testament. Oblong folio, old cf. neat.* 1644. [?]

201 BIBLE PRINTS. WEIGEL. BIBLIA ECTYPA. Bildnueszen anufz heilige Schrift der Alten Testaments, &c. 400 *fine old copperplate engravings, illustrating the Old Testament.* FINE IMPRESSIONS. *Oblong 4to. old cf. Scarce.*
Regensberg, Chr. Weigel, 1697.

* * BIBLE PRINTS. See Scheuchzeri Physica Sacra.

202 BIBLIA PAUPERUM. Reproduced in fac-simile from one of the Copies in the British Museum, with an Historical and Bibliographical Introduction by J. Ph. Berjeau. *Numerous Facsimiles printed with brown ink. Folio, half morocco, uncut.*
J. R. Smith, London, 1859.

ONLY 250 COPIES PRINTED. *Uniform with Sotheby's Principia Typographica, and the Canticum Canticorum.*

203 BIBLIA SACRA POLYGLOTTA, Textus Archetypos Virsiones que præcipuas ab Ecclesia antiquitus receptas necnon versiones recentiores Anglicanam, Germanicam, Italicam, Gallicam, et Hispanicam complectentia; accedunt Prolegomena in Textum Archetyporum Versionumque antiquarum Crisin literalem, autore SAMUELE LEE. 2 vols. *Stout folio, newly bound in hf. red morocco, gilt top, uncut edges.*
Londini, Samueles Bagster, 1869.

An excellent Polyglot edition of the Bible, in *Hebrew, Greek, Latin, English, French, German, Spanish, and Italian.* All of them are printed in 12mo. size, so that the Hebrew, Greek, Latin, and English occupy four quarters of each left hand page, and the others occupy the right hand. At the end of Vol. II. are, Variæ lectiones in versionem septuaginta virorum, Novum Testamentum Græcum, Pentateuchum Hebræo-Samaritanum, and the whole of the New Testament in *Syriac.*

204 BIBLIOTHECA AMERICANA. Catalogue of . . . . S. G. Deeth's Books. 8vo. *paper.* *New York,* 1865.

LARGE PAPER COPY.

205 BIBLIOTHECA AMERICANA VETUSTISSIMA: A Description of Works relating to America, published between the Years 1492 and 1551. With an Introduction, &c. (by Henry Harrisse). *Thick roy. 4to. new hf. morocco, extra, uncut.* VERY SCARCE. *New York,* 1866.

LARGE PAPER, *only* 99 *copies.*
A beautiful specimen of American typography, containing the titles of upwards of three hundred works, the greater part of which are in fac-simile, and for which the type was specially cast.
With a copy of a letter of the Publisher, Mr. Geo. P. Philes, with reference to the work, &c.

206 BIBLIOTHECA ANGLO POETICA; or, a Descriptive Catalogue of a Rare and Rich Collection of Early English Poetry. Illustrated by occasional extracts and remarks, critical and bibliograph-

ical. Compiled by A. F. Griffith. *Numerous portraits, initial letters, etc.* 8vo. *hf. russia, neat, edges untouched.*

London, 1815.

Fine Copy.
This was the Collection made by T. Park, with additions by Th. Hill.
" Deserving a place in every good library from the interesting information which it affords of the works of our early poets."—*Lowndes.*

207 Bibliotheca Chethamensis; sive Bibliotheca publicæ Macuniensis ab Humfredo Chetham armigero fundatæ Catologus exhibens libros varias classes pro varietate Argumenti distributos, edidit Johannes Radcliffe. *Fine portrait.* 3 vols. 8vo. *calf gilt, fine copy.* *Macunii*, 1791.

For an account of this library see Norton's Literary Gazette for Aug. and Sept., 1854.

208 **BIBLIOTHECA MAGNA VETERUM PATRUM,** et Anti-quorum Scriptorum Ecclesiasticorum; nunc vero Additione CC. circiter Authorum, tam Græcorum qui in Editioni Coloni-ensi, quam Latinorum qui Parisiensibus desiderabantur, locu-pletata, et accuratissime emendata; et in XVII. Tomos distri-buta (curante Ægidio Morello). 17 *vols. in 15, folio, calf, neat. Very scarce.* *Parisiis*, 1644.

Best Edition. *Sir Francis Palgrave's copy with his autograph on the title-page.*
Priced by Nutt, 1857, £11 11s. 0d.
The first edition of De la Bigne's collection of the Works of the Fathers appeared in 1576; the second in 1589; the third in 1609, reprinted in 1618 at Cologne; the fourth, in which the Greek Fathers were first added; and then the present edition (1644) was totally rearranged and edited by Morell, which forms the substratum of all the subsequent collections of the works of the Fathers.

209 Bichat, Xavier. Physiological Researches on Life and Death. 8vo. *sheep.* *Boston*, 1827.

210 Biddle, Daniel. The Spirit Controversy. Letters and Disserta-tions on the human Spirit and Soul. 12mo. *new cloth.*

London, 1869.

211 Big Bear's Adventures and Travels. *Illustrated.* 12mo. *cloth.*

Philadelphia, 1858.

212 Billings' Baronial and Ecclesiastical Antiquities of Scotland. *Upwards of* 240 *beautifully executed and highly interesting en-gravings of Ancient Castles, Abbeys, Churches, &c., besides nu-merous wood-cuts, with descriptive letter-press.* 4 *vols. royal 4to. cloth, uncut.* *Edinburgh*, 1852.

The finest series of Architectural plates yet published.
" This is a collection of the remains yet spared to Scotland. Mr. Billings is a masterly draughtsman, well skilled in the history and characteristics of architectural style, and uniting scrupulous fidelity to good taste. His en-gravers do him justice."—*Quarterly Review.*

213 Biographia Britannica; or, Lives of the Most Eminent Persons of Great Britain and Ireland. 7 vols. *folio, calf, gilt.* 1747.

Fine Copy.
" An indispensable work in every historical library."—*Lowndes.*

214 Bion, Moschus, etc. Idylles de Bion et de Moschus. Traduits en Français par J. B. Gail. *With the fine series of illustrations by Barbier, in two states, to wit :* The Etching, *and* Unletter-ed Proof. *Papier vélin.* 12mo. *half calf, gilt.*

Paris, L'An Troisième (1794).

Scarce in this state.

215 Birch, Samuel. History and Description of Ancient Pottery and Porcelain, Egyptian, Asiatic, Greek, Roman, Etruscan, and Celtic. *Colored plates, and several hundred wood-cuts.* 2 vols. 8vo. *new cloth.* London, 1858.
A new and valuable work, uniformly printed with Marryat's *Modern Pottery.*

216 Bishop, S. G. Eulogium on the Death of George Washington. *Royal 8vo. hf. green morocco, uncut, by Bradstreet.* Roxbury : *Privately Printed,* 1866.
One of 6 copies on Whatman's Drawing Paper.

217 Blackall, Bishop. Practical Discourses on the Lord's Prayer. 8vo. *old calf.* London, 1717.
W. Wordsworth's copy with his autograph on the title-page.

218 Blackburn, Henry. Travelling in Spain, in the present day, *printed on toned paper, and illustrated with wood cuts. 8vo. new cloth.* London, 1866.

219 Blackie, John Stuart. Homer and the Iliad. *4 vols. 8vo. new cloth.* Edinburgh, 1866.

220 Black-Letter Ballads. A Catalogue of an unique collection of Ancient English Brodside Ballads, printed entirely in the Black-Letter, post 8vo. hf. mor. uncut.
Russell Smith, London, 1856.

221 BLACKWOOD'S EDINBURGH MAGAZINE. A complete set from its commencement in April 1817 to and including Dec. 1854. *76 vols. thick 8vo. uniformly bound in hf. cf. neat.* Edinburgh, 1817–'54.

222 Blackwood's Edinburgh Magazine. Amer. Edition. July 1859 to Dec. 1861. *5 vols. 8vo. hf. russia.* N. Y. 1859–'61.
" No magazine has ever enjoyed a greater celebrity than ' Blackwood,' particularly for the ability of its Novels and Tales; " among the known writers are Bulwer, Alison, Lockhart, Prof. Wilson, S. Warren, and a host of others.

223 BLANC. GALERIE DES PEINTRES, German and Flemish Schools. *Upwards of two hundred portraits of artists, and engravings from their most esteemed works, beautifully executed on wood. Roy. 4to. new hf. green morocco, extra.* Paris, V. D.

224 Blair's Grave. A Poem, *illustrated by 12 engravings from the Designs of* Blake, *and a superb Portrait of that artist, engraved by Schiavonetti; fine* proof impressions. Folio, Large Paper. Bensley, *London,* 1813.
Large paper copies of the above are extremely rare, only four of them have ever been offered for sale in this country.

Blake, Wm. Life of, see Gilchrist.

225 Blake, William. Songs of Innocence and of Experience, showing the two contrary states of the Human Soul. Edited by R. H. Shepherd. *12mo. new cloth.* Pickering, *London,* 1868.

226 Blake, William. Poetical Sketches, reprinted from the original edition of 1783, edited by R. H. Shepherd. *12mo. new cloth.* Pickering, *London,* 1868.

227 Bledsoe, Rev. Albert T. A Theodicy; or, vindication of the Divine Glory as manifested in the Constitution and Government of the moral world. *8vo. hf. morocco, neat.* N. Y. 1853.

228 Bleeker, L. The Order Book of Capt. Leonard Bleeker, Major
of Brigade in the early part of the Expedition under James
Clinton, against the Indian Settlements of Western New York,
in the Campaign of 1779. Edited by Franklin B. Hough.
N. Y., 1865.

Large Paper. 50 *copies printed.* Imperfect—wants sigs. E and M.

229 Blondell, David. Treatise of the Sibyls, so highly celebrated,
as well by the Antient Heathens, as the Holy Fathers of the
Church; giving an accompt of the names and number of the
Sibyls, &c., &c. Folio, old cf., *very scarce.* *London*, 1661.

230 BLOUET, EXPEDITION SCIENTIFIQUE DE MOREE,
ordonnée par le Gouvernement Français, *with* 280 *large and
very fine engravings of Architecture, Sculpture, Inscriptions, and
views,* 3 vols. impl. folio, *new hf. morocco, gilt.*
Paris, Didot, 1831–4.

This magnificent work exhibits the most famous Temples and other Buildings
from actual admeasurement, with ground-plans, sections, and ornaments,
&c., a splendid series of Statues and other Sculpture and Inscriptions.
Among the contributors are Ravoisié, Poirot, De Gournay, and Trézel.

231 Bloodgood's Sexagenary; or Reminiscences of the American Revolution. *Portraits. Royal 8vo. paper, uncut.*
Munsell, Albany, 1866.

Large Paper; *only 50 copies.*

232 Bloodgood's Sexagenary; or Reminiscences of the American Revolution. *Portraits. 8vo. hf. crimson morocco, by Bradstreet.*
Munsell, Albany, 1866.

Printed on India Paper, *one of 3 (?) copies.*

233 ——Another Copy. *8vo. hf. crimson morocco, gilt top.*
Albany, 1866.

234 Blue Laws of Connecticut. The Code of 1650, being a compilation of the earliest laws of the general court of Connecticut, &c.
Frontispiece, 12mo. *cloth.* *Hartford,* N. D.

235 Boaden, James. Memoirs of Mrs. Siddons, interspersed with anecdotes of authors and actors. *Portrait,* 2 *vols.* 8vo. *hf. cf. gilt.*
London, 1827.

236 Boaden, James. Memoirs of Mrs. Inchbald, including her correspondence. *Fine portrait.* 2 *vols.* 8vo. *boards, uncut.*
London, 1833.

Boaden, Jas. Inquiry—see Shakespeare Portraits.

237 Boccaccio's Decameron, freely Translated with Life, etc., (by Du-
bois). *Fine portrait, and a complete set of Stothard's Illustrations, inserted.* 8vo. *sprinkled calf, extra, marbled edges by Bedford. Fine copy.* *London,* 1845.
Best 8vo. Edition.

238 Boccaccio, Giovanni. Decameron, or ten days' entertainment, to
which are prefixed Remarks on the Life and Writings of Boccaccio, &c. *Fine portrait, and a beautiful set of Stothard's
plates.* Proofs, *inserted.* 8vo. *polished calf, extra, yellow edges.*
London, 1820.

Fine Copy. Best Library Edition.

239 Bocquet, Henry. An Historical Account of the Expedition

against the OHIO INDIANS in 1764, with Preface by Francis Parkman. *Maps and plates. 8vo. new cloth, uncut.*
Cincinnati, 1868.

240 ——— The Same. Impl. 8vo. *cloth, uncut.*   *Cincinnati, 1868.*
LARGE PAPER.

241 BOISGELIN, CHEV. LOUIS de. ANCIENT and MODERN MALTA, with the History of the Knights of St. John of Jerusalem, and the Conquest of the Island by the English. *Large map and fine plates of antiquities, portraits of the Grand Masters, &c.* 2 vols. 4to. *calf gilt.*   *London, 1805.*
ORIGINAL MSS.

242 BOKER, GEORGE H. PODESTA'S DAUGHTER, a Dramatic Sketch. THE ORIGINAL MANUSCRIPT. 28 pp. folio, *morocco gilt.*

Presented to the "Central Sanitary Fair," May 4th, 1864.
"The age has not produced a poem more graceful than the Podesta's Daughter, nor scarcely one so distinguished for its simple and genuine, but deep and thrilling, pathos. The reader who can forbear to drop upon the page the tribute of a tear to the gentle Giulia,
'Sweeter far
Than rose or lily, violet or vine,
Though they could gather all their charms in one,'
would weep for nothing."   R. T. CONRAD.

243 ——— ... comprising WORKS edited by Goldsmith, 8 vols. CORRESPONDENCE and STATE LETTERS, edited by Parke, 4 vols. LIFE AND TIMES, by Thos. Macknight, 1 vol., together, 13 vols. 8vo. *new and uniformly bound in hf. calf extra, gilt tops, uncut edges.*
London, 1809–'63.

BEST EDITIONS.

244 BONNEY, T. G. The ALPINE REGIONS of Switzerland and the Neighboring Countries, their Physical Features, Scenery and Natural History. With *engravings on wood by Whymper.* 8vo. *new cloth.*   *London, 1868.*

245 BOOK OF COMMON PRAYER. The Order of Daily Service, the Litany, the Holy Communion, the PSALTER or PSALMS, and Special Services of the Church, WITH THE ANCIENT MUSICAL NOTATIONS, beautifully printed in red and black, within ornamented borders. 2 vols. *Royal 4to. boards, uncut.*
London, 1843–44.

LARGE PAPER.

This elegant and unique work (Edited by Dyce), contains the ancient Music as adapted to the First Prayer Book of Edw. VI., by J. Marbecke, with the Litany Chant, and other portions of *Gregorian Music,* thus forming a complete Choral Book for the Services of the English Church.

246 BOOK OF COMMON PRAYER. LITURGIA, seu Liber precum communium et Administrationis Sacramentorum,—una cum Psalterio seu Psalmis Davidis (Sternhold and Hopkins). *Beautiful portrait of Charles II. Ruled throughout with red lines, also a fine series of old engravings.* 8vo. (12mo.) *original old dark blue morocco, gilt leaves.*   *London, 1670.*

Fine old copy, *very scarce.*

247 BOOK OF COMMON PRAYER (called Q. ELIZABETH'S PRAYER-BOOK) and Administration of the Sacraments according to the use of the United Church of England and Ireland, together with the

Psalms of David. PICKERING'S BEAUTIFUL REPRINT, *with Portrait of the Queen, woodcut borders, and all the illustrations of* ALBERT DURER AND HOLBEIN, *thick post 8vo. cloth.*
London, 1853.

248 BOOK OF COMMON PRAYER, &c., for the use of the Protestant Episcopal Church in the CONFEDERATE STATES OF AMERICA. 24*mo. morocco gilt.* *Richmond, Va.,* 1863.

249 BOOK OF MORMON. Translated by Joseph Smith, Jr. 12mo. cloth, *scarce.* *New York,* N. D.

250 BOOK OF MORMON. EVIDENCES IN PROOF of the BOOK OF MORMON being a DIVINELY INSPIRED RECORD; written by the forefathers of the natives whom we call Indians (who are a remnant of the Tribe of Joseph) by Charles Thompson. 16mo. cloth, *rare.*
Battavia, N. Y., 1841.

251 BOOK OF VARIETIE, collected by Dr. Thomas Purland, *consisting of rare and curious old engravings, and woodcuts, views, portraits, old newspapers,* 1610, *&c., cuttings, &c.,* also 4 AUTOGRAPHS :— GEORGE III., *Lord Palmerston, Chas. Dickens, and Duchess of Sussex. all neatly mounted* in a scrap-book, *thick 4to. hf. morocco.*

252 BORROW, GEORGE. BIBLE IN SPAIN; or, the Journeys, Adventures, and Imprisonments of an Englishman, in an attempt to circulate the Scriptures in the Peninsula. 3 vols. post 8vo. *hf. green morocco, uncut.* *London,* 1843.

253 BORROW, GEORGE. The Zincali: or, an account of the Gipsies of Spain. 2 *vols. in one.* 12*mo. hf. mor.* *New York,* 1842.

254 BORROW, GEORGE. Wild Wales; its People, Language and Scenery. 12*mo. cloth.* *London,* 1868.

255 BORROW, GEORGE. Lavengro; the Scholar; the Gipsey; the Priest. *Portrait,* 12*mo. cloth.* *New York,* 1851.

256 BORUWLASKI, COUNT. (The celebrated Dwarf.) MEMOIRS OF, containing a sketch of his Travels, with an account of his reception at the different Courts of Europe, by himself. *Portrait.* 8*vo. hf. morocco, uncut.* *Durham,* 1820.
Fine copy, with an autograph letter of Boruwlaski inserted.

257 BOSSOLI'S SCENERY THROUGHOUT THE CRIMEA; within the City and Harbor of Sebastopol, Perekop, Eupatoria, Balaklava, Simferopol, Bakchi-Sarai, Kertch, Fort Arabat, &c., and on the Rivers Alma, Katcha and Salghir, taken prior to the War, *a series of* 52 *large and fine lithographic drawings, in double tints, on* 30 *plates,* imp. folio, *new hf. morocco.*
London, 1855.

258 BOSSUET, JACQUES BENIGNE. SERMONS. *Portrait.* 17 *vols.* 12*mo. hf. cf. gilt.* *Paris,* 1772.

259 BOSWELL, JAMES. LIFE OF SAMUEL JOHNSON, including his Tour to the Hebrides, *with Notes and numerous engravings on wood.* 3 *vols. post 8vo. hf. cf. extra.* *London,* 1859.

260 BOURDALOUE. SERMONS. Nouvelle Édition, revue et corrigée. 13 *vols.* 12*mo. old cf. gilt.* *Liege,* 1784.

261 Bourne, Vincent. Poetical Works, Latin and English. *Post
8vo. smooth morocco extra, gilt leaves.*
Pickering, London, 1826.
Large Paper. (?)

262 Bower, Arch. History of the Popes from the Foundation of the
See of Rome to the Present Time, 7 *vols. 4to. calf.*
London, 1750.

"This famous work was written after the author's renunciation of the Catholic Faith, and gave great offence to the Roman Catholics from the freedom of its exposures."

263 Boxiana; or, Sketches of Pugilism. *A series of upwards of 70
portraits of Celebrated Pugilists and members of the P. R. from
the earliest time. Imp. 8vo. hf. morocco.* N. D.

264 BOYDELL'S SHAKESPEARE GALLERY. 100 *very large
and beautifully executed plates to illustrate Shakespeare, from
Paintings by Northcote, Smirke, (including the Seven Ages),
Westall, Reynolds, Opie, Fuseli, Stothard, West, etc.* Brilliant
Impressions, *each plate mounted on guards. 2 vols. in one, imp.
folio, handsomely bound; red morocco, neat.*
London, 1803.

A fine copy, *the impressions of the plates being almost equal to proofs.*

265 Boynton, Capt. E. C. History of West Point and its Military
Importance during the American Revolution; and the Origin
and Progress of the United States Military Academy. *Numerous Maps and Illustrations, many on India paper. Imperial 8vo.
cloth, uncut.* *New York, 1864.*
Large Paper; *only 100 copies printed.*

266 Brabrook, E. W. The law relating to Industrial and Provident
Societies, also remarks on Trades Unions. *12mo. new cloth.*
London, 1869.

267 Bradford, Alden. History of Massachusetts, from 1764 to July,
1775, when General Washington took command of the American
Army, and a continuation from 1790 to 1820. *8vo. boards,
uncut edges.* *Boston, 1822.*
Scarce.

268 Bradford, Alex. W. Reports of cases argued and determined in
the Surrogate's Court of the County of New York. 4 *vols.
8vo. law sheep.* *New York, 1859.*

269 BRADFORD CLUB PUBLICATIONS. Complete. Comprising:
1. Papers relating to the Attack on Hatfield and Deerfield, 1859.
2. The Croakers, 1860. 3. Operations of the French Fleet
under De Grasse, 1864. 4. Anthology of New Netherland,
1865. 5. Narrative of the Career of De Soto in Florida, 1866.
6. Northern Invasion, 1866. 7. Laurens Correspondence and
Allen Memorial (by E. A. Duyckinck), together 7 *vols. roy.
8vo. uncut. (Part 3 in cloth, uncut.)*
New York, 1859–'67.
Fine Set, *only 150 copies printed.*

270 Bradstreet's, Gen., Statement upon Indian Affairs, edited by
F. B. Hough. *Small 4to. hf. crimson morocco, gilt top, by
Bradstreet.* (*London, 1764*) *Munsell, Albany, 18—.*
One of 5 copies on India Paper.

271 [BRAITHWAITE, RICHARD.] DRUNKEN BARNABY'S FOUR JOURNEYS to the North of England, in Latin and English metre. *Engravings on copper;* 3d edition, with ' Bessy Bell.' 16mo. (*8vo.*), *crimson morocco gilt, style of Roger Payne. Very scarce.*
London, 1723.
BEAUTIFUL COPY.

272 BRANT, SEBASTIAN. THE SHIP OF FOOLES, WHEREIN IS SHEWED THE FOLLY of all States, with divers other workes adioyned unto the same, very profitable and fruitfull for all men. Translated out of Latin into Englishe by ALEXANDER BARCLAY, Priest. *Folio.* Black letter. *Numerous rude woodcuts.* MAGNIFICENT COPY. *Very tall. Bound by Clarke and Bedford in red russia, extra gilt.*
VERY RARE. *Joseph Lilly advertised a copy in the same style of binding as above, at 18l. 18s. On the title-page of this copy are the autographs of Isaac D'Israeli and O. Gilchrist.*
Imprinted at London in Paules Churchyarde
by Iohn Cavvood printer to the Queenes
Maiestie. An. Do. 1570.

" The ' divers other workes adioyned ' to this edition are also by Alexander Barclay, viz: The Mirrour of Good Manners (which, as well as the Ship of Fools in this and Pynson's edition, has the Latin text) and Certayne Egloges, which by Wharton are supposed to have been the first that appeared in the English Language."—*Bib. Ang. Poetica.*
" All antient satirical writings, even those of an inferior cast, have their merit, and deserve attention, as they transmit pictures of familiar manners, and preserve popular customs. In this light, at least, Barclay's Ship of Fools, which is a general satire on the times, will be found entertaining. His author, Sebastian Brandt, appears to have been a man of universal erudition ; and his work, for the most part, is a tissue of citations from the ancient poets and historians."— *Warton.*
" The design of this work was to ridicule the prevailing follies and vices of every rank and profession, under the allegory of a ship freighted with fools, and in his metrical translation BARCLAY HAS GIVEN A VARIETY OF CHARACTERS DRAWN EXCLUSIVELY FROM HIS OWN COUNTRYMEN, and added his advice to the various fools, which possesses at least the merits of good sense and sound morality." In Dibdin's Typographical Antiquities, vol. ii. p. 431 and following, will be found a full description of this curious work with fac-similes of the woodcuts.

273 BRANTOME, PIERRE de BOURDELLE, *Abbé de.* Œuvres complètes. Édition revue et augmentée d'après les manuscrits de la Bib. Royale par J. A. C. Buchon. 2 vols. *impl. 8vo. hf. cf.*
Paris, 1838.

274 BRAY, CHARLES. PHILOSOPHY of NECESSITY; or, Natural Law as applicable to Moral, Mental, and Social Science. 2d edition, *8vo. new cloth.*
London, 1863.

275 BRAYLEY'S LONDINIANA, or Reminiscences of the British Metropolis, historical, antiquarian, topographical, and anecdotal. 100 *engravings of famous Buildings, &c.* 4 *vols. post 8vo. new hf. calf, gilt.*
London, 1829.

276 BREE'S, C. R., HISTORY OF THE BIRDS OF EUROPE not observed in the British Isles; *with 238 large and beautiful* COLORED PLATES OF BIRDS AND THEIR EGGS. 4 vols. imp. 8vo. *hf. green mor.*
London, 1863·

277 BRENNER, DAVID. The INDUSTRIES of SCOTLAND, their Rise, Progress, and Present Condition. *Thick 8vo. new cloth.*
Edinburgh, 1869.

278 BRIDGEWATER TREATISES.—A complete set of these highly valuable
Works, on the Power, Wisdom, and Goodness of God, as man-
ifested in the Creation. 12 *vols. 8vo. elegantly bound in tree-
marbled calf, super-extra, marbled edges. Pickering, 1835, etc·*
AN UNUSUALLY FINE COPY.
Comprises Chalmers on the Moral and Intellectual Constitution of Man, 2
vols. ; Kidd on the Physical Condition of Man, 1 vol. ; Roget's Animal and
Vegetable Physiology, 2 vols. ; Buckland's Geology and Mineralogy, 2 vols. ;
Kirby's Habits and Instincts of Animals, 2 vols. ; Prout's Chemistry, Meteorology, etc., 1 vol.

279 Brief Disquisition concerning the Early History of Printing in
America [extracted from the Bib. Am. Vetustium.] *Roy. 8vo.
bds. uncut.* New York, 1866.
Only 25 copies.

280 BRINTON, D. G. MYTHS of the NEW WORLD, *handsomely printed on
heavy toned paper.* Impl. 8vo. new cloth, *uncut.*
New York, 1868.
LARGE PAPER, 56 *copies printed.*

281 BRITISH MUSEUM. SYNOPSIS OF. A curious and interesting volume ; comprising a catalogue of the Antiquities, &c., mounted
on close-ruled writing paper completely filled with manuscript
revisions, additions, &c., &c., evidently intended for a new
edition ; also numerous wood cuts, cuttings, &c. *Thick 8vo. cf.
London, N. D.*

282 BRITISH NOVELISTS ; comprising every work of acknowledged merit,
usually classed under the denomination of Novels, with Biographical Sketches of the Authors, &c., by Wm. Mudford, *numerous
engravings.* 5 vols. 8vo. *hf. cf. neat.* London, 1810.
Contains the novels of Fielding, Smollett, Sterne, Swift, Goldsmith, Richardson, &c., &c.

283 BRITISH POETS. A complete collection of the British Poets, from
Chaucer to Wordsworth, accompanied with Biographical, His-
torical and Critical Notices. *New Edition,* with numerous ad-
ditions. PORTRAITS ON INDIA PAPER. 130 *vols. post 8vo. cloth,
uncut.* Boston, 1865.
LARGE PAPER (No. 19) *only* 100 *copies.*
Includes the Ballads, 8 vols.
BRITISH POETS, Portraits of ; see Portraits.

284 BRITISH ESSAYISTS ; with Prefaces, Historical and Biographical, by
A. Chalmers. 38 vols. post 8vo. *cloth, uncut.*
Boston, 1866.
LARGE PAPER, 100 *copies printed.* (No. 18).

285 BRITTON. The French text carefully revised, with an English translation, Introduction and Notes, by Francis Morgan Nichols. 2
vols. *impl. 8vo. new cloth.* Clarendon Press, Oxford, 1865.
One of the earliest text-books on English law.

286 BRITTON, JOHN. FINE ARTS of the ENGLISH SCHOOL, with Biographical and Critical Descriptions, 20 *fine engravings from
Paintings and Sculptures of eminent English Masters,* roy. 4to.
hf. calf, gilt. London, 1812.
Fine copy, with Portrait of Britton, and Autograph Letter inserted.
Contains specimens of Sir J. Reynolds, Flaxman, Westall, Romney, Nolle-
kens, Northcote, West, &c.

287 BRITTON, JOHN. AUTO-BIOGRAPHY, in Three Parts. SUBSCRIPTION EDITION. I. Personal and Literary Memoir of the author; II. Descriptive Account of his Literary Works; III. Biographical, Topographical, Critical and Miscellaneous Essays. COPIOUSLY ILLUSTRATED. *2 parts in one vol. thick roy. 4to. calf extra.*
London, 1850.

Printed only for presents to the subscribers to the *Britton Testimonial*. J. H. Markland's copy, who has inserted numerous fine portraits, several autograph letters of the author, newspaper cuttings, &c., &c.

288 BRITTON, JOHN. The AUTHORSHIP of JUNIUS, elucidated, including a memoir of Lieut-Col. Isaac Barre, M. P. *Portrait inserted. Roy. 8vo. cloth, uncut, scarce. For the Author, London,* 1848.

Presentation copy from the author to Geo. L. Craik.

289 BROCQUURE, BERTRANDON DE LA. TRAVELS OF, to Palestine, and his return from Jerusalem overland to France during the years 1432 and 1433, edited by Le Grand D'Aussy, translated by Thomas Johnes. *Folding map. 8vo. crimson morocco, in the style of Roger Payne. Hafod Press,* 1807.

Printed at the private Press of the translator.

290 BROOKLYN SANITARY FAIR. History of. *Profusely illustrated with colored plates. 4to. morocco,* extra. *Brooklyn, N. Y.,* 1864.

291 BROMHALL, T. TREATISE on SPECTRES; or an History of Apparitions, Oracles, Prophecies, and Predictions and the Cunning Delusions of the Devil, &c. *Folio, old cf. Scarce. London,* 1658.

292 BROTHERHEAD'S BOOK OF THE SIGNERS; *containing fac-simile letters of the Signers of the Declaration of Independence, also illustrated with* 61 *Engravings from Original Photographs and Drawings of the Residences, Portraits &c. Roy. 4to. hf. morocco, uncut.*
Philadelphia, 1861.

Limited Edition.

293 ———— The same, (another edition), *numerous plates,* thick roy. 4to. *sheets folded. Philadelphia,* 1865.

294 BROUGHAM, HENRY, Lord. WORKS, Biographical, Critical, Historical, and Miscellaneous, corrected and enlarged by HIMSELF, with many new lives of Philosophers, Men of Letters, and Statesmen. 11 *vols. post 8vo. polished calf, extra, marbled edges.*
London, 1862.

FINE COPY.

295 BROUGHAM, HENRY, Lord. LIVES OF THE STATESMEN AND MEN OF LETTERS OF THE TIMES OF GEORGE III. Both series, *numerous fine steel portraits.* 5 vols. roy. 8vo. new hf. cf. gilt.
London, 1839, *&c.*

FINE COPY.

296 BROUGHAM, HENRY, Lord. Critical and Miscellaneous Writings. 2 *vols. 12mo. cloth. Philadelphia,* 1841.

297 BROWN, ANDREW. Letter concerning Family History. Small 4to. uncut. N. D.

298 BROWN, JOHN. Historical Gallery of Criminal Portraitures, foreign and domestic, or a selection of the most impressive cases of Guilt and Misfortune to be found in Modern History. *Portraits, &c.* 2 *vols. 8vo. hf. vellum, red edges.*
Manchester, 1823.

99 BROWN, THOMAS. WORKS in Prose and Verse, serious, comical, and moral, with his Character by N. Drake, also the REMAINS, *engravings.* 5 vols. 12mo. *calf.* *London, 1720, &c.*
The life and popular manners of his time are vividly depicted in the pages of Tom Brown. His genius is acknowledged by Dr. Johnson.

300 BROWN, THOMAS. Hydriotaphia, Urne-burial, or a Discourse of the Sepulchrall Urnes lately found in Norfolk, with the Garden of Cyrus, &c. *4to. antique morocco, red edges.* *London, 1658.*
FINE COPY of the *1st edition.*
"One of the most beautiful works of this admirable author."—*Quarterly Review.*

301 BROWN, THOMAS. Lectures on the Philosophy of the Human Mind, with a memoir of the author by David Welsh. *Portrait.* 4 vols. 8vo. *calf, extra.* *Edinburgh, 1846.*
"An inestimable book."—*Dr. Parr.*

302 BROWN UNIVERSITY. Celebration of the One Hundredth Anniversary of the Founding of, Sept. 1864. *Portrait of James Manning.* Roy. 4to. *uncut.* *Providence, 1865.*
LARGE PAPER.

303 BROWNE, D. J. TREES OF AMERICA, Native and Foreign, Historically and Botanically delineated. *Numerous engravings.* 8vo. *new cloth.* *New York, 1857.*

304 BROWNE, JAMES. HISTORY OF THE HIGHLANDS and of the Highland Clans, *numerous portraits and engravings of arms, &c.* 4 vols. 8vo. *hf. cf. neat.* *Glasgow, 1828.*

305 —— Another copy. 8 parts, 8vo. cloth. *Glasgow, 1828.*

306 BROWNING, ELIZABETH BARRETT. POETICAL WORKS, complete, new Edition, *fine portrait.* 5 vols. 16mo. *tree-marbled* calf, extra marbled edges. *London, 1869.*

307 —— Another copy. 5 vols. 16mo. cf. extra. " "

308 BROWNING, ROBERT. POETICAL WORKS. Miscellaneous Poems, 6 vols., and Ring and the Book, 4 vols., together 10 vols. f. cap. 8vo. *tree marbled, calf extra, marbled edges.* *London, 1868.*

309 BRUCE, JAMES. TRAVELS in EGYPT, NUBIA, ABYSSINIA, &c. to discover the Source of the Nile. *Numerous engravings by Heath,* 5 vols. 4to. hf. calf. *Edinburgh, 1790.*
A large portion of this valuable work is devoted to the Natural History of Abyssinia.
WITH THE ORIGINAL DRAWINGS.

310 BRUMOY, THEATRE DES GRECS, edition augmentée, A LARGE PAPER COPY with the ORIGINAL DRAWINGS, *most beautifully executed, many in colors, and also a set of Proof Plates,* 13 vols. 4to. *half bound, red morocco, cloth sides, uncut.* *Paris, 1785–89.*
A most carefully compiled work by the following eminent scholars: Ch. Brotier for the translation of Aristophanes ; G. de la Porte-Dutheil for Aeschylus ; Rochefort for Sophocles, and Prevost for Euripides.
The original drawings included in the above set are exquisitely fine.

311 BRYDGES, SIR E. CENSURA LITERARIA, containing Titles, Abstracts, and Opinions of Old English Books, with original Disquisitions, Articles of Biography, etc. 10 *vols.* 8vo. *half calf, neat.* *London, 1805-9.*

312 BRYDGES, SIR E. RESTITUTA, or, Titles, Extracts, and Charact;
of Old Books in English Literature, revived. 4 vols. 8vo.
neat. Scarce. *London*, 18.
ONLY 250 COPIES PRINTED, *fine copy with proof leaves.*
" Works justly held in high estimation by all antiquaries in literature."

313 BRYDGES, SIR EGERTON. ARCHAICA, containing a reprint of scarce
old English Prose Tracts with Prefaces, Critical and Biographical. 2 vols. 4to. *hf. calf, extra, edges untrimmed, scarce.*
London, 1815.
ONLY 150 COPIES PRINTED.

314 BRYDGES, SIR EGERTON. RES LITERARIÆ, Bibliographical and
Critical. 3 vols. in 2. *8vo. new hf. green morocco, gilt tops,
uncut edges.* *Naples, Rome, and Geneva*, 1821, &c.
FINE COPY. Only 75 copies printed.
" Not more than 50 sets can be made complete."—See note in vol. 3 p. ix.

315 BRYDGES, SIR EGERTON. POLYANTHEA Librorum vetustiorum, Itali-
corum, Gallicorum, Hispanicorum, Anglicanorum, et Latinorum. *Thick 8vo. calf, extra.* *Geneva*, 1822.
Only 75 copies printed.

316 BRYDGES, SIR EGERTON. CIMELIA; seu examen criticum librorum
ex diaris literaris lingua præcipue gallica ab anno 1665 usque
ad annum 1792, scriptis selectum. *8vo. hf. morocco, uncut,
scarce.* *Geneva*, 1823.
Only 75 copies printed.
Forms a supplement to the works mentioned in the two preceding lots.

317 BRYDGES, SIR EGERTON. GNOMICA; detached Thoughts, Sententious,
Axiomatic, Moral and Critical. *8vo. hf. calf, neat, scarce.*
Geneva, 1824.
Only 75 copies printed.

318 BRYDGES, SIR EDGERTON. Phillips, Edward, THEATRUM POETARUM
ANGLICANORUM; containing brief characters of the English Poets
down to the year 1675. Edited with notes by Sir Egerton
Brydges. *8vo. hf. roxburgh morocco, uncut.* *Geneva*, 1824.
ONLY 100 COPIES PRINTED. *Very scarce.*
Presentation copy from the Editor.

319 BRYDGES, SIR EGERTON. *Lee Priory Press.* CŒLIA; containing
Twenty Sonnets by W. Percy, first printed in 1594. 4to. pp.
21, hf. morocco, neat.
John Warwick, Lee Priory Press, Kent, 1818.
ONLY 100 COPIES. The original was sold for £45, and would now bring £100.

320 BRYDGES, SIR EGERTON. *Lee Priory Press.* SELECT POEMS. Roy.
4to. pp. 40, *vignette, limp covers.*
Lee Priory Press, Kent, 1814.
LARGE PAPER. *Only 100 copies.*

321 BRYDGES, SIR EGERTON. *Lee Priory Press.* OCCASIONAL POEMS,
written in the year 1811. Vignette, roy. 4to. *sheets, stitched,*
pp. 18. *Lee Priory Press, Kent*, 1814.
LARGE PAPER.

322 BRYDGES. AUTOBIOGRAPHY, Times, Opinions, and Contemporaries.
Portraits. 2 vols. 8vo. hf. calf, extra. *London*, 1834.
A FINE and EXTENSIVELY ILLUSTRATED copy.

22? **BRYAN'S DICTIONARY OF PAINTERS, ENGRAVERS, and ARCHITECTS,** with Lists of their Works, their Ciphers, Monograms, and Marks, &c., *used by each engraver.* 2 vols. roy. 4to. LARGE PAPER, *extended to 4 thick vols. full bound in russia, gilt.* *London,* 1816.

A very interesting and valuable copy; the illustrations are UPWARDS of 900 in NUMBER, and comprise specimens of nearly every artist mentioned in the work, including many rare etchings, and engravings in every style of the art. ALL SELECTED IMPRESSIONS.

The plates are arranged in such a manner as to be easily taken out and others substituted in their place, when in the judgment of the collector, superior impressions or more desirable subjects were obtained. The result in this copy, is, that a series of plates, which for their general excellence and fine condition, has seldom been seen in a work of this character.

324 BRYANT, JACOB. ANCIENT MYTHOLOGY, *with nearly 50 fine engravings,* 6 vols. 8vo. *hf. calf, gilt, fine clean copy.* *London,* 1807.

An excellent edition, with Life of the Author, Vindication of the Apamean Medal, and copious Index.

325 BRYANT FESTIVAL at the "Century." *Illustrated edition, with 23 fine Portraits and views.* Roy. 4to. *hf. roxburgh morocco, uncut.* *New York,* 1868.

Only 150 copies printed. (No. 40).

326 BUCHAN, GEORGE. HISTORY of SCOTLAND, translated from the Latin, with notes and a continuation to the Union in the Reign of Queen Anne, by James Aikman. *Portraits, Map,* &c. 4 vols. 8vo. *cf. neat.* *Glasgow,* 1827.

327 BUCHANAN'S ADMINISTRATION ON THE EVE OF THE REBELLION. 8vo. cloth. *New York,* 1866.

328 BUCHOZ, M. HERBIER COLORIÉ DE L'AMÉRIQUE, représentant les Plantes les plus rares et les plus curieuses, qui se trouvent dans celle nouvelle partie du monde. *A series of 200 very large and finely colored plates, after nature.* Roy. folio, hf. morocco, *uncut.* *Paris,* 1783.

FINE LARGE COPY. *Scarce.*

329 BUCKLE, HENRY THOMAS. History of Civilization in England. 2 vols. 8vo. *new hf. cf. extra.* *New York,* 1864.

330 BUFFON. Histoire Naturelle, générale et particulière. Many Hundred *beautifully engraved* Plates. *38 vols. 4to. fine copy in old red morocco, extra, gilt edges.* *Paris,* 1770–80.

Contents. I. Histoire Naturelle et générale, 15 vols. II. Supplement, 7 vols. III. Oiseaux, 9 vols. IV. Minéraux, 5 vols. V. Ovipares et Serpents, par de Lacipede, 2 vols.

331 BULFINCH, THOMAS. AGE OF FABLE; or Beauties of Mythology. *Numerous vignettes on wood.* Crown 8vo. *new hf. cf. extra.* *Boston,* 1870.

332 BULFINCH, THOS. LEGENDS OF CHARLEMAGNE; or Romance of the Middle Ages. *Numerous wood cuts, post 8vo. new hf. cf. extra.* *Boston,* 1869.

333 BUMSTEAD, FREEMAN J. PATHOLOGY AND TREATMENT OF VENEREAL DISEASES, including the results of recent investigations upon the subject. *Numerous illustrations.* 8vo. *new cloth.* *Philadelphia,* 1868.

"Well known as one of the best authorities on the subject."—*Brit. and For. Med. Review.*

334 Bunsen, Christian C. J. Egypt's Place in Universal History;
an Historical investigation, in five books. Translated from the
German by Chas. H. Cottrell. 2d Edition, with Notes and additions by Samuel Birch. *Plates of Egyptian Divinities, Hieroglyphical writings, &c.* 5 vols. *thick 8vo. new cloth.*
London, 1848–67.

Published at £8 11s.
Includes an Egyptian Grammar and Dictionary, and a complete Hieroglyph-
ic Grammar and Lexicon by Birch.

335 Bunsen, Christian C. J. Hyppolytus and His Age; or, the Beginnings and Prospects of Christianity. 2d Edition. With
Appendix, containing his letters to Archdeacon Hare. 2 *vols.*
8vo. new cloth. *London,* 1854.

336 Bunsen, Christian C. J. God in History; or the Progress of
Man's faith in the moral order of the world, translated by
Susanna Winkworth, with a Preface by Dean Stanley. 2 *vols.*
8vo. new cloth. *London,* 1868.

337 Bunsen, C. J. *Baron.* Analecta Ante-Nicæna. 3 vols. 8vo. *new*
cloth. *London,* 1854.

338 Bunsen, C. J. *Baron.* Outlines of the Philosophy of Universal
History, applied to Language and Religion. 2 thick vols. 8vo.
new cloth. *London,* 1854.

339 Bunsen, C. J. Signs of the Times; Letters to Moritz Arndt on
the Dangers to Religious Liberty in the present state of the
World. 8vo. *new cloth.* *London,* 1856.

340 Bunsen, C. J. *Baron.* The Constitution of the Church of the
Future, a practical explanation of the correspondence with the
Rt. Hon. W. Gladstone. *Post 8vo. cloth.* *London,* 1847.

341 Bunsen, *Baron.* Memoir of, drawn chiefly from his family papers,
by his widow, Frances Bunsen. *Portraits and tinted plates.* 2
thick *vols. 8vo. new cloth.* *London,* 1868.

342 Bunyan, John. Miscellaneous Works, *portrait, &c.* 2 vols. 8vo.
hf. cf. gilt. *London,* 1827.

343 Burgess, Hon. T. Battle of Lake Erie, with notices of Commodore Eliot's conduct, &c. 12*mo. cloth.* *Boston,* 1839.

344 Burgess, William R. The Relations of Language to Thought.
12*mo. cloth.* *London,* 1869.

345 Burgoyne, Lieut.-Gen. Orderly Book; from his entry into the
State of New York, until his surrender at Saratoga, Oct. 16,
1777. Edited by Dr. E. B. O'Callaghan. *Portrait inserted.*
Sml. 4to. new hf. red morocco, gilt top, by Bradstreet.
Munsell, Albany, 1860.

One of 5 copies on India Paper, Munsell's Series, No. VII.

346 Burgoyne, Lieut.-Gen. Dramatic and Poetical Works, to which is
prefixed Memoirs of the Author. 2 *vols.* 12*mo. cf. neat.*
Chiswick Press, 1808.

347 Burke, Edmund. The Works of the Right Honorable Edmund
Burke. Revised Edition. *Portrait.* 12 *vols. royal 8vo. cloth uncut.*
Large Paper : *only* 100 *copies.* *Boston,* 1866.
Best edition of the works of this eminent statesman.

348 BURNET, GILBERT. HISTORY of the REFORMATION. *Numerous fine portraits. 3 vols. folio, old cf.* *Dublin,* 1730.

349 BURNET, BP. History of his Own Time. 2 vols. *folio, calf.* *London,* 1724.

350 BURNET, GILBERT. LIVES of Sir MATTHEW HALE and JOHN, Earl of Rochester. 12mo. bds. *uncut. Scarce.* *Pickering, London,* 1820.

One of the earliest of the late Mr. Pickering's publications.

351 BURNET, GILBERT. Court Sermon, 1670. Beautifully printed on toned paper. 8vo. *new cloth.* *Cincinnati,* 1868.

Only 150 *copies printed.*

352 BURNET, THOMAS. Sacred Theory of the Earth; containing an account of its original creation, &c. *Portrait and curious copper-plates.* 2 vols. 8vo. cf. *London,* 1759.

353 BURNEY (CHAS.) and HAWKINS (SIR JOHN.) GENERAL HISTORY of MUSIC from the earliest ages to the present time. BOTH WORKS. *Portraits, and numerous beautiful engravings by* BARTOLOZZI, *from designs by Cipriani. Together,* 9 vols. Roy. 4to. *uniformly bound in new hf. cf. antique, red edges, cloth sides.* A FINE UNIFORM SET, *very scarce.* *London,* 1776.

"Between the rival histories, the public decision was loud and immediate in favor of Dr. Burney. Time has modified this opinion, and brought the merits of each work to their fair and proper level—and adjudging to Burney the palm of style, arrangement, and amusing narrative, and to Hawkins the credit of minuter accuracy and deeper research; more particularly in the points interesting to the antiquary and the literary world in general."—*Life of Burney.*

354 BURNEY, CAPT. JAMES. CHRONOLOGICAL HISTORY of the DISCOVERIES in the SOUTH SEA or PACIFIC OCEAN. *Numerous maps, charts, and plates.* 4 vols. roy. 4to. hf. bound. *London,* 1803–17.

"A masterly digest of the Voyages in the South Sea, displaying a rare union of Nautical science and literary research."—*Quarterly Review.*

355 BURNEY, CAPT. JAMES. History of the Buccaneers of America. *Maps and Charts,* 4to. hf. morocco. *London,* 1816.

356 BURNS, ROBERT. POEMS and SONGS. *Illustrated Edition, with beautifully executed engravings on wood from designs by Birket Foster, Harrison, Weir, &c.,* printed on toned paper, thick 4to. *green levant morocco,* extra, *gilt edges.* *London,* 1867.

357 BURR, AARON. REPORTS OF THE TRIAL OF COLONEL AARON BURR FOR TREASON and for a Misdemeanor, in preparing the means of a Military Expedition against Mexico, a Territory of the King of Spain, with whom the United States was at Peace, &c. By David Robertson. 2 *vols.* 8vo. hf. calf, gilt, *gilt top, uncut edges, scarce in this condition.* *Philadelphia,* 1808.

358 BURR, AARON. MEMOIRS OF, with Miscellaneous selections from his Correspondence by Mat. L. Davis. *Portrait, &c.* 2 vols. 8vo. *cloth.* *New York,* 1837.

359 BURRILL, LADY. Poems. 2 vols. 8vo. *calf, gilt.* *London,* 1793.

"THE LEARNED BLACKSMITH."

360 BURRITT, ELIHU. Walks in the Black Country and its green borderland. *front.* 12mo. *new cloth.* *London,* 1869.

361 BURTON, ALFRED. ADVENTURES OF JOHN NEWCOME in the NAVY. A Poem in four cantos, with *colored plates by* ROWLANDSON, *8vo. hf. cf. extra.* *London,* 1818.

362 BURTON, JNO. HILL. THE BOOK HUNTER, his Nature, his Functions, his Club, Book-Club Literature, etc. Edited by R. Grant White. *Beautifully printed. Post 8vo. cloth.* *New York,* 1863.

363 BURTON, JNO. HILL. Narratives from Criminal Trials in Scotland. *2 vols. crown 8vo. new cloth.* *London,* 1852.

364 BURTON, CAPT. RICHARD F. THE HIGHLANDS OF BRAZIL; with an account of the Gold and Diamond Mines, &c. *Frontispiece, &c.* 2 vols. 8vo. *new cloth.* *London,* 1869.

365 BURTON, RICHARD. HISTORY of the KINGDOM of IRELAND; being an account of all the Battles, Sieges, and other considerable transactions; till the entire reduction of that country by King William, with a Brief account of the Ancient Inhabitants and the first conquest of that Nation by King Henry II. *Numerous fine portraits engraved on wood.* 2 vols. 4to. *elegantly bound in russia extra, gilt edges.* *Westminster,* 1811.
LARGE PAPER. *Only 50 copies printed.*

366 BURTON, ROBERT. THE ANATOMY OF MELANCHOLY, what it is, with all the Kinds, Causes, Symptoms, Prognostics, and several Cures of it. A new Edition, corrected and enriched by Translations of the numerous Classical Extracts. 3 *vols.* 8vo. *half morocco, extra, edges uncut, by Matthews.* BEST EDITION.
Riverside Press, Cambridge, 1861.
LARGE PAPER. Only 75 copies printed. Scarce.

367 BURTON, ROBERT. Anatomy of Melancholy. *Portrait and front.* 8vo. *cloth.* *Philadelphia,* 1855.

368 BURTON, W. E. Cyclopedia of Wit and Humor, of America, Ireland, Scotland and England. *Numerous fine portraits, woodcuts, &c., 3 parts, roy. 8vo. cloth.* *New York,* 1858.

369 BURTY, PHILIPPE. CHEFS D'ŒUVRE of the INDUSTRIAL ARTS, Pottery and Porcelain, Glass, Enamel, Metal, Jewelry, and Tapestry. Edited by W. Chaffers. *Profusely illustrated;* thick 8vo. new cloth, *uncut.* *New York (London),* 1869.

370 BURY, (DE), RICHARD. PHILOBIBLON. A Treatise on the Love of Books. First American Edition, with the Literal English Translation of John B. Inglis. Collated and Corrected with Notes by Samuel Hand. Crown 8vo. *cloth, uncut.*
Albany, Joel Munsell, 1861.
"His book relates the measures he took, the difficulties he encountered, and all the art he exerted to gratify his favorite passion. When Chancellor and Treasurer of England, he took his perquisites and new-year's gifts in books." *See* Burton's "Leicestershire," fol. 1622, p. 300. Gough's "Topography," II. p. 120.

371 BUSHNELL, C. J. CRUMBS FOR ANTIQUARIANS. Complete.
I. Early New York Business Tokens. 1859.
II. Memoirs of Samuel Smith, 1776–1786, written by himself, 1860.
III. Journal of Solomon Nash, 1776–1777. 1861.

IV. Memoirs of Tarleton Brown, Captain of the Revolutionary Army, 1862.

V. Narrative of the Life and Adventures of Levi Hanford.
  1863.

VI. Journal of the Expedition against Quebec, under
  Col. Benedict Arnold in 1775, by Maj. Return J.
  Meigs. 1864.

Vol. 2. I. Narrative of the Exertions and Sufferings of
  Lieut. James Moody. 1865.

II. Narrative of Major Abraham Leggett. 1865.

III. Adventures of Christopher Hawkins, and details of his Captivity, &c. 1864.

Together 9 parts, 8vo. sheets folded, with portraits and engravings.
New York, 1859, &c.

PRIVATELY PRINTED, *only 30 copies.*

372 BUTLER, SAMUEL. Hudibras, with Notes and Life of the Author
by Nash; *fine plates and vignettes, further illustrated by the addition of Hogarth's original set, brilliant impressions ; 3 vols. roy.
4to. hf. cf. extra,* SCARCE. *London,* 1793.

An elegant edition, *of which only* 200 *copies were printed.* Edited by Dr.
Nash, the Historian of Worcestershire, who has added a variety of entertaining notes ; Stanley's copy sold for £14 14s., and Dent's for £16 5s. 6d.

373 BUTLER, SAMUEL. HUDIBRAS, reprint of the edition of 1779. 12mo.
limp cloth. *London,* 1869.

374 BYRD, WM. WESTOVER MANUSCRIPTS; containing a History of the
Dividing Line betwixt Virginia and North Carolina; A Jour-
ney to the Land of Eden, 1733 ; and a Progress to the
Mines, 1728–36. *2 vols. 4to. uncut. Privately Printed.*
Richmond, 1866.

LARGE PAPER, *only 40 copies.*

375 BYRD, WILLIAM. History of the Dividing Line and Other Tracts.
From the Papers of William Byrd, Esquire, of Westover, in
Virginia. 2 vols. *small 4to. uncut. Richmond, Va.* 1866.

200 COPIES PRINTED.

376 BYRON, LORD. WORKS. LIBRARY EDITION, *printed on laid paper.
Portrait.* 6 vols. 8vo. cloth, *uncut. Murray, London,* 1823.

VERY SCARCE in *this state.*

377 BYRON, LORD. COMPLETE WORKS, with his Letters and Journals,
and his Life, by Thomas Moore. *Portraits and Vignettes on
steel, from drawings by Turner and Stanfield.* 17 vols. f. cap. 8vo.
hf. *crimson morocco,* extra. *Murray, London,* 1847.

Has all the variorum notes.

378 BYRON, LORD. HOURS OF IDLENESS. *Original Edition. Post 8vo.
elegantly bound in crimson morocco, extra, gilt edges, by* WRIGHT.
Scarce. *Newark,* 1807.

The first publication of Lord Byron, written between the ages of 16 and 19.
The following prophecy by the critic of the *Edinburgh Review,* in an article
on the "Hours of Idleness," has hardly been realized : "But whatever
judgment may be passed on the poems of this noble minor, it seems we must
take them as we find them, and be content ; for *they are the last we shall ever
have from him.*"

379 BYRON, LORD. HOURS OF IDLENESS ; a Series of Poems, original
and translated. *Post 8vo. calf. Scarce. London,* 1820.

First genuine edition.

380 Byron, Lord. Childe Harold. A Series of 30 *illustrations after drawings by Gilbert, Duncan, Cope, Goodall, Corbould, Faed, &c, &c., finely engraved on wood.* 4to. bds.

Art Union, London, 1855.

381 Byron, Lord. English Bards and Scotch Reviewers. With Preface and Notes by E. A. Duyckinck. *Roy. 4to. bds. uncut.*

New York, 1865.

Large Paper, 75 copies.

382 Byron. The True Story of Lord and Lady Byron, as told by Lord Macaulay, Thos. Moore, Countess of Blessington, Lady Byron, &c., in answer to Mrs. Beecher Stowe. *Sq. 16mo. vellum cloth.* *London,* 1869.

383 Byron. Countess of Blessington's Journal of Conversations with Lord Byron, with a sketch of the Author's Life. *12mo. new cloth.* *Boston,* 1869.

384 CÆSAR'S COMMENTARIES, translated in English, to which is prefixed a Discourse concerning the Roman Art of War, by William Duncan. Original Edition, *with portraits and 86 large and spirited engravings, including the Fine Buffalo Plate.* Large and fine copy, russia extra, *marbled edges.* *London,* 1753.

From the Library of the Marquis of Hastings. Brilliant impressions of the plates.

385 Cabot, Sebastian. The Remarkable Life, Adventures, and Discoveries of Sebastian Cabot, of Bristol, the founder of Great Britain's maritime power, &c., by J. F. Nicholls. *Portrait. Sq. 12mo. new cloth.* *London,* 1869.

Handsomely printed.

386 Caledonian Poetry. Poetry of Nature, comprising a selection of the most sublime and beautiful Apostrophes, Histories, Songs, Elegies, &c., from the Works of the Caledonian Bards. *The Typographical execution in a style entirely new, (?) printed with script characters.* 4to. old cf. neat. *Scarce.*

London, 1789.

Very curious.

387 Calmet, Augustine. Phantom World; or, the Philosophy of Spirits and Apparitions, with Introduction, &c., by the Rev. Henry Christmas. *2 vols. crown 8vo. hf. vellum, uncut.*

London, 1850.

388 Calmet's Dictionary of the Bible, Historical, Critical, Geographical and Etymological, Revised, Augmented and Corrected by C. Taylor. *5 vols. 4to. half roan, uncut. Charlestown,* 1812.

In its improved state, Mr. Taylor's edition of Calmet's Dictionary is indispensably necessary to every Biblical Student.

389 Cambridge Portfolio; or, Sketches of the Scenery, Antiquities, Public Buildings, &c., of Cambridge. Edited by the Rev. J. J. Smith. Nearly 100 large and fine engravings, and numerous woodcuts, facsimiles, &c., &c. *2 vols. roy. 4to. cloth, uncut.*

London, 1840.

Large Paper, *few printed.*

390 Camden's Britannia, translated and enlarged by Bp. Gibson, *portrait and numerous engravings of Coins, and maps,* 2 vols. folio, calf gilt. *London,* 1722.

Best edition of Bp. Gibson's translation.

391 CAMDEN, WILLIAM. Remains concerning Britain; 7th Edition, ammended by the Industry and care of John Philpot. *Fine Portrait by White.* 12mo. (8vo.) *mottled calf, extra, yellow edges.* *London,* 1674.
Beautiful copy.

392 CAMDEN. The Historie of the Most renouned and Victorious princess Elizabeth, late Queen of England, contayning all the Important and Remarkable Passages of State, both at home and abroad, during her long and prosperous Raigne. *Beautiful impression of the portrait.* Folio. *Handsomely bound in mottled calf, super-extra, yellow edges.* *London,* 1630.
BEAUTIFUL COPY. Original Edition.

393 CAMOENS' LUSIAD, or the Discovery of India, a Poem, translated from the Portuguese, in Verse, by Mickle, 4to. *calf, neat.*
London, 1778.
This elegant translation is extolled by Mathias in the " Pursuits of Literature."

394 CAMPAN, MADAME. MEMOIRS of the PRIVATE LIFE of MARIE ANTOINETTE, with Recollections, Sketches and Anecdotes, illustrative of the Reigns of Louis XIV, XV, and XVI. *Portraits.* 2 vols. 8vo. hf. cf. gilt. *London,* 1823.

395 CAMPBELL, J. F. FROST and FIRE; Natural Engines, Tool-Marks and Chips, with sketches taken at home and abroad by a traveller. *Profusely Illustrated.* 2 thick vols. 8vo. new cloth.
Edinburgh (Phila.) 1865.

396 CAMPBELL, JOHN, LORD. LIVES OF THE LORD CHANCELLORS and Keepers of the Great Seal of England, from the earliest times till the reign of King George IV, *complete.* LARGE TYPE, LIBRARY EDITION. 7 vols. 8vo. *elegantly bound in polished calf, extra, marb. edges.* *Murray, London,* 1845–47.
ORIGINAL EDITION, *very scarce.*

397 CAMPBELL, JOHN, *Lord.* LIVES of LORD LYNDHURST and LORD BROUGHAM. *8vo. new cloth.* *London,* 1869.
*** Forms the concluding volume to the preceding lot.

398 CAMPBELL, JOHN, *Lord.* LIVES of the LORD CHANCELLORS and Keepers of the Great Seal of England. 4th Edition. 10 *vols. crown 8vo. new hf. cf. extra.* *Murray, London,* 1858.

399 CAMPBELL, JOHN, *Lord.* LIVES of the CHIEF JUSTICES of ENGLAND, from the Norman Conquest till the death of Lord Tenterden. 3 *vols. 8vo. hf. cf. extra.* *London,* 1858.
LIBRARY EDITION.

400 CAMPBELL, DR. JOHN. NAVAL HISTORY of GREAT BRITAIN, including the History and Lives of the British Admirals, with a continuation to the close of the year 1812. 8 *vols. impl. 8vo. hf. cf. neat, edges uncut.* *London,* 1813.
Enlarged Edition, containing many additional lives of Naval Commanders and their achievements during the important period from 1779 to 1813.

401 CAMPBELL, MAJOR WALTER. Old Forest Ranger; or Wild Sports of India. *Numerous fine steel plates.* Crown 8vo. cloth.
London, 1863.

402 CAMPBELL, DR. THOMAS. Strictures on the Ecclesiastical and Literary History of Ireland, from the most ancient times. 8vo. calf, *scarce.* *Dublin,* 1789.

403 CANADA. GEOLOGICAL SURVEY, Report of Progress from its commencement to 1863. *Nearly 400 wood-cuts. Very thick 8vo. cloth.* *Montreal, 1863.*

404 CANOVA'S WORKS in SCULPTURE and MODELLING, with Descriptions by the Countess Albrizzi, and Life by Cicognara, 100 *beautiful outline engravings by H. Moses, and portrait by Worthington,* 3 vols. impl. 4to. *new hf. morocco, neat,* LARGE PAPER.
London, 1824.

This extensive and fine series of engravings exhibits in great perfection Canova's most magnificent works of sculpture.

405 CARDINAL DE RETZ. A Literary Curiosity, by the author of " The Maid's Husband," &c. 2 vols. post 8vo. *hf. vellum, gilt.*
London, 1844.

406 CAREY, HENRY C. PRINCIPLES of SOCIAL SCIENCE. 3 vols. 8vo. *hf. morocco, neat.* *Philadelphia, 1858.*

407 CAREY, HENRY C. The SLAVE TRADE, Domestic and Foreign ; why it exists, and how it may be extinguished. 12mo. *hf. morocco, neat.* *Philadelphia, 1862.*

408 CARICATURES. DON PIRLONE a ROMA, *a series of upwards of* 300 *caricatures by Italian Artists, engraved on copper, very curious. Oblong 4to. hf. morocco.* S. A. et L.

409 CARICATURES by GILLRAY, ROWLANDSON, CRUIKSHANK, and other celebrated artists, 100 *large and very satirical or humorous engravings, the greater portion in* COLORS, folio, *hf. bound.*
London, 1782–1823.

A very curious and interesting collection ; the caricatures of the Royal Family, Pitt, Fox, &c., are broadly humorous.

410 CARLETON, W. TRAITS and STORIES of the IRISH PEASANTRY, NEW EDITION, with Autobiographical Introduction and Explanatory Notes, *embellished with numerous spirited etchings and woodcuts,* 2 vols. thick 8vo. new cloth. *London, 1856.*

" Admirable, truly, intensely Irish ; never was the outrageous whimsicalities of that strange, wild, imaginative people so characteristically described."—*Blackwood.*

411 CARLISLE, FREDERICK, *Earl.* The FATHER'S REVENGE, a Tragedy ; with other Poems. *8vo. the Text neatly inlaid throughout, and illustrated by the insertion of numerous fine Portraits, Views, and Scenes. Roy. 4to. hf. morocco, uncut.*
Bulmer, London, 1800.

PRIVATELY PRINTED.
This copy was illustrated by W. Turner, who did the Dibdin's "Bibliomania," belonging to the library of John Allan.
Lord Carlisle was in early life the British envoy to the Colonies at Philadelphia during the American War, and guardian to Lord Byron. See " *English Bards and Scotch Reviewers.*"

412 CARLISLE, WILLIAM. ESSAY ON EVIL SPIRITS ; or reasons to prove their existence, &c. 12mo. *bds. Scarce.*
For the author, London, 1825.

413 CARLYLE, THOMAS. COMPLETE WORKS. LARGE TYPE, LIBRARY EDITION, comprising Miscellaneous Essays, 6 vols. FRENCH REVOLUTION, 3 vols. Life of Schiller, 1 vol. Sartor Resartus, 1 vol. Lectures on Heroes, 1 vol. Past and Pres-

ent, 1 vol. *Together 13 vols. 8vo. elegantly bound in tree-mar-bled calf extra, marbled edges, contents lettered. London, 1869–70.*
Elegant copy of the Best Edition—will be completed in about 20 volumes.

414 Carlyle, Thomas. Works, complete uniform edition, *handsomely printed,* 16 vols. *post 8vo. new hf. calf extra.*
London, 1859–60.

415 Carpenter, S. D. Logic of History. 500 Political Texts; being concentrated extracts of Abolitionism, &c. 8vo. cloth.
Madison, Wis., 1864.

416 Cartwright, W. C. On the Constitution of Papal Conclaves, *frontispiece. 12mo. vellum cloth, yellow edges.* Edinburgh, 1868.

417 Cary, Alice. Ballads, Lyrics, and Hymns. *Illustrated Edition. fine portrait, and numerous engravings on wood, sqr. 8vo. blue levant morocco antique.* New York, 1866.

418 CASANOVA, Jacques de Seingalt. MEMOIRES écrites par lui-même. Edition Originale, la sense complète: 6 vols. 12mo. hf. calf, neat. Bruxelles, 1860.

Fine copy, *very scarce.*
" J'ai cherché à découvrir le véritable auteur de ces mémoires si amusants, si spirituels et si curieux, qui ne sont pas et ne peuvent être de Jacques de Casanova, lequel était incapable d'écrire en français et surtout de composer un ouvrage de cette espèce ; car s'il était assez instruit, il n'entendait rien à une œuvre d'imagination et de style. Il est certain, cependant que ce fameux chevalier d'industrie avait laissé des notes et même des mémoires originaux, mais ces manuscrits étaient certainement indignes de voir le jour, et il fallut un habille homme pour les mettre en œuvre. Cet habile homme fut, nous en avons la certitude morale, Stendahl, ou plutôt Beyle, dont l'esprit, le caractère, les idées, et le style se retrouvent à chaque page dans les Mémoires imprimés." Bibliophile Jacob ; *note dans le catalogue Dutacq, page 60.*

419 Castiglione, Baldassar. The Courtier, translated into English, with other pieces in prose and verse, with a Life of the Author by A. P. Castiglione, *fine portrait after Raphael by Virtue,* thick 4to. calf, neat. W. Boyer, London, 1727.

"The treatise, 'Il Cortigiano' (The Courtier), of Count Castiglione, was written by the author while a resident at the Court of Urbino, which happened to be a very favorable specimen of courts. The work has been much and long admired in Italy, both for the thoughts and the style, and it still ranks among the classical works of the sixteenth century."—Eng. Cyclop.

420 Castlereagh, Viscount. Memoirs and Correspondence of, edited by his brother, Charles Vane, Marquis of Londonderry, *portraits,* 4 vols. 8vo. calf, gilt. London, 1848.

420* Catalogue. Bibliotheca Heberiana. The library of Richard Heber, complete. 13 *parts, 8vo. boards.* London, 1834, &c.
The most extensive, curious, and interesting library ever formed by one collector, rich in the rarest articles in every class of literature, in most languages.

421 Catalogue of a rare and extensive collection of books relating principally to America, forming the library of Joel Munsell, Esq. *8vo. tinted paper, uncut.* New York, [1865].
Large Paper.

422 Catalogue of the library of A. Wight, of Philadelphia. Prepared by J. Sabin. Roy. 8vo. *boards, uncut.* New York, 1684.
Large Paper.

423 CATALOGUE of the Private Library of the late William, J. Davis
    Royal 4to. uncut.   *New York*, 1865
      LARGE PAPER; *only 75 copies.*

424 CATALOGUE of the Private Library of John W. Grigg, of Phila
    delphia. *Imp. 8vo. pp.* 50, *half green morocco, gilt top, by Brad
    street.*   *Privately printed*, 1867
    Only 10 *copies printed.*

425 CATALOGUES. WOODWARD'S COIN SALES, *nearly a complete series, th
    greater portion with the printed prices, one on large paper, 4to.* 1
    catalogues, 8vo. and 4to. *paper.*   *New York*, 1862–67

426 CATLIN, GEORGE. ILLUSTRATIONS OF THE MANNERS, CUSTOMS, AN
    CONDITION OF THE NORTH AMERICAN INDIANS. *Upwards . o
    Three Hundred and Sixty engravings, from the Original Drawings
    by the Author. 2 vols. imperial 8vo. cloth, scarce.*
                                 London, 1857

427 CATLIN, GEORGE. O-KEE-PA. A religious ceremony; and othe
    customs of the Mandan Indians, *with* 13 *colored illustrations
    from drawings by the author,* 4to. new cloth.   *London*, 1867

428 CATHEDRALS. MURRAY'S HAND-BOOK TO THE ENGLISH CATHE
    DRALS. FOUR SERIES *complete,* profusely illustrated with finel
    executed engravings on wood, of *views, elevations, interiors
    groundplans, ornaments, &c., &c.* 6 *vols. post 8vo. handsomely boun
    in polished calf, extra, gilt edges.*   *London*, 1861--64

429 CATTERMOLE, GEORGE. ILLUSTRATED HISTORY OF THE GREAT CIVI
    WAR between Charles I. and the Parliament, 28 *highly finishe
    engravings of the most important events, by Heath, &c., royal 8vo
    cloth, gilt leaves.*   *London*, 1844--45

430 CAUSSIDIERE. MEMOIRS OF CITIZEN CAUSSIDIERE, ex-prefect of police
    and representative of the people (Revolution, 1848). 2 *vols. i
    one, crown 8vo. half vellum, gilt, uncut.*   *London*, 1848
    "Citizen Caussidiere subsided into a wine merchant in Broadway, Ne
    York."

431 CAUSSIN, NICHOLAS. HOLY-COURT. Treating of the motives whick
    should excite men of quality to Christian perfection; Maxim
    of Christianity against Profaneness, translated by Sir Thoma
    Hawkins. *Fourth Edition. Numerous old copperplate portraits
    thick folio, calf, neat.*   *London*, 1678
    Includes a Life of Mary, Queen of Scots, Cardinal Pole, &c.

432 CAVE, WILLIAM. History of the Lives, Acts, Death, and Martyr
    doms of those who were contemporary with or immediately suc
    ceeded the Apostles. Also the most eminent of the Primitiv
    Fathers, with Chronology, &c., *frontispiece, portraits,* 2 vols
    folio, calf, *very neat.*   *London*, 1687

433 CERVANTES. Don Quixote de la Mancha, LORD CARTERET'S EDITION
    In Spanish. *Good impressions of the beautiful set of* 68 *plates b
    VANDERGUCHT, 4 vols. 4to. calf gilt.*
                            Tonson, London, 1738
    "A splendid and excellent edition, with plates, two of which are b
    Hogarth."—*Lowndes.*

434 CERVANTES. DON QUIXOTE. ILLUSTRATIONS TO. *The complet

series of the celebrated engravings after designs by SMIRKE, *including the vignettes.* ARTIST PROOF IMPRESSIONS ON LARGE PAPER. *Folio, elegantly bound in pale brown morocco, super-extra, extra gilt sides, back, the inside panels elaborately ornamented with tooling to a Grolier pattern, gauffred gilt edges, &c., &c.* London, 1817.

BEAUTIFUL COPY, *few issued in this form.*

435 CÉRÉMONIES DES MARIAGES DES ROYS ET AUTRES GRANDS, Ordre des Séances des États-Généraux et des Notables. MSS. Folio. Old calf, gilt.

These historical collections commence with the marriage contract of Louis XII., 1498, and are transcripts from original records. They detail the marriage ceremonies of all the Royal personages of France, from that date to 1626. This volume was originally among the archives of the French government. They describe, in the minutest detail, the marriage ceremonies of the Royal personages, for 128 years. Some passages of these narratives, though in keeping with the style and manners of the times, would rather shock our sense of propriety. I shall notice one or two instances, omitting such circumstances as would not be tolerated in print in our day. Louis XIII. was married, in Bordeaux, on the 18th of October, 1615, at the premature age of fourteen, to Anne of Austria, of the same age. Therefore, they may well be called, in the language of the narrative, "the little King and the little Queen." The ceremonies on the occasion are circumstantially described, concluding, naturally, with the wedding night. The bridegroom and bride, immediately after an early supper, went to their respective rooms. The Queen-Mother, Mary of Medicis, remained with the little Queen until eight o'clock, when she went to the little King's room, and said to him, "My son, it is not enough to be married: you must go and see your wife, who is waiting for you." As a dutiful son, he answered, "Madame, I was only waiting for your command; and, to prove it, I will now go along with you." He then got up, and accompanied by his mother, went to the bridal chamber, where the bed, having been previously consecrated by one of the King's Chaplains, was already occupied by the bride. The little King, with his mother, nurse, wife's nurse, and five or six household officers, entered the room. The Queen-Mother, approaching the nuptial bed, told the little Queen, "Daughter, this is the King, your husband, whom I bring to you: love him well, I beg you." The bride answered in Spanish, that she had no other wish but to obey and please him and her, both. Mary of Medicis and the officers then went out of the room, leaving the two nurses with the young couple. Two hours after, the young King awoke, and called to his nurse for his night-gown and boots. As soon as they were put on, she took him back to his own room, where his officers were in waiting. He betook himself to bed, and slept soundly until morning. The little Queen went, likewise, to her own chamber, and slept on the small bedstead she had brought from Spain, &c., &c.

436 CHALMERS' (ALEX.) GENERAL BIOGRAPHICAL DICTIONARY : containing a Historical and Critical Account of the Lives and Writings of the most eminent persons of every nation, from the earliest accounts to the present time. EXTENDED AND ILLUSTRATED BY THE INSERTION OF NEARLY 1000 PORTRAITS, MANY OF WHICH ARE OF GREAT RARITY, ALL PROPERLY ARRANGED. 32 *vols. thick 8vo. half calf, gilt.* London, 1812–17.

To illustrate in a proper way a book of the above character, more is required than to accumulate indiscriminately a mass of engravings, to be bound in with the volumes, thereby swelling their bulk without increasing their artistic or literary value. Great care should be taken to *select* the portraits, also keeping in view the importance of the biographies with which they are to be placed. It is believed that these latter considerations were invariably borne in mind in the formation of the above fine collection. It may also be added, in commendation of this set, that the Biographical Dictionary of Chalmers, on account of its completeness and general merit, will always be considered invaluable as a standard authority and a work of reference for scholars.

437 CHAMBERS, ROBERT. CYCLOPEDIA OF ENGLISH LITERATURE. A History, Critical and Biographical, of British Authors from the

earliest to the present times; *numerous portraits on wood; 2 vols. imp. 8vo. new hf. cf. extra.* (*Edinburgh,*) *Phila.* 1863.

438 CHAMBERS, ROBERT. BOOK OF DAYS. A miscellany of Popular Antiquities, in connection with the Calendar, including Anecdote, Biography, and History, Curiosities of Literature, &c. *Profusely illustrated, 2 thick vols. imp. 8vo. tree calf, extra.*
Edinburgh.

439 CHAMIER, CAPT. R. M. Bent Brace, and Ayesha. 2 vols. in one. *8vo. hf. morocco, gilt.* *Paris,* 1836.

440 CHAPMAN, GEORGE. SONNETS attached to Chapman's translation of Homer's Iliad; *handsomely printed, sm. 4to. hf. morocco, gilt.*
Cheswick Press, 1857.

EXCESSIVELY RARE, *only 6 copies printed,* to wit: No. 1, Rev. John Mitford. —No. 2, Rev. Alexander Dyce.—No. 3, S. W. Singer.—No. 4, J. R. Smith. No. 5, D. Whittingham, and No. 6, Rev. Richard Hooper, (the editor.) The above is No. 1, Mitford's copy, with his autograph.

441 CHAMPFLEURY. Histoire de l'Imagerie populaire. *Profusely illustrated with facsimiles, &c., post 8vo. new hf. morocco, extra.*
Paris, 1869.

441* CHARLES I. WORKS. Reliquiæ Sacræ Carolinæ, or the Works of that great monarch and glorious martyr King Charles I. PROOF IMPRESSION *of the rare portrait.* 16mo. *crimson morocco, gilt.*
Hague, 1650.

FINE COPY of a rare edition unknown to Lowndes, who quotes only the later one of 1651.

442 CHARLES I. EIKON BASILIKE. The Pourtraicture of his most sacred Maiestie in his Solitudes and Sufferings. *Fine copy of the rare frontispiece by* MARSHALL. 12mo. (8vo.) *sprinkled calf extra, yellow edges.* *S. L.,* 1648.

FIRST EDITION, *beautiful copy.*
"So great was the interest which it excited, that 47 editions, 48,000 copies, were speedily absorbed."—*Allibone.*

443 CHARLESTON, THE SIEGE OF, by the British Fleet and Army, under the Command of Admiral Arbuthnot and Sir Henry Clinton, which terminated with the Surrender of that place on the 12th May, 1780. *Small 4to. uncut.* *Albany: J. Munsell,* 1867.
100 *copies printed.*

444 CHARLEVOIX, P. Histoire et Description Generale de la Nouvelle France, *numerous maps, &c. 2 vols. 4to. calf gilt.* *Paris,* 1744.

445 CHARLEVOIX, REV. P. F. X. History and General Description of New France, translated with Notes, &c. by Jno. G. Shea. *Fine portrait. Impl. 4to. uncut.* *New York,* 1866.
LARGE PAPER, few printed.

446 CHATTERTONIANA; comprising LIFE AND WORKS by Southey and Dr. Gregory. *Best edition, with plates, fac-similes, &c. 3 vols.* BRYANT (Jacob) on ROWLEY'S POEMS, 1 vol.—GREGORY'S LIFE, WARTON, and DAMPIER ESSAYS on ROWLEY, 3 vols. in one.—LIFE by JOHN DIX. *Large paper,* 1 vol. *together 6 vols. 8vo. newly bound in half calf, extra.* *London,* 1789–1836, &c.
A FINE SERIES.

447 CHAUCER. CANTERBURY TALES, with an Essay on his language and versification and an Introductory Discourse, together with Notes

and Glossary by Thomas Tyrwhitt. *Illustrated with a beauti-
ful series of engravings from designs by* MORTIMER. BRIL-
LIANT IMPRESSIONS. *2 thick vols. 4to. calf, extra, marbled edges.*
CLARENDON PRESS, *Oxford,* 1798.

LARGE PAPER, BEST EDITION.
.*. The illustrations were inserted only in the L. P. copies.

448 CHAUMONOT, PIERRE JOSEPH M. La Vie de, Missionnaire dans la
Nouvelle France. *Small 4to. bds. uncut.*
Cramoise Press, New York, 1858.

449 CHESTER, JOSEPH L. Notes upon the Ancestry of William Hutchinson and Anne Marbury, pp. 24. *4to. uncut. Boston,* 1866.

450 CHESTERFIELD, Earl of. LETTERS AND MISCELLANEOUS WORKS,
with Memoirs of his Life by Dr. Maty. *Portrait, 4 vols. 4to.
calf, neat.* *London,* 1777.

451 CHEVALIER BAYARD. The right joyous and pleasant History of
the Feats, Gests, and Prowesses of, by the Loyal Servant. 2
vols. crown 8vo. cloth, uncut. *London,* 1825.

452 CHILD, MAJ. J. New England's Jonas cast up at London, 1647,
with Introduction and Notes by W. T. R. Marvin. *Small 4to.
uncut.* *Boston,* 1869.
150 *copies.*

453 CHITTENDEN, L. E. Report of the Debates and Proceedings in the
Secret Session of the Peace Convention ; *thick 8vo. cloth.*
New York, 1864.

454 CHODOWIECKE, DANIEL N. (The German Wilkie.) ETCHINGS.
A series of nearly 100 *etchings by this celebrated German artist,
all neatly mounted on plate paper, including many fine and rare
specimens ; 4to. hf. green morocco.* *V. D.*

455 CHODOZKO, ALEX. SPECIMENS of the POPULAR POETRY of Persia, as
found in the adventures and Improvisations of Kworoglou ;
thick 8vo. cloth. *Oriental Society, London,* 1842.

456 CHRONICLE of the KINGS of ENGLAND, and MEMOIR of GUY, EARL of
WARWICK, reprinted from a Monastic MS. with Glossaries,
&c. ; sml. 4to. cloth. *London,* 1840.
PRIVATELY PRINTED, *by an amateur.*

457 CHRONICLES of RABBI JOSEPH BEN JOSHUA BEN MEIR. The Sphardi,
translated from the Hebrew by C. H. F. Bialloblotzky. 2 vols.
8vo. cloth. *Oriental Society, London,* 1836.

458 CHRYSOSTOM, JOANNIS. OPERA, quæ hactenus versa sunt omnia, ad
Græcorum codicum collationem multis in locis per utrusque
linguæ peritos emendata. *5 vols. in 3, thick folio, vellum.*
Basileæ in Officina Froberiana, MDXXX.

459 CHUNDER BHOLANAUTH. TRAVELS of a HINDOO to various parts of
Bengal and Upper India, with an Introduction by J. T. Wheeler.
Map ; 2 vols. post 8vo. new cloth. *London,* 1869.

460 CHURCH, BENJ. HISTORY OF KING PHILIP'S WAR, with an Introduction and Notes by Henry M. Dexter. *Maps. 2 vols. roy. 4to.
uncut.* *Boston,* 1865.
LARGE PAPER, *one of 4 copies on* DRAWING PAPER.

461 CHURCHILL'S COLLECTION of VOYAGES AND TRAVELS, *with several*

hundred engravings and maps, 6 vols. folio, hf. calf gilt, fine uniform set. London, 1744–7.

Unfortunately some of the plates are wanting, otherwise in fine condition.

These extensive collections comprise many Travels here first printed from the original MSS. and others first published in English, with a full account of the progress of Trade and Navigation from the beginning.

462 Cibber, Colley. Plays. *Subscription Edition.* 2 vols. roy. 4to. *calf, extra.* London, 1721.
Fine copy, *scarce.*

463 Cibber, Colley. Apology for the Life of, written by himself; with an historical view of the Stage during his Own Time. 4to. *half, neat, scarce.* London, 1740.
Original Edition.

464 Cleveland, John. Works, containing his Poems, Orations, and Epistles; also The Rustick Rampant, or, Rural Anarchy affronting Monarchy in the Insurrection of Wat Tyler, with Life of the Author. *Fine old portrait.* 12mo. (8vo.) *crimson morocco, gilt edges, in the style of Roger Payne.* London, 1699.
Fine copy. The famous Royalist Poet of the Commonwealth era.

465 Cleveland, John. Poems, J. C., with additions never before Printed. *Portrait.* 12mo. (8vo.) old cf. neat, *scarce.*
(London,) Printed in the yeare 1657.
" A genial artist, pure latinist, exquisite orator, and excellent Poet."—*Fuller.*

466 Clapperton's Second Expedition into the Interior of Africa; with the Journal of Richard Lander, *portrait and map, 4to. bds.* London, 1829.
See also, Denham and Clapperton.

467 Clarendon, Edward, Earl. History of the Rebellion and Civil Wars in England, begun in the year 1641. *Fine portrait after Lely.* 3 vols. thick folio, old cf. neat. Oxford, 1707.
Large Paper.

468 Clarendon, Earl. Characters of Eminent Men in the Reigns of Charles I. and II. Including the Rebellion, from the works of Lord Chancellor Clarendon. *Thick 12mo. calf, gilt.*
London, 1793.

Extra Illustrated, upwards of 60 rare and curious portraits and etchings inserted, many of which are very scarce.

469 Clarendon, Earl. State Papers, containing the materials from which his History of the Rebellion was composed, also, Life by himself, containing a continuation of his History of the Rebellion. 4 vols. roy. folio, hf. calf, gilt.
Oxford, Clarendon Press, 1759–67, *&c.*

470 Clark, Geo. H. Undertow of a Trade-Wind Surf, a series of fugitive poems, *handsomely printed on heavy toned paper, sm. 4to. cloth.* Hartford, 1860.
Only a limited edition, presentation copy from the author.

471 Clark, Col. Geo. Rogers. Campaign in Illinois in 1778–9, with an Introduction by the Hon. Henry Pirtle. *Portrait. 8vo. new cloth, uncut.* Cincinnati, 1869.

472 ——— Another copy. Imp. 8vo. *new cloth, uncut. Cincinnati,* 1869.
Large Paper.

473 CLARKE, ADAM. Account of the Infancy, Religious and Literary Life of, by himself, with additions by one of his daughters. *Portrait. 8vo. hf. calf neat.* *For the Author, London,* 1841.

474 CLARKE, DR. E. D. TRAVELS in VARIOUS COUNTRIES of EUROPE, Asia, and Africa. *Portrait, maps, and engravings.* BEST EDITION. 11 vols. 8vo. hf. calf *extra, fine copy.* *London,* 1816–24.

475 CLARKE, GEORGE. VOYAGE to AMERICA, with Introduction and Notes, by E. B. O'Callaghan. *Frontispiece. Sm. 4to. uncut.*
Munsell, Albany, 1867.
Only 100 copies.
N. Y. Colonial Tracts, No. II.

476 CLARK, HENRY JAMES. MIND in NATURE; or the origin of Life, and the Mode of Development of Animals; *upwards of 200 illustrations. 8vo. new cloth.* *New York,* 1865.

477 CLARKE, MARY COWDEN. THE COMPLETE CONCORDANCE TO SHAKESPEARE; being a Verbal Index to all the passages in the Dramatic Works of the Poet. *Portraits, Newspaper cuttings, etc. Very thick royal 8vo. half red morocco, gilt top, uncut edges.* *London,* 1847.
UNIQUE, from the Balmanno Collection.
This interesting volume (considered by its late owner as one of the gems of his collection), *contains a selection of upwards of 50 closely written pages of the* ORIGINAL MANUSCRIPT, *together with a long and exceedingly interesting Autograph letter (10 pp.), giving a minute and detailed account of the progress of the work from its first inception, through the twelve years occupied in its compilation, and four more of Press corrections, to its final publication. Also copies of a congratulatory letter from Douglas Jerrold; the Author's application for the Privilege of dedicating the work to the Queen; the Queen's reply. Also, numerous Newspaper cuttings, etc., all neatly mounted.*
The Author gives the following account of the origin of the idea of a Shakespeare Concordance:—"One fine morning, the 15th of July, 1829, at the breakfast-table of some friends in Somersetshire, the subject of Cruden's Concordance to the Bible was started, its vast utility discussed, and a regret expressed that no work existed for the quoters of Shakespeare. The hope of facilitating the use of his universal axioms, of helping to spread still further the knowledge of his wondrous wisdom and truth, fired my ambition; the desire to be myself the means of supplying a Concordance to the Bible of the Intellectual world, seized upon my imagination. That very day, I began my glorious task; with a pencil and the 'Tempest' in my hand, I accompanied my friends in their morning walk, thus offering the first lines of my work in honor of nature's poet on nature's own shrine—in the face of nature herself—in the open air."
Mr. Balmanno was a regular correspondent with Mrs. Cowden Clarke, under the *nom de plume* of the "Enthusiast," and was also the projector of the well-known American Testimonial to that lady, the contributors to which comprised many of the leading literary men of the day.

478 [CLARKE, WM.] REPERTORIUM BIBLIOGRAPHICUM; or, some Account of the most celebrated British Libraries, *numerous fine portraits, including the portrait of Francis I. engraved by W. Behns the sculptor* (the only plate he ever executed), *also the private plate of the Roger Payne monument.* Roy. 8vo. hf. green morocco, gilt top, *uncut edges.* *London,* 1819.
FINE CLEAN COPY.

479 CLARKSON, THOMAS. History of the Rise, Progress, and Accomplishment of the Abolition of the Slave Trade. 2 *vols. 8vo. russia.* *London,* 1808.

480 CLAY, HENRY. WORKS. Edited by Calvin Colton. 6 *vols. 8vo. sheep.* *New York,* 1863.

481 CLINTON, SIR HENRY. Narrative of the Campaign of 1781 in North America. *Folio, uncut.* J. Campbell, Philad., 1865. LARGEST PAPER, *only 25 copies.*

482 CLINTON, SIR HENRY. Answer to Sir Henry Clinton's Narrative of the Campaign of 1781. *Folio, uncut.* Philadelphia, 1865. LARGEST PAPER, 25 *copies.*

483 CLINTON, LIEUT. GEN. SIR HENRY. Observations on Mr. Steadman's History of the American War. *Fine photographic portrait. Royal 4to. sheets, folded. Privately reprinted,* New York, 1864. *Only* 50 *copies.*

484 CLOUGH, ARTHUR HUGH. The Bothic of Toper-na-Fwosich. A long vacation pastoral. 12mo. *bds.* Cambridge, Mass., 1849.

485 COBBETT, WILLIAM. WORKS of Peter Porcupine. New Edition. 2 vols. 8vo. hf. cf. Thomas Bradford, Philadelphia, 1796.

486 COCHRANE, CLARK B. MEMORIAL OF. *8vo. new hf. morocco, gilt top, by Bradstreet.* Munsell, Albany, 1867. ONE OF 3 COPIES *on India paper.*

487 COGHLAN, MRS. Memoirs of, written by herself. With an Introduction and Notes. LARGE PAPER. *Royal 4to. uncut.*

New York, 1864.

ONLY 20 COPIES PRINTED.

488 COHN, ALBERT. Shakespeare in Germany in the XVIth and XVIIth Centuries; and Account of English Actors in Germany and the Netherlands, &c. *4to. new cloth.* London, 1865.

489 COLDEN, CADWALLADER. THE HISTORY of the FIVE INDIAN NATIONS of Canada, which are Dependent on the Province of New York in America, etc. *Fine map, 8vo. handsomely bound in Cambridge calf, extra, carmine edges.* London, 1747. FINE TALL COPY.

490 COLERIDGE, SAMUEL TAYLOR. WORKS, comprising the FRIEND, edited by Henry N. Coleridge, 2 v. NORTHERN WORTHIES, 3 v. ESSAYS ON HIS OWN TIMES, edited by his daughter, 3 v. NOTES on ENGLISH DIVINES, 2 v. DRAMATIC WORKS, 1 v. LAY SERMONS, 1 v. POEMS, 1 v. CHURCH and STATE, 1 v. CONFESSIONS of an INQUIRING SPIRIT, 1 v. NOTES, Theological, Political and Miscellaneous, 1 v., and LECTURES on SHAKESPEARE and MILTON, 1 v. 8vo. LETTERS, CONVERSATIONS, and RECOLLECTIONS by Alsop, 1 v., together 18 vols. f. cap, 8vo. and 8vo. *uniformly bound in hf. blue morocco extra, gilt top, edges uncut, contents lettered. Moxon and Pickering, London,* 1850, *&c.* A very fine uniform set.

491 COLERIDGE, S. T. THE FRIEND; A Literary, Moral, and Political weekly paper, excluding personal and party politics and the events of the day, conducted by S. T. Coleridge. 27 nos. *complete, 8vo. sprinkled calf extra.* FINE COPY.

London, 1809–'10.

ORIGINAL NUMBERS *as published.* EXCESSIVELY RARE.

492 COLERIDGE, SAMUEL TAYLOR. Specimens of the Table-Talk of. *Portrait.* 12mo. *tree calf extra, marbled edges. Scarce.*

London, 1836.

53 COLERIDGE, SIR JOHN DUKE. Speeches delivered in the Court of Queen's Bench, in the case of Saurin *vs.* Star~ 8~~ ~~~~ *cloth.* L~~~~~, ~~~~.

An action brought by a professed Sister of the Order of Mercy against the Mother Superior of the Convent of Hull, to recover damages for assault and conspiracy to drive her from the convent, and have her expelled from the Order.

54 COLESON, MISS ANN. Narrative of her Captivity among the Sioux Indians. *Woodcuts. Imp. 8vo. bds.* Philadelphia, 1864.

55 Collectanea Græca Majora, ad usum Academicæ Juventutis, cum Notes, &c., Andreas Dalzel. 3 vols. 8vo. hf. morocco.
Boston, 1835.

56 COLLIER, JEREMY. Short View of the Immorality and Profaneness of the English Stage. *8vo. hf. mor. gilt.* London, 1698.

57 COLLIER, J. PAYNE. A BIBLIOGRAPHICAL AND CRITICAL ACCOUNT OF THE RAREST BOOKS IN THE ENGLISH LANGUAGE, alphabetically arranged, which during the last fifty years have come under the observance of J. P. C. *4 vols. crown 8vo. cloth.*
Riverside Press, (New York,) 1868.

57* ———— Another copy. LARGE PAPER. 4 vols. *8vo. new hf. rox. morocco, uncut.* New York, 1868.
ONLY 75 COPIES PRINTED.

58 COLLIER, J. PAYNE. POETICAL DECAMERON; or ten conversations of English Poets and Poetry, particularly of the Reigns of Elizabeth and James I. *2 vols. post 8vo. new, hf. green morocco, gilt.*
Edinburgh, 1820.

59 COLLINS' PEERAGE OF ENGLAND; Genealogical, Biographical and Historical, greatly augmented and continued to the present time, by SIR EGERTON BRYDGES. BEST EDITION. 9 vols. 8vo. *polished calf, extra, marbled edges.* London, 1812.

FINE COPY, *very scarce.*
The standard work of English Nobility and Family History. "Sir Egerton Brydges brought to his task the imagination of a Poet and the industry of an Antiquary."

60 COLLINSON, REV J. LIFE OF THUANUS, with some account of his Writings. *Portrait. 8vo. hf. cf.* London, 1807.

61 COLEMAN, GEORGE. (The Elder.) COMPLETE WORKS. Dramatic Works, 4 vols. Miscellaneous Works, 3 v. *Fine portrait after Gainsborough,* together 7 vols. 12mo. calf, full gilt, *fine copy.*
London, 1787.

62 COLMAN, GEO. (The Younger). Eccentricities for Edinburgh; containing Poems. *12mo. hf. mor. uncut, scarce.*
Edinburgh, N. D.

63 COLMAN, GEORGE (*The Younger*). BROAD GRINS, Tales in Verse. *16mo. calf gilt.* London, 1804.

64 [COMBE, WILLIAM.] ENGLISH DANCE OF LIFE and DANCE OF DEATH. Poems by the Author of Doctor Syntax, *with early impressions of the celebrated colored engravings,* by ROWLANDSON. *3 vols. 8vo. calf gilt.* London, 1815–17.

ORIGINAL EDITIONS, *very scarce.*
"The success of 'Doctor Syntax' prompted this, and similar works. Rowlandson supplied the illustrations during the first half of the month preceding

7

publication, and Combe wrote the text between the 16th and ?0th, descri?
the Artist's designs."

    Wm.) All the Talents; A Satirical Poem, in t?
Dialogues, by Polypus. 3d Edition. 8vo. pp. 81, *hf. ?orou*
uncut. London, 180?.
A scarce Political satire, attributed to Mr. Combe, author of Dr. Syntax. The
above copy has numerous ms. additions, newspaper cuttings, &c., inserted.

506 Comte, Auguste. Positive Philosophy, translated by Harriet
Martineau. *Thick post 8vo. cloth.* New York, 1858.

507 Comte de Paris. The Trades Unions of England, translated by
N. J. Senior, edited by Thomas Hughes. 12mo. new cloth.
London, 186?

508 Confederate Documents, Nos. 1 to 54. Official publications,
one vol. 8vo. hf. sheep. Richmond, 1861, &c.

509 Condorecourt, A. de. Les Prétendants de Catherine. *5 vols. in*
2. 16mo. hf. mor. Bruxelles, 1853.

510 Congreve, William. Dramatic and Poetical Works. *3 vols.*
12mo. cf. neat, scarce. Ewing, Dublin, 1773.

511 Convention of Delegates from several New England States held
at Boston, 3, 9, 1780, with Introduction, &c. by F. B. Hough.
Small 4to. uncut. *Munsell*, Albany, 1867.
100 copies.

512 Conybeare and Howison. Life and Epistles of Saint Paul.
Illustrated Edition, with numerous highly finished engravings on
steel, maps, woodcuts, &c. 2 vols. roy. 4to. *elegantly bound in*
tree-marbled calf extra by Riviere. London, 1866.
A beautiful copy.

513 Cooper, J. Fenimore. Works. *Illustrated Library Edition* elegant-
ly printed in large type. *Engravings from designs by* F. O. C.
Darley, woodcuts, &c., with a Biographical Essay by Wm.
Cullen Bryant. 32 *vols. crown 8vo. cloth.* New York, 1861.
Original Issue, *scarce.*

514 COOPER, Jas. Fenimore. LIFE of CAPT. RICHARD
SOMERS. The Original Manuscript. 21 *pp. folio, bound*
with the text as published in Graham's Magazine, Oct. 1847.
Folio, half morocco.
Presented to Mr. Balmanno by Rufus W. Griswold, with his autograph attestation.
In addition to the above, this volume contains 10 autograph letters, signed,
to J. D. P. Ogden, Esq., his lawyer, concerning his lawsuit against J. Watson
Webb, and others, for libel, 1839–40; also an unsigned letter to the Editor of
the *Commercial Advertiser*, 4to., with notes and newspaper cuttings inserted
by Mr. Balmanno.

515 Cook, Captain. Voyages Round the World, *complete*, with Life,
by Kippis, comprising First Voyage, 3 vols. Second Voyage,
2 vols. Third Voyage, 3 vols. and Life, 1 vol. *Several hun-*
dred maps, charts, and engravings; together 9 vols. 4to. *uniformly*
bound in calf gilt. London, 1773–84.

516 Copeland, R. Morris. Country Life; a Handbook of Agriculture,
Horticulture, and Landscape Gardening. *Several hundred en-*
gravings on wood, thick 8vo. new cloth. Boston, 1863.

517 Copland, James. Dictionary of Practical Medicine; comprising
General Pathology, Nature and Treatment of Diseases, &c. 3
thick vols. 8vo. sheep. N. Y. 1855.

518 Corneille, P. Œuvres, avec les notes de tous les Commentateurs (par Parrelle), *fine portrait*. Best Edition. 12 *vols. 8vo. green morocco, gilt.* Impr. de J. Didot l'aine, Paris, 1824.

" Edition de la collection des classiques français ; c'est la plus belle en ce format ; elle reproduit le texte de 1682, avec les nombreuses variantes des premières éditions ; et l'on y a ajouté plusieurs piéces de vers ainsi que huit lettres inédites."—*Brunet.*

519 Cornwallis, Charles, *Marquis.* Correspondence, edited with notes by Charles Ross, Esq. *Portraits.* 3 vols. 8vo. *tree-calf, extra, marbled edges.* London, 1859.

Contains much valuable information relating to the Revolutionary War, in which Lord Cornwallis was engaged from 1776–1781, and to India, of which he was twice Governor-General, 1786–93, the Irish Rebellion, 1798, &c.

520 Cory, I. P. Treatise on Accounts, Mercantile, Private, and Official, &c., &c. *8vo. bds. uncut.* Pickering, London, 1840.

**** Presentation copy from the author.

521 Cosevelt, W. G. Gallery of Pictures, with an Introduction by Mrs. Jameson. *A series of 90 fine outline plates after pictures by the old masters.* India proofs. Roy. 4to. new hf. *crimson morocco, extra.* London, 1836.

522 Cotton, Charles. Scarronides ; or Virgil Travestie. A mock Poem on the First and Fourth Books of Virgil's Æneid. 12*mo. boards, uncut.* Durham, 1807.

523 Couch, J. Fishes of the British Empire ; *with* 183 beautifully colored *engravings, comprising accurate figures of Fishes from Drawings by the Author,* with Scientific and Popular Descriptions. 4 vols. imp. 8vo. hf. morocco. London, 1867.

524 Council of Trent. Historia del Concilio Tridentino di Pietro Soare Polano. Seconda editione, *with the front. containing a view of the Council. Small 4to. vellum.* Rome, 1629.

525 Cousin, Victor. Course of the History of Modern Philosophy. 2 vols. 8vo. cloth. New York, 1852.

526 Covell, Silas L. Memorial, Minute and Resolution adopted by the Irving Club, July 22, 1867. *8vo. hf. green morocco, gilt top, by Bradstreet.* Albany, 1867.

One of 5 copies on Holland Paper.

527 Cowper, William. Poems. 3d Edition. 2 vols. 8vo. *cf. neat.* London, 1787.

From the library of William Hayley, the Friend, Editor and Biographer of the Poet, with his mss. notes, corrections, &c., and the following note on fly-leaf: " My first copy of Cowper's Poems, bought before I had the delight of knowing that dear interesting Bard, and carried with me to Weston in my first visit to him."—W. H.

528 Coxe, P. Social Day, a Poem, *with 32 most beautiful engravings, chiefly by J. Scott, roy. 8vo. calf, extra.* London, 1823.

This beautiful volume contains engravings after Wilkie, Stothard, Smirke, Cooper, Hill, &c. The exquisite plate of the " Broken Jar," by Wilkie, " the first plate executed on steel," engraved by Warren, has alone been sold for £3. 3s.

529 Cox, S. S. Eight Years in Congress—1857–65. Memoir and Speeches. *Portrait, 8vo. cloth.* New York, 1865.

530 Craig, A. R. The Book of the Hand ; or, the Science of Modern

Palmistry, chiefly according to the systems of D'Arpentigny and Desbarrolles, *with diagrams, &c.* *Crown 8vo. new cloth.*
London, 1867.

531 CRISIS (The). A Weekly Newspaper, edited by Sam. Medary, from its commencement, Jan. 1861 to Jan. 1864. 3 *vols. folio, hf. sheep.* Columbus, 1861–64.

The editor was, at the commencement of the war, Governor of Kansas, and subsequently became notorious by his advocacy of Southern principles during the late war.

532 Croker, T. Crofton. Fairy Legends. 2d Edition, *vignette,* 16*mo. cloth.* London, 1838.

533 Cromwell. Life of Oliver Cromwell, Lord Protector of the Commonwealth of England, Scotland, and Ireland. *Fine portrait by Virtue.* 8vo. hf. cf. gilt. London, 1725.

534 CROMWELLIANA. A Chronological Detail of Events in which Oliver Cromwell was engaged, from the year 1642 to his death in 1658; with a continuation of other Transactions, to the Restoration.

Largest Paper, *few copies printed for illustration.*

Extra Illustrated Copy. *Formerly belonging to* Robert Southey, *with his autograph on the title-page.* Nearly three hundred extra plates inserted, comprising Rare and Curious Portraits, Old Views, Facsimiles of Warrants, Genealogical Tables, &c., &c. *All neatly inlaid. Thick folio. Cambridge-calf, extra, yellow edges.* Westminster, 1810.

A very interesting volume, evincing good taste on the part of the illustrator.

535 Cronise, Titus F. Natural Wealth of California, with a detailed description of each county. Thick *roy.* 8vo. *new cloth.*
San Francisco, 1868.

536 Crosby, Brass (*Lord Mayor of London*). Memoir of, *Illustrated, with portraits and numerous Autographs, Original Documents, &c., &c., many on vellum, with seals attached, &c., &c. Roy. 4to. hf. morocco, uncut.* London, 1829.

Large Paper, *privately printed.*

537 Crowe, Catherine. The Night-Side of Nature; or, Ghosts and Ghost Seers. 12*mo. new hf. morocco.* London, 1863.

538 Cudworth's True Intellectual System of the Universe, *frontispiece by White,* 2 vols. in one, folio, *calf.* London, 1678.

" The vastest Magazine of reasoning and learning which ever appeared against Atheism."

539 Cundall, Joseph. Ornamental Art applied to Ancient and Modern Book-binding, *illustrated with specimens of various dates and countries.* (12) with 23 *extra plates inserted.* 4to. *hf. olive morocco, neat.* London, 1848.

John Allan's copy with his book-plate, &c.

540 CUPID and PSYCHE. *A series of* 33 *rare and curious engravings on copper by Ant. Salaert.* Early impressions. *Neatly mounted on heavy paper, roy.* 4to. *hf. cf. neat.*
(Brussels), *circa* 1630.

Rare and Curious.

541 Cussans John E. Handbook of Heraldry ; with Instructions

for tracing Pedigrees and deciphering Ancient MSS. also rules for the appointment of Liveries. *Profusely illustrated*, post 8vo. *new cloth*. London, 1868.

542 Custodis. Patriciarum Stirpium in S. Rom. Imp. vrbe Augusta Vindelicor Quarum quædam, à IV. et ultra, seculis hucusque superstites; &c., &c. Text in Latin and German. 122 *fine copperplates, of Knights, Armor, &c.* Sml. 4to. cf. gilt.
Auguspburg, 1613.

543 Custos, John. Sufferings of, for Free-Masonry, and from his refusing to turn Roman Catholic. *Portrait and curious plates of Tortures*, 8vo. calf gilt. London, 1846.

544 Cutts, J. Madison. Brief Treatise upon Constitutional and Party Questions, and the History of Political Parties. 12mo. *new cloth*. New York, 1866.

545 Cuvier's Animal Kingdom, arranged after its Organization. Translated and Enlarged by Carpenter and Westwood, *with upwards of 300 Colored and other Engravings. Imp. 8vo. green calf extra, marbled edges.* London, 1863.

546 Cyclopedia of American Literature; embracing Personal and Critical Notices of Authors, and selections from their writings, from the earliest period to the present day, by Evert A. and George L. Duyckinck. *Numerous fine portraits on India paper, and several hundred wood-cuts. 5 parts. Royal 4to. uncut.*
New York, 1866.

Large Paper; *only 100 copies.*

547 Cymbalum Mundi; or Satirical Dialogues on various subjects by Bonaventure des Pierriers, with a Critical Letter, &c., *frontispiece*, 8vo. *hf. mor. gilt.* London, 1723.

Very curious.
"Ces dialogues, composés à la manière de Lucien, son de Bonaventure des Periers, qui, dans une lettre à un prétendu Pierre Tryocan (Croyant), placée au commencement du livre, a prise le nome de Thomas du Clevier (pour du Clenier, ou l'incrédule). C'est un ouvrage allégorique assez piquant, et, surtout, beaucoup mieux écrit qu'on ne le faisait alors. Malheureusement, l'autorité crut apercevoir, dans les allégories du faux Thomas du Clevier, des impiétés et des hérésies condamnables, et le livre fut déféré au parlement de Paris, qui en ordonna la suppression, et fit mettre en prison le libraire Morin."
—*Brunet.*

548 Cyprian, St. Genuine Works, together with his Life written by his own Deacon Pontius, translated into English with Notes, &c., by Nathaniel Marshall. *Frontispiece*, folio, calf.
London, 1717.

549 Dabistan (The), or School of Manners, translated from the original Persian with notes and illustrations by David Shea and Anthony Troyer. 3 vols. 8vo. *new cloth.*
Oriental Society, London, 1843.

550 Dabney, Rev. R. L. Life and Campaign of Lieut.-Gen. Thos. J. Jackson (Stonewall Jackson). *Portrait and Diagrams, 8vo. cloth.*
New York, 1866.

551 D'Abrantes, Duchess (Madame Junot). Memoirs. *Portraits,* 8 vols. 8vo. new hf. calf, extra. London, 1831.
Best Edition, *scarce.*

552 Dagley, R. Death's Doings; consisting of original compositions

in Prose and Verse, intended as illustrations of the 24 *plates designed and etched by R. Dagley*. 8vo. hf. red morocco, *neat*.
London, 1826.

553 D'ALEMBERT, JEAN LE-ROND. ŒUVRES COMPLÈTES avec un Éloge par Condorcet. 5 *vols. 8vo. paper*. Paris, 1821.

554 (DALRYMPLE, SIR D. *Lord Hailes*). Opinions of Sarah, Duchess of Marlborough, from original MSS. 12*mo. hf. mor. uncut, very scarce*. (London), 1788.
White Knights, £1.10s.

555 DANA, R. H., JR. An Address upon the Life and Public Services of Edward Everett. *Roy. 4to. uncut*. Cambridge, 1865.
LARGE PAPER.

556 DANCE OF DEATH, exhibited in Elegant Engravings, with a Dissertation on the various Representations of that subject, particularly those of MACABRE and HOLBEIN, by FR. DOUCE, *upwards of 60 engravings*, 8vo. *new hf. morocco, uncut. Pickering*, London, 1833.
This edition is a faithful and beautiful facsimile of the celebrated woodcuts of Holbein, which have always been ranked amongst his finest productions.

557 DANCE OF DEATH, *exhibited in elegant engravings on wood*, with a Dissertation on that subject, particularly those ascribed to MACABRE and HANS HOLBEIN, by Francis Douce, *profusely illustrated*. 8vo. cloth, *uncut*. *Pickering*, London, 1833.

DANCE OF DEATH, see Combe, Wm.

558 DANGEAU, MARQUIS. Memoirs of the Court of France from the year 1684 to the year 1720, translated with Historical and Critical Notes. 2 *vols. 8vo. calf, gilt*. London, 1825.

559 DANIELL'S PICTURESQUE VOYAGE TO INDIA by way of China, with Descriptions, 50 *plates*, BEAUTIFULLY COLORED *in imitation of Drawings, on stout cardboards*, roy. 4to. *hf. russia, gilt*.
London, 1810.

560 DANIELL, GEORGE. MERRIE ENGLAND in THE OLDEN TIME. 2 *vols. crown 8vo. hf. olive morocco, gilt top, uncut edges*.
London, 1842.
EXTRA ILLUSTRATED COPY, by *William Upcott*.
Upwards of 200 *Curious and Rare Portraits, Views, &c.*, also 2 *Beautiful* DRAWINGS *in water-colors*, curious old cuttings from contemporary newspapers, &c., &c., neatly mounted and arranged.
This copy cost its present owner $100.
The author was the celebrated collector of Old English Literature, the sale of whose library realized £14,000.

561 DANTE. L'ENFER, traduction Française de Pier Angelo-Fiorentino, *with the illustrations from designs by* GUSTAVE DORÉ, *folio, new hf. green morocco, gilt top, uncut edges*. Paris, 1862.

562 D'ARBLAY, MME. DIARY AND LETTERS complete, including the period of her Residence at the *Court of Queen Charlotte*. *Portraits*, 7 *vols. post 8vo. polished calf, extra, yellow edges, by Bedford*.
London, 1842–46.
ORIGINAL EDITION, beautiful copy.
"Sparkling with wit, teeming with lively anecdotes and delectable gossip, and full of sound and discreet views of persons and things."

563 D'ARGENS, MARQUIS. New Memoirs, establishing a true knowledge of mankind, &c., being a critical Inquiry into the nature of Friendship and Happiness, &c., &c. 2 *vols.* 12*mo. cf. neat, scarce*.
London, 1747.

564 DARLEY, F. O. C. SKETCHES ABROAD with Pen and Pencil. *Small 4to. new cloth.* New York, 1869.

565 DARNELL, ELIAS. Journal of the Hardships, Captivity, Battles, &c. of the Volunteers and Regulars commanded by General Winchester, 1812–13. *16mo. boards.* Philadelphia, 1854.

566 DARWIN, ERASMUS. TEMPLE OF NATURE; or the Origin of Society; A Poem, with Philosophical Notes. *Illustrated with a fine series of Plates by* FUSELI. Roy 4to. calf, gilt. London, 1803.
LARGE PAPER.

567 DART, J. HISTORY AND ANTIQUITIES OF CANTERBURY CATHEDRAL, and the Adjoining Monastery, with Lives of the Archbishops, Priors, &c. 61 *large and fine plates, including every monument in the Cathedral, Tail-pieces, &c. Folio, russia extra.*
London, 1726.
FINE COPY, *original edition.*

568 DARWIN, CHARLES. VARIATION OF ANIMALS AND PLANTS under Domestication, *numerous fine engravings on wood.* 2 *vols.* 8*vo. polished calf, extra, marbled edges.* London, 1868.

569 DARWIN, CHARLES. ON THE ORIGIN OF SPECIES by means of natural selection, or the preservation of favored races in the struggle for life. *Crown 8vo. new cloth. Murray,* London, 1869.

570 DARWIN, CHARLES. Journal of Researches into the Natural History and Geology of Countries visited during the Voyage of H. M. S. Beagle round the World. *Thick crown 8vo. cloth.*
London, 1860.

571 DARWIN, CHARLES. Various contrivances by which British and Foreign Orchids are Fertilized by Insects. *Numerous cuts, post 8vo. new cloth.* London, 1862.

572 DASENT, GEORGE WEBBE. THE STORY OF BURNT NJAL; or Life in Iceland at the end of the Xth century, from the Icelandic of Njal's Saga. *Numerous maps, plans, &c.* 2 *vols. post 8vo. new cloth.*
Edinburgh, 1861.

573 DAVENANT, SIR WM. THE RIVALS, a Comedy. *Sm. 4to. pp. 56, hf. vellum.* Wm. Cademan, London, 1668.
"This Play is printed without any author's name; but Langbaine, with authority of Cademan, the publisher, ascribes it to Sir William Davenant." —*Baker's Biog. Dram.*

574 DAVIDS, T. HISTORY of INK, including its Etymology, Chemistry, and Bibliography. *Facsimiles, 12mo. bds.* N. Y., N.D.

575 DAVIES, C. M. HISTORY of HOLLAND from the beginning of the Tenth to the end of the Eighteenth Century. 3 *vols.* 8*vo. hf. calf, extra.* London, 1841–4.
" A valuable work, chiefly compiled from Original Documents, State Papers, &c."

576 DAVILA, H. C. Historie of the Civil Warres of France, with the CONTINUATION, containing the Life of the Duke of Espernon. *Portrait.* 2 vols. *folio, calf.* London, 1647–70.

577 DA VINCI. TREATISE on PAINTING, translated from the Italian by Dr. J. Rigaud, with a new Life of the Author by J. S. Hawkins. *Illustrated with a series of 23 outline plates on copper, Portrait, &c. Roy. 8vo. new hf. morocco, uncut.* London, 1802.
LARGE PAPER. *Best Edition.*

578 Davis, Hugh. De Jure Uniformitatis Ecclesiasticæ; or three Books of the Rights belonging to an Uniformity in Churches. *Folio, old calf, neat.* London, 1669.

579 Davis, Wm. J. In Memoriam, by H. B. Dawson. *Roy. 4to. uncut. Privately printed.* N. Y. 1865.

580 DAVISON, Francis. POETICAL RHAPSODY, with a Preface by Sir Egerton Brydges. The second volume containing the Poems of A. W. and Sir Walter Raleigh. 2 vols. in one, 8vo. hf. *crimson morocco, extra.* Lee Priory Press, Kent, 1814, &c.

Unique (?) Lowndes says *one* copy on India paper.
The present is a fine copy, elegantly printed throughout on fine India paper, on one side only.
"The collection of Elizabethan Poetry, now introduced to the curious through the *Lee Priory Press,* has long been a desideratum among lovers of Old English Literature; for though it passed through four editions in the Reign of James I., it has, for the last century, been so rare, that but few have been gratified with a perusal of it."
"The most estimable of our Early Metrical Miscellanies."

581 Dawson, Henry B. Major-General Israel Putnam; a Correspondence on this Subject with the Editor of "The Hartford Daily Post" by "Selah" of that City and Henry B. Dawson, of White Plains, N. Y. *Royal 8vo. new hf. morocco, gilt top, uncut, by Bradstreet.*
Privately Printed, Morrisania, N. Y., 1860.

582 Dawson, Henry B. The Assault on Stony Point by General Anthony Wayne, July 16, 1779. Prepared for the N. Y. Historical Society, and read at its regular monthly meeting, April 1, 1862. *Map and numerous fac-similes. Royal 8vo. boards.*
Morrisania, N. Y., 1863.

Only 250 copies printed. No. XI of the "Gleanings."

583 Dawson, Henry B. Correspondence between John Jay and Henry B. Dawson, and between Jas. A. Hamilton and Henry B. Dawson, concerning the Federalist. *Roy. 4to. boards.*
Large Paper [No. 25.] New York, 1864.

584 Dean, John W. Memoir of the Rev. Nathaniel Ward, author of the "Simple Cobbler of Agawam," with notices of his Family. Roy. 8vo. *new cloth, uncut.* Munsell, Albany, 1868.

585 Dean, Silas. Papers relating to the Case of, now first Published from the Original Manuscripts. *8vo. boards, uncut.*
Seventy Six Society, Philadelphia, 1855.

586 [Deane.] Bibliographical Tracts. Number One. Spurious Reprints of Early Books. *8vo. uncut.* Boston, 1865.
Edition, 131 copies.

587 Decimal Coinage. A series of Eleven Tracts, Papers, &c., on Currency, Uniform Decimal System, &c., collected by John Dillon (deputy chairman of the Decimal Association). *Autograph Letters inserted; one vol. roy. 8vo. new hf. morocco.*
London, V. D.

588 Decker, T. The Gull's Hornbook, edited from the scarce edition of 1609, with Glossary and Notes, by Dr. Nott. 4to. boards, uncut. Bristol, 1812.
Only 100 Copies Printed.
"This work affords a greater insight into the fashionable follies and vulgar habits of Queen Elizabeth's day than perhaps any other extant."

589 DE CORDOVA, R. J. The Prince's Visit; A humorous description of the Tour of his Royal Highness. *8vo. paper.*
New York, 1861.

590 DE COSTA, B. F. Pre-Columbian Discovery of America by the Northmen, illustrated by translations from the Icelandic Sagas, Notes, &c. *Map, 8vo. cloth, uncut.* Albany, 1868.

591 DEE, Dr. JOHN, on SPIRITS. A Relation of what passed for many Years between Dr. John Dee and some Spirits; also the Letters of sundry great men and Princes to the said Dr. Dee. With a Preface by Meric Casaubon, D. D. *Folio cf. gilt, very scarce.* London, 1659.
" This work made a great noise on its publication, and the credit of it was revived a long time afterwards by Dr. Hook."—*Lowndes.*

592 DE FOE, DANIEL. Novels and Miscellaneous Works, with Prefaces and Notes, including those attributed to Sir Walter Scott. 6 *vols. 12mo. cloth.* *Bohn,* London, 1854.

593 DE FOE, DANIEL. Memoirs of the Life and Adventures of Signor Rozelli at the Hague, *numerous copperplate engravings, 8vo. calf, very neat.* London, 1709.

594 [DE FOE, DANIEL.] CARLETON, CAPT. GEORGE. MEMOIRS OF, including anecdotes of the War in Spain under the Earl of Peterborough, and many interesting particulars relating to the manners of the Spaniards in the beginning of the last century, by himself. *Roy. 8vo. hf. morocco, gilt top, uncut.* Edinburgh, 1808.
LARGEST PAPER. Edited by Sir Walter Scott.
" The best account of Lord Peterborough that I have happened to meet with, is in Captain Carleton's Memoirs."—*Dr. Johnson.*

595 DEFOE. Life and Newly-Discovered Writings of Daniel Defoe. Comprising Several Hundred Important Essays, Pamphlets, and other Writings, now first brought to light, after many years' diligent search. By William Lee, Esq. With Fac-Similes and Illustrations. 3 vols. 8vo. *new cloth.* London, 1869.
VOL. I.—A NEW MEMOIR OF DEFOE. VOLS. II. and III.—HITHERTO UNKNOWN WRITINGS. A most valuable contribution to English History and English Literature.
" There can be no two opinions as to the importance of the materials which Mr. Lee's industry and zeal have placed at our disposal." * * * * *
" Articles and narratives are accumulated here in the most graphic and charming style." * * * * " The new list of Defoe's writings, included by Mr. Lee in his first volume, may be pronounced by far the most exhaustive and trustworthy that has been ever compiled."—*The Saturday Review,* 15th May, 1869.

596 DE GENLIS, *Countess.* MEMOIRS, illustrative of the History of the XVIIIth and XIXth centuries; also, ROMANCES (Duchess de la Vallière and Mme. de Maintenon). *Portrait, together* 10 *vols. in 5, crown 8vo. hf. cf. extra,* fine copy. London, 1825.

597 D(ELONEY) T. THOMAS of READING; or the sixe worthie Yeomen of the West. *4to. hf. morocco, uncut.* London, 1632.
Only a limited edition. [Reprinted, Edinburgh, 1812.]

598 DE LA BECHE, SIR HENRY. Geological Observer; many hundred illustrations, *very thick 8vo. cloth, scarce.* London, 1851.

599 DE LA MOTRAYE'S TRAVELS through Europe, Asia, and into Part of

Africa; *profusely illustrated with Maps and engravings on copper.* 3 *vols. folio, calf,* [*rebacked*] *extra.*
Printed for the Author, London, 1723.

600 DE LA MOTTE. Vie de Jeanne de St. Remy de Valois, ci-devant Comtess de la Motte, confidente et favorite de la Reine de France, avec particulieres relatives au Collier de Diamans. 2 *vols. p. 8vo. cloth.* Paris, [1798.]

601 DELEPIERRE, OCTAVE. Analyse des Travaux de la Société des Philobiblon de Londres, *printed on dutch paper, post 8vo. hf. mor. uncut.* London, 1862.
"Tiré à 300 exemplaires seulement."

602 DE LASTEYRIE, *Count* C. P. HISTORY of AURICULAR CONFESSION, Religiously, Morally and Politically Considered. 2 vols. in one, *post 8vo. new hf. vellum, extra, uncut.* London, 1848.
Now scarce.

603 DEMOCRATIC REVIEW and UNITED STATES MAGAZINE. A complete set from its commencement in October, 1838, to and including July, 1859. *Profusely illustrated with fine portraits on steel of eminent statesmen, &c.* BOTH SERIES. 31 *vols. 8vo. hf. sheep, uniform.* New York, 1838–59.
This set includes the very scarce "Historical Register" forming the 4th vol. of the first series, which being published as supplements to the various numbers, running through several years, *is wanting in most sets.*

604 DEMOCRITUS in LONDON, with the Mad Pranks and Comical Conceits of Motley and Robin Good-fellow. 12*mo. cloth.*
Pickering, London, 1852.

605 DEMOSTHENES. ORATION UPON the CROWN, translated with notes by Henry, Lord Brougham. *Post 8vo. new hf. vellum, extra.*
London, 1840.

606 DE PEYSTER, GEN. J. WATTS. Historical Tracts, viz., Practical Strategy, Secession in Switzerland, and in the United States. Dutch Battle of the Baltic, History of Carausius, &c. 4 pamphlets, 8vo. paper. Poughkeepsie, &c., 1858.

607 DE PEYSTER, J. W. The Dutch at the North Pole, &c. 8vo. paper. New York, 1857.

608 DE PILES, ART OF PAINTING, and the Lives of the Painters, containing a compleat Treatise of Painting, Designing, and the use of Prints, with reflections on the works of celebrated Painters, translated from the French, with an essay on the English School. 8*vo. calf, rebacked with red morocco,* gilt.
UNIQUE COPY. London, 1706.
With 30 old drawings in india ink, of painters' heads (including the artist ?), also a rare portrait, (etching) of Hollar, by himself.

609 DE RETZ, CARDINAL. MEMOIRS OF, containing the particulars of his own Life, with an account of the Secret Transactions of the French Court. 4 *vols. 12mo. new hf. morocco extra.*
London, 1774.

610 DESCRIZIONE DE GIARDINO REALE detto DI BOBOLI, *large map and* 48 *fine engravings on copper by Vasscellini of the celebrated Statuary, &c.* Roy. 4*to. hf. russia, uncut.* Florence, N. D.
LARGE PAPER.

611 DEVIL UPON TWO STICKS IN ENGLAND; being a continuation of Le
Diable Boiteaux of Le Sage. 6 vols. 12mo. *new hf. cf. gilt,
scarce.* *Logographic Press*, London, 1791.
Attributed to Wm. Combe, author of "Dr. Syntax."

612 DE VIRIVILLE, VALLET. HISTOIRE DE L'INSTRUCTION PUBLIQUE EN
EUROPE, et principalement en France, *many hundred illustrations
on wood, armorial bearings, illuminated in gold and colors, &c., 4to.
hf. red morocco, extra, scarce.* Paris, 1849.

613 D'EWES, SIR SIMOND. AUTOBIOGRAPHY AND CORRESPONDENCE,
during the Reigns of James I. and Charles I.; edited by J. O.
Halliwell, *portrait*, 2 vols. 8vo. *hf. cf. neat.* London, 1845.

614 DENHAM, CLAPPERTON, and OUDNEY'S Travels and Discoveries in
Northern and Central Africa, *numerous engravings by Finden, and
map*, 2 vols. 8vo. *calf extra.* London, 1828.
Fine copy from the library of J. H. Markland, with his autograph.

615 DENNISTOUN, J. MEMOIRS OF THE DUKES OF URBINO, illustrating the
Arms, Arts, and Literature of Italy, from 1440 to 1630, with
appendix of Original Documents, Poetry, &c. *Finely illustrated with engraved views, portraits, &c.* 3 vols. sq. 8vo. *new hf.
vellum antique, red edges.* London, 1851.
One of the most elegant and interesting works on Italy ever published; it
contains copious details of the Literature of the times.

616 DENS, PERTRI. Theologia Moralis et Dogmatica, editio nova, et ab-
solutissima. 9 vols. post 8vo. paper. Dublin, 1832.
The famous text-book of the Catholic Clergy.

617 DENTON, DANIEL. A BRIEF DESCRIPTION OF NEW YORK, (1670)
formerly called New Netherlands, with the Places thereunto
Adjoining. Likewise a Brief Relation of the Customs of the
Indians there. Edited with Notes by Gabriel Furman. 4to.
cloth, uncut. New York, 1845.
LARGE PAPER. 100 *copies.*
See also MILLER.

618 DIARY of the SIEGE of DETROIT, in the War with Pontiac, &c.,
edited by F. B. Hough. *Sm. 4to. hf. crimson morocco, gilt top,
by Bradstreet.* Munsell, Albany, 1860.
One of 25 copies on INDIA PAPER, Munsell's Series, No. 4.

619 DIBDIN, CHARLES. Songs. Chronologically arranged with Notes,
historical, Biographical, and Critical, WITH THE MUSIC, and
memoir of the Author by George Hogarth. *Thick 8vo. hf.
green morocco, gilt.* London, 1848.
Comprises over 1000 different songs.

620 DIBDIN, REV. T. F. BIBLIOGRAPHICAL, ANTIQUARIAN and PICTURESQUE
TOUR IN FRANCE and GERMANY, *with fine early impressions of the
numerous beautiful engravings, the Vignettes on* INDIA PAPER. 3
vols. royal 8vo. *half russia, gilt top, uncut edges.* London, 1821.
This copy contains the extra plate of the "Halt of the Pilgrims."

621 DIBDIN, REV. T. F. LIBRARY COMPANION; or the Young Man's
Guide and the Old Man's Comfort in the Choice of a Library.
8vo. *hf. calf, neat, uncut edges.* London, 1825.

622 DIBDIN, REV. T. F. THE BIBLIOMANIA; or, Book Madness, Con-

taining some Account of the History, Symptoms, and Cure of this Fatal Disease. In an Epistle addressed to Richard Heber, Esq. *Roy. 8vo. new hf. morocco, gilt top, uncut.*
Privately reprinted for the Club of Old Sticks,
57 *copies printed.* 1864 (London, 1809.)

623 ———— THE SAME. LARGEST PAPER. Atlas 4to. on *Whatman's Drawing Paper,* only 5 copies. 1864.

624 DIBDIN, REV. T. F. Introduction to the Knowledge of the Rare and Valuable Editions of the Greek and Latin Classics, with an account of Polyglot Bibles, Psalters, &c., &c. 4th Edition. 2 *vols. 8vo. hf. morocco, uncut.* London, 1827.

Dawson Turner's copy, with long autograph letter of Dr. Dibdin, and Portrait from a private plate etched by Turner, inserted.

ORIGINAL MSS. BY CHAS. DICKENS.

625 DICKENS, CHARLES. "HUNTED DOWN." The ORIGINAL MANUSCRIPT. 15 *pp. 4to. neatly mounted on writing paper, handsomely bound in full green crimped morocco, extra, by* MATTHEWS.

A highly characteristic and interesting specimen.
Presented to the Metropolitan Sanitary Fair by Robert Bonner, Esq.

626 DICKENS, CHARLES. WORKS. HOUSEHOLD EDITION ON LARGE PAPER. *Illustrated with Proof Impressions from designs by Darley, Gilbert, Cruikshank, Phiz, &c.* 54 vols. 8vo. *new cloth, uncut.* Cambridge: Printed at the Riverside Press, 1862, &c.

LARGE PAPER. 100 COPIES ONLY PRINTED. This edition contains the PLATES issued with the English edition, in addition to those by Darley.

627 ———— Another copy, *with designs by Darley and Gilbert.* 50 vols. crown 8vo. *green vellum cloth.* New York, 1862, &c.

Wants Uncommercial Traveller, 2 v., Master Humphrey's Clock, 1 v., and American Notes, 1 v. to complete the set.

628 DICKESON, M. W. The American Numismatical Manual of the Currency or Money of the Aboriginal, Colonial, State, and United States Coins. *Illustrated by 19 plates of fac-similes, executed in gold, silver, and copper. 4to. cloth, uncut.*
Philadelphia, 1859.

629 DILKE, CHARLES WENTWORTH. GREATER BRITAIN; A Record of Travel in English-Speaking Countries, during 1866–67. *Maps, &c.* 2 *vols. 8vo. new cloth.* L[ondon, 18]68.

630 DUNLOP, JOHN [illegible]. History of the [illegible] Reign of [illegible], King of Castile and Leon. Map, &c. 2 vols. [illegible] 8vo. *sprinkled calf, extra, yellow edges. Fine copy.* London, 1788.

Southey's copy, with his autograph.

631 DIPLOMATIC CORRESPONDENCE. Question between the United States and Peru, in consequence of the seizure of the two American Vessels, Lizzie Thompson and Georgiana. *Folio, sheets.*
Lima, 1858.

632 DIRCK, HENRY. LIFE AND TIMES OF THE MARQUIS OF WORCESTER, with a reprint of his "Century of Inventions," 1663, and a commentary thereon. *Handsomely printed on toned paper, portraits, &c., thick impl. 8vo. new hf. morocco, gilt top, uncut edges.* London, 1865

LARGE PAPER, *only 25 copies.*

633 DIRCK, HENRY. NATURE STUDY; or, the art of attaining those excellencies in Poetry and Eloquence which are mainly dependent on the manifold influences of universal nature. *Portrait. Beautifully printed. Thick 8vo. new cloth.* London, 1869.

634 D'ISRAELI, ISAAC. WORKS. A REMARKABLY FINE SERIES of the ORIGINAL EDITIONS, comprising: CURIOSITIES OF LITERATURE. *Both Series.* 6 vols. 8vo. AMENITIES OF LITERATURE, 3 vols. 8vo. COMMENTARIES on the LIFE and REIGN of CHARLES I. 5 vols. 8vo. QUARRELS OF AUTHORS, 2 vols. *crown 8vo.* CALAMITIES OF AUTHORS, 2 vols. *crown 8vo.* LITERARY CHARACTER, 2 vols. *cr. 8vo.* LITERARY MISCELLANIES, including a dissertation on Anecdotes, 1 vol. CHARACTER OF JAMES I. 1 vol. FLIM-FLAMS, or the Life and Errors of my Uncle, &c. 3 *vols.* 12*mo.; together 26 vols.* 12*mo. and 8vo. uniformly bound in new hf. calf extra, marbled edges.* London, 1801, &c.

ALL BEST LIBRARY EDITIONS, *very scarce.*
"His works must live in honor, and in freshness, as long as our history and literature survive, and no man will turn over their pages three hundred years hence, without saying to himself, 'This was a man of indefatigable zeal, of elegant feelings, and, above all, of lofty purity of character."—*Blackwood's Magazine.*
"That most entertaining and searching writer, D'Israeli, whose works in general I have read oftener than perhaps any other English writer whatever."— *Lord Byron.*

635 D'ISRAELI, ISAAC. CURIOSITIES OF LITERATURE, with a View of the Life and Writings of the Author, by his Son. *Portrait.* 4 *vols.* 8*vo. half roxburgh morocco, uncut.*
Riverside Press, Boston, 1864.

LARGE PAPER: *only* 100 *copies printed.*
Uniform in size and style of binding with the *large paper* editions of Lamb, Bacon, Montagu, &c.

636 D'ISRAELI, ISAAC. AMENITIES OF LITERATURE, consisting of Sketches and Characters of English Literature. New Edition, edited by his son, the Right Hon. B. D'Israeli. 2 *vols.* 8*vo. half morocco, uncut, by Matthews.* Boston, 1864.

LARGE PAPER: *only* 100 *copies.*
Uniform with the preceding lot.

637 D'ISRAELI. REVOLUTIONARY EPIC. 12*mo. new cloth.*
London, 1864.

638 DIXON, WM. HEPWORTH. SPIRITUAL WIVES. *Portrait,* 2 *vols.* 8*vo. new cloth.* London, 1868.

639 DIXON, WM. HEPWORTH. Her Majesty's Tower. Library Edition. 8*vo. new cloth.* London, 1870.

640 DOBSON, SUSANNA. LIFE OF PETRARCH, with a fine series of plates after Kirk, by Ridley. 2 vols. roy. 8vo. *crimson morocco, extra.* *Bensley,* London, 1797.

LARGE PAPER, *fine copy.*

641 DOBSON, MRS. LITERARY HISTORY OF THE TROUBADOURS, containing Lives, Extracts from their Works and particulars relating to the Customs, Morals, and History of the XIIth and XIIIth centuries. 12*mo. hf. vellum, gilt.* London, 1807.

642 DOCTRINE OF DEVILS proved to be the grand Apostacy of these later times. An Essay tending to rectifie those undue notions and

apprehensions men have about Dæmons and Evil Spirits. 12*mo.*
hf. cf. antique, curious. London, 1676.

643 DODSLEY, ROBERT. OLD PLAYS. A Select Collection; new
edition, with Additional Notes and Corrections by Isaac Reed,
Octavius Gilchrist, and the Editor (John Payne Collier). 12
vols. 8vo. half calf, gilt, marbled edges.
LARGE PAPER. *Prowett and Pickering,* London, 1825–33.
Extremely scarce.
"This valuable work contains 60 of our best and scarcest Early Plays, begin-
ning with the first Dramatic Performances, entitled, "Moralities or Myste-
ries." Interspersed with much valuable information respecting our early
Dramas and Poetry."

644 DODSLEY, ROBERT. SELECT COLLECTION OF OLD PLAYS. *Second
Edition,* corrected and collated with the old copies, with Notes,
Critical and Explanatory (by Isaac Reed), *front.* 12 *vols. in* 14,
post 8vo. calf, neat. London, 1780.
A large portion of this edition was destroyed by fire. "This *second edition*
contains a single Play by Ford, "'Tis a Pity she's a Whore,' and three by
Shirley, viz., The Bird in a Cage; The Gamester, and Andromana; not given
in the *third edition.*"—*Lowndes.*

645 DODSLEY. COLLECTION OF POEMS, in 6 vols. 8*vo. hf. russia, gilt.*
London, 1765.

646 (DODSLEY, ROBERT). THE ŒCONOMY OF HUMAN LIFE, translated
from an Indian Manuscript, written by an ancient Bramin.
Illustrated with an exquisite series of vignettes by Harding. 12*mo.*
cf. neat. London, 1806.

647 DOMAT, JEAN. THE CIVIL LAW IN ITS NATURAL ORDER; together
with the Public Law. Translated into English, by William
Straham; with Remarks on some Differences between the Civil
Law and the Law of England; Edited by the Hon. Luther S.
Cushing. Fourth edition. 2 vols. 8vo., *law sheep.*
Boston, 1861.

648 DONALDSON, JAMES. A Critical History of Christian Literature and
Doctrine, from the Death of the Apostles to the Nicene Council.
3 vols. 8*vo. new cloth.* London, 1864.

649 DON PIRLONE a Roma, Memorie di un Italiano, per Michelangelo
Pinto, 3 vols. 4to. illustrated with 306 *extraordinary Political
Caricatures, very severe on the Papal and French Governments, half
calf, neat,* SCARCE, SUPPRESSED. (Rome), 1850.

650 DORÉ, GUSTAVE. CERVANTES; DON QUICHOTTE DE LA
MANCHÉ, traduit par Louis Viardot, avec un notice sur la Vie
et les Ouvrages de l'auteur. *With upwards of* 360 *large illustrations and vignettes by* DORÉ, *engraved by Pisan, fine impressions.*
2 *vols. atlas folio, cloth, uncut.* Paris, 1863.
FINE COPY.

651 DORÉ, GUSTAVE. LA FONTAINE, FABLES DE, avec un notice sur la
Vie de Jean La Fontaine, par Geruzez. *Illustrated with upwards
of* 300 *large engravings and vignettes from designs by Doré.*
PROOF IMPRESSIONS *on* INDIA PAPER. 2 vols. atlas folio, cloth,
uncut. Paris, 1867.
The present copy has an Artist proof impression of the Portrait of La Fontaine, engraved on steel by Delonnoy.

652 DORÉ, GUSTAVE. THE HOLY BIBLE. *A complete set in numbers as published, with fine impressions of the* 230 *engravings from the celebrated designs by Doré, forming 2 vols. Folio.*
London, 1866.

653 DORÉ. LA LÉGENDE du JUIF ERRANT, avec un notice par Pierre Dupont, *a series of* 12 *very large and characteristic engravings on wood, by Roget, Gauchard, &c., after the celebrated designs of Doré, folio, bds.* Paris, 1862.

654 DORÉ. LA LÉGENDE de CROQUE-MITAINE, recueille par Ernest L'-Épine, *illustrated with* 177 *vignettes on wood, from the inimitable designs of* GUSTAVE DORÉ. 4to. new hf. morocco, extra.
Paris, 1863.

655 DORÉ. CONTES DROLATIQUES (DROLL TALES COLLECTED FROM THE ABBEYS OF LORAINE). Par BALZAC. With Four Hundred and Twenty-five Marvellous, Extravagant, and Fantastic Wood-cuts, by GUSTAVE DORÉ. 8vo. half morocco, gilt top.
Paris, 1864.

The most singular designs ever attempted by an artist. This book is a fund of amusement. So crammed is it with pictures, that even the contents are adorned with thirty-three Illustrations.

656 DORÉ, GUSTAVE. HISTORICAL CARTOONS from the First Century to the Nineteenth, with descriptive text by Thomas Wright. *Oblong 4to. bds.* London, N. D.
DORÉ. See Dante.

657 DORAN, DR. Annals of the English Stage, from Betterton to Kean. 2 vols. crown 8vo. cloth. New York, 1865.

658 DORAN, DR. ANNALS OF THE STAGE, from Thomas Betterton to Edmund Kean.—Actors, Authors, Audiences, with numerous Portraits, etc. *2 vols. imp. 8vo. hf. green morocco, uncut.*
New York, 1865.

LARGE PAPER: *only 160 copies printed.*

659 DOUCE, FRANCIS. ILLUSTRATIONS OF SHAKESPEARE, and of Ancient Manners; With Dissertations on the Clowns and Fools of Shakespeare; on the collection of Popular Tales entitled Gesta Romanorum; and on the English Morris Dance. *The engravings on wood by Jackson. 8vo. half green morocco, gilt tops, uncut edges.* London, 1839.

"I look upon this work as a sort of Hortus Shakespearianus; the research and learning bestowed on it are immense."—*Dibdin.*

660 DOUGLAS, STEPHEN A. Life of, by James W. Sheahan. *Portrait,* 12mo. *cloth.* New York, 1860.

661 DOUGLASS, HON. THOMAS. Autobiography of, *portrait,* 12mo. *sheets stitched.* New York, 1856.

662 DOYLE, JOHN ANDREW. THE AMERICAN COLONIES previous to the Declaration of Independence (Arnold Prize Essay). 8vo. *vellum cloth.* London, 1869.

663 DOYLE, RICHARD. THE FOREIGN TOUR of MESSRS. BROWN, JONES, and ROBINSON, *a series of upwards of* 100 *humorous designs by Doyle. Roy. 4to. cloth, scarce.* London, 1854.

664 DRAKE, SAMUEL G. HISTORY AND ANTIQUITIES OF BOSTON, from its Settlement in 1630 to the Year 1770, with An Introductory

History of the Discovery and Settlement of New England
With Notes, &c. *Large folding Maps and Plans, upwards of 4
fine portraits, and numerous woodcuts.* 2 vols. *folio, boards.*

Boston, 185[?]

Large Paper.

665 —— Another Copy. Impl. 8vo. *new cloth.* Boston, 185[?]

666 Drake, Samuel G. The Old Indian Chronicle; being a collectio[n]
of Exceeding Rare Tracts, written and published in the Tim[e]
of King Philip's War, by Persons residing in the Countr[y]
To which are now added an Introduction and Notes. 4to. *clot[h]
uncut.* Boston, 186[?]

667 Drake, Samuel G. The Witchcraft Delusion in New England
its Rise, Progress, and Termination, as exhibited by Dr. Cotto[n]
Mather in the Wonders of the Invisible World; and by M[r]
Robert Calef, in his More Wonders ... with a Preface, Intr[o]
duction, and Notes. 3 vols. roy. 4to. *uncut.*
Printed for W. E. Woodward. Roxbury, 186[6]

Large Paper. 50 *copies.*

668 —— Another Copy. 3 vols. roy. 8vo. *uncut.* Roxbury, 186[6]

669 —— Another Copy. *Printed throughout on* India Paper. 3 vol[s]
sm. 4to. *new hf. crimson morocco, gilt top, by Bradstreet.*

Roxbury, 186[6]

.*.* Only 5 copies printed.

670 Drake, S. G. Founders of New England. Result of some R[e]
searches among the British Archives for Information relatin[g]
to. Made in the years 1858, '59 and 1860. *Third Editio[n]
Map and portraits. Royal 4to. new hf. morocco, gilt top.*
Privately Reprinted. Boston, 186[5]

Only 75 *copies.*

671 —— Another Copy. *Impl. 4to. boards.* Boston, 186[5]

672 Drake, S. G. Brief Memoir of Sir Walter Raleigh. *Portrai[t]*
Sm. 4to. *uncut.* *Privately Printed.* Boston, 186[?]

673 Drake, Sam'l G. Memoir of, by John H. Sheppard. *Portrai[t]*
Small 4to. boards, uncut. *Munsell,* Albany, 186[3]
Printed for Private Distribution.

674 Drama. A Pleasant Conceated Comedy, wherein is shewed ho[w]
a man may choose a good Wife from a bad. Sm. 4to. *inter[
leaved, hf. cf.* London, 162[1]
Original Edition. *W. E. Burton's* copy.

675 Drama. Hecuba. A Tragedy, as it is acted at the Theatre Roya[l]
in Drury-Lane. *Sm. 4to. pp.* 36, *hf. vellum.* London, 172[6]
The author was Richard West, Lord Chancellor of Ireland.

676 Drama. Romulus and Hersilia; or, the Sabine War. A Tra[
gedy acted at the Duke's Theatre. 4to. *pp.* 64, *hf. red morocc[o]
gilt, scarce.* London, 168[3]
The Epilogue to this play was written by Mrs. Aphra Behn.

677 Drama. The Metamorphosis; or, the Old Lover Outwitted. [A]
farce. (*Title-page in MS.*) Sm. 4to. *hf. vellum.*

London, 170[4]

An adaptation from Molière, by John Corey, the comedian.

678 DRAPER, J. WM. History of the Intellectual Development of Europe. *Thick 8vo. new hf. mor.* New York, 1864.

679 DRAPER, J. WM. History of the American Civil War. 2 vols. 8vo. new cloth. New York, 1867.

680 DRAPER, J. W. Thoughts on the Future Civil Policy of America. *8vo. new cloth.* New York, 1865.

681 DRAWINGS BY RAPHAEL. A series of 33 Photographs from the OXFORD COLLECTION, *mounted on card-board, folio, in portfolio.*

682 DRAYTON, MICHAEL. POEMS, newly corrected and augmented. *Engraved title.* 12mo. (*8vo.*) *sprinkled calf extra, yellow edges* (the margins of several leaves are closely trimmed, but complete). London, Printed by Willi Stansby for John Smetherick, N. D. (1605).

FINE COPY, *scarce.*

683 DRUMMOND, Sir WM. ORIGINES; or, Remarks on the Origin of several Empires, States, and Cities. Maps. 4 vols. 8vo. cloth, *uncut, scarce.* London, 1824.

" Sir William Drummond is well known to the world as an ingenious Oriental scholar. In the present work he has put forth his whole strength, and among many erudite discussions, his conjectures on the Stadium of Herodotus and others, who have written on the extent of Babylon, are curious and valuable."—*British Critic.*

684 DRYDEN, JOHN. PLAYS, OPERAS AND ESSAY ON DRAMATIC POETRY. *Original Editions*, collected and bound in 2 vols. *sml. 4to. hf. cf. extra, red edges.* London, 1683, &c. *All in fine order, very rare.*

685 DRYDEN, JNO. Fables from Boccaccio and Chaucer, with a Memoir. *16mo. cloth.* *Blanchard*, New York, 1857.

686 DUBLIN UNIVERSITY MAGAZINE. A Literary and Political Journal. From its commencement in 1833 to 1862, inclusive. 60 vols. *8vo. cloth, uncut.* Dublin, 1833–62.

Contains the Tales of Lover, Carleton, Lever, &c., besides articles by W. Archer Butler, Bp. Fitzgerald, Anster, Mangan, Petrie, Waller, Wilde, Mrs. Savage, Eliot Warburton, and many others.

687 DU CHAILLU, PAUL B. JOURNEY TO ASHANGO-LAND; and further penetration into Equatorial Africa. *Map and illustrations, thick 8vo. new cloth.* New York, 1867.

688 DUDLEY, EDMOND. The TREE of COMMON WEALTH, written by him while a Prisoner in the Tower, under sentence of Death for High-Treason, in 1509–'10. *Printed from the original MS. 4to. hf. morocco, uncut.* Manchester, 1859.

Only 140 *copies, privately printed.*

689 DUMAS, ALEX. TALES OF ALGERIA, or Life among the Arabs; from the " Véloce " of Dumas. 12mo. cloth. Philadelphia, 1868.

690 DUMAS, ALEXANDER, NOVELS. 12 vols. 8vo. new cloth. Philadelphia, V. D.

Comprising : Three Guardsmen, Iron Mask, Twenty Years After, Iron Hand, Bragelonne Son of Athos, Diana of Meridor, Louise la Valliere, Forty-five Guardsmen, Memoirs of a Physician, Andree de Favernay, Adventures of a Marquis, Count of Monte Christo.

691 DUNCAN, GEO. The Various Theories of the relation of Mind and Brain, reviewed. *12mo. new cloth.* London, 1869.

692 DUNLOP, JOHN. HISTORY OF FICTION; being a Critical Account of the most celebrated Prose Works of Fiction, &c. *Roy. 8vo new cloth.* London, 1845.

693 DUNTON, JOHN. LIFE AND ERRORS, with the Lives and Characters of more than a Thousand Contemporary Divines, &c., edited by NICHOLS. *Portrait.* 2 vols. 8vo. in one, *calf, gilt, fine copy.* London, 1818.

BEST EDITION.

694 DUPIN, L. E. HISTORY OF ECCLESIASTICAL WRITERS; containing an Account of the Authors of the several Books of the Old and New Testament; and the Lives and Writings of the Primitive Fathers; Catalogue of all their Works, with a Compendious History of the Councils from the 1st to the 17th century. 16 vols. in 8; Canon of the Old and New Testaments, 2 vols. in 1. Together 9 vols. folio, calf, gilt, red edges. London, 1696–1725.

A very fine, clean, and perfect set. *Very Scarce.*
"Those who quarrel most with the boldness of Dupin, must still allow the greatness of his literary endowments."—*C. Butler.*
"Dupin's work was condemned by the Archbishop of Paris, on the complaint of the celebrated Bossuet, as 'containing several propositions that are false, rash, scandalous, capable of offending pious ears, tending to weaken the arguments which are brought from tradition to prove the authority of the canonical books of holy scripture, erroneous and leading to heresy.' This sentence upon the work, however, proves its highest recommendation to the Protestant reader."—*Chalmers.*

695 D * * *(ULAURE), J. A. DES DIVINITÉS GÉNÉRATRICES, ou du culte du Phallas chez les anciens et les modernes; Des cultes de *dieu de Lampsaque*, de Pan, de Venus, &c., par J. A. D * * * *. *8vo. hf. red morocco, extra, uncut edges.* Paris, 1805.

ORIGINAL EDITION, said to contain much matter that was afterwards suppressed by the author in his second edition.
"L'on trouvera le rapprochement d'un grand nombre de traits épars dans un immensité de livres peu communs, dont l'ensemble offrir une face nouvelle."—*Preface.*

696 DUNTON, JOHN. Letters from New England. Thick royal 4to. *uncut.* *Prince Society,* Boston, 1867.

LARGE PAPER, 20 *copies printed* (10).

697 DURER, ALBERT. PASSIO CHRISTI; THE LITTLE PASSION. A complete set of the Thirty-seven Wood Cuts, by Albert Durer. Reproduced in fac-simile. Edited by W. C. Prime. One volume, royal 4to. (thirteen by ten and one half inches.) *Printed on heavy glazed Plate Paper*, full morocco antique, gilt edges. J. W. Bouton, New York, 1868.

THE LITTLE PASSION of Albert Durer, consisting of thirty-seven Wood Cuts, has long been regarded as one of the most remarkable collections of Illustrations known to the world. Complete sets of the entire series are excessively rare. The editions which have been published in modern times in Europe are defective, lacking more or less of the Plates, and are of an inferior and unsatisfactory class of workmanship.

698 D'URFEY, TOM. Wonders in the Sun; or, the Kingdom of the Birds. A Comick Opera. 4to. pp. 70, hf. morocco. London, 1706.

699 D'URFEY, TOM. THE MODERN PROPHETS; or, New Wit for a Husband. A Comedy. 4to. pp. 42, *hf. cf.* London, 1709.

Fine, clean copy, *scarce.*
"The pieces of this author are remarkable for licentiousness, looseness of sentiment, and indelicacy of wit, yet are very far from being devoid of merit."

700 DURKEE, DR. S. Treatise on Gonorrhœa and Syphilis, *with colored illustrations, 8vo. new cloth.* Philadelphia, 1867.

701 DUSSELDORF GALLERY : GALERIE ELECTORALE de DUSSEL- DORF, où Catalogue raisonné et figuré de ses Tableaux, par ME- CHEL et PIGAGE, *with* 30 *beautiful plates, containing* 365 *small ones, engraved by* MECHEL, *original and* BRILLIANT IMPRESSIONS, 2 *vols. oblong imp. 4to. in the original half binding, uncut edges.*
Basle, 1778.
A FINE COPY, formerly in the collection of Mr. Bryan, the well-known Amer- ican connoisseur and collector.
The plates being small, it is very important that the impressions be clear, otherwise they are very unsatisfactory.

702 DUYCKINCK, E. A. and GEORGE. CYCLOPEDIA OF AMERICAN LITER- ATURE, embracing Personal and Critical notices of Authors and selections from their writings, from the earliest period to the present day. *Portraits and numerous engravings on wood.* 2 *vols. impl. 8vo. new hf. calf, extra.* New York, 1866.

703 DWIGHT, HENRY E. Travels in the North of Germany in the years 1825–26. *8vo. boards, uncut.* New York, 1829.

704 DYER, DAVID. HISTORY of ALBANY PENITENTIARY. *8vo. hf. crimson morocco, gilt top, by Bradstreet.* *Munsell*, Albany, 1867.
One of 5 *copies on* INDIA PAPER.

705 EARLY VOYAGES UP AND DOWN THE MISSISSIPPI, by Cavelier, St. Cosme, Le Sueur, &c., with Introduction, &c., by John Gilmary Shea. *4to. hf. crimson morocco, gilt top, by Bradstreet.*
Munsell, Albany, 1861.
One of 5 *copies on* INDIA PAPER. Munsell's Series, No. 8.

706 EARLY VOYAGES UP AND DOWN THE MISSISSIPPI, by Cavelier, St. Cosme, Le Sueur, Gravier, and Guignas, with An Introduction and Notes, &c., by J. Gilmary Shea. *Sml. 4to. uncut.*
Munsell, Albany, 1861.
Munsell's Historical Series, No. 8.

707 EASTLAKE, CHARLES L. HINTS ON HOUSEHOLD TASTE in Furniture, Upholstery, and other details, *profusely illustrated, crown 8vo. new cloth, gilt.* London, 1868.

708 EASTWICK, EDWARD B. THE ANIVAR-I SUHAILI ; or the Light of Canopus ; being the Persian Version of the Fables of Pilpay, literally translated into Prose and Verse. *Impl. 8vo. new cloth.*
Hertford, 1854.

709 EARLY ENGLISH TEXT SOCIETY, complete.—I. Arthur and other Romances. II. Works illustrating our Dialects and the History of our Language. III. Biblical Translations and Religious Treatises. IV. Miscellaneous. 36 *parts, 8vo. uncut.*
London, 1864–70.
Contents.—I. Early English Alliterative poems, in the West-Midland Dialect of the XIVth Century. Edited by R. Morris.
II. Arthur ; a short sketch of his Life and History, in Eng. Verse.
III. Office and Dewtie of Kyngis, by William Lander.
IV. Sir Gawayne and the Green Knight.
V. Hume's Orthographie and Congruitie of the Britain Tongue.
VI. Lanclot of the Laik. Scottish Metrical Romance. (1490.)
VII. The Story of Genesis and Exodus, an Early English Song (1250).
VIII. Morte Arthure, from Thornton's MS. (1440.)

IX. Chaucer. Animadversions uppon the Annotacions, &c., 1598.
X. Merlin, or Early History of King Arthur, Pt. I.
XI. Lindsay, Sir D. The Monarche, &c.
XII. The Wright's Chaste Wife.
XIII Sainte Macherete, the Meiden and Martyr.
XIV. King Horn, with fragmonts of Floriz and Blaunchfleur.
XV. Political, Religious, and Love Poems.
XVI. Book of Quinte Essence ; or the Fifth Being.
XVII. Extracts from 20 MSS. of Piers Plowman.
XVIII. Hali Meidenhad, an Alliterative homily.
XIX. Lindsay's Monarche and other Poems.
XX. Hampole's Short Prose Treatises.
XXI. Merlin, &c. Pt. II.
XXII The Romans of Pastenay.
XXIII. Dan Michell's Ayenbit of Imvyt, A. D. 1340.
XXIV. Hymns to the Virgin and Christ, &c.
XXV. The Stacions of Rome.
XXVI. Religious Pieces in Prose and Verse. (1440.)
XXVII. Manipulus Vocabulorum ; a Rhyming Dictionary.
XXVIII. Langland's Vision of Piers Plowman, &c.
XXIX. Old English Homilies, &c.
XXX. Pierce the Ploughman's Creed.
XXXI. Myers' Instructions for Parish Priests.
XXXII. The Babees Book ; Manners and Meals in Olden Time, with
woodcuts, &c. (in 2 parts.)
XXXIII. Knight of La Tour Landry, &c.
XXXIV. Early English Homilies, Pt. II.
XXXV. Lindsay's Sqvyer Meldrum.

The ONLY COMPLETE SET of these important publications offered at public sale in this country.

The early numbers of the Society's Publications are out of print, and difficult to procure.

710 EARLY ENGLISH TEXT SOCIETY. EXTRA SERIES, 5 parts, *impl. 8vo. uncut.* London, 1868.
LARGE PAPER.
Comprising :—William of Palerne ; Early English Pronunciation ; Caxton's Book of Curtesye ; Havelock the Dane ; Romance of the Chevelere Assigne.

711 ECLIPSE of FAITH ; or, A Visit to a Religious Sceptic. 12*mo. cloth.* Boston, 1860.

712 EDICT of NANTES. HISTORY of the FAMOUS EDICT ; containing an account of all the Persecutions that have been in France, from its first publication, &c., translated from the French. 2 *vols. sm. 4to. calf, very neat, scarce.* John Dunton, London, 1694.

713 EDINBURGH REVIEW, complete from its commencement in 1802, to April, 1859, inc. with Indexes. 111 *vols. 8vo. new hf. cf. neat.* Edinburgh, 1802–59.
Fine uniform set.

714 EDMUNDS, F. Traces of History in the Names of Places, with a vocabulary, &c. *Post 8vo. new cloth.* London, 1869.

715 EDUCATION. Report of the Committee of Council on Education, 1868–69. *Thick 8vo. paper.* London, 1869.

716 EDWARDS, EDWARD. COLLECTION OF TRACTS, REPORTS, and MISCELLANEOUS TREATISES, on PUBLIC LIBRARIES, LIBRARY ECONOMY, BIBLIOGRAPHY, ART, PICTURE COLLECTIONS, &c., &c., *comprising nearly 100 tracts in different languages, but principally English, with autograph letters, MS. Notes, &c. &c. by Mr. Edwards.* Uniformly bound in 10 vols. 8vo. and 12mo. *hf. calf, neat.* V. D.
A UNIQUE COLLECTION, comprising several privately printed tracts, Catalogues of the British Museum, and Priced Catalogues of Important Book sales, &c., &c., the private collection of Mr. Edwards, author of "Memoirs of Libraries," and the recently published History of the British Museum.

717 EDWARDS, EDWARD.   MEMOIRS OF LIBRARIES; including a handbook
of Library Economy, *with Diagrams, fac-similes, &c.* 2 thick
vols. 8vo. *new cloth, uncut.*   London, 1859.
"Of the industry bestowed upon this extensive compilation, and of the
marvellous condensation of fact which it supplies, it is difficult to speak
in terms of proper commendation; even to the most accomplished bibliographer it cannot fail to be of great service, but how much more to the tyro or
ordinary bibliographer."—*Brownson's Review.*

718 EDWARDS, EDWARD.   FREE TOWN LIBRARIES, Their Formation,
Management, and History; in Britain, France, Germany, and
America.   *Thick 8vo. new cloth.*   London, 1869.

719 EDWARDS, EDWARD.   LIFE OF SIR WALTER RALEIGH, based on contemporary documents, together with his Letters; now first collected.   *Portraits, &c.* 2 thick vols. 8vo. *new cloth, uncut.*
                                                  London, 1868.

720 EDWARDS, H. S.   LIFE OF ROSSINI.   *Portrait. 8vo. new vellum
cloth.*   London, 1869.

721 EDWARDS, JNO. H.   SHELBY AND HIS MEN; or the War in the West.
Portrait. 8vo. cloth.   Cincinnati, 1867.

722 EDWARDS, JONATHAN.   WORKS.   A reprint of the Worcester Edition, with Additions and a copious general Index. 4 *vols.*
8vo. *cloth.*   New York, 1858.

723 EGAN, PIERCE (the younger).   REAL LIFE IN LONDON; or, the Adventures of Bob Tallyho and his cousin Hon. Tom Dashall
through the Metropolis, &c.   *Profusely illustrated with a series
of colored plates, by Rowlandson, Heath, Alken, &c.* 2 vols. 8vo.
hf. cf. neat.   London, 1824.
ORIGINAL EDITION, *scarce.*

724 EGLOFFSTEIN, BARON F. W. VON.   Contributions to the Geology and
Physical Geography of Mexico.   *Maps and Plates.* Imp. 8vo.
cloth.   New York, 1864.

725 ELIOT, REV. JOHN.   Brief Narrative of the Progress of the Gospel
among the Indians of New England, 1670.   With Note, &c.,
by W. T. R. Marvin.   Small 4o. *uncut.*   Boston, 1868.
150 *Copies Printed.*

726 ELIOT, SAMUEL.   History of Liberty.   *Both Series.* 4 *vols. post.*
8vo. *cloth.*   Boston, 1853.

727 ELLESMERE, EARL OF.   The Pilgrimage and other Poems.   *Illustrated Edition.* 4to. *cloth, gilt.*   *Murray,* London, 1856.

728 ELLIOTT, REV. CHARLES.   Sinfulness of American Slavery, with
Observations on Emancipation, &c. 2 *vols.* 12mo. *cloth.*
                                                  Cincinnati, 1857.

729 ELLIOTT, REV. CHARLES.   Delineation of Roman Catholicism, drawn
from the authentic and acknowledged standards of the Church
of Rome. 2 *vols.* 8vo. *sheep.*   New York, 1841.

730 ELLIOT, SIR H. M.   HISTORY OF INDIA, as told by its own Historians,
edited from the posthumous papers of Sir H. Elliot, by Prof.
John Dowson. 2 *vols.* 8vo. *new cloth.*   London, 1867.

731 ELLIOT, JONATHAN.   DEBATES in the several CONVENTIONS on the
ADOPTION of the FEDERAL CONSTITUTION; together with the

Journal of the Federal Convention, with Supplement containing the Madison Papers. *5 vols. 8vo. law cf. neat.*
Philadelphia, 1859.

732 ELLIS, SIR H. ORIGINAL LETTERS of Sovereigns and other distinguished Personages, illustrative of English History, with Notes and Illustrations. THE THREE SERIES COMPLETE. *Engravings and fac-similes.* 11 vols. post 8vo. *uniformly bound in calf, gilt.* Fine copy. London, 1825–46.

"With delight we recommend them for curious illustration; correctness of long-received historical theories; developments of famous characters; discovery of new and important facts;—in short, for everything that renders such a collection interesting."

733 ELLIS, REV. WM. WORKS, comprising POLYNESIAN RESEARCHES, 2 vols. HISTORY OF MADAGASCAR, 2 vols. VISITS TO MADAGASCAR, 1 vol. TOUR THROUGH OWYHEE, 1 vol. *Profusely illustrated with Maps and Engravings.* 6 vols. 8vo. *uniformly bound in new hf. cf. extra, uncut.* London, 1826, &c.

FINE SET. Best Library Editions.

734 ELVIN, C. N. ANECDOTES OF HERALDRY, in which is set forth the origin of the armorial bearings of many families. *Numerous wood cuts, 12mo. new cloth.* London, 1864.

735 EMANUEL, HARRY. DIAMONDS AND PRECIOUS STONES; their History, Value, and Distinguishing Characteristics, with tests for their identification. *Plates, beautifully printed on toned paper. 4to. hf. roxburg morocco, uncut.* London, 1865.

LARGE PAPER; *only* 35 *Copies.*

736 EMBLEMS. NUÑEZ DE CEPEDA, FRANCIS. Idea de el Buen Pastor Copiada por los S.S. Doctores Representada en Empresas Sacras, con Avisios Espirituales, Morales, Politicos, y Economicos, para el Govierno de un Principe Ecclesiastico. *Fifty fine copper-plates of emblems. 4to. vellum.* Leon, 1687.

From the Library of John Allan ; see also GREEN, J.

737 EMERSON, GEO. B. REPORT ON THE TREES AND SHRUBS growing naturally in the Forests of Massachusetts. *Plates, 8vo. cloth, scarce.* Boston, 1850.

738 EMORY, WILLIAM H. REPORT OF THE UNITED STATES AND MEXICAN BOUNDARY SURVEY. *Numerous Maps and plates; including also a complete Natural History of those regions, with copious illustrations, those of Costume and Ornithology beautifully colored. 3 vols. 4to. law calf.* Washington, 1857.

739 EMORY, W. H. NOTES OF A MILITARY RECONNOISSANCE from Fort Leavenworth, Mo. to San Diego, Cal. *Profusely illustrated, and large folding map. 8vo. cloth.* Washington, 1848.

740 ENCYCLOPEDIA BRITANNICA; or, Dictionary of Arts, Sciences, and General Literature. *Eighth and last Edition. Complete. Several hundred fine engravings.* 22 *thick vols. and Index,* 4to. cloth. Edinburgh, 1861, etc.

741 ENCYCLOPÉDIE OU DICTIONNAIRE RAISONNÉ des SCIENCES, des Arts, et des métiers. . . . mis en ordre par DIDEROT et D'ALEMBERT, avec supplément, Tables, &c. Complete. 36 vols. of Text and 8 vols. of *Plates, together* 39 *vols. 8vo. calf, neat.*
Lausanne et Berne, 1781.

"This famous French 'Encyclopédie' ought to be in every Public Library.
It formerly fetched high prices, to wit, Edwards, £24. 3s. Talleyrand, £29.8s.
J. Smith, £17, Marquis of Lansdowne, £43. 1s, &c.

742 ENGLISH LIBERTIES; or, The Free-born Subject's Inheritance, contain-
ing Magna Charta, Abstracts of the Penal Laws, Work and
Power of Parliament, Office Duties of Constables, Church-
Warden, Surveyors, &c., &c. 16mo. (8vo.), *calf.*
London, 1691.

743 ENNEMOSER, JOSEPH. HISTORY OF MAGIC, translated from the German by Wm Howitt. 2 vols. 12mo. cloth. London, 1854.

744 ENGRAVINGS. *A complete set of upwards of Three Hundred Portraits, and Character Illustrations to the* BRITISH POETS, AND ESSAY-
ISTS, *beautifully engraved after designs by Stothard, Westall, Thurston, Corbould, &c.* PROOFS IMPRESSIONS. *4 vols. 8vo. maroon
morocco extra, gilt leaves.* London, 1796.

745 ENGRAVINGS. ENGLISH SCHOOL, *upwards of Two hundred* fine plates,
after designs by Stothard, Corbould, Loutherbourg, Neagle,
&c., &c. ALL BRILLIANT IMPRESSIONS, *including many* PROOFS,
illustrating the English classic authors, neatly mounted in a scrap-
book. 4to. hf. calf, gilt. London.
A CHOICE COLLECTION.

746 ENGRAVINGS. *A Series of Magnificent Engravings to illustrate the
folio or quarto Editions of the Works of* SHAKESPEARE AND MILTON,
upwards of 50 large plates, *folio, blue morocco, extra.*
London, 1818.

747 ENGRAVINGS. LIVERSEEGE, HENRY. *A series of 37 large and beau-
tifully executed engravings in mezzotint, by Bromley, Cousins,
Ward, &c., comprising illustrations to the Waverley Novels,
Shakespeare, Don Quixote, &c. &c.* BRILLIANT IMPRESSIONS.
Folio, hf. morocco, gilt. London, 1832.

748 ENGRAVINGS. A miscellaneous collection of 50 *large plates, in lithography, on steel, &c. including many fine proofs. Roy. 4to. hf.
cf. neat.* V. D.

749 ENGRAVINGS. *A series of 34 plates, principally Views of English
Cities, engraved by Storer;* loose in a portfolio.

750 EPICURE'S Year Books for 1869. 16mo. new cloth.
London, 1869.

751 EPIGRAMS. THE FESTOON. A collection of Epigrams, Ancient and
Modern. Panegyrical, Satyrical, Amorous, Moral, Humorous,
and Monumental, with an Essay on that species of Composition.
Vignette. 8vo. sprinkled calf, extra, yellow edges.
London, 1766.

A RARE COLLECTION. Fine copy from Mr. Dillon's library, with numerous
MS. additions in the *autograph of* HORACE WALPOLE, also numerous old cuttings inserted.

752 EPISODES OF INSECT LIFE, by *Acheta Domestica* (MISS L. M.
BUGDEN). THREE SERIES COMPLETE. *Frontispiece and numerous
singularly beautiful vignettes, all* ELEGANTLY COLORED. 3 vols.
crown 8vo. cloth, gilt leaves. London, 1849.
ORIGINAL EDITION, *colored copies, are very scarce.*

753 ERASMUS. Twenty-two SELECT COLOQUIES pleasantly representing

several superstitious levities that were crept into the Church of Rome, trans. by Sir Roger L'Estrange, portrait, &c.   *8vo. calf, neat.   Fine Copy.*   *London*, 1699.

Bound with the above is Cicero's "Offices," by the same translator.

754 ERSKINE, LORD. THE FARMER'S VISION, a poem. *Post 8vo. bds. Very Rare.*   *London*, 1819.

PRIVATELY PRINTED, with the autograph presentation of Lord Erskine to James Perry, Esq. (Editor of the Morning Chronicle).

In the Preface the author says of his subject, "It is, indeed, so capable of being made interesting that I would have prolonged the vision and worked it up into a Poem, but for an insuperable objection, viz. THAT I AM NOT A POET. It is not fit for publication, and few copies are only printed for friends who asked for them, as it was too long to make them in writing."

755 ESSAYS AND REVIEWS. Recent Inquiries in Theology by eminent English clergymen, with Introduction, &c. by Rev. F. H. Hedge. 12mo. cloth.   *Boston*, 1862.

756 ESSAYS ON RELIGION AND LITERATURE, by various writers, edited by Archbp. Manning. 2 vols. 8vo. new cloth, uncut.

London, 1865.

757 ESPY, JAMES P. Philosophy of Storms. 8vo. cloth.

Boston, 1841.

758 ETCHINGS. A COLLECTION OF ORIGINAL ETCHINGS by Rembrandt, and after Rembrandt by Vivares, CLAUDE, DOMINIQUE BARRIERE, HORIZONTI, HOLLAR, THEODORE VAN KESSEL, RUNCIMAN, CORNELIUS BEGA, CASTILIOGNE, SYLVESTRE, DELLA BELLA, and others. *200 beautiful etchings, fine impressions on India paper*, neatly mounted. Roy. 4to. *crimson morocco, extra gilt sides, back, and gilt leaves.*   London, N. D.

759 ETCHINGS. A Quarto Volume, containing *upwards of* 150 *fine and rare old etchings, and engravings, by early German and Flemish masters,* to wit, ALDEGREVER, LUCAS VAN LEYDEN, HANS SEBALD BEHAM, JOST AMMAN, REMBRANDT, GOTTZEUS, &c., *&c., including many brilliant impressions, some on India paper,* all neatly mounted on heavy Dutch paper. Impl. 4to. hf. morocco.   V. D.

760 ETCHINGS. ORIGINAL ETCHINGS FROM ANCIENT AND MODERN MASTERS, *a series of* 100, FROM ORIGINAL PLATES *by Della Bella, Bega, Claude, Hollar, Peter de Laire, Van Kessel, Du Jardin, Ostade, Van Vliet, Wicke, Rembrandt, Wierotter, and J. S. Smith.* Fine impressions. Oblong 4to. *hf. crimson morocco, extra, yellow edges.*   S. L. et A.

A FINE SERIES.

ETCHINGS, see also Hamerton, P. G., Chodowiecki.

761 ETHERIDGE, J. W. The Targums of Onkelos and Jonathan Ben Uzziel on the Pentateuch; with the Fragments of the Jerusalem Targum; from the Chaldee. 2 vols. crown 8vo. *new cloth.*   *London*, 1862.

762 ETRURIA PITTRICE, OVVERO STORIA DELLA PITTURA TOSCANA, dal Secolo X. fino al presente; *containing* 120 *fine engravings (some printed in tint) exhibiting select specimens of as many differ-*

ent Italian Masters, especially of the early periods ; with vignette portraits, and biographical sketches of each. *2 vols. roy. folio, original hf. vellum, boards.* Firenze, 1791.
Very Rare.
The greater part of these paintings are not engraved in any other collection ; but many of them are described in Lanzi's History of Painting in Italy.

763 Eustace, Rev. Jno. C. Classical Tour through Italy, its Scenery, Antiquities, Monuments, &c., with descriptions of the recent Spoliations of the French, *engravings of ground plans of Churches,* 2 vols. 4to. *calf, neat,* (pub. £5. 5s). London, 1813.

764 Evans, D. Morier. Speculative Notes and Notes on Speculation, crown *8vo. new cloth.* London, 1864.
Presentation copy from the author.

765 EVELYN and PEPYS' MEMOIRS, with Evelyn's Silva and Terra, edited by Hunter, and Miscellaneous Works, edited by Upcott, *profusely illustrated with fine portraits and plates,* together 7 vols. roy. 4to. *new and elegantly bound in tree-marbled calf, extra, by Clarke.* London, 1819-'25.
A fine set. (Published at £18. 18s. *in boards.*)
The Best Editions of these delightful performances, giving us a rare insight into the manners and customs of the Courts of Charles I. and II.

766 Evelyn, John. Sculptura ; or the History and Art of Chalcography, and engraving in copper, to which is annexed a new manner of engraving, or Mezzotinto, communicated by Prince Rupert. *Fine impression of the etched portrait of Evelyn, by Worlidge, and fac-simile of the Mezzotinto by Prince Rupert.* 12mo. hf. cf. neat. London, 1769.

767 Everett, Edward. Memorial. *India Proof Portrait and View of Mr. Everett's Library. Roy. 4to. boards.*
N. E. H. & G. Society, Boston, 1865.
Large Paper ; *one of 4 copies, on Whatman's Drawing Paper.*

767* ———— Another. *Roy. 4to. boards.* Large Paper. Boston, 1865.

768 Everett, Edward. Eulogy on Thomas Dowse, of Cambridgeport. *Portraits and a View of the Dowse Library. 8vo. cloth.*
Boston, 1859.

769 Ewald, Heinrich. History of Israel, translated from the German with Preface, &c., by Russell Martineau. *2d Edition Revised.* 2 vols. *8vo. new cloth.* London, 1869.

770 Excursion of the Putnam Phalanx, to Boston, Charlestown, and Providence, 1859. *8vo. cloth.* Hartford, 1859.

771 Faber, Geo. Dissertation on the Mysteries of the Cabiri ; or the great Gods of Phœnicia, Egypt, Troas, Greece, etc., etc., *front.* 2 vols. 8vo. *calf, neat.*
Printed for the Author, Oxford, 1803.
" This work establishes the justice of the remark made on the author's profound acquaintance with Antiquity. In this respect it is second only to the Ancient Mythology of Bryant."—*Bibl. Bib.*

772 Fable for Critics ; or better (I like as a thing that the reader's first fancy may strike, an old-fashioned title-page, such as presents a tabular view of the volume's contents.) A glance
10

at a few of our Literary Progenies from the tub of Diogenes. 12mo. pp. 80, bds. *uncut, scarce.* New York, 1848.
The author of this amusing little squib was James Russell Lowell.

773 FABLES. ÆSOP'S SELECT FABLES, with selections from those of other Fabulists. *Dodsley's beautiful edition printed by Baskerville, and illustrated with medallion cuts. 12mo. polished calf, extra, yellow edges.* London, 1761.
Choice copy, *scarce.*

774 FACETIÆ. ART OF INGENIOUSLY TORMENTING. Essay on. New Edition, with 5 humorous illrstrations in colors by G. M. Woodward. *12mo. new hf. morocco, scarce.* London, 1809.

775 FACETIÆ, COMICAL PILGRIM; or Travels of a Cynick Philosopher through the most wicked parts of the World, with his merry observations on the English Stage, Gaming Houses, Beaux, Women, Courtezans, &c. &c. *Front. sm. 8vo. hf. cf. neat, very scarce.* London, 1720.

776 FACETIÆ. History of some of the Penitents in the Magdalen-House, as supposed to be related by themselves. 2 vols. 12mo. cf. gilt. *Scarce.* London, 1760.

777 FACETIÆ. LE MOYEN DE PARVENIR. Nouvelle Édition. Corrigée (par François Béroalde). *2 vols. 12mo. calf.* (Paris), A Chinon, de l'imprimerie de François Rabelais. N. D.

778 FACETIÆ. VIRGIN IN EDEN; or, Pilgrim's Progress, by Way of Dialogue, represented by a Nobleman, Student, and Heiress, on their Journey from Sodom to Canaan, by C. Porey. *8vo. boards, rare.* London, 1769.

779 FAIRBAIRN, JAMES. CRESTS OF THE FAMILIES OF GREAT BRITAIN AND IRELAND. Compiled from the best authorities by James Fairbairn, and revised by Laurence Butters. 2 vols. 4to. *cloth.* Edinburgh, [1860?]
LARGE PAPER; INDIA PROOF IMPRESSIONS OF THE PLATES.
The most complete work on the subject.

780 FAIRFAX, EDWARD. GODFREY OF BOULOGNE; or, the Recovery of Jerusalem. Done into English Heroicall Verse by Edward Fairefax, Gent. Together with the Life of the said Godfrey. *Engraved title, folio, elegantly bound in mottled calf, extra, yellow edges.* London, *Printed by John Bill,* 1624.
FINE COPY. Original Edition.

781 FAIRHOLT, F. W. COSTUME IN ENGLAND. A History of Dress from the earliest period until the close of the XVIIIth century. *Nearly 700 engravings on wood, thick post 8vo. new cloth.* London, 1860.

782 FALCONER, WILLIAM. SHIPWRECK, a Poem, with a Life of the Author by J. S. Clarke. *Illustrated with a series of engravings on steel, by Fitler, after drawings by N. Pocock, the Marine painter.* Roy. 8vo, russia, full gilt. London, 1811.
LARGE PAPER.

783 FALSTAFF, SIR JOHN. Original Letters of, now first made public by a gentleman, a descendant of Dame Quickly, from Original MS. *Front. 12mo. hf. cf. gilt. Scarce.*
For the Author, London, 1796.

By James White, a school companion of Charles Lamb's, who said of it, "The whole work is full of goodly quips and rare fancies, all deeply marked like hoar antiquity—a bundle of the sharpest, queerest, and profoundest humors of any these juice-drained times have spawned."

784 FANE, SIR FRANCIS. SACRIFICE. A Tragedy. 3d Edition. 4to. *hf. morocco, red edges.* London, 1687.

Sir F. Fane was a grandson of the Earl of Westmorland, temp. Charles II. and Governor of Doncaster and Lincoln. He wrote the comedy " Love in the Dark; or, The Man of Business," 1675. "Tis not in Dramatick Poetry alone that our author is a Master, but his Talent is equal also in Lyricks."— *Langbaine.*

785 FANNING, COLONEL DAVID. Narrative, Giving An Account of his Adventures in North Carolina from 1775 to 1783, as written by himself, with An Introduction and Explanatory Notes. *4to. uncut.* New York, 1865.

LARGE PAPER : *only 50 copies in this size.*
Fanning was a Tory in the Revolutionary War. The above forms No. I. of Mr. Jos. Sabin's Reprints.

788 FANSHAWE, CYRIL A. BOOK OF BATTLE SONGS. A collection of the War Songs of various nations, by various translators, and Remarks on the Poetry of Martial Enthusiasm. *Small 4to. cloth, gilt.* London, N. D.

789 FANSHAWE, LADY. MEMOIRS, written by herself, with Extracts from the Correspondence of Sir R. Fanshawe, Ambassador from Charles II. to Madrid. *Portraits. 8vo. handsomely bound in polished calf, extra, yellow edges.* London, 1829.

BEST EDITION. Edited by Sir Harris Nicholas.
"These Memoirs may be ranked among the most interesting specimens of Autobiography."

790 FANSHAW, SIR RICHARD. (GUARINI) Il Pastor Fido ; the Faithful Shepherd, with an addition of several other Poems, and a discourse of the Civil Wars of Rome. *12mo. (8vo.) hf. cf. neat.*
London, 1676.

First translation of Guarini's famous Pastoral. See Bib. Anglo. Poetica, p. 105.

791 FARADAY, MICHAEL. Lectures on the Physical Forces. *16mo. cloth.* *New York, 1860.*

792 FARQUHAR, GEORGE. WORKS, comprising all his Poems, Letters, Essays and Comedies. *2 vols. 12mo. old cf. neat. Scarce.*
London, 1742.

793 FARRAR, REV. F. W. Seekers after God. 12mo. new hf. cf. extra.
Philadelphia, (1869).

794 FARRAR, REV. F. W. Essays on a Liberal Education. *8vo. new cloth.* *London, 1867.*

795 FASTES DE LA NATION FRANÇAISE par Ternisien d'Haudricourt. *A series of upward of 500 finely executed engravings on steel of celebrated events in the history of France, with descriptive text engraved throughout. 3 vols. roy. 4to. hf. mor.* *Paris, N. D.*

796 FATHER TOM AND THE POPE, or, a Night at the Vatican, as edited by Mr. Michael Heffernan. *Small 4to. uncut.*
Privately Printed, Philadelphia, 1861.

Only 98 copies.
Attributed to William Magenin, Jno. Fisher Murray, Rev. Francis Mohoney, and others.

797 Federalist, on the New Constitution, written in 1788 by Messrs. Hamilton, Madison, and Jay, with Appendix, &c. *8vo. sheep.*
Hallowell, 1857.

798 Fœderalist: A Collection of Essays, Written in Favor of the New Constitution, as Agreed upon by the Fœderal Convention, September 17, 1787. Reprinted from the original text, with an Historical Introduction and Notes by H. B. Dawson. *Portrait of Hamilton on India Paper. Imperial 8vo. cloth. Vol. I.* *Morrisania, N. Y.*, 1864.
Large Paper; *only 250 copies printed. Vol. II. is not yet published.*

799 Fellowes, W. D. Visit to the Monastery of La Trappe, in 1817, with Notes taken during a Tour through Le Perche, Normandy, Bretagne, &c., *numerous beautiful colored engravings. Impl. 8vo. blue morocco, extra.* *London*, 1823.
Large and Thick Paper.

800 Female Life in London. Evelina; being the History of a young lady's introduction to Fashionable Life and the gay scenes of the metropolis. *Numerous colored plates, by Heath, &c.* 8vo. *hf. cf. gilt, very scarce.* *London*, 1822.

801 Female Review. Life of Deborah Sampson, the Female Soldier in the War of the Revolution, with an Introduction and Notes by Jno. A. Vinton. *Portrait. Small 4to. uncut.* *Boston*, 1866.
Only 250 copies.

802 ———— Another copy. *Roy. 4to. uncut.* *Boston*, 1866.
Large Paper, *only 35 copies.*

803 FERGUSON, James. TREE and SERPENT WORSHIP; or, Illustrations of Mythology and Art in India, in the First and Fourth Centuries after Christ, from the Sculptures of the Buddhist Topes at Sanchi and Amravati, prepared under the authority of the Secretary of State for India. With Introductory Essays and Descriptions of the Plates. 99 very large and beautifully *executed Photographs, from the original monuments, also numerous woodcuts, &c., &c. Thick roy. 4to. new hf. red morocco, gilt top, uncut edges.* *India Museum, London*, 1868.
*** Only 100 copies printed, *pub'd at $75 gold.*
Now out of print and scarce.
"One of the most important contributions to the subject ever made."

804 Ferguson, James. History of Architecture in all Countries, from the earliest times to the present day; also History of the Modern Styles of Architecture. *Upwards of 1,000 beautifully executed engravings on wood. 3 vols. thick 8vo. new hf. mor. gilt top, uncut edges.* *London*, 1865.

805 Ferguson, Robert. The Teutonic Name-System applied to the Family Names of France, England, and Germany. *Thick 8vo. new cloth.* *London*, 1864.

806 Fielding, H. Works, Complete, with an Essay on his Life and Genius, by Murphy. *Fine portrait. 10 vols. 8vo. hf. calf, extra, fine clean copy, scarce.* *London*, 1806.

807 Fielding, Henry. Complete Works, comprising his Novels, Plays and Miscellaneous Writings, with a Memoir by Thos. Roscoe. *Illustrated with 20 etchings by George Cruikshank. Thick roy. 8vo. new calf, extra.* *London*, 1866.

808 Figuier, Louis. The Vegetable World; being a History of Plants, with their Botanical descriptions and peculiar properties. *Nearly* 500 *beautifully executed engravings on wood. Thick 8vo. new hf. cf., extra.* London, (N. Y.), 1867.

809 Figuier, Louis. Ocean World; being a Descriptive History of the Sea and its living Inhabitants. *Upwards of four hundred engravings on wood. Thick 8vo. new hf. cf. extra.* London, (N. Y.), 1868.

810 Figuier, Louis. The Insect World; being a popular account of the Orders of Insects, the Habits and Economy of some of the most interesting species. *Profusely illustrated, upward of* 560 *engravings on wood. 8vo. new hf. cf. extra.* (London), N. Y., 1868.

811 Figuier, Louis. The World before the Deluge. New Edition edited by Henry W. Bristow. *Profusely illustrated. Thick 8vo. new hf. cf. extra.* London, (N. Y.), 1867.

812 FINDEN'S Landscape and Portrait Illustrations to the Life and Works of Lord Byron, with Descriptions by Brockedon. *Upwards of* 150 *highly finished engravings, early impressions.* 3 *vols. royal 4to. full dark blue levant morocco, richly gilt.* London, 1833–4.

Large Paper.
These beautiful engravings are from drawings by Stanfield, Roberts, Cattermole, Callcott, Westall, etc.

813 Finden's Landscape Illustrations to the Bible, with Descriptions by Hartwell Horne. 100 *highly finished engravings from drawings by* Turner, Stanfield, Callcott, Roberts, &c. Proof Impressions *on India Paper.* 2 vols. in one, *Roy. 4to. crimson morocco extra, gilt leaves.* London, 1836.

Largest Paper, *fine copy.*

814 Finden's Ports, Harbors, Watering Places, and Coast Scenery of Great Britain. 120 *highly finished engravings after drawings by Bartlett, Harding, Creswick, &c. Fine impressions;* with Descriptions by Dr. Beattie. 2 *vols. 4to. half morocco gilt.* London, (1840).

Original Copy.

815 Finlay, G. Historical Works on Greece, Rome, and the Byzantine Empire, complete, 7 vols. 8vo. *new polished calf, extra.* Edinburgh, 1857.

Fine Copy, *best Edition.* Comprising Greece under the Romans, 1844—Mediæval Greece and Trebizond, 1851—History of the Byzantine Empire, from 716 to 1057—History of the Byzantine and Greek Empires, from 1057 to 1454—History of Greece under Othoman and Venetian Domination.
"In the essential requisites of fidelity, accuracy and learning, Mr. Finlay bears a favorable comparison with any historical writer of our day."—*N. A. Review.*

816 Fitzgerald, Percy. A famous Forgery, being the Story of "the unfortunate" Doctor Dodd. *Portrait, post 8vo. new hf. morocco, uncut.* London, 1865.

817 Flaxman's Compositions from Homer's Iliad and Odyssey. 74 *large and spirited engravings, by Piroli, Blake, Neagle, &c. Original impressions.* 2 *vols. in one, oblong fol. new hf. morocco, gilt.* 1805

818 FLEMING, GEORGE. HORSE-SHOES and Horse-Shoeing; their origin, history, uses and abuses. *Colored frontispiece,* and *upwards of two hundred illustrations on wood. Thick 8vo. new cloth, uncut.*
London, 1869.

"Though but of minor importance in archæology, yet the discussion of this subject has attracted much notice at times, and engaged a large share of attention on the part of men much celebrated as antiquarians and scholars."

819 FLETCHER, REV. JOHN. CHECKS to ANTINOMIANISM, in a series of letters to the Rev. Mr. Shirley, &c. 2 *vols. 8vo. sheep.*
New York, N.D.

820 FLINT, AUSTIN. Physiology of Man; designed to represent the existing state of Physiological Science, &c. *8vo. new cloth, uncut.*
New York, 1869.

821 FLORENCE GALLERY. TABLEAUX, STATUES, BAS-RELIEFS, et CAMAES de la GALERIE de FLORENCE et du PALAIS PITTI, dessinés par Wicar, avec explications par Mongez, imprimées sur PAPIER VELIN. 4 *vols. in three, impl. folio, containing* 400 *beautiful engravings of first-rate Pictures, Statues, Bas-reliefs, and Gems,* ORIGINAL *and* BRILLIANT IMPRESSIONS, *with descriptive letter-press.* 3 *vols. original hf. binding.* 1789–1802.

" Nothing can exceed the brilliancy of the impressions in this beautiful work." *The present copy was formerly in the collection of Mr. Bryan, the well-known collector of the Bryan Gallery, now in the rooms of the N. Y. Historical Society*

822 FLOYER, SIR JOHN. The Sibylline Oracles, translated from the best Greek copies, and compared with the sacred Prophecies, especially Daniel and Revelation. 12mo. (8vo.) *maroon morocco, neat, scarce.*
London, 1713.

823 FOLK-LORE, MYTHOLOGY, AND TRADITION. A HIGHLY INTERESTING AND VALUABLE SERIES OF WORKS, ILLUSTRATING THE FOLK-LORE, TRADITIONS, SUPERSTITIONS, and LEGENDS OF VARIOUS COUNTRIES. *Numerous illustrations on steel and wood. Together* 42 *volumes,* 12mo. *post 8vo. and 8vo. elegantly and uniformly bound in half morocco extra, gilt tops, edges uncut, contents lettered.*
Various places and dates.

Many of the works included in this fine series are very scarce, and in every instance the best edition has been selected.

THE SET COMPRISES THE FOLLOWING :
Arabian Tales. [Not included in the Arabian Nights.] 1 volume.
Arabian Fables. By Bidpai. 1 vol.
African Tradition and Stories. By Callaway. 1 vol.
African. Hottentot Fables and Tales, by Bleek. 1 vol.
English Ancestral Traditions. By Timbs. 1 vol.
English. Lancashire Folk-Lore, by Henderson. 1 vol.
English. Legends of the Lintel and the Ley. By Dendy. 1 vol.
English. Folk-Lore of the West of England, by Hunt. 2 vols.
German. The Book of Were-Wolves; being an account of a terrible superstition, by Baring Gould. 1 vol.
German. Chronicle of Gudrun. A Story of the North Sea. 1 vol.
Icelandic. Story of Burnt Njal, by Dasent. 2 vols.
Icelandic Legends. By Arnason. Illustrated. 2 vols.
Icelandic. Gisli the Outlaw, by Dasent. Illustrated. 1 vol.
Icelandic. The Oxonian in Iceland, by Metcalfe. 1 Vol.
Icelandic. Popular Tales from the Norse, by Dasent. 1 vol.
Icelandic. The Edda of Saemund the Learned. 1 vol.
Icelandic. Viga Glum's Saga, by Head. 1 vol.
Irish. Killarney Legends, by Crofton Croker. 1 vol.
Irish. Fairy Legends and Traditions, by Crofton Croker. Illustrated. 1 vol.
Irish. Legendary Fictions of the Irish Celts, by Kennedy. Illustrated. 1 vol.

Middle Ages. Curious Myths of the Middle Ages, by S. Baring Gould. 2 vols.
New Zealand. Traditions and Superstitions of the New Zealanders. 1 vol.
Persian. The Anvar-i Suhaili; or, The Lights of Canopus, by Eastwick. 1 vol.
Russian. Krilof and his Fables, by Ralston. Illustrated. 1 vol.
Scandinavian Traditions and Superstitions, by Thorpe. 3 vols.
Scottish. Popular Tales of the West Highlands, by Campbell. 4 vols.
Scottish. Traits and Stories of the Scottish People, by Rogers. 1 vol.
Scottish Life and Character. By Ramsay. 1 vol.
Scottish. Peasant Life in Glenaldie. 1 vol.
Welsh. Wild Wales, by George Barrow. 1 vol.
Washingtons (The). A Tale of the Seventeenth Century, by Simpkinson. Illustrated. 1 vol.
Witch Stories of Scotland and England. By Linton. 1 vol.

824 FOLK-LORE. HENDERSON, WM. Notes on the Folk-Lore of the Northern Counties of England and the Borders, *colored front.* 12*mo. new cloth.* London, 1866.

825 FOLK-LORE. O'BRIEN, DENOCH. Fictions of the Irish Celts. *Frontispiece.* 12*mo. new cloth.* London, 1866.

826 FONBLANQUE, ALBANY. England under seven Administrations. *Portraits.* 3 *vols. post 8vo. new hf. calf, extra, very scarce.*
London, 1837.

827 (FOORD, ED.) The Famous History of Montelion, Knight of the Oracle, son to the true Mirror of Princes, the most renouned King of Assyria. 𝕭𝕷𝕬𝕮𝕶 𝕷𝕰𝕿𝕿𝕰𝕽. Sm. 4to. hf. mor. *very scarce.* London, 1695.

828 FORD'S DRAMATIC WORKS; with Notes critical and explanatory, by WILLIAM GIFFORD. NEW EDITION revised with additions to the text and to the notes, by the Rev. ALEX. DYCE. *Beautifully printed.* 3 *vols. 8vo. cloth, uncut.* Toovey. London, 1869.
Large paper; few printed for subscribers, and already out of print.

829 (FORDE, EDWARD.) The most Famous, Delectable, and Pleasant History of Pariemus, the most renouned Prince of Bohemia. *Two Parts, with very curious portraits on wood.* 𝕭𝕷𝕬𝕮𝕶 𝕷𝕰𝕿𝕿𝕰𝕽. 2 vols. sm. 4to. *hf. morocco, extra.*
London, 1681.

FINE COPY of this once popular Romance of Chivalry; the above is the eleventh impression.

830 FOREIGN QUARTERLY REVIEW. A JOURNAL of the BEST FOREIGN LITERATURE. Complete from its commencement in July, 1827, to July, 1846, inclusive, (all pubd.) 37 vols. 8*vo. calf, very neat.* London, 1827-46.
FINE COPY.
A Journal of the highest reputation, and contains numerous articles by T. Carlyle, and other authors of the first standing.

831 FORSTER, JOHN. WALTER SAVAGE LANDOR. A Biography. *Portraits, &c.* 2 thick vols. *crown 8vo. new cloth.* London, 1869.

832 FORSTER, J. W. THE MISSISSIPPI VALLEY; its Physical Geography. Maps, &c. 8*vo. new cloth.* Chicago, Ill., 1869.

833 FORSTER and WHITNEY's Report on the Geology of the Lake Superior Land District, *numerous plates.* 2 vols. 8*vo. cloth.*
Washington, 1851.

834 FORSYTH, WILLIAM. The Life of Marcus Tullius Cicero. *With Illustrations.* 2 *vols. imp. 8vo. cloth, uncut.* New York, 1865.
LARGE PAPER. *Only 75 copies printed.*

835 —— Another Copy. 2 vols. Large Paper.   N. Y. 1865.

836 Forsyth, William. Cases and Opinions on Constitutional Law, and various points of English Jurisprudence. *Thick roy. 8vo. new cloth.*   London, 1869.

837 Fosbrooke's Encyclopædia of Antiquities, and Elements of Archæology, Classical and Mediæval, 107 *plates*, 2 vols. roy. 8vo. British Monachism, new edition, 15 *plates*, roy. 8vo. *Together 3 vols. roy. 8vo. hf. cf. antique, red edges.*   London, 1843.

> Contents: 1. Manners and Customs of Ancient Pilgrims. 2. Consuetudinol of Anchorets and Hermits. 3. Some Account of the Continentes, or persons who had made vows of chastity. 4. Select Poems in various styles.

838 FOSCOLO, UGO. Essay on Petrarch. Impl. 8vo. cloth. Very Rare.   *Printed for the Author*, London, 1821.

> Privately Printed, and only 16 copies.
> See Martin's Catalogue of Privately Printed Books (Ed. 1824), p. 534.

839 Foss, E. Judges of England, with Sketches of their Lives, and Notices connected with the Courts of Westminster, from the Norman Conquest. 4 vols. 8vo. *cloth.*   London, 1848–57.

> A most valuable and important work, forming a suitable accompaniment to Lord Campbell's Lives of the Lord Chancellors and Chief Justices.

840 Foulkes, Edmund S. Christendom's Divisions, being a philosophical sketch of the divisions of the Christian Family in East and West. *2 vols. post 8vo. new cloth.*   London, 1865.

841 Fourier, Charles. The Social Destiny of Man, or theory of the four movements, translated by Henry Clapp, Jr., with Introduction, &c., by Albert Brisbaine. *Fine portrait.* 8vo. *hf. roan. Scarce.*   New York, 1857.

842 Fox, C. J. History of the early part of the Reign of James Second. *Fine portrait.* Large and thick paper. Roy. 4to. calf, gilt. *Fine copy.*   London, 1808.

> "There is no work in our language that in point of excellence approaches Fox's History as a profound and masterly exposition of the British Constitution, and in which the minutest facts are most sacredly and accurately detailed."

843 Fox, Mary. The Country-House. Beautifully printed, with 5 large tinted lithographic plates and beautiful woodcuts. *4to. cloth, uncut.*   London, 1843.

> Privately Printed, *and only* 170 *copies.*

844 Foxe's Book of Martyrs. Acts and Monuments of Matters most Special and Memorable, happening in the Church, with an Universal History of the same. 𝕭𝕷𝕬𝕮𝕶 𝕷𝕰𝕿𝕿𝕰𝕽. *Numerous curious engravings of martyrdoms, &c.* 3 vols. folio, old calf, gilt.   London, 1632.

> "The Book of Martyrs was, and yet is, one of the most extraordinary and popular Church Histories in the World."

845 FRAGMENTS OF ANTIQUITIE, gathered by T. Purland. A large 4to. Scrap-book, *containing reports of various Antiquarian Societies, Newspaper cuttings, and many hundred woodcuts, etchings, and steel plates, Illustrating the Antiquities of Great Britain, all neatly arranged, with a complete* ms. *Index. Roy. 4to. hf. morocco, uncut.*   London.

845* France and the French Revolution; A collection of Authentic narratives of the horrors committed by the Revolutionary

Government of France under Marat and Robespierre, trans. from the French. *3 vols. 8vo. cloth.* London, 1826.

845 FRANCIS, JNO. W. OLD NEW YORK; or, Reminiscences of the past sixty years, with a memoir of the author by Henry T. Tuckerman. *Portraits on India Paper. Imp. 8vo. hf. green morocco, gilt top.* New York, 1865.
LARGE PAPER ; *only* 100 *copies printed.*

846 FRANCIS, SIR PHILIP. MEMOIRS OF, with Correspondence and Journals, by Joseph Parkes and Herman Merivale. *Portraits. 2 vols. 8vo. new hf. calf, extra, marbled edges.* London, 1867.

847 FRANCKLIN, REV. THOS. Sermon preached before the Honorable Trustees for establishing the COLONY OF GEORGIA in America. *4to. hf. mor. uncut edges.* London, 1750.
Fine copy ; see also Watts, (Rev. T.)

848 FRANKLIN, BENJAMIN. AUTOBIOGRAPHY, edited from his MSS., with Notes and an Introduction by John Bigelow. *Portrait, post 8vo. new hf. cf. extra.* Philadelphia, 1868.

849 FRANKLIN, BENJ. Letters to, from his Family and Friends, 1751–1790. *Portraits. Roy. 8vo. bds. uncut.* New York, 1859.

850 FRASER, JAMES BAILLIE. Journal of a Tour through part of the Snowy Range of the Himālā Mountains, and to the Sources of Rivers Jumna and Ganges. *Large folding map. Roy. 4to. hf. russia, neat.* London, 1821.

851 FRAUDS OF ROMISH MONKS AND PRIESTS, a series of Letters from a Gentleman in Italy. *12mo. calf, scarce.* London, 1691.

852 FREEMAN, FREDERICK. THE HISTORY OF CAPE COD, the Annals of Barnstable County, including the District of Marshpee. *Many portraits. 2 vols. imp. 8vo. boards, uncut.* Boston, 1858.

853 FRENCH HISTORICAL LETTERS. 5 vols. foolscap, containing *upwards of* 1000 *MS. translations of important Letters in the great Historical Collection, principally to and from Napoleon, Joseph, King of Spain, Murat, King of Naples, Louis XVII and Louis XVIII.* 5 vols. folio, paper. V. D.
A curious series.

854 FRENCH ANAS. *Engraved titles. 3 vols. 16mo. hf. morocco.*
London, 1805.

855 FRENCH, JAMES CLARK. The Trip of the Steamer Oceanus to Fort Sumter and Charleston, S. C., April 14th, 1865. *8vo. uncut.*
Brooklyn, 1865.

856 FRENEAU, PHILIP. POEMS relating to the American Revolution, with An Introductory Memoir and Notes by Evert A. Duyckinck. *Portrait on India paper. Imperial 8vo. cloth, uncut.*
New York, 1865.
LARGE PAPER ; *only* 100 *copies.*

857 FRITHIOF'S SAGA: A legend of the North; by Elias Tegnér, translated from the Swedish by G. S. Revised and illustrated, with an Introductory Letter by the Author. *Illustrated with* 17 *engravings and numerous musical accompaniments. 8vo. cloth, scarce.* Stockholm, 1839.
Best Edition, by Prof. George Stephens, of Copenhagen.

858 Froissart, Sir John. Chronicles of France, England, Spain, &c., from the latter part of the reign of Edward II to the Coronation of Henry IV, translated by Thos. Johnes. *Numerous wood-cuts.* 2 vols. *Imp. 8vo. new hf. cf. antique.*

London, 1855.

859 FROUDE, James Anthony. HISTORY of ENGLAND, from the Fall of Wolsey to the Death of Queen Elizabeth. Large type, Library Edition. 10 vols. 8vo. new cloth. London, 1867, &c.

860 Froude, Jas. Anthony. History of England. *Riverside Edition.* 10 *vols. crown 8vo. new hf. cf. extra.* New York, 1868.

861 Froude, James Anthony. History of England, from the Fall of Wolsey. *Printed on toned paper, 4 vols. imp. 8vo. new cloth, uncut.* New York, 1865, &c.

Large Paper, *few printed.*

862 Froude, Jas. A. Inaugural Address delivered to the University of St. Andrews, March 19, 1869. *8vo. cloth.* London, 1869.

863 Fugitive Pieces, on Various Subjects, by several Authors. 2 vols. 12mo. cf. gilt. London, 1761.

864 Fuller, Thomas. Holy and Profane State. *Third Edition*, with frontispiece (including portrait of Charles I), and *portraits of Joan of Arc, Cardinal Wolsey, Joan of Naples, Edward the Black Prince, Queen Elizabeth, Francis Drake, Scaliger, Duke of Alva, Bp. Ridley, Lord Burleigh*, &c., &c., by William Marshall. *Folio, hf. calf, gilt. Very scarce.*

(London, 1652), Cambridge, 1648.

865 Fuller, Thomas. Good Thoughts in Bad Times, and other papers. *Handsomely printed, with rubricated title, &c. 8vo. cloth, uncut.* Boston, 1863.

Large Paper, *only 30 copies.*

866 Fuller, Thomas. David's Hainous Sinne. Heartie Repentance. Heavie Punishment. *Post 8vo. ant. vellum, uncut.*

B. M. Pickering, London, 1869.

Only 100 copies printed. The work is a literatim copy of the original, even the typographical errors being reproduced.

867 Furman, Gabriel. Notes, Geographical and Historical, Relating to the Town of Brooklyn, Long Island, with Notes, and a Memoir of the Author. *4to. hf. morocco, gilt top.*

Brooklyn, *Reprinted for the Faust Club*, 1865.

Only 120 copies.

868 ——— Another copy. *Imp. 4to. boards, uncut.* Brooklyn, 1865.

Large Paper, *only 20 copies.*

869 Furman, Gabriel. Biographical Sketch of. Imp. 8vo. uncut.

Only 25 copies. N. D.

870 Gabell, Rev. J. H. L. The Accordance of Religion with Nature. *8vo. cloth, uncut, scarce. Pickering*, 1842.

871 Gadbury, J., *Astrologer*. Doctrine of Nativities, containing the whole Art of Directions whereby any man may discover the most Remarkable and Occult Accidents of his Life, &c., *fine portrait by Cross*, folio, *new hf. calf, gilt, scarce.* London, 1658.

Includes also Tables for calculating Planets, and the Doctrine of Horarie Questions.

874 GAGE, W. L. Life of Félix Mendelssohn-Bartholdy, *portrait*, 12mo. *hf. cf. extra.* New York, 1866.

875 GAIESS. Commentaries on the Roman Law, with an English Translation, &c., by F. Tomkins and W. Geo. Lemon. Part I. 8vo. *paper*, pp. 496. London, 1869.

876 GALERIE AGUADO: Choix des principaux Tableaux de la Galerie du *Marquis de las* Marismas del Guadalquivir, par C. Gavard. *Atlas folio.* 38 *very fine engravings after exquisite specimens by* Murillo, Velasquez, Carlo Dolce, Rubens, Rembrandt, Raphael, Correggio. Large Paper. *Folio, hf. morocco, neat.* Paris, 1839.
Brilliant Proof Impressions, *with the artist's stamp.*
"Admirable in illustration, as far as it goes, of the Spanish School of Art." —*D. Turner.*

877 Galerie de L'Ermitage gravée au trait d'après les plus beaux Tableaux qui la composent, avec la Description Historique par Camille de Geneve. *A series of 45 finely executed engravings in outline.* *Roy. 4to. hf. red morocco, extra.* St. Petersburgh, &c., 1805.
Very Scarce, *fine copy.*

878 Galerie du Florence, et du Palais Pitti. Tableaux, Statues, Bas-Reliefs et Camées, désinés par Wickar, &c., avec les explications, &c. 52 *large and beautifully engraved plates, comprising upwards of* 100 *pictures.* Fine Impressions. *Atlas folio, hf. red morocco.* Paris, 1789.
A selection of the choicest examples from this celebrated gallery.

879 GALERIE de MUSÉE NAPOLÉON, publiée par Filhol, graveur contenant 792 *graveurs, d'après les tableaux des peintres les plus célèbres de toutes les écoles et des belles statues de l'antiquité, avec un texte explicatif par Lavellée.* Fine Impressions *of the plates.* 10 vols. impl. 8vo. *hf. green morocco, gilt,* Paris, 1804.
Original Edition, *scarce.*
This fine work is the only one which contains engravings of *all* the magnificent paintings and sculpture, &c., concentrated by Bonaparte from Italy, Spain, and other countries, before they were again dispersed.

GALLERY OF THE GREAT PAINTERS.

880 GALERIE COMPLÈTE des TABLEAUX des PEINTRES les plus célèbres de toutes les Epoques, ou recueil des plus belles compositions tirées des Saintes Ecritures, de l'Histoire Ancienne, et autres objets, *comprising* 1300 *plates, beautifully engraved in outline, with Lives of each Painter by Landon,* 12 vols. roy. 4to. in 6, *new hf. crimson morocco, extra, gilt tops, uncut edges.* Paris, Didot.

This beautiful work is the only one that contains in a single work the chefs-d'œuvre of all the Great Masters which are dispersed in different Galleries of Europe. It comprises the works of the following painters:

Raphael, 4 vols.	Domenichino.
Michael Angelo.	Albano.
Baccio Bandinelli.	Leonardo da Vinci.
Volterra.	Titian.
Correggio.	Guido.
Le Sueur.	Paul Veronese.
Poussin, 2 vols.	Paintings of the Ancients.

881 GALERIA REALE DI FIRENZE, illustrata da Zanoni, Montalvi, &c., *with upwards of* 650 *plates, containing all the Paintings, Portraits, Bas-Reliefs, Statues, Gems, &c. in the Florence Gallery.* 13 vols. 8vo. *hf. calf, gilt,* (pub. £16. 16s.) *scarce.*   Firenze, 1817–33.

882 GALERIE DE PALAIS ROYAL, dite d'Orleans, gravée d'après les tableaux des differentes écoles qui la composaient par Couché, avec un description historique de chaque tableaux.   354 *very fine engravings, from the most beautiful collection of Paintings ever formed, brilliant impressions.* 3 *thick vols. royal folio, half morocco, gilt.*   Paris, 1786–1808.

PROOFS ON INDIA PAPER.
This Collection, known as the Orleans Gallery, is one of the scarcest and most pleasing of all the Collections.

883 GALLERIA PITTI (L'Imperiale e Reale) illustrata per cura di Luigi Bardi.   *Containing five hundred plates from the celebrated pictures of the old masters, finely engraved by the best Italian artists,* with Descriptions.   4 vols. royal folio, *new half morocco, extra, gilt leaves.*   Florence, 1837–42.

A very beautiful work, which must not be confounded with one of nearly the same title.

884 GALLERY.   CABINET GALLERY OF PICTURES, selected from the Splendid Collections of Art, Public and Private, which adorn Great Britain, with Descriptive Notices by Allan Cunningham. *Upwards of* 70 *beautiful line engravings from pictures by celebrated masters, ancient and modern.* BRILLIANT PROOF IMPRESSIONS ON INDIA PAPER. 2 *vols. impl. 8vo. hf. green morocco, gilt top, uncut edges.*   Major, London, 1833.

LARGE PAPER: *scarce in this condition.*

885 GALLERY.   NATIONAL GALLERY OF PICTURES by the Great Masters, with Descriptions, *nearly* 120 *highly finished engravings, fine early impressions.* 2 vols. 4to. *hf. morocco, gilt.*
London, (1833.)

INDIA PROOF IMPRESSIONS, *scarce in this state.*

886 GALLERY OF MUNICH.   GALLERY OF THE OLD GERMAN MASTERS, formerly at Stuttgart, in the possession of the Brothers Boisseree, now removed to Munich.   *Engraved in lithography, heightened by tints, and so admirably executed as to be scarcely distinguishable from the most perfect line engravings,* mounted on drab-colored drawing paper, forming 2 *vols. thick, elephant folio, bound, hf. turkey morocco, gilt.*
Munich, 1800–'36.

Among the painters are :

Van Eyck, M. Coxie,	Albert Dürer, B. von Orley,
I. von Mechenem, J. Hemling,	Lucas Cranach, J. Walch,
H. Heemskerck,	M. Grünewald, Holbein,
J. Patenier,	Martin Schön, Mabuse,
Hugo van der Goes,	Lucas van Leyden,
J. von Melem, W. von Köln,	Van Assen, Hans Asper,
J. Schwarz, B. de Brüyn,	Quintin Metsys,
J. von Calcar, J. Schoorel,	Engelbrechtsen,

and various other Painters whose names are unknown.

Published at 100 guineas, unbound.   Priced by Bohn, £63.

₊ This work is the admiration of the most fastidious connoisseurs.   It is impossible to conceive the perfection which lithographic engraving has attained at Munich, without seeing this *chef d'œuvre.*   The stones, from their uncommon size, being valuable, were cleaned off, and used as the work proceeded ; and as a very limited number were struck off, sets are now scarce.

87 GALLERY. ANGERSTEIN GALLERY, (*now National Gallery.*) Catalogue of the Celebrated Collection of Pictures of the late John Julius Angerstein, accompanied with Historical and Biographical Notices by John Young. 41 *beautifully finished etchings after the celebrated pictures of the old masters.* INDIA PROOF IMPRESSIONS, *folio, hf. morocco, extra, edges uncut.*

London, 1823.

LARGE PAPER, *scarce.*

88 GALLERY of *Modern British* ARTISTS; consisting of a series of *engravings on steel from pictures by Turner, Roberts, Stanfield, Harding, Fielding, Cox, Prout, &c.,* fine impressions. *4to. hf. russia, gilt.* London, 1834.

89 GALLERY of BRITISH and FOREIGN PORTRAITS, with Memoirs by distinguished Biographers, 168 *fine portraits beautifully engraved on steel, original impressions.* 7 *vols. impl. 8vo. dark green morocco, super-extra, gilt edges.* C. *Knight*, London, 1833–8.

CHOICE COPY.

A very interesting series, engraved in the highest style of the Art, in the same manner as Lodge's portraits, to which it forms an excellent companion, the portraits being different.

90 GALLERY. CABINET de POULLAIN, *containing* 120 *beautiful engravings after the Old Masters.* FINE IMPRESSIONS, with Biographical Notices and Descriptions by Count D'Orsay. *Royal 4to. calf, gilt.* Paris, 1781.

SCARCE.

91 GALLERY. LEUCHTENBERG GALLERY OF PICTURES AT MUNICH, 262 *spirited etchings after the Great Masters,* ancient and modern, with Lives of the Painters and Descriptions of each Picture, by J. D. Passavant, thick roy. 4to. *hf. morocco, scarce.*

Frankf., 1851.

The LEUCHTENBERG GALLERY is one of the finest in existence. The etchings in the above work are executed by Herr Muxel, the Curator of the Gallery, and exhibit with fidelity the peculiar method of treatment of each painter.

92 GALLERY. NATIONAL GALLERY of PICTURES by the Great Masters, with Descriptions. 120 *highly finished engravings on steel.* 2 vols. in one, *4to. cloth, uncut.* London, (1833.)

FINE EARLY COPY.

GALLERY. See DUSSELDORF, MUSEUM FLORENTINUM, ETTRURIA PITTRICE, FLORENCE, STAFFORD, COSEVELT, &c.

93 GALLOWAY, J. The Examination of Joseph Galloway, Esq. By a Committee of the House of Commons. Edited by Thomas Balch. *Two hundred and fifty copies Printed. 8vo. boards, uncut. Philadelphia : Printed for the Seventy-Six Society,* 1855.

94 GAMBRA, COUNT P. (*A Brother of the Countess Guiccioli.*) Narrative of Lord Byron's last Journey to Greece. *8vo. hf. cf. neat.*

London, 1825.

95 GARDEN, ALEXANDER. ANECDOTES OF THE AMERICAN REVOLUTION, Illustrative of the Talents and Virtues of the Heroes and Patriots who acted the most conspicuous parts therein. 3 *vols. folio, boards, uncut.* Brooklyn, 1865.

LARGE PAPER, *only 30 copies.*

896 ——— Another copy. 3 vols. 4to. *boards.* Brooklyn, 1865.

897 Gardiner, Samuel Rawson. Prince Charles and the Spanish
Marriage; 1617–1623. A chapter of English History. *8vo.*
London, 1869.
"We thank Mr. Gardiner much for his able, intelligent and interesting book.
We will do him the justice to say it is the best history of the period which
it covers; *it is the only history.*"—*Spectator.*

898 Gardiner, Samuel J. Autumn Leaves, *handsomely printed on laid
paper. 8vo. new cloth, uncut.* New York, 1865.
Large Paper. *Only 50 copies.*

899 Garrick, David. Life of, from original family papers, and unpublished documents, by Percy Fitzgerald. *Portrait, &c.* 2
thick vols. *8vo. new hf. calf, gilt.* London, 1868.

900 Garrick, David. Life of, from Original Family Papers, and numerous published and unpublished sources, by Percy Fitzgerald. *Portrait.* 2 thick *vols. 8vo. new cloth.* London, 1868.
Published at $18 in cloth.

901 GARRICK. The manner pointed out in which the Common
Prayer was read in private by the late Mr. Garrick, for the instruction of a young clergyman, by J. W. Anderson. *8vo. hf.
mor.* London, 1797.
Excessively Rare.

902 Garland, Hugh A. Life of John Randolph of Roanoke. 2
vols. 8vo. cloth. New York, 1866.

903 Gaspey, Thos. Life and Times of the Good Lord Cobham (Sir
John Oldcastle), *portrait inserted.* 2 vols. in one. *Thick post
8vo. hf. mor. uncut.* London, 1844.
The first Protestant Martyr.

904 GAY, JOHN. Fables, with a Life of the Author. Illustrated
Edition, *with nearly 70 finely engraved plates by Neagle, frontispiece, &c.* Roy. 8vo. *handsomely bound in crimson morocco, gilt
edges, in the style of Roger Payne.* London, 1793.
Very Scarce. Not mentioned by Lowndes.

905 Gay, John. Fables. *Front. and numerous engravings on copper.*
12mo. *old cf. neat.* London, 1767.
Scarce edition.

906 Gazetteer of the World, or Dictionary of Geographical Knowledge, *illustrated with an extensive series of highly-finished engravings, colored maps, and many wood-cuts,* 7 thick vols. impl. 8vo.
new half calf, marbled leaves (pub. in *bds.* £10). Edinb., 1858.
A valuable work, forming a complete body of modern Geography, physical,
political, statistical, historical, and ethnographical.

907 Gell and Gandy's Pompeiana; The Topography, Edifices
and Ornaments of Pompeii. Both Series complete, *with upward of 200 fine plates, maps, vignettes, by Cook, Heath, &c., early
impressions.* 4 vols. *impl. 8vo. new hf. morocco, gilt tops, uncut
edges, scarce.* London, 1824.
Large Paper. *Best Edition.*

908 Gell, Sir William. Topography of Troy and its Vicinity, illustrated and explained by Drawings and Descriptions, 45 *large
and fine engravings,* beautifully colored *like drawings,* folio,
hf. green morocco, gilt edges. (Pub. in bds. £15. 15s.)
London, 1804.
Fine Copy. *Only a limited edition.*

909 " GERMAN POPULAR STORIES." Collected by the Brothers Grimm, from Oral Tradition, and Translated by EDGAR TAYLOR. Edited by JOHN RUSKIN. With twenty-two Illustrations after the inimitable designs of George Cruikshank. Both series complete. *Proof impressions of the plates on India paper.* Thick 4to. half morocco, gilt top. *London*, 1869.

₊ These are the designs which Mr. Ruskin has praised so highly, placing them far above all Cruikshank's other works of a similar character. So rare had the original book (published in 1823–26) become, that £5 to £6 per copy was an ordinary price.

LARGE PAPER EDITION. Only a very few copies printed.

910 GERMAN THEATRE, translated by Benjamin Thompson. *Illustrated with steel plates, 6 vols.* 8vo. calf, gilt. *London*, 1801.

LARGE PAPER.
Contains the Plays of Kotzebue, Schroeder, Goethe, Lessing, Schiller, Ifland, and others.

911 GESSNER, SOLOMON. WORKS, translated from the German with Notes, Critical and Explanatory, with a Memoir of the author, *fine engravings by Worthington, &c.* 2 vols. crown 8vo. calf, gilt.
London, 1805.

912 GESSNER, SOLOMON. WORKS, with Life, &c., *fine plates by Stothard.* 3 vols. crown 8vo. cf. *Liverpool*, 1802.

913 GESSNER, S. NEW IDYLLES, translated by W. Hooper. ILLUSTRATED EDITION, *engraved frontispiece, and numerous beautiful copper-plates, and vignettes from Gessner's own designs. Roy. 8vo. new hf. calf, extra, scarce.* *London*, 1776.

914 GIBBON, EDWARD. WORKS, complete, viz.: DECLINE AND FALL OF THE ROMAN EMPIRE, edited by MILMAN, 12 vols. MISCELLANEOUS WORKS, by Lord Sheffield, 5 vols., and LIFE AND CORRESPONDENCE, by Milman, 1 vol. BEST LIBRARY EDITION, together 18 vols. 8vo. *elegantly bound in tree-calf, extra, marbled edges.* *London*, 1839, &c.

A fine uniform set.

915 GIBBON, EDWARD. History of the Decline and Fall of the Roman Empire, with Notes by Dean Milman. *6 vols. post 8vo. new hf. cf. extra.* *Riverside Press, Boston*, 1862.

916 GIFFORD, JOHN. HISTORY OF FRANCE from the Earliest Times to the present important era, with Notes, critical and explanatory, *several hundred illustrations.* 5 vols. 4to. calf, gilt, *fine copy.*
London, 1791.

917 GIFFORD, WILLIAM. BAVIAD AND MŒVIAD. A Satirical Poem. *Engraved frontispiece. Roy. 8vo. dark blue morocco, gilt.*
London, 1797.

LARGE PAPER, fine copy.

918 GIFFORD, WILLIAM. THE BAVIAD and MŒVIAD. Post 8vo. calf, neat. *London*, 1811.

919 GILBART, JAS. W. Practical Treatise on Banking. New Edition, by J. Smith Homans. 8vo. cloth. *Philadelphia*, 1860.

920 GILBERT, JOSIAH. CADORE; or, Titian's Country. *Profusely illustrated with fac-similes from the Drawings and Pictures of Titian, and engravings on wood, of scenery, &c. Printed on toned paper*, 4to. new cloth, *uncut.* *London*, 1869.

921 GILBERT, WILLIAM. LUCRÈZIA BORGIA, Duchess of Ferrara. A Biography, illustrated by rare and unpublished documents. *Portrait.* 2 vols. post 8vo. *new cloth.* London, 1869.

922 GILCHRIST, ALEXANDER. LIFE OF WM. BLAKE (" Pictor Ignotus "), with selections from his Poems and other writings. *Illustrated from Blake's own works, in fac-simile, by W. J. Linton, and in photo-lithography, with a few of Blake's original plates.* 2 vols. 8vo. half morocco, roxburgh style. London, 1863.

923 GILCHRIST, JAMES P. A BRIEF DISPLAY of the ORIGIN AND HISTORY OF ORDEALS, with a Chronological Register of the Principal Duels, 1762–1820 (172 in number). *8vo. new hf. morocco, gilt.* For the Author, London, 1821.

924 GILLRAY'S CELEBRATED CARICATURES, comprising the best Political and Humorous Satires of the Reign of Geo. III. 1779–1810, 600 LARGE and HIGHLY SPIRITED ENGRAVINGS, *printed from the original plates.* Also THE SUPPRESSED CARICATURES. 2 vols. ATLAS FOLIO, *hf. morocco, gilt back, and gilt leaves, with an 8vo. vol. comprising illustrative Descriptions of every plate.* London, 1850.

Gillray is undoubtedly the prince of English Caricaturists, and is considered by many as superior even to Hogarth.

925 GILPIN, REV. WM. WORKS on the FINE ARTS, the PICTURESQUE, LANDSCAPE SCENERY, and GARDENING, comprising Observations and Artistical Remarks on the Picturesque Beauty of various parts of England, Wales, and Scotland. *With upwards of One hundred and eighty fine aquatinta engravings. Together 12 vols. uniformly bound in calf, gilt.* London, 1794, &c.

FINE COMPLETE SET, from the Library of Lord Farnham.

Comprising : 1. Northern Tour.—Mountains and Lakes of Cumberland and Westmoreland, 2 vols.
2. Southern Tour.—Hampshire, Sussex, and Kent.
3. Western Tour.—Hampshire, Isle of Wight, Wiltshire, Surrey, Somersetshire, Devon, Dorset.
4. Eastern Tour.—Cambridge, Norfolk, Suffolk, Essex, and North Wales.
5. Scottish Tour.—The Highlands, 2 vols.
6. River Wye, and several parts of South Wales.
7. Forest Scenery and other Woodland Views, chiefly in New Forest, Hampshire, 2 vols.
8. Five Essays—On Picturesque Beauty ; on Picturesque Travel ; on Sketching Landscape, &c.
9. Essay on Prints and Early Engravers.

"Gilpin has described, in several justly-esteemed tours, the Picturesque Beauties of Great Britain. All his volumes are accompanied by engravings aquatint, executed by himself with the taste and feeling of a painter. All his works abound with ingenious reflections, proper to enrich the theory of the arts, and to guide the practice of them."—*Biographie Universelle.*

925* GILPIN, WILLIAM. The Central Gold Region. The Grain, Pastoral, and Gold Regions of North America. *Numerous maps,* 8vo. cloth. Philadelphia, 1860.

926 GINSBURG, CHR. D. THE KABBALAH ; its Doctrines, Development, and Literature. An Essay. *8vo. cloth.* London, 1865.

927 GIRARD COLLEGE and its founder ; a Biography of Mr. Girard, &c. by Henry W. Arey. *Portrait. 12mo. cloth.* Philadelphia, 1866.

928 GISLI THE OUTLAW, from the Icelandic by George Webbe Dasent, with illustrations by C. E. Mildenay. *Small 4to. new cloth.* Edinburgh, 1866.

929 GLADSTONE GOVERNMENT, being cabinet pictures, by a Templar. *8vo.* new cloth, *uncut.*   London, 1869.

930 (GLANVIL) BARTOLOMEUS, de PROPRIETATIBUS RERUM. *Finely printed with gothic character in double columns, small folio, leather.*
Colophon. Explicit de pprietalbs rerū editus a fratre Bartho lomeo anglico ordinis fratrum mino 4. Impressus Argentine Anno dñi MCCCCXCI. finitus altera die post sestum sancti Laurentii martyrés.
FINE CLEAN COPY.
"It will be seen in the course of these notes that Shakespeare was extremely well acquainted with this work." *Douce's Illus. to Shakspeare.*

931 GLANVIL, JOSEPH. Sadducesimus Triumphatus; or, a full and plain Evidence concerning Witches and Apparitions. *Front. 8vo.* old cf.   London, 1726.

932 GLAPTHORNE, HENRY. THE HOLLANDER. A comedy written in 1635. *Original 4to. edition.* Small 4to. hf. mor.
               London, 1640.

933 GLAPTHORNE, HENRY. ARGALUS AND PARTHENIA. As it hath been Acted at the Court before their Majesties. Small 4to. hf. mor. pp. 55.   London, 1639.
"One of the chiefest dramatic poets of that age."— *Winstanley.* See Retrospective Review, Vol. X. 122–159.

934 GLIDDON, GEORGE R. ANCIENT EGYPT, a series of chapters on Early Egyptian History, Archæology and other subjects connected with Hieroglyphical Literature. *Both series.* Small folio, hf. mor. *scarce.*   Philadelphia, 1848.
Over 18,000 copies of this work were disposed of in three years. "Mr.Gliddon, in this cleverly-written publication, brings forward matter of great importance to all who admire antiquity, or who are interested in history."—*London Chronicle.*

935 GLOVER, RICHARD. LEONIDAS, a Poem. *Beautifully printed by* BENSLEY, *with numerous fine plates by* STOTHARD. 2 vols. post morocco, *gilt.*   London, 1798.

936 GODFREY OF BULLOIGNE, translated by Sir Edmund Fairfax. *Small folio, hf. vellum.*   London, 1624.
Imperfect—wants title and two pages, which are supplied by MSS.

MANUSCRIPT BY WILLIAM GODWIN.

937 GODWIN, WILLIAM. CLOUDSLEY : A Novel. (Three volumes), *the* ORIGINAL MANUSCRIPT, *throughout in the author's autograph,* each leaf mounted on guards. 4to. hf. morocco.   (*London,* 1830.)
UNIQUE !
An interesting literary curiosity by the celebrated author of "Caleb Williams."
"Cloudsley is better written than Caleb Williams. The expression is everywhere terse, vigorous, and elegant—a polished mirror without a wrinkle."— *Edinburgh Review.*
"A work of genius which will be read by all who possess genius, or respect it in others."—*Scotsman.*

938 GODWIN, WILLIAM. WORKS, comprising POLITICAL JUSTICE, 2 vols. ADVICE TO A YOUNG AMERICAN on his Studies, with Cobbett Papers against gold, 1 vol. ENQUIRY CONCERNING THE POWER OF INCREASE in the *Numbers of Mankind,* 1 vol. And
12

ENQUIRER, 1 vol., together 5 vols. 8vo. new hf. morocco, *gilt top, uncut edges.* *London,* 1797, &c.

939 GOFFE, THOMAS. THREE EXCELLENT TRAGEDIES, viz. The Raging Turk; or, Bajazet the Second; The Courageous Turk; and the Tragœdie of Orestes. 12mo. old cf. neat. *Scarce.*
London, 1656.

Bound with the above is the original uncastrated edition of Chas. Cotton's SCARRONIDES; or *Virgile Travestie,* 1664, which is rare.

940 GOFFE, COL. WM. PLAN FOR SEIZING AND CARRYING TO NEW YORK COL. WM. GOFFE THE REGICIDE, as set forth in the Affidavit of John London, April 20, 1678, from the Original in the Office of the Secretary of State at New York, by Franklin B. Hough. 12mo. pp. 17, *cloth.* *Albany,* 1855.

941 GOLD. A Legendary Rhyme, *illustrated with twelve outlines, by Alfred Croquill.* Oblong 4to. new cloth. *London,* N. D.

942 GOUGE, WM. M. Journal of Banking from July 1841 to July 1842, containing Essays on various questions relating to Banking and Currency. Impl. 8vo. bds. *uncut. Scarce.*
Philadelphia, 1842.

943 GOULD, S. BARING. THE BOOK OF WERE WOLVES, being an account of a terrible superstition. *Front. post 8vo. new cloth.*
London, 1865.

944 GOULD, S. B. Curiosities of Olden Time. *16mo. new cloth.*
London, N. D.

945 GOULD, THOMAS R. The Tragedian; an essay on the Histrionic genius of Junius Brutus Booth. *Portrait,* 12mo. new cloth.
New York, 1868.

946 GOWER, JOHN. CONFESSIO AMANTIS, edited and collated with the best MSS. by Dr. Reinhold Pauli. *Elegantly printed with an antique character, uniform with Pickering edition of Milton.* 3 vols. 8vo. *tree-marbled calf, super-extra.* *London,* 1857

947 GRAMMAR of HOUSE PLANNING; hints on arranging and modifying Plans of Cottages, Street and Farm Houses, Villas, Mansions, &c. *Profusely illustrated.* 12mo. *cloth.*
Edinburgh, 1866.

948 GRAMMONT'S MEMOIRS, by HAMILTON. Translated, with Life, etc. *Fine portraits of the Court Beauties and notorious characters of the Court of Charles II.* 3 vols. 8vo. *calf, rebacked with red morocco.* London, 1869.

949 GRAMMONT. Secret History of the Court of Charles II., including the Amours of the Duke of Buckingham and the Earl of Rochester. *Frontispiece.* 12mo. *cloth.* New York, 1864.

950 GRANGER (REV. JAMES). BIOGRAPHICAL HISTORY OF ENGLAND, from Egbert the Great to the Revolution. BEST EDITION. 6 *vols. in 3, folio, hf. russia, gilt.*
London, 1824.

LARGEST PAPER, *scarce.*
This copy has, in addition to the numerous portraits published with the book, a large number of fine portraits inserted loosely throughout the work, many of which are very scarce, and for the most part in fine condition.

951 [GRANT, MRS. *of Laggan.*] Essays on the Superstitions of the Highlanders of Scotland. 2 *vols.* 12*mo. hf. cf. gilt.*
London, 1811.

952 GRAVES, W. Two Letters from W. Graves, Esq., Respecting the Conduct of Rear-Admiral Thomas Graves in North America, during his Accidental Command there for Four Months in 1781. *Roy. 4to. new hf. maroon morocco, gilt top, by Bradstreet.*
Morrisania, N. Y., 1865.

953 GRAY, ASA. GENERA of the PLANTS of the UNITED STATES, illustrated by figures and analyses from nature, *nearly* 200 *plates.* 2 *vols. 8vo. cloth.*
New York, 1849.

954 GREEK CLASSICS. BIBLIOTHEQUE des CLASSIQUES GRECS, avec la traduction latine en regard, et les index latins. 16 *vols. imp. 8vo. new hf. cf. neat.*
Didot, Paris, 1841, &c.

Comprising: Fragmenta Historicorum Græcorum, (Muller),4 vols. Plutarchi Vitæ, (Doehner), 2 vols. Arrianus, (Muller), 1 vol. Zenophon, 1 vol. Herodotus, (Muller), 1 vol. Polybius, 1 vol. Appianus, 1 vol. Josephus, (Dindorf), 2 vols. Diodori Siculus, (Muller), 2 vols., and Thucydides, (Haas), 1 vol.

955 GREEK TESTAMENT. VETUS TESTAMENTUM GRÆCE secundum septuaginta interpretes, ex auctoritate sixti quinti Pontificis Maximi editum ad exemplar Vaticanum, &c., cura Leander Van Ess. *8vo. hf. cf.*
Leipzig, 1855.

956 GREEN, HENRY. SHAKESPEARE and the EMBLEM WRITERS : An Exposition of their Similarities of Thought and Expression. Preceded by a View of the Emblem-Book Literature down to A. D. 1616. Illustrated by nearly 250 woodcuts and Photolithographic Plates. *Impl. 8vo. new cloth, extra.*
LARGE PAPER, few printed.
London, 1869.

This work, which has been printed with great care, abounds in ornamental, illustrative, fac-simile woodcuts and photo-lithographs, taken from the works of Authors with several of whom Shakespeare was personally acquainted. The Students and Scholars of the great dramatist will here find illustrations, until now unquarried, from his marvellous writings. And in the first three chapters of the work Bibliophilists will discover information, once lying widely scattered, now brought into compass and order.

957 GREEN, HORACE. Treatise on Diseases of the Air-Passages, Bronchitis, &c., &c. *8vo. cloth.*
New York, 1853.

958 GREENHILL, THOMAS. ART. of EMBALMING; wherein is shewn the Right of Burial, the Ceremonies, and the several ways of Preserving Dead Bodies in most Nations of the World. *Numerous copperplates, folio, old calf, neat.*
For the Author, London, 1705.
The author was a 39th child.

959 GRETTIS, SAGA. The Story of Grettir the Strong, translated from the Icelandic by E. Magusson and William Morris. *Crown 8vo. new cloth.*
London, 1869.

960 GRIMM, HERMAN. Life of Michael Angelo, translated by Fanny E. Bunnett. *Portrait on India Paper.* 2 *vols. imp. 8vo. new cloth.*
Boston, 1866.
LARGE PAPER, only 50 copies.

961 GROSE'S VULGAR DICTIONARY. A CLASSICAL DICTIONARY of the

Vulgar Tongue. By Francis Grose. *Beautifully printed on toned paper.* 8vo. half roxburg mor. gilt top.

London, 1867.

A genuine unmutilated reprint of the much sought after First Edition, of Captain Francis Grose's "Classical Dictionary of the Vulgar Tongue," and contains words and explanations which in the later editions have been either omitted or softened.

962 [Grose, Capt.] Gambado, Geoffrey. Annals of Horsemanship: containing accounts of Accidental Experiments, and Experimental Accidents, both successful and unsuccessful, *with Bunbury's series of humorous engravings. Folio, hf. mor. uncut.*

London, 1791.

Fine large copy.

963 Grose's Antiquities of England and Wales. *Good impressions of the several hundred fine engravings of Castles, Abbeys, Churches, etc., etc. 8 vols. 4to. russia, gilt.* London, 1797.

964 Grote, George. History of Greece, *maps, &c. complete.* 8 vols. 8vo. *handsomely bound in new hf. green calf, extra, marbled edges.*

Murray, London, 1862.

Large type, Library Edition.
"A great literary undertaking, equally notable whether we regard it as an accession to what is of standard value in our language, or as an honorable monument of what English scholarship can do."—*Athenæum.*

965 Grote, George. History of Greece. 12 vols. *post 8vo. new hf. cf. antique.* New York, 1861.

966 Grote, George. Plato, and the other Companions of Socrates. 2d Edition. 3 vols. *8vo. polished calf, extra, marbled edges.*

Murray, London, 1867.

Intended as a supplement and sequel to the History of Greece by the same author.

967 Grotius, Hugo. Rights of War and Peace, translated into English by Wm. Evats. Folio, old cf. *neat, scarce.* London, 1682.

968 Grotius, Hugo. The Truth of the Christian Religion, with a Seventh Book, with notes, &c., by Le Clerc, translated by Dr. John Clarke. *8vo. hf. morocco, neat.* London, 1793.

Best Edition.

969 Gualdo, Priorato. Historia di Leopoldo Cesare, continente le cose più memorabili successe en Europe da 1656 sino al 1670. *Several hundred large folding maps, and Portraits of celebrated personages, finely engraved on copper.* 2 vols. *folio, calf, neat, arms impressed on the sides.* Vienna, 1670.

970 Guiccioli, Countess. My Recollections of Lord Byron. *Portrait.* 2 *vols. 8vo. new cloth.* London, 1869.

971 Guild, Reuben A. The Librarian's Manual: a Treatise on Bibliography, comprising a Select and Descriptive List of Biographical Works; to which are added Sketches of Public Libraries, *illustrated with engravings. Sm. 4to. boards.*

New York: *Printed by Munsell.* 1858.

972 —— Another Copy. Large Paper. *Roy. 4to. boards.*

New York, 1858.

Only 20 copies.

973 GUILLEMIN, AMÉDÉE. The Heavens; An Illustrated Hand-

book of Popular Astronomy, 3d Edition. Edited by J. N. Lockyer. *Several hundred plates, diagrams, &c., thick impl. 8vo. new hf. morocco, extra, gilt edges.* London, 1868.

The most exhaustive popular treatise yet published.

974 GUIZOT, M. Saint Louis and Calvin. *Frontispiece. 12mo. new hf. cf. extra.* Philadelphia, 1869

975 GYLLIUS, ANTONIUS, de Bosporo Thracio. Lib. III. *Front. 32mo. old cf.* Lugduni Bataviorum. *Apud Elzeirios*, 1632.

976 HABEAS CORPUS, MARTIAL LAW, &c. Tracts on, comprising: 1. The Writ of Habeas Corpus and Mr. Binney, *pp.* 29. 2. Remarks on Mr. Binney's Treatise on the Writ of Habeas Corpus, *pp.* 19. 3. Answer to Mr. Binney's Reply to "Remarks, &c.," by G. M. Wharton, *pp.* 8. 4. The Suspending Power of the Writ of Habeas Corpus, *pp.* 48. 5. Decision of Chief Justice Taney in the "Merryman Case," *pp.* 16. 6. Habeas Corpus and Martial Law, A Review of the Taney Decision by Joel Parker, *pp.* 55. 7. Privilege of the Writ of Habeas Corpus under the Constitution, *pp.* 50. 8. Martial Law; What is it? and Who Can Declare it? *pp.* 19. 9. Martial Law, by S. S. Nichols, *pp.* 32. 10. A Letter to A Friend in a Slave State by a Citizen of Pennsylvania, *pp.* 60. And two others. *Together* 12 *tracts, royal 4to. uncut.*
J. Campbell, Philadelphia, 1862–63.

LARGE PAPER, *only* 49 *copies.*

977 HABINGTON, WILLIAM. CASTARA, with a Preface and Notes by Charles A. Elton. *12mo. hf. vellum, gilt top, edges uncut.*
J. M. Gutch, Bristol, (1812).

"'Castara' well deserves a place in the library of every lover of English poetry."—See *Brydges*' "*Censura.*"

978 HAGENBACH, DR. K. R. TEXT-BOOK OF THE HISTORY OF DOCTRINES. The Edinburgh translation, revised and augmented by Dr. H. B. Smith. 2 *vols. 8vo.* new cloth. New York, 1867.

979 HAIG, JAMES. Symbolism; or Mind, Matter, Language as the elements of Thinking and Reasoning, &c. *Thick, post 8vo. vellum cloth.* Edinburgh, 1869.

980 HAKLUYT SOCIETY PUBLICATIONS, from the commencement in 1847 to 1869. 41 vols. 8vo. *many maps and plates, new in cloth, printed for subscribers only.* 1847–69.

List of the volumes, making a set:

1 Hawkins' (Sir. Richd.) Observations in his Voiage into the South Sea in 1593, 1622; edited by Capt. C. R. Bethune. 1847.
2 Columbus, Select Letters with other original documents relating to his Four Voyages, translated and edited by R. H. Major. 1847.
3 Ralegh's Discoverie of Guiana in 1595, 1596; ed. by Sir R. N. Schomburgk, *map.* 1847.
4 Sir Francis Drake, his Voyage, 1595, by Thomas Maynarde, edited from the original MSS. by W. D. Cooley. 1849.
5 Rundall (Thos.) Narrative of a Voyage towards the North-West in search of a Passage to Cathay and India, 1496 to 1631, 3 *maps.* 1849.
6 Strachey (Wm.) Historie of Travaile into Virginia Britannia, edited from the MS. by R. H. Major, *map, facsimiles, and fine plates.* 1849.
7 Hakluyt (Ed.) Divers Voyages touching the discovery of America and the Islands adjacent, 1582; edited by J. Winter Jones, *facsimile and* 2 *maps.* 1850.

8 Rundall's Collection of early Documents on Japan.   1850.
9 Coats' Geography of Hudson's Bay, edited by Jno. Barrow.   1851.
10 Hakluyt (Rd.) Discovery and Conquest of Terra Florida by Don Ferdinando de Soto; 1611; edited by W. B. Rye, *map*.   1851.
11, 12 Herberstein, Rerum Moscovitarum Commentarii: Notes upon Russia, translated and edited by R. H. Major, 2 vols. *2 facsimile maps and 4 plates.*
1851-52.
13 De Veer (Gerrit) Three Voyages by the North-East to China, 1594-6, edited by C. T. Beke.   1852.
14, 15 Mendoza (Juan Gonzalez de) Historie of China, transl. by Parke, 1588; edited by R. G. Staunton, 2 vols.   1853-4.
16 D'Orléans (Pierre Joseph) History of the Tartar Conquerors of China, *Paris*, 1688; transl. & edited by Earl of Ellesmere.   1854.
17 Fletcher (Francis) The World encompassed by Sir Francis Drake; edited by W. S. W. Vaux, *map*.   1854.
18 Middleton (Sir Hen.) Voyage to Bantam and the Maluco Islands, 1606; ed. by B. Corney, *map and 5 plates*.   1855.
19 White (Adam) Collection of early Documents on Spitzbergen and Greenland.   1855.
20 Bond (Edw. A.) Russia at the Close of the 16th Century.   1856.
21 Benzoni (Girolamo) History of the New World; Travels, 1541-56, *Venice*, 1572, translated and edited by Adml. W. H. Smyth, *facsimiles of old woodcuts.*
1857.
22 Major (R. H.) India in the 15th Century.   1857.
23 Champlain, Voyage to the West Indies, 1599-1602; transl. by A. Wilmere, edited by N. Shaw, 4 *colored and* 4 *plain facsimiles.*   1859.
24 Expeditions into the Valley of the Amazon, 1539, 1540, 1639; transl. and edited by C. R. Markham.   1859.
25 Gonzalez de Clavijo, Embassy to the Court of Timour at Samarcand, 1403-6, by R. Markham, *map*.   1859.
26 Hudson (Hen. *the Navigator*) by G. M. Asher, 2 *maps*.   1859.
27 Early Voyages to Terra Australis, now called Australia, edited by R. H. Major, *maps*.   1859.
28 Ursua and Aguirre, Expedition in search of El Dorado, 1560-61, by Bollaerts and Markham.   1861.
29 Guzman's Life and Acts, by Markham.   1862.
30 Galvano's Discoveries of the World, *Portuguese and English*, by Bethune.
1862.
31 Jordanus' Mirabilia descripta, by Yule.   1863.
32 Varthema's Travels by Jones & Badger.   1863.
33 Cieza de Leon (Pedro de) Travels, A. D. 1532-50, contained in the First part of his Chronicle of Peru; translated and edited, with notes and an introduction, by C. R. Markham, 8vo. *map*, *cloth*.   1864.
34 Andagoya's Narrative of proceedings in Tierra Firme, etc. by Markham.
1865.
35 Barbosa's East Africa and Malabar, by Stanley.   1866.
36, 37 Cathay and the way thither, by Yule, 2 vols.   1867.
38 Frobisher's Three Voyages in Search of a Passage to Cathaia and India, by the North-West, 1576-8, edited by Admiral R. Collinson, *portrait*.   1867.
39 Morga's (Ant. de) Philippine Islands, Moluccas, Siam, Cambodia, Japan, and China at the close of the 16th century; translated from the Spanish by the Hon. Henry Stanley, 8vo. *cloth*.   1868.
The original edition: "Sucesos de las Isles Philippinas," was printed at Mexico in 1609, and is extremely rare.
40 Gayangos (Don P. de) the Fifth Letter of Cortes to the Emperor Charles V.   1868.
41 First part of the Royal Commentaries of the Yncas, by the Ynca G. de la Vega, transl. by Markham, Vol. I.   1869.
COMPLETE SETS ARE VERY SCARCE.

"The Hakluyt Society never has sold nor ever intends to sell its productions. Members alone can obtain them.   When such ceases to be the case, the Hakluyt Society will cease to exist."
R. H. Major, Hon. Sec. to the Hakluyt Society, pro tem.

981 Haliburton, Judge. Yankee Stories, *with illustrations.* 12mo. *cloth.*
Philadelphia.

982 HALLAM, HENRY. WORKS, viz: Europe during the Middle Ages, 3 vols.   Constitutional History of England, 3 vols.   Literature of Europe, 4 vols.   *In all* 10 *vols.* 8vo. *vellum cloth, uncut.*
Boston, 1865.
LARGE PAPER.   *Only* 100 *copies printed.*

983 HALLAM, HENRY. WORKS: comprising Literature of Europe, Europe during the Middle Ages, and Constitutional History of England. *4 vols. 8vo. cf.* New York, 1847.

ORIGINAL MSS. BY HALLECK.

984 HALLECK, FITZ-GREENE. "YOUNG AMERICA." THE ORIGINAL MANUSCRIPT. *14 pp. folio, neatly mounted on writing paper, with extra blank leaves. Folio, bound in full green crimped morocco, by Matthews.*

A fine specimen of the delicate peculiar hand-writing of Halleck, doubtless the most valuable manuscript from his pen in existence. "Young America" was his latest published Poem, or rather series of Poems. It includes a number of choice lyrics and several of the Author's most eloquent and humorous descriptive passages. The Poem appeared in the *Ledger*, in 1864; Mr. Bonner paying for it the handsome price of $500.00. It was subsequently published in book form, with illustrations.

985 HALLECK, FITZ-GREENE. FANNY; a Poem. *Portrait on India paper. Imperial 8vo. uncut.* New York, 1866.

PRIVATELY PRINTED; 70 *copies.*

986 HALLIWELL, J. O. LETTERS OF THE KINGS OF ENGLAND, edited from the originals in the Royal Archives, &c., with Introduction and Notes, *portrait,* 2 vols. post 8vo. *cloth.* Lond. 1846.

987 HALLIWELL, J. O. DICTIONARY OF ARCHAIC and PROVINCIAL WORDS, obsolete phrases, proverbs, and ancient customs from the fourth century. *2 vols. 8vo. new cloth.* London, 1865.

988 HALLIWELL, J. O. The YORKSHIRE ANTHOLOGY, a Collection of Ancient and Modern Ballads, Poems, and Songs, relating to the County of Yorkshire. *Fine rubricated title-page. Plate representing Mother Shipton's Prophecy. 4to. cloth, uncut.*
London, 1851.

PRIVATELY PRINTED; *and only 110 copies, 10 copies being printed on very thick paper. See the printer's autograph attestation on the fly-leaf.*
Contains a Glossary of Yorkshire words.

989 HALLIWELL, J. O. Historical Sketch of the Provincial Dialects of England, Illustrated by numerous Examples. *Beautifully printed. Imperial 8vo. cloth, uncut. Munsell,* Albany, 1863.

990 HALLIWELL, J. O, NOTES OF FAMILY EXCURSIONS IN NORTH WALES, taken chiefly from Rhyl, Abergele, Llandudno, and Bangor. *Handsomely printed by Whitingham.*
For the Author, London, 1860.

PRIVATELY PRINTED.

991 HALL, BENJ. H. HISTORY OF EASTERN VERMONT, from its earliest settlement to the close of the eighteenth century. With A Biographical Chapter and Appendixes. *Frontispiece. 2 vols. royal 8vo. uncut. Munsell,* Albany, 1865.

LARGE PAPER; 50 *copies printed.*

992 HALL, CAPT. BASIL. VOYAGE OF DISCOVERY to the West Coast of Corea, and the Great Loo Choo Island, WITH VOCABULARY BY CLIFFORD, *colored engravings and map, 4to. hf. calf, gilt.*
London, 1818.

993 HALL, CHAS. FRANCIS. ARCTIC RESEARCHES, and Life among the Esquimaux; narrative of an expedition in search of Sir John Franklin, 1860, '61 & '62. *Maps, and 100 engravings. Thick 8vo. cloth.* New York, 1865.

994 HALL, JOSEPH, BP. Virgidemiarum. Satires in Six Books.
12mo. calf, *neat.* Oxford, 1753.

995 HALL, MR. AND MRS. S. C. IRELAND, its Scenery, Legends,
Tales. *Superbly Illustrated with 500 beautiful engravings on
steel and wood, after drawings by Creswick, Harvey, &c. 3 large
vols. roy. 8vo. polished calf extra, marbled edges.*
London, (1850).
FINE COPY.

996 HAMERTON, PHILIP GILBERT. ETCHING AND ETCHERS. Critical Notices of the English, Dutch, French and other schools, and details of the Art. *Profusely Illustrated with etchings* (original
plates) *by Rembrandt, Callet, Paul Potter, Waterloo, Du Jardin,
Hillemacher, Haden, Cope, Redgrave, Palmer, &c., &c.* (35 in
number). *Thick roy. 8vo. hf. morocco, carmine edges.*
London, 1868.
"The best treatise extant; by the genial author of the ' Painter's Camp in
the Highlands.' "

997 HAMILTON, J. C. THE FEDERALIST; A commentary on the Constitution of the United States; A collection of Essays by Alex.
Hamilton, Jay, and Madison. Also the Continentalist and
other Papers, Edited by John C. Hamilton. *Portrait. 2 vols.
imperial 8vo. cloth, uncut.* Philadelphia, 1865.
LARGE PAPER; 100 *copies printed.*

998 HAMILTON CLUB SERIES :
No. I. Life of Alexander Hamilton by John Williams (*An-
thony Pasquin*).
II. Observations On Certain Documents in the " History of
the United States for the Year 1796," by Alex. Hamilton
" *Reynold's Pamphlet* ").
III. The Hamiltoniad by Anthony Pasquin (John Williams).
IV. Letters to Alexander Hamilton, King of the Feds. Ci-
devant secretary of the Treasury, &c., by Tom. Callender. 4
vols. royal 4to. uncut. New York, 1866.
LARGE PAPER ; *only* 20 *copies*, and 40 copies in 8vo.

999 ———— Another copy, except part three. *Small paper,* Roy. 8vo.
uncut. New York, 1866, &c.

1000 HAMILTON, SIR WILLIAM. LECTURES ON METAPHYSICS AND LOGIC,
edited by Mansel and Veitch. 2 *thick vols.* 8vo. cloth.
Boston, 1860.

1001 HAMILTON'S COLLECTION of VASES, mostly of pure Greek
Workmanship, with Descriptions in French, *upwards of* 200
fine large engravings. 3 vols. impl. folio, *hf. bound.*
Naples, 1791–5.
A fine and interesting work; the pictures of the splendid Vases are accu-
rately engraved in outline by Tischbein, the director of the Academy of Painting at Naples.

1002 HAMMOND, GEORGE. ΠΝΕΥΜΑΤΟΛΟΓΙΑ. A Discourse of Angels ; also something touching Devils, Apparitions, and Im-
pulses. Sm. 4to. old calf, *neat.* London, 1701.

1003 HAMOR, RAPHE. A True Discourse of the Present Estate of Virginia, and the successe of the Affaires there till 18 June 1614.

Together with a Relation of the severall English Townes and Fortes, &c., &c. *Folio, boards, uncut.*

London, 1615. *Albany*, 1860.

ONLY 200 COPIES. Reprinted for Dr. Barney, of Richmond, Va.

1004 HANCOCK, JOHN. Ten Chapters in the Life of. 8vo. cloth.

Privately printed, New York, 1857.

1005 HANGER, COL. GEORGE. LIFE, ADVENTURES, and OPINIONS of, by himself. To which is added Advice to lovely Cyprians; Matrimony, Compulsive Wedlock, Polygamy, etc. *2 vols. 8vo. hf. calf.* London, 1801.

1006 HANLEY, SYLVANUS. Illustrated and Descriptive Catalogue of Recent Bivalve Shells, with 960 *figures by Wood and Sowerby,* COLORED. *Roy. 8vo. new cloth.* London, 1842–56.

1007 HANMER, MEREDITH, D.D. ANCIENT ECCLESIASTICAL HISTORIES of the First Six Hundred Years after Christ. EUSEBIUS, SOCRATES, and EVAGRIUS, translated into English. *6th Edition, folio, hf. cf. neat.* London, 1663.

1008 HANWAY, JONAS (the celebrated Philanthropist). Ode to the Memory of Mr. George Peters, Jr., of St. Petersburgh, merchant. *Numerous vignettes, &c., added. 4to. calf, neat. Very scarce.* London, 1780.

PRIVATELY PRINTED.

1009 HARASZTHY, A. GRAPE CULTURE, WINES, and WINE-MAKING; with Notes on Agriculture and Horticulture. *Numerous illustrations.* 8vo. cloth. New York, 1862.

1010 [HARDWICKE, COUNTESS OF]. THE COURT OF OBERON; or, The Three Wishes. A Drama in three Acts. *Colored frontispiece. 4to. hf. morocco, gilt. Privately printed,* London, 1831.

1011 (HARDING, SAMUEL). SICILY and NAPLES; or, The Fatal Union. A Tragedy by S. H. A. B. è C. exon. *Sm. 4to. pp. 96, vellum, scarce.* Oxford, 1640.

The Play is recommended by verses to the author by N. Downey, R. Stapylton, Rich'd Doddridge, Edw. and Joh. Hall.

HARDING'S SHAKESPEARE ILLUSTRATIONS. *Large Paper.* See Shakespeare.

1012 HARINGTON, SIR JOHN. ORLANDO FURIOSO in English Heroical Verse by Sir John Harington of Bathe, Knight; now thirdly revised and amended with the additions of the Author's Epigrams. Engraved title, containing portraits of Harington and Ariosto, *by Coxon, also numerous curious engravings 'shewing the principal incidents described by the poet, at one view.' Folio, elegantly bound in mottled calf, extra, yellow edges.*

London, *printed by G. Miller for J. Parker,* 1634.

A very fine copy. Best edition, and the first in which the Epigrams appear. —*Bib. Angl. Poetica,* £4. 4s.

1013 HARLEIAN MISCELLANY; a Collection of scarce, curious, and entertaining Pamphlets and Tracts, as well in Manuscript as Print, selected from the Library of the Earl of Oxford, with Historical, Political, and Critical Annotations by Oldys, 8 *vols. 4to. cf. neat.* London, 1744–46.

This edition used to sell formerly for upwards of £12. 12s.

1014 HARPER'S NEW MONTHLY MAGAZINE. A complete set of this interesting magazine from its commencement in June, 1850, to May, 1867, *many thousand illustrations on wood.* 34 *vols. 8vo. neatly bound in hf. brown morocco, extra.*
New York, 1850–67.

1015 HARPER'S WEEKLY. A JOURNAL OF CIVILIZATION, complete from its commencement in Jan. 1857 to December, 1868, *many thousand engravings on wood.* 12 *vols. folio, new hf. morocco, gilt.* New York, 1857–68.
A perfectly new copy, fresh from the Publishers.

1016 HARSHA, D. A. LIFE OF PHILIP DODDRIDGE, D. D. With Notices of some of his Contemporaries, and Specimens of his style. *Portrait on India paper, and wood-cut view of his Church. 8vo. paper.*
LARGE PAPER; *only* 40 *copies printed,* 10 *of which were destroyed.*
J. *Munsell, Albany,* 1864.

"The pressman worked them (the 40 copies of the above book) so badly, that I culled the sheets, and they did not hold out 30 copies."—*Extract from a letter of the Printer.*

1017 HARSHA, D. A. Life of Philip Doddridge, D. D., with notices of some of his contemporaries, and specimens of his style. *Portrait, &c. 8vo. paper, uncut. Munsell,* Albany, 1864.
LARGE PAPER.

1018 HARSHA, D. A. Life of the Rev. George Whitfield. *8vo. new hf. green morocco, gilt top, by Bradstreet. Munsell,* Albany, 1866.
ONE OF 5 COPIES ON INDIA PAPER.

1019 ———— Another copy. 4to. uncut. Albany, 1866.
LARGE PAPER, 50 *copies.*

1020 HARSHA, D. A. Life of the Rev. James Hervey. *4to. uncut.*
Munsell, Albany, 1865.
LARGE PAPER, 50 *copies.*

1021 Hartford Convention. History of, with a Review of the Policy of the U. S. Government, &c. *8vo. cloth.* New York, 1833.

1022 HARTWICK SEMINARY. Memorial Volume of the Semi-Centennial Anniversary of, August, 1866. *8vo. hf. crimson morocco, gilt top, by Bradstreet. Munsell,* Albany, 1867.
One of 5 copies on INDIA PAPER.

1023 HARRINGTON, ALFRED W. Memorial of. *4to. new cloth.*
Chicago, 1868.

1024 HARRIS, GEORGE. THEORY OF THE ARTS; or Art in relation to Nature, Civilization, and Man, with an investigation into the Rise, Province, Principles and Application of each of the Arts. 2 *vols. 8vo. new cloth.* London, 1869.

1025 HARRIS, JAMES. WORKS; with an account of his Life and Character by his son, the Earl of Malmesbury. *Portraits.* 2 vols. roy. 4to. hf. vellum, gilt top, uncut edges. London, 1801.
BEST EDITION. Comprises Hermes—Philosophical Arrangements—Three Treatises—Philological Enquiries—and Miscellaneous Pieces.

1026 HARRIS, T. W. Treatise on some of the Insects injurious to Vegetation. New Edition, edited by Chas. L. Flint, *several hundred woodcuts, and numerous* EXQUISITELY COLORED *plates. 8vo. cloth, red edges.* Boston, 1863.

1027 HARRIS' COMPLETE COLLECTION OF VOYAGES and Travels, comprising above Six hundred authentic Writers, *numerous large maps, and engravings.* BEST EDITION. 2 *thick volumes,* folio, calf, *neat.* *London,* 1764.

A valuable collection, including Hakluyt, Purchas, Ramusio, De Bry, Herrera, &c.

1028 HARVARD COLLEGE CONGRATULATORY VOLUME. PIETAS ET GRATULATIO COLLEGII CANTABRIGIENSIS apud novanglos. *4to. elegantly bound in crimson morocco, gilt back, broad borders of gold on the sides, with the Royal Arms impressed in the field, gilt edges.* *Bostoni, Massachusettensium, typis J. Green & J. Russell, MDCCLXI.*

*** THE PRESENTATION copy TO HIS MAJESTY GEORGE III., *in fine condition.* Among the contributors were President Holyoke, John Lovell, Stephen Sewell, John Lowell, Samuel Deane, Benjamin Church, Governor Francis Barnard, Dr. Samuel Cooper, &c.
For a long and very interesting account of this work, see Duyckinck's Cyclopedia of American Literature, Vol. I. pp. 11-14.

1029 HAYES, DR. I. I. THE OPEN POLAR SEA ; a narrative of a Voyage of Discovery towards the North Pole, in the Schooner "United States." *Portrait, maps, &c. 8vo. new cloth.* *New York,* 1867.

1030 HAYLEY, WILLIAM. Life of George Romney, *fine impressions of the numerous beautiful engravings after Romney's paintings, some by* BLAKE. *4to. hf. cf. extra.* *Chichester,* 1809.

1031 HAZARD, ROWLAND G. Causation and Freedom in Willing. Two Letters addressed to Jno. Stuart Mill. *Crown 8vo. new cloth.* *London,* 1869.

1032 HAZLITT, W. CAREW. ENGLISH PROVERBS AND PROVERBIAL PHRASES, collected from the most authentic sources, alphabetically arranged and annotated. Imperial *8vo. new cloth, uncut.* *London,* 1869.

LARGE PAPER. *Only 50 copies.*

1033 ———— ANOTHER COPY. *8vo. new cloth.* *London,* 1869.

Edition of 300 copies only.

BIBLIOGRAPHY OF OLD ENGLISH LITERATURE.

1034 HAZLITT, W. CAREW. Hand-Book to the Popular, Poetical, and Dramatic Literature of Great Britain, from the Invention of Printing to the Restoration. *Thick imperial 8vo. hf. morocco, uncut.* *London,* 1867.

1035 HEARD, F. F. The Legal Acquirements of William Shakespeare. *Rubricated Title. 4to. uncut.* *Boston: J. K. Wiggin,* 1865.

ONLY 64 COPIES PRINTED.

1036 HEARNE, THOMAS. ROBERT OF GLOUCESTER'S CHRONICLE, with Glossary, &c. 2 vols. PETER LANGTOFF'S CHRONICLE, 2 vols. transcribed from the original MSS. *4 vols. 8vo. hf. cf. neat.* *Oxford,* 1724-5.

These editions of these Chronicles are very rare, and have been sold at auction as high as £12.

1037 HEARNE, THOMAS. Collection of Curious Discourses, by eminent Antiquaries. *2 vols. 8vo. calf.* *London,* 1775.

1038 HEATON, MRS. CHARLES. HISTORY OF THE LIFE OF ALBRECHT

Dürer of Nürnberg, with a translation of his Letters and Journal, and some account of his works. *Illustrated with upwards of 30 fine plates by the autotype process, in permanent tints, in fac-simile of his most celebrated works.* Beautifully printed. *Imp. 8vo. new cloth, extra, gilt edges.* London, 1870.

1039 HEEREN, ARNOLD H. L. HISTORICAL WORKS, comprising Ancient Greece, 1 vol. Asiatic Nations, 2 vols. Carthaginians, &c. 1 vol. Europe, &c. 1 vol. and Ancient History, 1 vol.; together 6 vols. 8vo. *uniformly bound in hf. cf. extra.*
London, 1847-55.

"We look upon Heeren as having breathed new life into the dry bones of ancient history."—*Edinburgh Review.*

1040 HEEREN, A. H. L. Manual of the History of the Political System of Europe and its Colonies. 2 vols. *8vo. cloth.*
Oxford, 1834.

1041 HEETOPADES OF VEESHNOO-SARMA, in a series of connected Fables, interspersed with Moral, Prudential, and Political Maxims, translated from an ancient Sanskrit MSS. by Charles Wilkins. *8vo. new hf. green morocco, uncut.* Bath, 1787.

The oldest known collection of Fables, attributed to Bidpai, the original of Æsop, &c., &c.

1042 HEGEL, G. W. F. Lectures on the Philosophy of History, translated by J. Sibree. *12mo. cloth.* Bohn, London, 1857.

1043 HELVETIUS, C. A. TREATISE ON MAN; his intellectual faculties, and his education, 2 vols.; also DE L'ESPRIT, or Essays on the Mind and its several Faculties, translated from the French by D. W. Hooper. *Portrait.* 3 vols. *impl. 8vo. new hf. cf. extra, uncut edges.* London, 1809-10.

LARGE PAPER, *scarce.*
These works were burnt by order of the Parlement of Paris, and the author driven out of the Kingdom.

1044 HEMANS, MRS. F. ("*Felicia Dorothea Browne* "). POEMS. *Original Edition,* with beautiful vignettes on wood by Clennell. *Roy. 4to. cloth, uncut edges.* Liverpool, 1808.

LARGE PAPER, *very rare;* "written between the ages of eight and thirteen years," her first publication with list of subscribers, &c.

1045 HENRIETTA, MARIA, QUEEN. LETTERS, including her private correspondence with Charles I. edited by Mary A. E. Green. *12mo. new hf. morocco.* London, 1857.

1046 HENTZNER, PAUL. JOURNEY into ENGLAND, in the year MDXCVIII. *Vignette, view of Strawberry-Hill. 12mo. (4to.) mottled, calf, extra.* Printed at Strawberry-Hill, 1757.

FINE COPY, *scarce.*

1047 HERALDIC ANOMALIES. 2d Edition. 2 vols. *crown 8vo. boards, uncut, scarce.* London, 1824.

By Archdeacon Nares.

1048 HERBERT, GEORGE. WORKS in Verse and Prose. PICKERING'S HANDSOME LIBRARY EDITION, *in large antique type, by Whittingham. Fine portrait.* 2 vols. *8vo. morocco antique, gilt edges.*
Pickering, London, 1853.

FINE COPY.
This edition contains the Proverbs, and many pieces never before printed, with Notes, by S. T. Coleridge, and Life, by his Biographer, Barnabas Oley.

1049 Herbert, W. Antiquities of the Inns of Court and Chancery ; with a concise History of English Law. 24 *fine copper-plate illustrations.* Royal 8vo. *new hf. green morocco, gilt top.*
London, 1804.

Large Paper, *scarce.*

1050 HERCULANUM ET POMPEI: recueil Général des Peintures, Bronzes, Mosaiques, &c. découverts jusqu'à ce jour et reproduits d'après tous les ouvrages publiés jusqu'à présent, avec un Texte explicatif de M. Barré, *with* 700 fine engravings, 8 vols. impl. 8vo. (including the Musée Secrète). *French bds. lettered.* *Paris, Didot,* 1863.

This is the most complete work on the discoveries at Herculaneum and Pompeii, exhibiting all the paintings, bronzes, miniatures, &c. hitherto published in rare or expensive works, with the addition of many others which have not previously appeared.

1851 HERCULANEUM. The Antiquities of Herculaneum ; translated from the Italian by Thomas Martyn and John Lettice. 50 *large and beautifully executed plates, comprising over one hundred examples of the Monuments, Frescoes, &c., &c., excavated at Herculaneum, a large number illustrating the Ancient Priapeian Worship.* Impl. 4to. *new hf. red morocco, edges uncut.*
London, 1773.

Fine copy, *very scarce.*

1052 Herder, John Godfrey. Outlines of a Philosophy of the History of Man. Translated from the German by T. Churchill. 2 *vols.* 8vo. *new hf. morocco, uncut, very scarce.*
London, 1803.

1053 Herndon and Gibbon, Lieuts. Reports on the Exploration of the Valley of the Amazon. *Maps and plates.* 4 *vols.* 8vo. *cloth.* Washington, 1853.

1054 Herodotus. History. A new English version, edited with copious Notes and Appendices, illustrating the History and Geography of Herodotus, by George Rawlinson. 4 vols. 8vo. *cloth.* New York, 1859.

The Standard translation.

1055 HERRERA'S General History of the vast Continent and Islands of America, from their first Discovery, with the best account of their Antiquities, &c., translated by Stephens, *engravings and map,* 6 vols. 8vo. *calf, scarce.* London, 1725.

" Of all Spanish writers, Herrera furnishes the fullest and most authentic information of the Conquest of Mexico, as well as every other Transaction of America."—*Robertson.*

1056 Herschel, Sir J. F. W. Results of Astronomical Observations made during the years 1834–5–6–7, at the Cape of Good Hope, *with* 18 *plates.* Impl. 4to. *new cloth.* London, 1847.

Printed at the expense of the Duke of Northumberland.

1057 HERVEY'S Illustrations of Modern Sculpture, with Descriptions in Prose and Verse, 18 *highly finished engravings by the best artists, from Choice Works of Canova, Flaxman, Baily, Westmacott, &c.* India proofs, impl. 4to. *hf. morocco, gilt leaves.*
London, 1834.

1058 Hervey, Rev. James. Meditations and Contemplations on the

Starry Heavens, among the Tombs, &c., &c. HEPTINSTALL'S FINE EDITION, *with numerous fine plates from drawings by Corbould*. 2 vols. impl. 8vo. calf, gilt. London, 1796.

1059 HEYDON, SIR CHRISTOPHER. A DEFENCE of JUDICIALL ASTROLOGIE, in answer to a Treatise lately published by Mr. John Chamber. *Vignette title, sml. 4to. hf. cf. neat. (A few leaves reprinted.)* Printed by John Legat printer to the Universitie of Cambridge, 1603.

"A work full of no common reading, and carried on with no mean arguments."—*Ant. a Wood.*

1060 HICKOK, LAURENS P. Rational Psychology. *Thick 8vo. cloth.* Schenectady, N. Y., 1854.

1061 HICKCOX, JOHN H. History of Bills of Credit, or Paper Money issued by New York, from 1709 to 1789, &c. *Royal 4to. uncut.* Albany, 1866.

LARGE PAPER; *only 75 copies.*

1062 ―――― Another copy. *4to. uncut.*

1063 HICKCOX, JOHN H. HISTORICAL ACCOUNT of AMERICAN COINAGE. *With illustrations. 4to. boards.* Albany, N. Y., 1858.
LARGE PAPER; *only 50 copies printed.*

1064 HICKS, T. Eulogy on Thomas Crawford by Thomas Hicks, N. A. *Portrait and Views on India Paper. 4to. half morocco, uncut.* New York, 1865.

LARGE PAPER; *25 copies printed.*

1065 HIGGINS, GODFREY. ANACALYPSIS; an attempt to draw aside the veil of the Saitic Isis, or an Inquiry into the origin of Languages, Nations, and Religions. *3 vols. in 2. 4to. cloth, plates. Very scarce.* London, 1833-36.

On page vii. of the Preface this passage occurs: "I have printed only 200 copies of this work; of these two hundred only a few got at first into circulation. The tendency of the work is to overturn all the established systems of religion, to destroy received notions upon subjects generally considered sacred, and to substitute a simple unsacerdotal worship. Names hitherto looked upon with veneration by the world are stripped of their honors, and others are lifted from opprobrium to a position of reverence."

1066 HIGGINS, G. CELTIC DRUIDS; an attempt to shew that the Druids were the Priests of Oriental Colonies, who emigrated from India, 45 *fine plates of Druidical Remains*, on INDIA PAPER, *and numerous vignettes*, 4to. cloth. London, 1829.
Scarce.

1067 High Life in New York, by Jonathan Slick. *12mo. cloth.* Philadelphia, 1854.

1068 HILSOP, ALEX. PROVERBS of SCOTLAND, with Illustrative and explanatory Notes and a Glossary. Thick 12mo. new cloth. Edinburgh, 1868.

1069 HILTON, DAVID. Brigandage in South Italy. *2 vols. 12mo. new cloth.* London, 1864.

1070 HIPPOCRATIS eoi et CLAUDIANI GALENI. OPERA. Gr. et lat. cura et stud Renati Chaterii. *Portraits. 13 vols. in 10, folio, calf, neat.* Lutet, Paris, 1679.

1071 HISTOIRE SECRÈTE de la Cour de Berlin, ou correspondance d'un voyageur François. *2 vols. 8vo. old cf.* S. L. 1789.

1072 History of England ; from the text of Hume and Smollett, continued to the present time by Thomas Gaspey, Esq.. Large Type, Illustrated Edition, *with upwards of 500 large steel engravings, Portraits, &c., &c.* 6 *thick vols. imp. 8vo. new hf. morocco, gilt.* London, N. D.

1073 History of Hindostan, as connected with other Great Empires of Asia during the most ancient Periods, by Thomas Maurice. *Numerous plates, 3 vols. 4to. calf.* London, 1820.

1074 History of Modern Europe ; with an account of the Decline and Fall of the Roman Empire, and a view of the progress of society, &c., to the Peace of Paris in 1763. 6 *vols. 8vo. hf. cf. gilt.* London, 1827.

1075 HISTORY of PAINTING. *A fine series,* comprising Waagen's Hand-Book of Painting, German, Flemish and Dutch Schools, 2 vols.—Eastlake (Sir Chas.), Hand-Book of Painting, Italian Schools, 2 vols.—Early Flemish Painters by Crowe & Calvacaselle, 1 vol.—Jameson's (Mrs.) Memoirs of Early Italian Painters, 1 vol. *all profusely illustrated with portraits and engravings of the most celebrated pictures, &c., together 6 vols. crown 8vo. elegantly bound in polished calf, extra, gilt edges, by* Hayday. London, 1868.
A Fine Uniform Series.

1076 Hobbes' (T. *of Malmesbury*) Complete Works, *English and Latin,* now first collected, edited by Sir W. Molesworth, *portrait and plates, handsomely printed,* 16 vols. 8vo. new hf. calf, *extra, marbled edges* (pub. £9. 12s). London, 1839–46.
Fine Copy.
The only complete edition of the works of this celebrated writer, who will ever be regarded as one of the master spirits of English Literature.

1077 Hobbes, Thomas. Leviathan ; or, the Matter, Form, and Power of a Common-wealth, Ecclesiastical and Civil, *frontispiece, folio, old cf. neat.* London, 1651.

1078 Hodgson, W. B. Education of Girls and the Employment of Women of the upper classes, educationally considered. 2*d edition, post 8vo. new cloth.* London, 1869.

1079 HOGARTH'S Works, illustrated by J. Ireland, with the Supplement, *upwards of 120 engravings, good impressions,* 3 vols. royal 8vo. calf, gilt. London, 1793–8.
The supplemental volume contains numerous plates, not included in other editions.

1080 Hogarth, William. Works moralized by Dr. Trusler, *fine impressions of the cuts, 4to. hf. crimson morocco, gilt.*
London, N. D.

1081 Hogarth, William. Works, *consisting of 148 engravings, including many of the minor pieces not in any other edition, engraved by Messrs. Cooke & Davenport, with Descriptions by the Rev.* John Trusler. 2 *vols. roy. 4to. hf. cf. gilt.* London.

1082 Hogg, James. (Ettrick Shepherd). Works, complete. *New Edition,* revised at the instance of the author's family, by the Rev. Thomas Thomson. *Portraits and numerous engravings on steel. 2 vols. roy. 8vo. new hf. calf, extra.* London & Edn. 1866.
Best Edition.

1083 Hogg, Thos. Jefferson. Life of Percy Bysshe Shelley, *portrait*, 2 *vols. post 8vo. cloth* (all published). *London*, 1858.

1084 Holbein's Dance of Death, *illustrated by a series of photo-lithographic facsimiles* from the copy of the first edition in the British Museum, with Notices, &c., by H. Noel Humphreys. 12mo. cloth. (*Quaritch*), *London*, 1868.

1085 Holbein. Emblems of Mortality ; representing by numerous engravings of Death seizing all Ranks and Conditions of People. (Basle), *numerous wood-cuts* (*with the initials* A. A.) 16mo. *clo. bds.* *Charleston*, 1846.
Very scarce.

1086 Holmes, John. A Letter of Directions to his Father's Birthplace, &c. 8vo. *uncut.*
Printed for the U. Q. Club, N. Y. 1865.
Only 99 copies.

1087 Holmes, Hon. Nathaniel. The Authorship of Shakespeare, *portrait, crown 8vo. cloth.* *New York*, 1867.

1088 Holy Coat of Treves, John Ronge, and the New German Catholic Church. 16mo. *hf. cf. scarce.* *New York*, 1845.

1089 Homans, J. Smith. Cyclopedia of Commerce and Commercial Navigation. 2 *thick vols. impl. 8vo. hf. cf. antique.*
New York, 1858.

1090 Homer's Iliad, rendered into English Blank Verse by Edward Earl of Derby, *printed on heavy laid paper.* 2 vols. impl. 8vo. *new cloth, uncut.* *New York*, 1866.
Large Paper. *Only 50 copies.*

1091 Homeri quae exstant Omnia Ilias, Odyssea Batrachomyomachia, Hymni, Pœmatia aliquot, cum comm. Jo. Spondani, (Gr. et Lat.) *Folio, hf. cf.* Basileæ, per *Sebastianum Henricpetri*, 1606.
Contains the entire Commentary of Spondanus, with the Poetical Epitome of the Iliad by Pindar (the Theban), and the History of the Trojan Wars by Dares, the Phrygian.

1092 Homilies. Certain Sermons or Homilies, appointed to be read in Churches, in the Time of Queen Elizabeth, of famous memory; and now thought fit to be reprinted, &c. 𝔅𝔩𝔞𝔠𝔨 𝔏𝔢𝔱𝔱𝔢𝔯. *Folio, old calf.* *London*, 1676

1093 HONE'S POPULAR WORKS : Every-Day Book, Table-Book, and Year-Book, *with 550 woodcuts of Old Buildings, Old Customs, Remarkable Characters, Curiosities, &c.* 4 vols. 8vo. *hf. calf, neat.* *London*, 1838.
An everlasting fund of amusement and instruction, containing information not easily to be found elsewhere : commended by Lamb, Scott, Southey, &c.

1094 Hood, Thomas. National Tales. *Illustrated with a series of lithographic plates from drawings by T. Dighton.* 2 vols. post 8vo. *polished calf, extra, gilt edges, by* Bedford. *London*, 1827.
Fine Copy, *very scarce.*

1095 Hood, Thomas. Poems. *Illustrated with engravings on steel and wood from designs by Gustave Doré, folio, green cloth, gilt.* *London*, 1870.

1096 [Hook, Geo. W.] Puritan. A Poem in seven cantos, *tinted paper, 8vo. cloth.* *Cincinnati*, 1868.

1097 HOOK, WALTER F. (Dean of Chichester.) LIVES OF THE ARCH-
BISHOPS OF CANTERBURY. Both series, 8 vols. 8vo. new cloth,
uncut. *London,* 1861–68.

1098 HOPE, T. COSTUME OF THE ANCIENTS, *with* 300 *fine out-
line engravings by H. Moses, of Egyptian, Greek, and Roman
Habits and Dresses,* 2 vols. ROYAL 4to. new hf. russia, neat, *scarce.*
Bulmer, 1812.

BEST EDITION; LARGE PAPER: an indispensable book to artists, &c.

1099 HOPKINS, CHARLES. FRIENDSHIP IMPROV'D; or, the Female War-
riour. A Tragedy, acted at the Theatre in Lincoln's-Inn-
Fields. *Sml. 4to. pp.* 56, *hf. vellum.* *London,* 1700.

1100 HOUBRAKEN AND VIRTUE'S HEADS OF ILLTSTRIOUS PER-
SONS OF GREAT BRITAIN, with their Lives and Characters, by
Birch. 108 *large and beautifully engraved portraits.* BRILLIANT
IMPRESSIONS. Folio, hf. crimson morocco, extra, uncut edges.
1757.

Fine copy, much superior to the subsequent issues. "A most interesting
series of portraits after Holbein, Vandyke, Kneller, Lely," &c.

1101 HOUGH, F. B. History of Duryea's Brigade, during the Campaign
in Virginia under Gen. Pope, and in Maryland under Gen. Mc-
Clellan, in 1862. *Portrait. Rl. 8vo. half morocco, gilt top, uncut, by Bradstreet.* Albany, Munsell, 1864.

300 copies printed.

1102 HOUGH, FRANKLIN B. History of St. Lawrence and Franklin
Counties, N. Y., from the earliest period. *Portraits, &c. thick
roy. 8vo. boards, uncut.* Albany, 1853.

1103 HOUGH, F. B. Notices of Peter Penet, and of his operations among
the Oneida Indians. *Map. Impl. 8vo. uncut.*
Lowville, N. Y., 1866.

Edition 50 *copies.*

1104 HORNE, T. HARTWELL. INTRODUCTION TO THE STUDY OF BIBLIO-
GRAPHY, with Memoir on the Public Libraries of the Ancients.
Engraved facsimiles. 2 *vols. 8vo. new half crimson morocco, gilt
tops, uncut edges.* FINE COPY. London, 1814.

From the Library of John Allan.
The second volume contains a most complete list, and description of works
on Bibliography and Literary History.

1105 HORNE, Rev. T. HARTWELL. REMINISCENCES, Personal and Bibliographical, with Notes by his daughter. *Portrait, post 8vo. cloth.*
London, 1862.

1106 HORNECK, ANTHONY. The Great Law of Consideration; or a Discourse, wherein the Nature, Usefulness of Consideration in order to a truly serious and Religious Life, is laid open. *Front.
8vo. old cf.* London, 1729.

Wm. Wordsworth's copy, with his autograph on the title-page.

1107 HORNER, FRANCIS. Memoirs and Correspondence of, edited by his
brother. *Portrait.* 2 vols. 8vo. *cloth.* Boston, 1853.

1107* HORTICULTURAL TRANSACTIONS of the Society of London, *with*

14

RICHLY COLORED *engravings*, BOTH SERIES COMPLETE, 10 vols. roy. 4to. *hf. morocco, gilt* (pub. at upwards of £50).

London, 1812–47.

This valuable work comprises a collection of papers by the most eminent horticulturists and botanists of the day ; it is likewise embellished with an extensive series of the most beautifully colored plates of Fruits and Flowers, &c., by Mrs. Withers, equal to the finest Drawings.

1108 HOSMER. Catalogue of the Valuable and Choice Library of Zelote Hosmer, Esq., of Cambridge, Mass. *Imperial 8vo. uncut.*

Boston, May 7, &c., 1861.

LARGE PAPER. This collection was particularly rich in Early English Literature, Bibliography, and Rare Editions of the Greek and Latin Classics.

1109 HOTTEN and LARWOOD. HISTORY of SIGN-BOARDS. *Colored Frontispiece and* 100 *illustrations in Fac-simile, showing the various old signs which were formerly hung from Taverns and other houses. 4to. hf. morocco.* London, 1867.

LARGE PAPER, 100 *copies.*

1110 HOW, DAVID. DIARY OF, a Private in Colonel Paul Dudley Sargent's Regiment of the Massachusetts Line in the Army of the American Revolution, from the Original Manuscript, with a Biographical Sketch of the Author, and Illustrative Notes by Henry B. Dawson. *Royal 8vo. uncut.*

Morrisania, N. Y., 1865.

Only 250 *copies.* No. IV. of Dawson's " Gleanings."

1111 HOWE, SAML. G. The Cretan Refugees and their American Helpers. *Map, &c. 8vo. pp.* 64, *paper.* Boston, 1868.

1112 HOWELLS, W. D. Venetian Life. *Thick 12mo. hf. cf. extra.*

New York, 1867.

1113 HOWELLS, W. D. Italian Journeys. *12mo. hf. cf. extra.*

New York, 1867.

1114 HOWITT, WILLIAM. The NORTHERN HEIGHTS of LONDON ; or Historical Associations of Hampstead, Highgate, Muswell Hill, Hornsey, and Islington. *8vo. new cloth.* London, 1869.

1115 HUBBARD, REV. WILLIAM. The HISTORY of the INDIAN WARS in NEW ENGLAND, From the First Settlement to the Termination of the War with King Philip, in 1677. By Samuel G. Drake. 2 vols. 4to. *uncut.*

Printed for W. Eliot Woodward, Roxbury, MDCCCLXV.

LARGE PAPER ; 50 copies printed.

1116 HUBBARD. The Same. *2 vols. sml. 4to. uncut.* Roxbury, 1865.

1117 ——— Another copy. BEAUTIFULLY PRINTED on INDIA PAPER. (Only 6 copies.) *2 vols. roy. 8vo. hf. crimson morocco, gilt top.*

Roxbury, 1865.

1118 HUGHES *vs.* BRECKENRIDGE. Discussion of the Question : Is the Roman Catholic Religion inimical to civil and religious liberty ? *Thick 8vo. cloth, scarce.* Philadelphia, 1836.

1119 HUGHLINGS, I. P. Logic of Names, and Introduction to Boole's Laws of Thought. *12mo. new cloth.* London, 1869.

1120 HUGO, VICTOR. Napoleon the Little. *12mo. hf. mor. uncut.*

London, 1852.

Very scarce.

1121 HUGO, VICTOR. Les Misérables. Fantine, Marius, St. Dennis, Val-
jean, *complete in one vol. 8vo. cloth.* New York, 1862.

1122 HUDDESFORD, GEORGE. POEMS, including Salmagundi, Topsy Tur-
vy, Bubble and Squeak, &c.; also, The WICCAMICAL CHAPLET,
a Selection of Original Poetry. *2 vols. post 8vo. cf.*
London, 1801–4.

"The Wiccamical effusions manifest great sportiveness of genius, and no in-
considerable portion of that 'Broadgrin' which in the present age is preferred
to merely elegant poetry."—*Lon. Monthly Rev.*

The title "Wiccamical" denotes the fact that the contributors were educated
at Winchester School, founded by William of Wickham.

1123 HUISH, ROBERT. MEMOIRS of the PUBLIC and PRIVATE LIFE OF
GEORGE III., with a variety of secret anecdotes, &c., and an
Historical Memoir of the House of Brunswick, *numerous fine
portraits, &c. 4to. hf. cf. gilt, scarce.* London, 1821.

1124 HUME, DAVID. THE HISTORY OF ENGLAND from the Invasion of
Julius Cæsar, to the Revolution in 1688. A new edition with
the Author's last Corrections and Improvements, with Life, etc.
6 vols. royal 8vo. cloth. Boston, 1866.

LARGE PAPER; only 50 copies printed.

1125 HUMBOLDT, ALEXANDER VON. WORKS, comprising: POLITI-
CAL ESSAY on the KINGDOM of NEW SPAIN, *maps, &c.*, 4 vols.—
PERSONAL NARRATIVE of Travels to the EQUINOCTIAL REGIONS,
maps, plans, &c., 7 vols.—RESEARCHES concerning the INSTITU-
TIONS and MONUMENTS of the ANCIENT INHABITANTS of AMERI-
CA, *profusely illustrated*, 2 vols.—ESSAY on the SUPERPOSITION of
ROCKS, 1 vol. *Together 14 vols. 8vo. uniformly bound in new
bright calf, extra, yellow edges.* London, 1823, &c.

FINE COPY, *best Library Editions.*

1126 HUMPHREYS, H. N. ILLUMINATED BOOKS OF THE MID-
DLE AGES, with an Account of the development and progress of
the Art of Illumination from the IVth to the XVIIth centuries.
*Illustrated by a series of 31 examples of the size of the originals,
selected from the most beautiful of the MSS. of the various periods,
executed on stone, and most beautifully printed in gold, silver, and
colors, by* OWEN JONES. (Published at £16 16s.) *Impl. folio,
new hf. red morocco, gilt edges.* London, 1849.

FINE COPY, *scarce.*
The illustrations are all of the exact size of the originals, are from the most celebrated MSS. in the Imperial Royal Libraries of Vienna, Moscow, Paris, Naples, Copenhagen and Madrid, and other great Libraries of the Continent,
and from the rich Public, Collegiate and Private Libraries of Great Britain.

1127 HUMPHREYS, H. NOEL. HISTORY OF THE ART OF PRINTING; its Invention and Progress to the Middle of the Sixteenth Century, *with
105 plates, comprising facsimiles from the most remarkable Block-
Books, and from all the important Typographical Monuments of
Germany, Holland, Italy, France, England, &c. including 44 fac-
similes of the Press of Caxton, Wynkyn de Worde, Pynson, and of
the Earliest English and Foreign Bibles and Prayer-Books,* impl.
4to. extra cloth. London, 1868.

1128 HUMPHREYS, H. NOEL. MASTERPIECES OF THE EARLY PRIN-
TERS AND ENGRAVERS. *Seventy-two plates*, displaying eighty-one
examples of absolute facsimiles in Photo-Lithography from rare

and curious books, remarkable for illustrative devices, beautiful borders, decorative initials, printers' marks, elaborate title-pages, &c., &c. *Each subject accompanied by a full description, and a concise account of the Work from which it has been selected.* Complete in 12 *numbers, folio, uncut.* London, 1868–70.

Ornamental Borderings, elaborately enriched Initials, and Printers' Marks, of a decorative character, form prominent features in this series of facsimiles. But those illustrative Devices which often consist of important compositions, of an elaborate character, by one or another of the great artists whose respective careers shed so much artistic brilliancy over the close of the 15th and the opening of the 16th century, also necessarily form the more leading features of the work. Among these will be found a great variety of remarkable designs by Wohlgemuth, Dürer, Burgmair, Cranach, Jerome Resch, Hans Schaufelein of Nordlingen, Josse de Negkher, and others; and also specimens of works of scarcely less merit by artists whose names are at present unknown. An inspection of the examples selected will show that, within the space afforded by a single volume, such a variety of specimens, from books remarkable for the beauty of their printing and enrichments, has been got together as will serve to illustrate pretty generally the progress of the art during the last quarter of the 15th and up to the middle of the 16th century. It should be stated also, that by far the greater part of the examples are now published for the first time, and have never appeared in any other bibliographical work, many of the originals being of extreme rarity.

1129 HUNT, CHARLES HAVENS. LIFE OF EDWARD LIVINGSTON. With an Introduction by George Bancroft. *Portraits, on India paper, of Livingston and General Jackson. Imperial 8vo. vellum cloth, uncut.* New York, 1864.

LARGE PAPER; *only 50 copies printed.*

1130 HUNT, LEIGH. WORKS, comprising THE REFLECTOR, 2 vols. 8vo. LITERARY EXAMINER, 1 vol. 8vo. THE TOWN, 2 vols. crown 8vo. INDICATOR, 2 vols. crown 8vo. AUTOBIOGRAPHY, 3 vols. crown, 8vo. Memoirs of Kensington, 2 vols. cr. 8vo. STORIES FROM THE ITALIAN POETS, 2 vols. cr. 8vo. CORRESPONDENCE, 2 vols. cr. 8vo. MEN, WOMEN AND BOOKS, 2 vols. cr. 8vo., and POEMS, 1 vol. *Portraits and Engravings.* Together 19 vols. 8vo., *uniformly bound in dark blue morocco, gilt top, uncut edges.* London, 1823.

A FINE UNIFORM and very COMPLETE SERIES. *All best editions.*
"He is, in truth, one of the pleasantest writers of his time,—easy, colloquial, genial, humane, full of fine fancies, and verbal niceties, possessing a loving if not a 'learned spirit' with hardly a spice of bitterness in his composition." — *Whipple's Essays and Reviews.*

1131 HUNT, LEIGH. STORIES OF THE ITALIAN POETS, with Lives of the Writers. 2 *vols. post 8vo. new cloth.* London, 1846.

1132 HUNT, ROBERT. Popular Romances of the West of England; or, the Drolls, Traditions, and Superstitions of Old Cornwall. *Front.* 2 vols. *crown 8vo. new cloth.* London, 1865.

1133 HUNT, ROBERT. POPULAR ROMANCES of the West of England; or, The Drolls, Traditions, and Superstitions of Old Cornwall. *Front.* BOTH SERIES. 2 *vols. 12mo. cloth.* London, 1865.

1134 HUNT'S MERCHANTS' MAGAZINE AND COMMERCIAL REVIEW. A complete set from its commencement in July, 1839, to and including Nov. 1864. 51 *vols. 8vo. uniformly bound in hf. morocco, neat.* New York, 1839–'64.

Fine uniform set.

1135 HUSKINSON, RT. HON. W. SPEECHES, with a Biographical Me-

moir from Authentic sources. *Fine proof portrait.* 3 vols. impl.
8vo. polished calf, extra. London, 1831.

LARGE PAPER, *scarce in this state.*

1136 HUTCHINSON, FRANCIS. An Historical Essay concerning Witchcraft, with Observations, &c. 8vo. calf, *neat.* London, 1718.

See p. 72, for an account of the Salem Witchcraft in New England.

1137 HUTCHINSON PAPERS. Relative to the History of Massachusetts
Bay. *2 vols. roy. 4to. uncut.* (*Vol. I. in boards*).
Prince Society, Albany, 1865.

LARGE PAPER; *only 10 copies.*

1138 IAMBLICHUS ON THE MYSTERIES of the Egyptians, Chaldeans, and
Assyrians, translated from the Greek by THOMAS TAYLOR. 8vo.
boards, uncut, scarce. Printed for the Translator; Chiswick, 1821.

1139 ICONOGRAPHIC ENCYCLOPEDIA OF LITERATURE, SCIENCE
AND ART, by J. G. Heck, translated and edited by Spencer F.
Baird. 4 vols. thick 8vo. of text, and 2 vols. oblong 4to. *com-
prising over* 500 *plates,* together 6 vols. *hf. morocco, antique.*
New York.

1140 ILLINOIS REPORTS by Freeman. Vol. 44. 8vo. *law sheep.*
Chicago, 1869.

1141 IMPERIAL DICTIONARY OF UNIVERSAL BIOGRAPHY, comprising original Memoirs of distinguished Men of all Ages and Nations,
by eminent Writers. 24 *fine portraits,* 6 *vols. impl. 8vo. new
cloth.* Edinburgh, (1858.)

1142 INDAGINE, JOHANNES. DIE KUNST der CHIROMANTZEY, PHYSIOGNO-
MEY. Naturlichen Astrologey, Complexion eins jegklichen
menschens, etc., etc. *Portrait of the Author on reverse of title
and profusely illustrated with grotesque figures, Astrological signs,
etc., on wood,* folio, *boards.*
(Strasbourg, *Johannan Schott.* Anno MDXXIII.)

1143 INDIA. Historic Incidents and Life in India, by Caleb Wright
and J. A. Brainard. *Profusely illustrated, 8vo. cloth.*
Chicago, 1867.

1144 INDIAN AFFAIRS. Proceedings of the Commissioners of, &c., &c.
Map. 2 vols. small 4to. *hf. crimson morocco, gilt top, by Bradstreet. Munsell,* Albany, 1861.

One of 5 copies on INDIA PAPER.

1145 INGLIS, H. D. WORKS, a complete set, *with maps and engravings,
including the humorous series by G. Cruikshank,* 12 vols. post 8vo.
new hf. calf, gilt (pub. £6. 16s.) London, 1837, &c.

COMPRISING:

Channel Islands, Jersey, Guern-	Tyrol, with a Glance of Bavaria.
sey, &c.	Journey through Ireland.
New Gil Blas. 2 vols.	——————— Spain in 1830. 2 vols.
Rambles in the Footsteps of Don	Switzerland, South of France, &c.
Quixote.	Tales of Ardennes.
Solitary Rambles through many	Tour through Norway, Sweden, and Den-
Lands.	mark.

1146 INQUISITIONS, HISTORY OF, including the Secret Transactions of those
horrific Tribunals. (Stockdale), *with 12 engravings on copper.*
4to. *hf. cf. neat.* London, 1810.

1149 IRELAND. ANCIENT IRISH HISTORIES, by Spenser, Campion, Hanmer, and Marleburrough. 2 vols. *thick roy. 8vo. calf, neat.* 1809.

LARGE and THICK PAPER, *(but somewhat 'cut down.')* Comprises Spenser's View of the State of Ireland, 1596; Campion's Historie of Ireland, 1571; Hanmer's Chronicle of Ireland, 1571; Marleburrough's Chronicle, 1571.

1150 IRELAND. History of the Execrable Irish Rebellion, trac'd from many preceding acts, to the Grand Eruption October 23, 1641, (by Dr. Baglate?) . *Folio, old cf. neat.* London, 1680.

Autograph of Lord Rokeby.

1151 IRELAND, JOSEPH N. Records of the New York Stage from 1750 to 1860. *Vignette. 2 vols. 8vo. boards.*

New York, 1867.

Edition limited to 200 copies.

1152 IRELAND, WM. HENRY. CONFESSIONS, containing the particulars of his fabrication of Shakespeare manuscripts, with anecdotes, opinions, &c. *Post 8vo. cf. scarce.* London, 1805.

"It is mortifying (says Mr. Gifford in a note to his edition of Ford's Plays) to reflect that had this youth possessed but a single grain of prudence, *and known when and where to stop, his forgeries might, at this moment, be visited by anniversary crowds of devoted pilgrims,* in some splendid shrine set apart, in his father's house, for that pious purpose."

See also, SHAKESPEARE FORGERIES.

1153 [IRELAND, W. H.] CHALCOGRAPHIMANIA; or the Portrait-Collector and Printseller's Chronicle, with infatuations of every description. A Humorous Poem, with Notes, &c. by Satiricus Sculptor, Esq. *Illustrated by the insertion of 60 fine portraits, views, &c. 8vo. red morocco, gilt.* London, 1814.

From the Allan collection.

"Written by W. H. Ireland from information mostly furnished by T. Coram." —*Lowndes.*

1154 [IRELAND, W. H.] SCRIBBLEOMANIA; or the Printer's Devil's Polichronicon. A sublime Poem, edited by Ansee Pen-Dragon, Esq. *8vo. hf. green calf, neat.* London, 1815.

"Samson slew his thousands with the jawbone of an ass; then wherefore should not I perform similar exploits with the quill of a goose?"—*Preface.*

1155 IRVING, JOSEPH. HISTORY of DUMBARTONSHIRE, Civil, Ecclesiastical, Territorial, with Genealogical Notices of the Principal Families in the County, 4to. *finely printed on* THICK CLUB PAPER, *and illustrated with Maps, Views, Portraits, facsimiles of Original Documents, etc. etc. cloth. Dumbarton, for the Author,* 1860.

Of this important work, an impression limited to 280 copies was printed, and of these nearly 200 COPIES WERE DISPOSED OF TO ORIGINAL SUBSCRIBERS. To the high merits of the work, as the only worthy Scotch County History in existence, the " Edinburgh Review," "Gentleman's Magazine," " Saturday Review," have borne ample testimony, and when the original number of copies printed is considered, and the few remaining for sale, it is not surprising that in a short time the book has become scarce, and, like so many English County Histories, its value has thereby become greatly enhanced.

1156 IRVING, WASHINGTON. WORKS. *National Edition, printed on toned paper, and illustrated with engravings on steel.* 22 vols. *crown 8vo. cloth.* New York, 1861.

Includes Life of Washington.

1157 IOWA. REPORT ON THE GEOLOGICAL SURVEY of Iowa, embracing the results of investigations made during portions of the years

1855, '6, and '7, by James Hall and J. D. Whitney, *numerous maps and plates.* 2 vols. *impl. 8vo. cloth, scarce.*

By the Legislature, 1858.

1158 Iu-kiao-li: or, the Two Fair Cousins. A Chinese novel, from the French version of M. Abel Remusat. 2 vols. in one, *post 8vo. hf. mor. uncut.* *London,* 1827.
Very scarce.

1159 Ives, Lieut. Jos. C. Report on the Exploration of the Colorado River of the West, *numerous large folding maps, &c. and colored lithographic plates. Roy. 4to. new hf. green morocco, gilt.*
Washington, 1861.

1160 Jacob, J. J. A Biographical Sketch of the Life of the Late Captain Michael Cresap. *Sml. 4to. uncut.* *Cincinnati,* 1866.

1161 James, G. P. R. Life and Times of Louis XIV. *Numerous fine portraits. 4 vols. 8vo. new hf. cf. extra.* *London,* 1838.
" His accuracy both as to facts and the deductions flowing from them may be relied on. His works are always instructive; and we are sure to rise from their perusal with gratification."—*Athenæum.*

1162 James I. Secret History of the Court of, with Notes and Introductory Remarks. 2 vols. *8vo. cf. gilt.* *Edinburgh,* 1811.
Contains Osborne's Traditional Memoirs; Sir Anthony Weldon's Court of King James; Aulicus Cocquinariæ; and Peyton's Divine Catastrophe of the house of Stuarts.

1163 JAMESON, Mrs. LEGENDS of the MADONNA, as represented in the Fine Arts, *with 55 drawings by the author and 152 woodcuts. Sm. 4to.* *London,* 1867.

1164 Jameson, Mrs. Legends of the Monastic Orders. Second Edition enlarged, *with 11 etchings by the author and 88 woodcuts. Sm. 4to.* *London,* 1867.

1165 Jameson, Mrs. Sacred and Legendary Art. *Illustrated with 16 etchings and numerous woodcuts.* 2 vols. *sm. 4to.*
London, 1866.

1166 Jameson, Mrs. and Lady Eastlake's History of our Lord, as exemplified in Works of Art; with that of His Types, St. John the Baptist, and other Persons of the Old and New Testament. 31 *etchings and* 281 *wood engravings of Paintings, Mosaics, Ancient Ivory Carvings, Byzantine and other Miniatures.* 2 *thick vols. sm. 4to.* *London,* 1865.
The above four lots are all uniformly bound in tree-marbled calf, extra, gilt edges by Riviere.

1167 JAMESON, Mrs. WORKS, comprising Characteristics of Women, 2 vols.; Rambles in Canada, 2 vols.; Common-Place Book, 1 vol.; Romance of Biography, 2 vols.; Social Life in Germany, 2 vols.; Diary of an Ennuyé, 1 vol.: *engravings, &c.,* together, 10 vols. Post 8vo. *uniformly bound light blue morocco, extra, gilt top, uncut edges.* *London,* 1826, *&c.*

1168 Jameson, Mrs. Beauties of the Court of Charles II. Memoirs of, *with* 21 *beautiful portraits after Sir Peter Lely. Imperial 8vo. crimson cloth.* *London,* 1861.

1169 JARDINE, Sir W. NATURALIST'S LIBRARY complete, containing valuable works on every branch of Animated Nature,

by the most eminent naturalists, *with upward of* 1200 *beautiful colored plates.* 40 vols. fcap. 8vo. new hf. cf. very neat.
Edinburgh, 1833–40.

ORIGINAL COPY.

In the preparation of this valuable series, Sir Wm. Jardine was assisted by Swainson, Waterhouse, Magillivary, Bushnan, Selby, Schomburgh, Col. Hamilton Smith, Dr. Hamilton, and others.

"This book is, perhaps, the most interesting, the most beautiful, and the cheapest series ever offered to the public."—*Athenæum.*

1170 JARVES, DEMING. Reminiscences of Glass Making. 12mo. new cloth. *New York,* 1865.

1171 JARVES, J. ART-STUDIES; the Old Masters of Italy, Painting, etc. *Beautifully printed on heavy toned paper, with 43 outline engravings of Altar Pieces, Groups, etc.* selected from the Old Masters, 1200 to 1517. *2 vols. in one, 8vo. new hf. cf. extra. New York,* 1861.

Includes the Byzantine and best periods of Art in Italy.

1172 JARVES, JAMES J. Art-Thoughts; the experiences and observations of an American Amateur in Europe. *Post 8vo. new cloth.*
New York, 1869.

1173 JARVES, JAS. JACKSON. The Art-Idea; Sculpture, Painting and Architecture in America. 12mo. hf. rox. morocco, uncut.
New York, 1868.

1174 JEFFREY of MONMOUTH. BRITISH HISTORY, translated from the Latin, with a Preface concerning the Authority of the History by Aaron Thompson. *8vo. crimson morocco, gilt, in the style of Roger Payne.* London, 1718.

LARGE PAPER, *fine copy.*

1175 JERROLD, DOUGLAS. WORKS. Collected Edition, with an Introductory Memoir by his Son, W. Blanchard Jerrold. *Plates. 4 vols. crown 8vo. cloth.* London, 1863.

1176 JESSE, J. HENEAGE. MEMOIRS of the LIFE AND REIGN of KING GEORGE III. *2d Edition.* 3 thick vols. 8vo. new cloth.
London, 1867.

1177 JESUITS RELATIONS. Relations des Jésuites, contenant ce qui s'est passé de plus remarquable dans les Missions des Frères de la compagnie de Jésus dans la Nouvelle France, (ouvrage publié sous les auspices du Gouvernement Canadien). *3 thick vols. royal 8vo. hf. calf, gilt.* Quebec, 1858.

LIMITED EDITION. This is a new edition, and includes the whole series of Reports from 1632 to 1673, preceded by the Relations of Pierre Biard, originally printed at Lyons in 1616; and of Charles Lalemant, printed at Paris in 1626.

"When we consider that the missionaries and colonists of Gaul found their way to the Kennebec, the Mohawk, Central New York, Ohio, Michigan, Illinois, and Wisconsin, in the period embraced in these volumes, their great importance to our early history is at once evident."

1178 Jewell's (Bp. *of Salisburie*) Workes, newly set forth with additions and Life, *very thick folio, calf, neat, scarce,* (in a recent catalogue, £4. 4s.) J. Norton, London, 1611.

A CHOICE COPY.

"The first and indeed much the best writer of Queen Elizabeth's time was Bp. Jewell."—*Bp. Burnett.*

1179 JOE MILLER'S JESTS, or, the WIT'S VADE MECUM, being a collection of the most Brilliant Jests, the politest Repartees, the most elegant Bons Mots, and most pleasant short stories in the English language. An interesting specimen of remarkable fac-simile, 8vo. half morocco, old Dutch paper sides.

London : printed by T. Read, 1739. London, 1865.

The book is well known, or rather the Jests are, for the veritable *first edition* of Joe Miller is one of the rarest books in the English language. With regard to the contents of Joe Miller's *Jests*, the plain spoken words are neither better nor worse than those in any other similar collection of the period. It is to be regretted that the author did not employ expressions a little less coarse than he has done ; his wit and pungency, however, it is impossible to deny. *Only a very few copies have been reproduced.*

1180 JOHNSON, DR. SAMUEL. The RAMBLER. The ORIGINAL EDITION, as published in Nos. (at 2d each) every Tuesday and Saturday. *Complete. 2 vols. folio, calf, rebacked with dark-blue morocco, full gilt.* London, 1749–50.

SCARCE.
A fine, clean, and perfect copy ; in the subsequent editions the text was much altered.

1181 JOHNSON, DR. SAMUEL. RASSELAS. Illustrated Edition, *with four engravings by Raimbach after designs by* SMIRKE. 4to. hf. cf. neat. London, 1805.

1182 JOHNSON'S TYPOGRAPHIA, or the Printer's Instructor. Including an Account of the Origin of Printing, with Biographical Notices of the Printers of England from Caxton to the close of the Sixteenth Century, &c. &c. 2 *thick vols. 8vo. hf. cf. neat, scarce.* London, 1824.

LARGEST PAPER. Contains the essence of Dibdin's Typographical Antiquities and other valuable works.

1183 ———— Another copy. Small paper. 2 vols. thick 16mo. cloth, *uncut.* London, 1824.

1184 JOHNSTON, ALEX. KEITH. PHYSICAL ATLAS of Natural Phenomena, Geology, and Orography, Hydrography, Meteorology and Magnetism, Botany, Natural History, Ethnology, and Statistics. NEW AND ENLARGED EDITION. 42 *large* COLORED *plates*, with copious Index, &c. *Imp. folio, new hf. red morocco, gilt edges.* Edinburgh, 1856.

1185 [JOHNSTONE] CHRYSAL ; or the Adventures of a Guinea, with curious and interesting anecdotes, &c. 4 *vols. 12mo. calf, gilt.* London, 1783.

1186 JOMINI, BARON. LIFE of NAPOLEON, translated from the French, with Notes, &c. by H. W. Halleck, with Atlas, containing 60 *Maps, Plans of Battles, &c.,* together 5 vols. 8vo. &c. new cloth, New York, 1864.

1187 JONES, MAJ. GENERAL SIR JOHN. JOURNAL of SIEGES carried on by the DUKE of WELLINGTON in Spain during the years 1811 and 1814, with Notes and Additions, etc. THIRD EDITION. 3 *thick vols. 8vo. new cloth, uncut.* London, 1846.

1188 JONES, CHARLES C. JR. Historical Sketch of the Chatham Artillery during the Confederate Struggle for Independence. Imp. 8vo. *uncut.* *Munsell,* Albany, 1867.

LARGE PAPER.
15

1189 JONES, REV. DAVID. Journal of Two Visits made to some Nations of Indians. *Imp. 8vo. uncut.* J. Sabin, New York, 1865.
LARGE PAPER, 50 *copies.* Sabin's Reprints, No. 2.

1190 JONES, HUGH. Present State of Virginia, &c. *Roy. 8vo. uncut.*
London, 1724, *reprinted* New York, 1865
LARGE PAPER, 50 *copies.* Sabins Reprints, No. 5.

1191 JONES, OWEN. DETAILS and ORNAMENTS FROM THE ALHAMBRA, *a series of 26 large and exquisitely* COLORED PLATES, HEIGHTENED WITH GOLD. Folio, hf. cf. London, 1845.
With autograph letter of the Author inserted (4 pp.)

1192 JONES, OWEN. GRAMMAR of ORNAMENT. A Series of 112 *exquisitely* COLORED PLATES, *executed in Chromo-Lithography, comprising* 3000 *examples of the Decorations of all ages and nations,* with descriptive letter-press. Roy. 4to. *new cloth, gilt.* London, 1865.

1193 JONES, OWEN. EXAMPLES of CHINESE ORNAMENT. 100 *beautiful plates in* RICH COLORS, *executed in chromo-lithography, comprising near* 1000 *objects in the South Kensington Museum and other collections.* Imp. 4to. *new cloth.* London, 1867.
A companion, or second series of the " Grammar of Ornament."

1194 JONES, SIR W. COMPLETE WORKS, with the Supplement containing his Asiatic Researches, and Life by Lord Teignmouth, BEST EDITION, *portraits and numerous engravings of Oriental symbolical characters, &c.* 13 *vols. 8vo. mottled calf, gilt.*
London, 1807, &c.

1195 JONES, SIR WILLIAM. THE MUSE RECALLED, an Ode occasioned by the Nuptials of Lord Viscount Althorp and Lady Lavinia Bingham, Mch. VI. 1781. 4to. pp. 8, *hf. morocco, very scarce.*
Strawberry Hill, Printed by Thomas Kirgate, 1781.
ONLY 250 COPIES PRINTED.

1196 JONSON, BEN. WORKS, with a Biographical Memoir by William Gifford. *Portrait. Thick 8vo. cloth.* Boston, 1853.

1197 JORROCK'S JAUNTS and JOLLITIES. The Hunting, Shooting, Racing, Driving, Sailing, &c., of that renowned sporting citizen, Mr. John Jorrocks. *With* COLORED *illustrations by Henry Alken.* Impl. 8vo. *new cloth.* London, 1869.
The Author was Mr. R. S. Surtees.

1198 JOSEPHUS' WORKS, translated by William Whiston. *Portrait, Map, and Vignettes.* 4 vols. 8vo. calf, neat.
Cheswick Press, London, 1825.
Fine copy.

1199 JOSSELYN, JOHN. An Account of Two Voyages to New England, made during the years 1638, 1663. *Roy. 4to. uncut.*
Boston, 1865.
LARGE PAPER, 25 *copies printed.*

1200 JOSSELYN, JOHN. New England's Rarities Discovered in Birds, Beasts, Fishes, Serpents, and Plants of that Country, with Introduction and Notes by Edw. Tuckerman. *Roy. 4to. uncut.* Boston, 1865.
LARGE PAPER, 25 *copies printed.*

1201 **JOVIUS PAULUS. THE TURKES CHRON-ICLES.** A shorte treatise vpon the Turkes Chroni-cles, compyled by Paulus Iouius byshop of Nuerne, and dedicated to Charles the V. Emperour. Drawen oute of the Italyen tong in to Latyne, by Franciscus Niger Bassianates. And translated out of Latyne by Peter Ashton. 144 leaves. 16*mo.* (8*vo.*) *hf. green morocco.*

Colophon.—Imprinted in Fletestrete at the signe of the Sunne—By—The xii. day of Auguste,—M. D. XLVI. *cum privilegio—solum.*

A very fine, clean, and perfect copy. *Scarce.*
See Dibdin's Ames, vol. 3, p. 489.

1202 JULIAN, THE EMPEROR. Works ; also some pieces of the sophist Libanus, translated from the Greek, with Notes, &c., by John Duncombe. 2 *vols. 8vo. calf, gilt.* London, 1798,
The only translation.

1203 JOYCE, P. W. Origin and History of Irish names of Places. *Thick 12mo. new cloth.* Dublin, 1869.

1204 JUMEL, Mme. ELZA B. Obituary Notice from the N. Y. Times. July 18th, 1865. Impl. 8vo. *uncut.* New York, 1865.
Only 30 copies.

1205 JUNIUS' LETTERS, including those under other Signatures, and his Private Letters to Woodfall, with Notes, by Dr. Mason Good, *and facsimiles.* BEST EDITION. 3 *vols. 8vo. calf, extra. Fine copy. Scarce.* London, 1814.

1206 JUNIUS' LETTERS. 2 vols. 12*mo. calf, neat. Scarce.*
Woodfall, London, 1772.
"The first authorized edition."

1207 JUSTINIANUS, BERNARDUS. DE ORIGINE URBIS VENETIARUM, rebusque ab ipsa gestis historia 1492. Also, ORATIONES et EPISTOLÆ. pp. 66, *folio, vellum.*
Venetiis, per Bernardum Benalium, 1492.
EDITIO PRINCEPS.
Fine copy from the library of Wm. Roscoe.

1208 JUVENALIS et PERSIUS. Decii Junii Juvenalis Aquinatis Satiræ decem et sex. Auli Persii Flacci satiræ sex. *Beautifully printed by Whittingham, on laid paper within red borders. 4to. elegantly bound by* RIVIERE *in calf, extra.*
Chiswick Press, London, 1845.
Printed expressly for presents.

1209 KAMES, HENRY HOME, *Lord.* Sketches of the History of Man. 3 *vols. 8vo. cf.* Edinburgh, 1807.

1210 KANE, ROBERT. Elements of Chemistry, edited by Dr. William Draper. *Woodcuts, 8vo. cloth* New York, 1848.

1211 KAULBACH, WM. FEMALE CHARACTERS of GOETHE, with descriptive text by G. H. Lewes. *A series of* 20 *large and beautiful engravings on steel in the line manner, by the best German engravers from the celebrated designs of W. von Kaulbach. Fine Impressions. Atlas folio, crimson cloth, embossed.*
London.

1212 KEANE, MARCUS. TOWERS AND TEMPLES OF ANCIENT IRELAND; their Origin and History discussed from a new point of view. *Illustrated with one hundred and eighty-six engravings on wood from original drawings*, etc. 4to. cloth, *uncut*. Dublin, 1867.

The theory advanced by the author is directly opposite to that maintained by Dr. Petrie, to wit: That the Round Towers were erected for the purposes of heathen worship, several hundred years before the birth of Christ.

1213 KEATINGE, MAURICE. TRAVELS through FRANCE and SPAIN to MOROCCO, with a Residence at the Moorish Court, &c., *numerous engravings*, roy. 4to. *cloth, uncut*, (pub. £3. 3s).
London, 1817.

1214 KEATS, JOHN. ENDYMION; a Poetic Romance. *8vo. elegantly bound in dark green morocco, super-extra, by F. Bedford.*
London, 1818.

FIRST EDITION. *Very scarce.*

1215 KEATS, JOHN. ENDYMION; a Poetic Romance. *8vo. tree-marbled calf, extra, marbled edges.* London, 1818.

FIRST EDITION. *Very scarce.*

1216 KEATS, JOHN. POETICAL WORKS and LIFE and LETTERS. New Edition, edited by Lord Houghton, *handsomely printed.* Portrait. *2 vols. post 8vo. tree-marbled calf, extra, by* HAYDAY.
Moxon, London, 1867.

1217 KEATS, JOHN. POETICAL WORKS. With a Memoir by R. Monckton Milnes. ILLUSTRATED EDITION, *with* 120 *engravings from original drawings, and the antique by George Scharf, Jr. Proof Portrait.* 4to. *crimson gros-grained morocco, gilt edges.*
Moxon, London, 1854.

LARGE PAPER, *few printed.*

1218 KEITH, REV. ALEX. The Harmony of Prophecy, &c. **12mo. new** cloth. New York, 1860.

1219 KELLER, DR. FERDINAND. The LAKE DWELLINGS OF SWITZERLAND and other parts of Europe, translated and arranged by J. Edward Lee. 95 *plates. comprising upwards of* 1500 *examples of antiquities. 8vo. hf. calf, extra.* London, 1866.

1220 Kelley, Jonathan. Humors of Falconbridge. *12mo. cloth.*
Philadelphia, 1856.

1221 KEN, BISHOP. CHRISTIAN YEAR; or Hymns and Poems for the Holy Days and Festivals of the Church. *Illustrated with a beautiful series of photographs from celebrated pictures by the old masters. Crown 8vo. elegantly bound in cambridge calf, extra, gilt edges.* *Pickering*, London, 1868.

1222 KENDALL, GEO. W. Narrative of the Texan Sante Fé Expedition. *Map and Illustrations.* 2 vols. 12mo. *cloth.* New York, 1856.

1223 KENNION, EDWARD. ESSAY on TREES in LANDSCAPE; or, an attempt to shew the importance of characteristic expression in this branch of Art, and the means of producing it; 60 *large and beautiful plates, including four large unpublished landscapes and six picturesque studies etched by H. W. Williams. Atlas 4to. cloth, uncut, scarce.* London, 1844.

ELABORATELY ILLUSTRATED COPY.

1224 KEYSLER, John George. TRAVELS through Germany, Bohemia, Hungary, Switzerland, Italy, and Lorrain, giving a true relation of the present state of those countries; their Natural, Literary, and Political History; manners, laws, customs, commerce, antiquities, curiosities of art and nature, &c., &c. 4 vols. 4to. the TEXT NEATLY MOUNTED ON HEAVY DRAWING PAPER, and ARRANGED in 8 THICK VOLUMES, ROY. FOLIO, the WHOLE ILLUSTRATED by the INSERTION of UPWARDS of 2000 RARE AND CURIOUS PLATES, *comprising* PORTRAITS, VIEWS, ANTIQUITIES, MAPS, &c., &c., *mentioned in the work; a large proportion of which are excessively rare, all neatly mounted, and arranged with ruled borders, &c.   8 vols. roy. folio, new hf. russia, untrimmed edges.*
London, 1760.

UNIQUE. The work of some indefatigable "Graingerite" who appears to have spared neither time nor expense in gathering the materials necessary for such an undertaking.
The work is so arranged that it may be extended indefinitely. "J. G. Keysler was a distinguished savant of the last century, and the most accomplished Antiquarian of his time. He traversed Europe in prosecution of his studies on the Fine Arts, Antiquities, &c., and his Narrative was translated into nearly all the European languages, and ran through several editions in England."

1225 KEYSLER, George. TRAVELS through Germany, Bohemia, Hungary, Switzerland, Italy, and Lorrain. *Maps and numerous copperplate engravings.*   4 vols. 4to. calf, gilt.   London, 1766.

1226 KIDDER, F. THE EXPEDITIONS of CAPT. JOHN LOVEWELL, and his encounters with the Indians; including a Particular Account of the Pigwaket Battle, with a History of that tribe; and a Reprint of Rev. Thomas Symmes' Sermon. Roy. 4to. *uncut.*
LARGE PAPER, 25 *copies.*   Boston, 1865.

1227 ———— Another copy. Small paper. *Sml. 4to. uncut.*
Boston, 1865.

1228 [KILLIGREW, Thomas?] THE CHEATS and ILLUSIONS of ROMISH PRIESTS and Exorcists, discovered in the History of the Devils of Loudun, being an account of the pretended possession of the Ursuline Nuns. *8vo. old calf, scarce.*   London, 1703.

1229 KING, REV. DR. RITES and CEREMONIES of the GREEK CHURCH in Russia, containing an account of its Doctrine, Worship, and Discipline, *engravings of Ecclesiastical Costume, &c. Roy. 4to. hf. green morocco,* UNCUT.   London, 1772.
VERY SCARCE. "An elaborate and authentic work; the great source of information on the Ritual, Doctrines, &c., of the *Greek Church.*" The services are translated.

1230 KINGSBOROUGH'S (LORD) ANTIQUITIES of MEXICO. comprising fac-similes of Ancient Mexican Paintings and Hieroglyphics, preserved in the Royal Libraries of Paris, Berlin, and Dresden; in the Imperial Library of Vienna; in the Vatican Library; in the Borgian Museum at Rome; in the Library of the Institute of Bologna; and in the Bodleian Library at Oxford; together with the Monuments of New Spain, by M. Dupaix; illustrated by many valuable inedited MSS., *containing upwards of* 1000 *large plates, embracing all the Remains of*

Mexican Architecture, Art, Religion, etc. 9 *vols. impl. folio, hf. morocco, uncut, gilt tops,* WITH THE PLATES COLORED (pub. at £175.)   London, 1830-48.

Cet ouvrage de la plus grande magnificence, a été exécuté aux frais de Lord Kingsborough, qui en a fait hommage à plusieurs bibliothèques publiques du continent, particulièrement à la Bibliothèque royale, a Paris, et a celle de l'Institut de France. Le prix de chaque exemplaire était de 175 livres (2000 fr. Klaproth). Les quatre premiers volumes renferment les planches lithographiées au nombre de plus de 1000 ; les trois autres contiennent l'explication des planches et plusieurs mémoires inédits, écrits en différentes langues, ainsi que des appendices en anglais. Le septième volume est entièrement rempli par un ouvrage important qui a pour titre :—*Historia Universa de las cosas de Nueva Espana, por el M. R. P.Fr. Bernardino de Sahagun."—Brunet.*

After an interval of seventeen years two more volumes of this extraordinary work have been published, in every respect uniform with the preceding, consisting, 1. of Supplementary Notes in English and Spanish ; 2. of Extracts from the works of Torquemada, Acosta and Garcia, illustrating the last portion of the Mexican paintings, contained in the collection of Mendoza, and shewing the correspondence which exists between many of the Mexican and Hebrew laws ; 3. Adair's History of the North American Indians, their customs and descent from the Jews ; 4. Cartas ineditas de Hernando Cortez ; 5. Cronica Mexicana de Tezozomoe ; 6. Historia Chichimeca y Relaciones por Fernando de Alva Ixtlilxochitl.

" When, some four centuries ago, the enterprise of Spanish navigators opened the vast continent of America to the admiration of Europe, the civilization of the New World was found to be concentrated in two spots, and two only, of that enormous territory. One of these favored regions was Peru : the other was Mexico. IT WAS IN MEXICO ESPECIALLY THAT ART, POLITICS AND SCIENCE HAD RECEIVED THEIR GREATEST DEVELOPMENT. All the rest of North America, from the shores of Hudson's Bay to the mouths of the Mississippi, was desolate and barbarous, diversified only by swamp, forest, or prairie, and populated by savages without knowledge or laws. Mexico alone redeemed the character of the new continent, and presented to the eyes of the invaders a spectacle so marvellous as to satisfy even the expectations which the great discovery had raised. There the Spaniards found an organized State, an ancient polity, and opulent capital, an exalted dynasty, a formidable priesthood, and a people well skilled in mechanical and decorative arts. So great, in fact, was the proficiency of the Mexican workmen, so elaborate the system of government, and so impressive the whole evidence of wealth and grandeur, that for some time the civilization of Mexico was regarded as superior to that of Europe. Although, indeed, the researches of modern inquirers have enabled us to supply some corrective to these ideas, it is really probable that in certain respects the Spaniards found Mexico more advanced than Spain, and we have been recently assured on the authority of a comprehensive history that this civilization was the necessary incident of geographical and natural advantages. Such was the situation and configuration of Mexico that it could hardly fail to make progress, and all that was discovered there in the shape of national wealth or political order represented the extraordinary opportunities which nature had provided."—*Times,* Dec. 8, 1858.

1231 KINGSLEY, REV. CHARLES. The Hermits. *Frontispiece.* 12mo. hf. cf. extra.   Philadelphia, 1868.

1232 KINNEY, ELIZABETH C. POEMS. *Beautifully printed on heavy laid paper.* 8vo. hf. rox. morocco.   New York, 1867.
LARGE PAPER.

1233 KIPPIS, ANDREW. BIOGRAPHIA BRITANNICA ; or the Lives of the most eminent Persons who have flourished in Great Britain and Ireland. 5 *vols. folio, calf, neat.*   London, 1778.

1234 KIRBY. THE WONDERFUL MUSEUM ; or Magazine of Remarkable Characters ; including all the curiosities of nature and art, &c. *Profusely illustrated with portraits of celebrated characters.* 4 *vols. 8vo. hf. cf.*   London, 1803.

1235 KIRKLAND, FRAZER. Pictorial Book of Anecdotes and Incidents of the War of the Rebellion, Civil, Military, Naval, and Domestic, *with upwards of three hundred engravings on wood.* *Thick Impl. 8vo. sheep.* Hartford, 1866.

1236 KITTO, JOHN, D.D. CYCLOPÆDIA of BIBLICAL LITERATURE. *New Edition,* edited by William L. Alexander, D.D. *Profusely illustrated with large engravings on steel, several hundred wood-cuts, Maps, &c.* Printed on toned paper. *3 very thick volumes imp. 8vo. new cloth.* Edinburgh, 1869.

LAST AND BEST EDITION. Amongst the contributors to this valuable work are the most eminent Oriental and Biblical scholars of the present day.

1237 KITTO, JOHN. HISTORY OF PALESTINE, Physical and Biblical, also the Natural History. *Profusely illustrated with large and finely executed engravings on steel, and several hundred wood-cuts.* 2 *vols. imp. 8vo. new hf. cf. extra.* London, 1841.

1238 KNIGHT, C. PICTORIAL HISTORY OF ENGLAND, being a History of the People as well as a History of England, by C. Knight, Prof. Craik, C. Macfarlane, &c., *upwards of 2000 engravings, and numerous fine steel portraits.* 8 large vols. 8vo. *new hf. calf, extra, marbled edges.* London, 1860.

1239 KNIGHT'S PICTORIAL HISTORY OF LONDON, Ancient and Modern, *with 700 engravings of Celebrated Buildings, Antiquities, Costumes, Curiosities, etc.* 6 *vols. in 3. Thick imp. 8vo. hf. crimson morocco, gilt edges.* London, 1851.

1240 KNIGHT, MADAME. Private Journal of Journey from Boston to New York in 1704. *4to. new hf. red morocco, gilt top, by Bradstreet.* Albany, 1865.

LARGE PAPER; *only 50 copies.*

1241 ———— Another Copy, PRINTED ON INDIA PAPER. *8vo. hf. crimson mor. gilt top, by Bradstreet.* Albany, N. Y., 1865.

*** *One of 5 copies.*

1242 KNIGHT, RICHD. PAYNE. A DISCOURSE ON THE WORSHIP OF PRIAPUS, and its connection with the Mystic Theology of the Ancients. By Richard Payne Knight, Esq. A New Edition. To which is added AN ESSAY ON THE WORSHIP OF THE GENERATIVE POWERS DURING THE MIDDLE AGES OF WESTERN EUROPE. *Illustrated with 138 Engravings (many of which are full-page) from Ancient Gems, Coins, Medals, Bronzes, Sculpture, Egyptian Figures, Ornaments, Monuments, etc.* 1 *vol. royal 4to. half morocco, uncut.*
Privately printed, on heavy toned paper, at the Chiswick Press. LARGE PAPER; *only 20 copies.* London, 1866.

The extreme rarity of the original edition of Payne Knight's curious essay on the Mystic Theology of the Ancients is well known to collectors, copies having been recently sold at $150 in this city. This is a new and elegant edition, edited by two very distinguished English scholars, and embraces the original work entire, with much highly important additional matter.

1243 KNIGHT, WILLIAM. The Arch of Titus and the Spoils of the Temple, an historical and critical lecture. *Illustrated. Sml. 4to. new cloth.* London, 1867.

1244 KNOLLES, RICHARD. GENERAL HISTORIE of the TURKS, with continuation by Sir Paul Rycaut. 6th Edition, *with numerous*

well-engraved portraits. Best Edition. 3 *vols. folio, cf. rebacked.*
London, 1687.

"None of our writers can, in my opinion, justly contest the superiority ot Knolles, who, in his history of the Turks, has displayed all the excellencies that narration can admit."—*Dr. Johnson.*

1245 Knox, John. Historie of the Reformatioun of Religioun within the Realm of Scotland, &c., with Life of the Author, from the original MSS. in the University Library of Glasgow. *Fine portrait by Cooper. Folio, new calf, antique, gilt top,* uncut edges. Edinburgh, 1732.

Fine Copy, *excessively rare in this uncut state.*
Best Folio Edition. Edited by Dr. Ruddiman.

1246 Koops, Matthias. Historical Account of the Substances which have been used to describe events and to convey ideas, from the earliest date to the invention of paper. *Printed on yellow straw paper. 8vo. hf. cf. neat.* London, 1801.
Curious and scarce.

1247 Koran of Mohammed, translated from the original, with Explanatory Notes, from the most approved Commentators, and a Preliminary Discourse, by George Sale. 2 vols. 8vo. hf. cf. gilt.
London, 1812.

1248 Kortholt, Christian. Historia Ecclesia Novi Testamenti, à Christo nato usque ad seculum decimum, sistens Statum Ecclesiæ sub Imperatoribus, Schismata, Hæreses, &c. *Sml. 4to. vellum.* Lipsiæ, 1697.

1249 LABARTE, Jules. HISTOIRE DES ARTS INDUSTRIELS, au moyen age, et à l'époque de la Renaissance. 4 vols. 8vo. of text, and 2 vols. roy. 4to. *Comprising one hundred and fifty beautifully colored plates of Ornamental Sculpture, Goldsmiths' Work, Miniatures, Mosaic, Enamels, Armor, &c.* Together 6 vols. 8vo. *and* 4to. *new hf. mor. gilt tops, uncut edges.*
Paris, 1864.

Out of Print and scarce. A copy is priced by a bookseller of this city at $250 gold.

1250 La Bruyere, M. Works, translated from the French. By Nicholas Rowe. 2 vols. 12mo. cf. gilt. London, 1752.
Includes the "Characters of Theophrastus."

1251 Lackington, James. Memoirs of the first forty-five years of the Life of. Best Edition. *Fine portrait, 8vo. new hf. morocco, gilt top, uncut.* London, 1792.

1252 Lackington, J. Ode to the Hero of Finsbury Square; congratulatory on his late marriage, and illustrative of his genius as his own Biographer; with notes referential, by Peregrine Pindar, Gent. *Caricature front. 4to. hf. russia, neat.*
London, 1795.

Interesting copy, with Autograph Letter, Prospectus of his Memoirs, and an Interior View of his Store, inserted.

1253 Lacordaire, Rev. Père. Jesus Christ. Conferences delivered at Notre Dame, in Paris. 12mo. *cloth.* London, 1869.

UNIQUE COPY, EXTRA ILLUSTRATED.

1254 LACROIX (Paul. Bibliophile-Jacob.) Les Arts au Moyen Age, et a l'époque de la Renaissance. *Beautifully printed on heavy paper, and elegantly illustrated with nearly* 100 *fine lithographic plates,* by Kellerhoven, *and upwards of* 400 *engravings on wood, by the best engravers.* 1 vol. extended to 2 vols. thick Imperial 8vo. *handsomely bound,* by Hayday, *in hf. red levant morocco extra, gilt tops, uncut edges.* Paris, 1869.

This copy was selected by its owner with particular care with reference to the impressions of the plates belonging to the work.
No labor or expense has been spared to make these two volumes highly interesting and instructive ; nearly all the chapters have been extended by the insertion of rare and curious matter. Especial reference need only to be made to those on Armor, Musical Notation, Musical Instruments, Glass and other Painting, Architecture, and Manuscripts, in the latter of which, specimens on vellum of the XIIth century, besides some 70 *beautiful miniatures in colors are included. The Article on Printing has had special attention, among which will be found numerous quaint wood-cuts, from the celebrated Nuremberg Chronicle,* 1493, *from the Terence of* 1496, *with the curious representations of the stage costumes, etc., from the Bible. Venice,* 1498. *Very curious cuts from the Cologne Chronicle of* 1499, *and numerous specimens of typography, from that date to* 1554. *Also four sets of Alphabets of the Mediæval period, including Holbein's Alphabet of the Dance of Death.*
This is undoubtedly one of the most interesting as well as splendid works yet published on the arts of the Middle Ages, to which it serves as a sort of Encyclopædia. It exhibits choice specimens of Architecture, Sculpture, Painting, Furniture, Stained glass, Arms and Armor, Manuscripts, Missals, Tapestry, Gold and Silver Work, etc., etc.

1255 Ladies' Miscellany (*sic*). A collection of Poetical Tracts, &c., comprising : The Force of Religion, or, Vanquished Love, by E. Young, 1714 ; Art of Dress, by Jno. Durant, 1777 ; Apple Pie, by Dr. King ; Metamorphoses of the Town, &c., 1731 ; Duck's Poems ; The Thresher's Miscellany ; History of Mrs. Man'ey's Life and Times, 1725, with Key. *Copper-plates. In one vol. 8vo. cf.* A curious collection. London, V. D.

1256 LA FONTAINE. CONTES ET NOUVELLES, en vers. (*Edition exécutée aux frais* des fermiers generaux; *avec une notice par D. Diderot.*) Proofs before Letters *of the celebrated engravings by* Eisen. Original Edition. *Very scarce.* 2 vols. sm. 8vo. *old red morocco, gilt, gilt leaves.*
Amsterdam (Paris, Barbou), 1762.

Farmer General Edition, *with the plates in the first state, (before the Figleaf.)*
So fine a copy as the above very seldom occurs.

1257 La Fontaine. Œuvres Complètes. *Fine portrait after Le Brun, and* 120 *beautifully executed engravings after designs by Dessenne, Chaudet, Huet, &c.* (some rather free). 14 *vols.* 16mo. *green polished calf, extra, marbled edges.* Paris, 1820.
A choice copy.

1258 La Fontaine. Fables, translated from the French by Elizur Wright, *with* 240 *Illustrations by* **J. J. Grandeville.** *Frontispieces on India Paper.* 2 *vols.* roy. 8vo. *boards, uncut, scarce.*
Boston, 1841.

1259 Lafarge, Madame. Memoirs, by herself. *Portrait.* 2 vols. post 8vo. *hf. vellum, gilt.* London, 1841.

1260 La Hodde, Lucien de. The Cradle of Rebellions. A Histor
of the Secret Societies of France. *8vo. cloth.*
New York, 1864

1261 Laing, Malcolm. History of Scotland from the Union of th
Crowns on the accession of James VI to the Throne of Eng
land to the Union of the Kingdoms. *Front.* 4 vols. *8vo. ne*
hf. cf. neat. London, 1819
" Whether I consider his sagacity in explaining causes, his clearness in rela
ing facts, his vigor in portraying characters, I shall ever find reason to lamer
that the continuation of Hume's History of England was not undertaken by
writer so eminently qualified as Mr. Laing is for a work so arduous and s
important."—*Bib. Parriana.*

1262 Laing, S. Chronicle of the Kings of Norway, or Heims
kringla, from the Earliest Period to the Twelfth Century, fror
the Icelandic of Snorro Sturleson, 3 vols. 8vo. *cloth.*
London, 1844
" We owe all that is rational, certain, and connected in the ancient history o
these vast countries to the writings of Snorro Sturleson."

1263 Lamartine, A. de. History of Girondists; or, Personal Memoir
of the Patriots of the French Revolution. *Portraits.* 3 vol
f. cap. 8vo. hf. cf. extra. Bohn, London, 1856

1264 Lamartine, A. de. History of the Restoration of the Monarch
in France. *Portraits.* 4 vols. *f. cap. 8vo. new hf. cf. extra.*
Bohn, London, 1854

1265 Lamb, Chas. Complete Works, and Eliana. *Beautifully print*
ed on toned paper. Together 5 *vols. 8vo. half morocco, uncu*
edges, by Matthews. Best Edition.
Riverside Press, Boston, 1865
Large Paper. Only 100 copies printed.
Uniform with the works of Bacon, Burton, D'Israeli, Montaigne, etc.

1266 Lamb, Charles. Essays of Elia. *Handsomely printed, portrai*
8vo. new cloth, uncut. Boston, 1860
Large Paper, *few printed.*

1267 Lambert, Marchioness de. Works of. Translated from th
French. *Vignettes.* 2 *vols.* 16mo. *new hf. vellum, gilt.*
London, 1781

1268 LANDMANN, George. PORTUGAL, Historical, Military
and Picturesque. Observations on, with 75 *fine colored engra*
ings of the Peninsular Battles and Sieges, Towns, Scenery, &c.
large vols. impl. 4to. *hf. morocco, uncut* (pub. £15. 15s.).
Bulmer, London, 1818
This is by far the most beautiful book on Portugal; and the Narrative of th
Campaign of the British Army is acknowledged to be the most accurate ye
published.

1269 Landon, C. Life and Works of Dominichino. 60 *large outlin*
plates after the most celebrated pictures by Dominichino. 4to. h
cf. gilt. London, 1804

1270 Landor's, W. Savage, Works complete, Imaginary Conversation
Pentameron, Pericles and Aspasia, Plays, Poems, &c. 2 vol
royal 8vo. *cloth. Moxon,* London, 1858

1271 Lanzi, Luigi. History of Painting in Italy, from the period o
the Revival of the Fine Arts to the end of the Eighteent

Century, translated by Thomas Roscoe. 6 vols. IMPERIAL 8*vo.*
elegantly bound in claret morocco, gilt edges. London, 1828.
LARGE PAPER (Pub'd at £6 6*s.* in boards).
" The arts owe a debt of the deepest gratitude to the man with whom Mr.
Roscoe has, by this excellent translation, put it into the power of every English reader to become familiarly acquainted."—*Lit. Gazette.*

1272 LAOCOON ; or, the LIMITS of POETRY and PAINTING, translanted
from the German of G. E. Lessing, by William Ross. *8vo. new
hf. cf. extra, fine copy.* London, 1838.
VERY SCARCE.

1273 LA ROCHE, R. Pneumonia ; its supposed connection, pathological and etiological, with Autumnal Fevers. *8vo. cloth.*
Philadelphia, 1854.

1274 L'ART POUR TOUS. ENCYCLOPÉDIE de L'ART INDUSTRIEL et
DÉCORATIF, par Claude Sauvageot. A complete set from its
commencement in 1861, to June, 1868, inclusive. *Profusely
illustrated with engravings on wood, chromo-lithographs, &c., &c.,
comprising specimens of ancient and modern masterpieces of Ornamental and Decorative Art.* 7 *vols. folio, new hf. red morocco,
gilt.* Paris, 1861–68.
The text is in English, French, and German ; an indispensable work to Engravers, Silversmiths, Metal Workers.

1275 LAURENS CORRESPONDENCE, with Notes, &c., by Frank Moore.
Portrait. 4to. bds. uncut. *Zenger Club,* New York, 1861.

1276 LAVATER, J. CASPER. ESSAYS ON PHYSIOGNOMY,
and LAVATER'S PHYSIOGNOMICAL SKETCHES. Translated by
Hunter. *Numerous beautiful engravings, by Holloway, Bartolozzi, and others. Original and brilliant impressions. Together*
5 *vols. impl. 4to. russia, extra, marbled leaves.* London, 1810.
So fine a copy of this splendid work as the above seldom occurs.
The ordinary copies with the worn plates are hardly worth possessing.

1277 LAVATER, J. C. Essay on Physiognomy. *Several hundred engravings. 4 vols. 8vo. hf. mor.* London, 1797.
From the Library of Rufus Choate, with his autograph in each volume.

1278 LAVATER, J. GASPARD. L'ART DE CONNAITRE les HOMMES
par la PHYSIONOMIE. *Nouvelle Edition,* corrigée et disposée
dans un ordre plus méthodique, precédée d'une Notice Historique sur l'auteur ; augmentée d'une exposition des recherches ou
des opinions de la Chambre, de Porta, de Camper, de Gall, &c.,
&c. par M. MOREAU. *Upwards of 500 finely executed engravings,
with* INDEX. 10 *thick vols. 4to. new hf. calf, extra.*
Paris, 1806.

BEST FRENCH EDITION, containing much additional matter, and a larger number of plates than any other edition.

1279 LAYARD, AUSTEN H. MONUMENTS OF NINEVEH, *Drawings of the Buildings, Sculptures, Bas-Reliefs, &c.* discovered during
his Excavations among the Ruins of Nineveh, and other ancient
cities of Assyria, 170 *large and curious outline and tinted plates,*
LARGE PAPER, BOTH SERIES, in 2 impl. folio volumes, *hf. morocco, gilt* (pub. £21). London, 1849–53.

1280 LAYARD, A. H. NINEVEH AND ITS REMAINS, with an Account of a

Visit to the Chaldæan Christians of Kurdistan, and the Yezid-sor Devil Worshippers, &c., *engravings*, 2 vols. 8vo. *cloth.*

New York, 1849.

1281 LAW, REV. ROBERT. MEMORIALLS; or, the memorable things that fell out within this Island of Brittain from 1638 to 1684. Edited from the original MSS. by Charles K. Sharpe. *Frontispiece, 4to. hf. calf, neat, uncut edges.* Edinburgh, 1818.

LARGE PAPER. (?)
"This work forms a collection of perhaps the best-selected tales of Witchcraft and wizardry which has been yet published."

1282 LAWRENCE GALLERY OF DRAWINGS. DRAWINGS by MICHAEL ANGELO, selected from the matchless collection of Sir Thomas Lawrence. 30 *large and fine plates executed in exact imitation of the originals, mounted on impl. folio paper. Folio, hf. morocco.*

London, 1853.

These drawings are executed with great spirit and exactness, and form a most interesting accompaniment to Ottley's Drawings from the Italian School.

1283 LEA, HENRY C. HISTORICAL SKETCH OF SACERDOTAL CELIBACY in the Christian Church. *Thick 8vo. new cloth.*

Philadelphia, 1867.

1284 LEAKE, ISAAC Q. Memoir of the Life and Times of General John Lamb. *Portrait. 8vo. cloth.* Albany, 1857.

1285 LEAKE, WILLIAM MARTIN. TRAVELS IN GREECE, comprising TRAVELS in the MOREA, and SUPPLEMENT, *with large folding maps, plans, plates of inscriptions, &c.,* 4 *vols.* TRAVELS in NORTHERN GREECE, *maps, &c.,* 4 vols. TOPOGRAPHY of ATHENS, *plates,* 1 vol., and DEMI of ATTICA, 1 vol.; together 10 vols. 8vo. *elegantly bound in polished calf, extra.*

London, 1821–35.

FINE UNIFORM SET, *scarce.*
"ALL of COLONEL LEAKE'S WORKS are of GREAT INTRINSIC VALUE, and are highly deserving of a place in every good library."—*Edinburgh Review.*

1286 LECHFORD, T. PLAIN DEALING; or, News from New England. By Thomas Lechford. With an Introduction and Notes by J. Hammond Trumbull. *Roy. 4to. uncut.*

Boston: Wiggin & Lunt, 1867.

LARGE PAPER, *one of 4 copies, on Whatman's Drawing Paper.*

1287 LECKY, WILLIAM E. H. HISTORY of EUROPEAN MORALS from Augustus to Charlemagne. 2 *vols. 8vo. new cloth.*

London, 1869.

1288 LECKY, W. E. H. History of the Rise and Influence of the spirit of Rationalism in Europe. 2 vols. 8vo. new cloth.

New York, 1866.

1289 LEE, MAJ. GEN. Proceedings of a General Court-Martial held at Brunswick, in the State of New Jersey, by Order of General Washington, for the trial of Major-General Lee, July 4th, 1778, Major-General Lord Stirling, President. *8vo. hf. crimson morocco, gilt top, by Bradstreet.*

Privately Reprinted, New York, 1864.

Only 100 *copies.*

1290 LEE, HARRIET and SOPHIA. Canterbury Tales. New edition. 3 *vols. 12mo. new cloth.* New York, 1865.

1291 LEECH, John. GRAPHIC WORKS. *An extraordinary collection of the works of the celebrated caricaturist,* consisting *of fine early impressions of many hundred characteristic engravings on wood, etchings, &c. &c. from Punch and other periodicals; all neatly mounted and arranged, as far as possible in chronological order, together with the sale catalogue of his drawings* (priced and named), *Newspaper cuttings, &c., &c.* The whole comprised in two large 4to. scrap books, hf. bound in red morocco, London, V. D.
A UNIQUE COLLECTION.
Most of the plates in this collection are selected early impressions, and can only be obtained by destroying the original issues when they occur.

1292 LEECH, John. PICTURES OF LIFE AND CHARACTER, from the Collection of Mr. Punch. THE FOUR SERIES COMPLETE. *Comprising upwards of* 2000 *Humorous Sketches.* 4 *vols. oblong folio, half morocco.* London, 1865, &c.
"The truth, the strength, the free vigor, the kind humor, the John Bull pluck and spirit of Leech's hand, are approached by no competitor. The backgrounds of landscapes in his drawings are as excellently true to nature as the actors themselves. Our respect for the genius and humor which invented both, increases as we look again and again at the designs."— *W. M. Thackeray, in the Quarterly Review.*

1293 LEECH, JOHN, AND H. K. BROWNE. Sponge's Sporting Tour, Plain or Ringlets, Ask Mama, Handley Cross, and Mr. Romford's Hounds (by R. S. SURTEES). *All profusely illustrated with large colored plates and many hundred woodcuts from the inimitable designs of* LEECH *and* H. K. BROWNE. A complete set. 5 *vols. thick 8vo. new hf. cf. extra.* London, 1858, &c.

LEE PRIORY PRESS. See Brydges.

1294 LEGRAND D'AUSSY. FABLIAUX OU CONTES, FABLES ET ROMANS DU XIIe ET DU XIIIe SIÈCLE, traduits ou extraits par Legrand d'Aussy. Troisième édition, considérablement augmentée (avec un avis de l'editeur, signé Ant. Aug. Renouard). *Illustrated with* 18 *beautifully executed engravings, after Moreau and Desenne.* BRILLIANT IMPRESSIONS, *with the outline lettering.* 5 *vols. 8vo. half crimson morocco, gilt tops, uncut edges, by* HAYDAY. Paris, 1829.
"Belle Edition."—BRUNET.

1295 LE JESUITE SECULARISÉ, *engraved title.* 16mo. *vellum.* Very curious. Cologne, 1683.

1296 LELAND, CHAS. G. Hans Breitman's Ballads. *Printed on tinted paper, post 8vo. new cloth, gilt.* Philadelphia, 1869.

1297 LELAND, THOMAS. HISTORY OF IRELAND from the Invasion of Henry II. with a Discourse on the Ancient State of the Kingdom, 3 *vols. 4to. calf gilt.* London, 1773.

1298 LEMON, MARK. UP AND DOWN THE LONDON STREETS. *Profusely illustrated.* 8vo. *new cloth.* London, 1867.

1299 Lemon, Mark. The Jest Book. 16mo. hf. rox. mor.
Cambridge, 1865.

1300 LENFANT, JAMES. HISTORY OF THE COUNCIL OF CONSTANCE, translated from the French (by Stephen Whately). *Fine copperplates, Portraits, &c.* 2 vols. sml. 4to. cf. neat.
London, 1728.

1301 LE ROY. RUINES DES PLUS BEAUX MONUMENTS DE LA GRÈCE, considérées du côté de l'Histoire et du côté de l'Architecture. 60 *large and fine engravings in the style of Piranisi.* 2 *vols. in one. Impl. folio, calf.* Paris, 1758.

1302 LES IMITATEURS DE CHARLES NEUF, ou les conspirateurs Foudroyés. Drame en cinq actes, &c. *Curious copper-plates.* 8vo. pp. 128, *paper.*
Paris. *De l'Imprimerie du Clergé et de la Noblesse de France, dans une des caves ignorées des Grands Augustins.* 1790.
Very Curious.

1303 LE SAGE's ASMODEUS, or the Devil on Two Sticks, with Life by Jules Janin, translated by Thomas, ILLUSTRATED EDITION, *numerous spirited engravings by Tony Johannot,* royal 8vo. *new hf. cf. extra, gilt top, uncut edges.* London, 1841.
FINE COPY.

1304 LE SAGE. Bachelor of Salamanca, translated from the French by James Townsend. 2 *vols.* 16*mo. cloth.* Philadelphia, 1854.

1305 LESSONS OF THRIFT, published for the General Benefit by a member of the Save-all-Club. *Numerous humorous engravings in colors by Cruikshank.* 8vo. *hf. russia, gilt, scarce.* London, 1820.

1306 LETTER FROM THE NOBILITY, Barons, and Commons of Scotland in the year 1320 directed to Pope John. Sml. 4to. pp. 11, *uncut.*
Privately Printed, New York, 1861.

1307 LETTERS FROM BUENOS AYRES AND CHILI, with an original history of the latter country. *Numerous colored plates,* of costumes, &c. 8vo. *calf, gilt, with pictured panels.* London, 1819.
A fine specimen of pictorial binding.

1308 LEVI, LEONE. ANNALS OF BRITISH LEGISLATION; being a classified and analyzed summary of public bills, statutes, and of sessional papers generally, of the Houses of Lords and Commons, together with accounts of commercial legislation, Tariffs, and Facts relating to Foreign Countries. *Maps.* 6 *vols. impl.* 8*vo. hf. cf. neat.* London, 1856, &c.
A valuable work of reference; of prodigious labor and research.

1309 LEVER, CHARLES. WORKS. New and Revised Edition, *with upwards of* 150 *humorous etchings from designs by Phiz.* 22 vols. *Crown* 8*vo. new hf. red morocco, extra, marbled edges.*
Chapman & Hall, London, 1862, &c.
ONLY COMPLETE LIBRARY EDITION. Comprising: Dodd Family, Charles O'Malley, Harry Lorrequer, The O'Donoghue, Knight of Gwynne, Daltons, Roland Cashel, Jack Hinton, Martins of Cro Martin, Fortunes of Glencore, One of Them, Davenport Dunn, Barrington, Tom Burke, Luttrel of Arran.

1310 LEWES, GEO. HENRY. HISTORY OF PHILOSOPHY from Thales to Comte. *Third Edition.* 2 thick vols. 8*vo. new cloth.*
London, 1867.
Last and Best edition, completely rewritten.

1311 LEWIS XIV. PRIVATE LIFE OF, in which are contained the Principal Events, Remarkable Occurrences, and Anecdotes of his Reign, trans. by J. O. Justammond. *Portrait.* 4 *vols.* 8*vo. hf. cf. scarce.* London, 1781.

1312 LEWIS, GEN. ANDREW. The ORDERLY BOOK of that portion of the American Army stationed at or near Williamsburg, Va., from

March 18th, 1776, to August 28th, 1776. From the Original MS., with Notes and Introduction by Charles Campbell, Esq. *4to. uncut.* Richmond, Va., 1860.

1313 LEWIS, HON. SIR GEO. CORNEWALL. Essays on the Administrations of Great Britain from 1780 to 1830. Edited by Sir Edmund Head. *Portrait.* 8vo. new cloth, *uncut.*
London, 1864.

1314 LEWIS, SIR GEORGE C. An Essay on the Influence of Authority in Matters of Opinion. *8vo. boards, uncut, scarce.*
London, 1849.

1315 LEWIS, SIR GEO. C. An Inquiry into the Credibility of the Early Roman History. *2 vols. 8vo. new cloth.* London, 1855.

1316 LEWIS, SIR GEORGE C. A TREATISE on the METHODS of OBSERVATION and REASONING in POLITICS. 2 vols. *8vo. cloth, bds.*
London, 1852.

1317 LEWIS, SIR GEO. C. Dialogue on the Best Form of Government. *12mo. new cloth.* London, 1863.

1318 LEWIS, SIR GEO. C. Essay on the Origin and Formation of the Romance Languages. *Post 8vo. new cloth.* London, 1862.

1319 LEWIS, SIR GEO. C. LOCAL DISTURBANCES in IRELAND, and on the Irish Church Question. *8vo. cloth, bds.* London, 1836.

1320 LEWIS, SIR GEO. C. Remarks on the Use and Abuse of Political Terms. *8vo. cloth, bds.* London, 1832.

1321 LLOYD, H. HISTORY of CAMBRIA, now called Wales, a part of the most famous Yland of Britaine; translated and continued by D. Powell. *Folio, cloth, uncut.*
London, 1584; *reprinted, 1811.*
LARGEST PAPER; *few printed in this form.*

1322 LIANCOURT, *Count C. A. De Goddes.* PIUS the NINTH; or, the First Year of his Pontificate. *Portrait. 2 vols. post 8vo. new hf. vellum, extra.* London, 1847.

1323 LIBRARY of LOVE. AN EXTRAORDINARY COLLECTION of EROTIC LITERATURE; *uniformly bound in 24 vols. 8vo. and 12mo. with illustrations* (Lettered, Paul de Kock's Novels), *new hf. morocco, neat.* New York, &c., V. D.
It is doubtful if another collection, similar to the above, exists in the country; and it would certainly be impossible to form one at the present time, at any cost.
The following list comprises a few of the prominent works included in the series, *viz.:* History of a Rake, or the Lives and Amours of a general Lover. Amours of a Musical Student. Fanny. Amours of Napoleon. Amorous Intrigues of Aaron Burr. The Married Maid. Venus's Album. Melting Moments. Loves and Intrigues of Lord Byron. Amours of Marguerite of Burgundy. Fanny Greeley, or Free Love. Asmodeus, or the Iniquities of New York. Gay Girls of New York. Fast Life in London and Paris. Confessions of a Waiting-Maid. Sharps and Flats. The Ladies' Garter. The Fancy Man. Merry Wives of London. Amours of a Young Man of Leisure. Life of Kate Hastings. A Woman of Pleasure. Anna Mowbray, or Tales of the Harem. The Female Roué. The Grisettes of Paris. Memoirs of a Man of Pleasure. The Delights of Love. Adventures of a French Bedstead. Confessions of a Sofa—and *about* 50 *others.*

1324 LIBER VAGATORUM. The Book of Vagabonds and Beggars, with a Preface by Martin Luther; translated into English, with Introduction and Notes by John Camden Hotten. *Frontis-*

piece. Beautifully printed by Whittingham. Sm. 4to. *half morocco, uncut.* London, 1860.

As a picture of the manners and customs of the vagabond population of Central Europe before the Reformation, it is very interesting. The fact of Luther
writing a preface, and editing it, gives it at once some degree of importance.
Presentation copy from the translator.

1325 LIFE OF DAVID ROBERTS, R. A. Compiled from his
Journals and other sources, by James Ballantyne. *Illustrated
with etchings and fac-similes of pen-and-ink sketches by the artist.*
Roy. 4to. *new cloth, uncut.* Edinburgh, 1866.
*** *Only a limited Edition.*

1326 LIFE OF MOTHER MARGARET MARY HALLAHAN (*Foundress of the
English congregation of St. Catharine of Sienna*), of the Third
Order of St. Dominic, by her Religious Children; with Preface
by the Bp. of Birmingham. *Portrait.* 8vo. *new cloth.*
London, 1869.

1327 LIFE of a SOLDIER. A narrative and descriptive poem, *with eighteen
engravings by Wm. Heath.* COLORED. Roy. 8vo. *calf, gilt, scarce,*
London, 1823.

1328 LILLY, WILLIAM. ASTROLOGICAL TRACTS, comprising.
Supernatural Sights and Apparitions seen in London, June 30,
1644, interpreted, 1644. England's Propheticall Merline, for-
telling to all Nations of Europe untill 1663, the Actions depend-
ing upon the influence of the Conjunction of Saturn and Jupi-
ter, 1644. Ephemeris for 1645, &c., &c. *Wood-cuts, &c.* In
one vol. *sm.* 4to. *old cf. Very scarce.* London, 1644, &c.

1329 LILLY, WILLIAM. CHRISTIAN ASTROLOGY, modestly treated of, in
three books. *Numerous curious diagrams, &c.* Thick *sm.* 4to.
old cf. Soiled but *perfect. Very scarce.* London, 1647.

1330 LIMBORCH, PHILIP. HISTORY of the INQUISITION in France, Spain,
Italy, Portugal, Venice, Sicily, Sardinia, Poland, &c. *Engravings.* 2 vols. 4to. calf, neat. London, 1731.

1331 Lincoln and Douglas. Political Debates of. Roy. 8vo. cloth.
Columbus, O., 1860.

1332 LINCOLNIANA. In Memoriam. Sermons, eulogies, and speeches,
elegantly printed. 4to. *cloth, uncut.* Boston : *Spencer,* 1865.

1333 LIVERMORE, GEORGE. An HISTORICAL RESEARCH respecting the
Opinions of the Founders of the Republic on Negroes as
Slaves, as Citizens, and as Soldiers. Read before the Massa-
chusetts Historical Society, August 14, 1862. 4to. *uncut.*
Boston, 1862.

LARGE PAPER, *only 50 copies printed.* Presentation copy, with Autograph of
the Author.

1334 LIVINGSTON, JOHN H. Sermon delivered before the N. Y. Mission-
ary Society, April 3, 1804. 8vo. *calf, gilt.* New York, 1804.

1335 LIVINGSTONE, D. and C. NARRATIVE of an EXPEDITION to the
ZAMBESI and its Tributaries, 1858–61. *Map, wood-cuts,* thick
8vo. *new cloth.* New York, 1866.

1336 LOCKE, JOHN. WORKS, complete. *Fine portrait by Virtue.* 3 *vols.*
folio, cf. neat. London, 1727.

1337 [Lockhart, John G.] Peter's Letters to his Kinsfolk. 3 vols. 8vo. new hf. dark blue morocco, extra, gilt tops, *uncut edges.*
Edinburgh, 1819.

Extra Illustrated copy, *with nearly one hundred fine Portraits, Views, Facsimiles, &c., &c., inserted.* A choice copy.

" It gives us the pictures, mental and bodily, of some of the leading men of Scotland with great truth and effect. It is a singular hotch-potch, and full of wit and humor."— *Allan Cunningham.*

1338 Lodge's Portraits of Illustrious Personages of Great Britain, with Bibliographical Memoirs. 240 *portraits.* 10 parts. Impl. 8vo. cloth. London Pub. Co. Lond., N. D.

1339 LONDON ART JOURNAL and ART UNION from 1849 to July 1863, with all the Exhibition Catalogues, and including the Vernon, Turner, Wilkie, and Royal Galleries, *with several beautifully executed engravings on steel and wood.* 16 *vols.* 4to. new hf. green morocco, extra, gilt backs. London, 1846-69.

An original, subscribers' copy.
This beautiful and interesting work comprises the most extensive and elegant illustrations of the Modern British School of Painting and Sculpture, together with the best examples of Foreign Art ever published.

1340 London Directory. A Collection of the Names of the Merchants Living in and about the City of London : very useful and necessary. Carefully collected for the Benefit of all dealers that shall have occasion with any of them, directing them at the first sight of their name to the place of their abode. 16mo. cloth, gilt, after a pattern of the period.
London : Printed for Sam Lee, 1677. London, 1863.

This curious little volume has been reprinted at the Chiswick Press, from one of the only two copies known, one of which brought £30, at auction, in London. *Only a very few copies have been reprinted, on paper made to resemble the original.*

1341 LONDON and its Environs Illustrated, *nearly one hundred highly finished engravings, of Mansions, Public Buildings, &c. in London, Westminster, the Country 30 miles round,* with Descriptions, 2. vols. 4to. in one, *russia, extra.* London, 1842, &c.

1342 London Magazine. First series *complete.* 8 vols. 8vo. half calf, *very scarce.* London, 1820-26.

" Arrah ! honey, why did you die? Had you not an Editor and elegant prose writers—beautiful Poets and broths of boys for criticisms and classics, and wits and humorists—Elia, Cary, Procter, Cunningham, Bowring, Barton, Hazlitt, Elton, Hartley, Coleridge, Talfourd, Horace Smith, with a power besides? Hadn't you lions' heads with traditional tales—hadn't you an opium eater, and a dwarf, and a giant, and a learned Lamb, and a green man ? Arrah ! why did you die ?"—T. Hood.

1343 London Society, edited by Miss M. E. Braddon, from its commencement in February, 1862, to Jan. 1866, *with numerous full-page engravings and several hundred woodcuts.* 9 thick vols. 8vo. cloth, extra. London, 1862-66.

1344 Longfellow, Henry W. Complete Works, Revised Edition. *Portrait.* 7 vols. crown 8vo. *cloth, bds. uncut.* Boston, 1866.
Large Paper, 100 *copies printed,* (No. 38.)

1345 Longfellow, Henry W. Ballads and other Poems. 3d Edition. *Handsomely printed on thick paper.* Imp. 8vo. *boards, uncut.*
Cambridge, 1842.

Large Paper, *scarce.*
17

1346 Longfellow, H. W. Dante's Divine Comedy. Inferno, Purgatorio, Paradiso. *3 vols. roy. 8vo. new cloth, uncut.* Boston, 1867.

1347 Longinus. Dionysius on the Sublime, translated from the Greek, with notes, &c. by Wm. Smith, front. by *Vandergucht. 8vo. old cf. scarce.* London, 1793.
Sir Wm. Blackstone's copy with his Autograph.
"An excellent translation, made with great accuracy and judgment."

1348 Longman, William. History of the Life and Times of Edward III. *Front. and Maps. 2 vols. 8vo. new cloth.* London, 1869.

1349 Longus. Les Amours de Daphinis et Chloé, traduction nouvelle, *avec figures nouvellement dessinée, sur les peintures de M. le duc d'Orleans, Regent.* Roy. 4to. hf. red morocco, extra, edges uncut. Paris, *de l'imprimerie de monsieur,* 1787.
Large Paper, *very scarce.*

1350 Lossing, Benson J. Mount Vernon and its Associations, Historical, Biographical, and Pictorial, new edition with additions, *profusely illustrated and beautifully printed on toned paper. 4to. cloth, uncut.* New York, 1865.
Large Paper. *Only 100 copies printed.*

1351 Lossing, B. J. Pictorial Field-Book of the Revolution; or, Illustrations, by pen and pencil, of the History, Biography, Scenery, Relics, and Traditions of the War for Independence, *with several hundred engravings on wood. 2 vols. royal 8vo. new hf. calf, extra.* New York, 1860.

1352 LOUDON, J. C. Arboretum et Fruticetum Britannicum; or, the the Trees and Shrubs of Britain, native and foreign, Pictorially and Botanically delineated with their propagation, culture and management, *with upwards of 400 plates of Trees, and upwards of 2500 woodcuts of trees and shrubs. 8 vols. in 6, thick 8vo. tree-marbled calf, extra, marbled edges.* London, 1854.

1353 Loudon's Cyclopædia of Plants; comprising their specific character, Description, Culture, History, Application in the Arts, &c., &c. New Edition, edited by Mrs. Loudon, *several thousand engravings on wood, thick 8vo. pp. 1574, new cloth.*
London, 1855.

1354 Loudon, J. C. Encyclopædia of Cottage, Farm and Villa Architecture and Furniture, new edition by Mrs. Loudon, *with 2000 woodcuts,* thick 8vo. *new cloth.* London, 1853.

1355 Loudon, J. C. Encyclopædia of Gardening, comprising the Theory and Practice of Horticulture, Floriculture, Arboriculture, and Landscape Gardening, *with many hundred woodcuts,* new edition by Mrs. Loudon, thick 8vo. *new cloth.*
London, 1860.

1356 Louis XVIII. Private Memoirs of the Court of, by a Lady. *2 vols. 8vo. hf. mor. scarce.* London, 1830.

1357 LOWE, E. J. Ferns, British and Exotic. A complete History and Description of, with 479 *accurate and* beautifully colored plates. 8 vols. roy. 8vo. *new hf. morocco, gilt.*
London, 1856–60.
A most comprehensive and beautifully illustrated work on Ferns, comprising contributions from the most eminent botanists of the day.

358 LOWE, E. J. NATURAL HISTORY OF BRITISH GRASSES. With 74 COLORED ILLUSTRATIONS. *Roy. 8vo. new hf. morocco, gilt.* London, 1865.
This volume is very faithful and marvellously cheap, considering the beautiful manner in which it is produced.—*Literary Record.*

359 LOWE, E. J. NEW AND RARE FERNS. Natural History of (not included in the British Ferns). With 72 BEAUTIFUL COLORED PLATES. Roy. 8vo. new hf. morocco, gilt.
London, 1862.
"The most beautifully produced of any of the works recently published on this subject. It is not only the fullest and most accurate treatise on ferns extant, but it is also the cheapest."—*Floral World.*

360 LOWE, E. J. BEAUTIFUL LEAVED PLANTS; being a description of the most beautiful leaved plants in cultivation in this country, with an extended catalogue. *Sixty large and* BEAUTIFULLY COLORED PLATES. Roy. 8vo. new hf. morocco, gilt.
London, 1865.

361 LOWER, MARK ANTHONY. CURIOSITIES of HERALDRY, with Illustrations from Old English Writers, *illuminated front. and numerous woodcuts,* 8vo. *cloth.* London, 1845.

362 LOWER, MARK ANTHONY. PATRONOMICA BRITANNICA; A Dictionary of the Family Names of the United Kingdom, *portrait, impl.* 8vo. *new cloth.* London, 1860.

363 LOWNDES, WILLIAM THOMAS. The BIBLIOGRAPHER'S MANUAL of ENGLISH LITERATURE. New Edition, revised, corrected, and enlarged; with an Appendix relating to the Books of Literary and Scientific Societies. By Henry G. Bohn. 11 vols. *Post 8vo. new cloth.* London, 1865.

363* —————— Another copy. LARGE PAPER, (only 100 copies.) 6 vols. 8vo. hf. *mor. uncut.* London, 1869.

364 LOWVILLE ACADEMY, Semi-Centennial Anniversary celebrated at Lowville, N. Y. July, 1858. *Impl. 8vo. hf. mor.*
Privately Printed. Lowville, N. Y. 1859.

365 LUBBOCK, SIR JOHN. PRE-HISTORIC TIMES, as illustrated by Ancient Remains, and the manners and customs of modern savages. *Colored front. and numerous engravings on wood, thick 8vo. new cloth.*
London, 1869.

366 LÜBKE, DR. WILHELM. HISTORY of ART, translated by F. E. Burnett. *Handsomely printed, and most profusely illustrated with engravings on wood, &c.* 2 *thick vols. imperial 8vo. new cloth, uncut.*
London, 1868.
Published at $25.

367 LUCRETIUS. THE NATURE of THINGS; a Didascalic Poem, with commentaries, &c. by Thomas Busby. *Portrait, 2 vols. in one, atlas 4to. calf, gilt.* London, 1813.
LARGE PAPER, (covers loose).

368 LUDERS, ALEXANDER. Essay on the Character of Henry the Vth, when Prince of Wales. *Front. post 8vo. hf. mor. gilt top.*
London, 1813.

369 LURINE, LOUIS. Ici l'on Aime. (A collection of Novellettes.) 12mo. *hf. mor.* *Paris, 1854.*

1370 LYELL, SIR CHARLES. ELEMENTS of GEOLOGY ; or, the ancient changes of the Earth and its Inhabitants as illustrated by Geological Monuments, 6*th edition, upwards of* 700 *woodcuts, thick 8vo. cloth.* *New York,* 1866.

1371 LYELL, SIR CHARLES. PRINCIPLES of GEOLOGY ; or, the modern changes of the Earth and its Inhabitants. *Maps, and numerous cuts, thick 8vo. cloth.* *New York,* 1865.

1372 LYNTON, E. L. Witch Stories. Post 8vo. cloth. *London,* 1861.

1373 LYSONS, REV. SAMUEL. Our British Ancestors ; Who and What were They ? An Inquiry, serving to elucidate the Traditional History of the Early Britons, *post 8vo. new cloth.*
London, 1865.

1374 LYTTELTON, LORD. HISTORY of the LIFE of KING HENRY II. and of the Age in which he lived, 5 vols. royal 4to. *calf, gilt.*
London, 1767.

" An elaborate and highly important work. Dr. Johnson says he was thirty years in preparing his history."—*Lowndes.*

1375 LYTTON, LADY BULWER. The School for Husbands ; or, Molière's Life and Times. 3 vols. *post 8vo. cloth.* *London,* 1852.

1376 MACAULAY, LORD. COMPLETE WORKS. Comprising the History of England, Essays Contributed to the Edinburgh Review, Speeches, Miscellaneous Writings, and Poems. *Portrait. Riverside Press Edn.* 16 *vols. crown 8vo. new hf. calf, antique.*
New York, 1865–68.

1377 MACAULAY, LORD. HISTORY of ENGLAND from the accession of James II. *Beautifully printed on heavy* HOLLAND PAPER, *with rubricated titles, &c.* 8 *vols. thick crown 8vo. sheets stitched.*
Boston, 1866.

LARGE PAPER ; one of 5 copies printed on Holland paper.

1378 ———— Another copy, including the ESSAYS, together 14 vols. crown 8vo. *cloth, uncut.* *Boston,* 1866, &c.

LARGE PAPER. *Only* 75 *copies printed.*

1379 MACDONALD, GEORGE. England's Antiphon. *Front.* 12mo. *new hf. cf. extra.* *Phila.* 1869

1380 MACFARLANE, C. Lives and Exploits of Banditti and Robbers in all parts of the World. *Frontispiece, and numerous engravings.* 2 *vols. foolscap 8vo. polished calf, extra, yellow edges, by Bedford.*
London, 1833.

1381 MAC IAN. The CLANS of the SCOTTISH HIGHLANDS, illustrated by appropriate Figures, *displaying their Dress, Tartans, Arms, Armorial Insignia, and Social Occupations, from Original Sketches by* R. R. MCIAN, 72 *beautifully* COLORED *plates,* with descriptions by JAMES LOGAN, 2 vols. impl. 4to. *hf. bound green morocco extra, massive emblematical tooling on the backs and sides, gilt edges.*
London, 1845–47.

This splendid work, now out of print, was published at £20.
" One of the most valuable and interesting works of modern times. The portraits are painted by a veritable Highlandman—an artist of the true stamp, who is familiar with his subject."—*Art Union.*
" The Tartans given by Messrs. M'Ian and Logan we know have always been received as the veritable patterns."—*Post.*

1382 McIntosh, Charles. The Practical Gardener, and Modern Horticulturist, *numerous colored plates, &c.* 2 *vols. 8vo. calf, gilt.*
London, 1834.

1383 Mackay, Chas. Memoirs of Extraordinary Popular Delusions and the Madness of Crowds, *profusely illustrated,* 2 vols. in one, 12*mo. hf. cf. extra.* London, 1856.

1384 (McKean, Joseph.) A Plea for Friendship and Patriotism; in two discourses, preached at First Church in Boston, March 27 and April 7th, 1814. 12*mo. pp.* 56, *bds.*
Not published. Boston, 1814.

1385 Mackenna, B. Vicuiña. Francisce Morgen; or The Inquisition as it was in South America, translated from the Spanish by Dr. J. W. Duffy. *Fine portrait.* 8*vo. new cloth.* London, 1869.

1386 Mackie, Chas. Castles, Palaces, and Prisons, of Mary, Queen of Scots. History and Description of, *with* 48 *highly finished engravings. Thick royal 8vo. hf. green calf, extra.*
London, 1854.

1387 Mackintosh, Sir James. View of the Reign of James II from his Accession to the enterprise of the Prince of Orange. *4to. hf. morocco, extra, by Hayday.* London, 1835.
Extra Illustrated Copy.
From the Library of Sir Charles Price. Numerous fine portraits, &c., inserted, the greater portion being Proof, and some Artist's Proof Impressions.

1388 Maclaren, Charles, (Editor of the ' *Scotsman*.') Select Writings, Political, Scientific, Topographical, and Miscellaneous. Edited with a memoir by Robert Cox and James Nicol. *Portrait.* 2 *vols. crown 8vo. new cloth.* Edinburgh, 1869.

1389 Macklin, Chas. Comedies. Man of the World and Love à la Mode. *Fine portrait.* 4*to. cf. gilt.* London, 1793.
Fine edition, published by subscription for the author's benefit when he was 100 years old.

1390 McClellan, Maj. Genl. Geo. B. Report on the Campaigns of the Army of the Potomac, with an Account of the Campaign in Western Virginia. *Maps, &c. Printed on heavy paper. Imperial 8vo. cloth, uncut.* New York, 1864.
Large Paper; *only* 250 *copies.*

1391 Macleod. Henry Dunning. Theory and Practice of Banking. 2d Edition. 2 *vols. 8vo. new cloth.* London, 1866.

1392 McCoy, Jno. F. Catalogue of the Entire Collection of Coins, Medals, &c., Collected by Mr. J. F. McCoy. 8*vo. uncut.*
Roxbury, 1864.

1393 McPherson, Edw. Political History of the United States of America, during the Great Rebellion. 2d Edition. 8*vo. sheets, stitched.* Washington, 1865.

1394 Macpherson, John. The Baths and Wells of Europe; their Action and Uses, with hints on change of Air and Diet cures. *Map.* 12*mo. new cloth.* London, 1869.

1395 McCulloch, J R. Dictionary, Practical, Theoretical, and Historical, of Commerce and Commercial Navigation. *New Edition,* revised and corrected throughout by Hugh G. Reid,

numerous large folding Maps, &c.   Very thick 8vo. new hf. russia.
London, 1869.
Last and Best Edition.

1396 Maddan's Thelypthora; or, A Treatise on Female Ruin; in its Causes, Effects, Consequences, Prevention, and Remedy, Marriage, Whoredom, Fornication, Adultery, Polygamy, Divorce, &c. 3 *vols. 8vo. calf, neat, scarce.* London, 1781.

1397 Madden, R. R. Phantasmata; or, Illusions and Fanaticisms of Protean Forms Productive of Great Evils. *Fine frontispiece.* 2 *vols. 8vo. hf. morocco, neat.* London, 1857.

1398 MAGNA CHARTA, Regis Johannis XV du Junii Anno Regni XVII et D MCCXV. *The celebrated charter, most elegantly printed in* GOLD ON THE FINEST VELLUM, pp. 22. *Atlas 4to. hf. vellum.* Londini, *apud Johannion Whittaker,* MDCCXVI.
An Elegant Specimen of Typography; *very rare.*
"The most magnificent of all editions of MAGNA CHARTA WAS PRINTED IN LETTERS OF GOLD by JOHN WHITTAKER in 1816, and dedicated to the Prince Regent, afterwards George IV. The ordinary copies were printed on thick glazed cardboard, some white, and others tinted of various hues; these were published at £10 10s. Others had decorated borders and emblazoned arms, with portraits, &c.; these were much more expensive. Others again were printed on white or purple satin or VELLUM, in super-royal folio; these were published at from 50 to 100 guineas each. * * *"—*Lowndes.*

1399 Magna Charta. The Great Charter, and Charter of the Forest, with other authentic instruments, with an Introductory Discourse containing the History of the Charters, by William Blackstone. Roy. 4*to. calf, gilt, fine copy, scarce.*
Clarendon Press, Oxford, 1759.
Large and Thick Paper.

1400 Mahaffy, Jno. P. Twelve Lectures on Primitive Civilizations, and their Physical Conditions. 12*mo. new cloth.*
London, 1869.

1401 [Mahony, Rev. Francis.] Reliques of Father Prout, late P. P. of Watergrasshill, in the county of Cork. *Illustrated with numerous etchings on copper by Alfred Croquis* (D. Maclise). *Thick crown 8vo. calf, extra.* Bohn, London, 1866.

1402 Maine, Henry Sumner. Ancient Law; its connection with the early history of Society, and its relation to modern ideas. 8vo. cloth. New York, 1864.

1403 Maine. Catalogue of Original Documents in the English Archives, relating to the Early History of the State of Maine, including the "Defence of Sir Ferdinando Georges." *Roy. 8vo. paper, scarce.* *Privately Printed,* New York, 1858.

1404 Maine Historical Society. Collections of. First Series, 7 vols. Second Series, 1 vol. 8 *vols. 8vo. new cloth.*
Portland, 1865–69.

1405 Maine in the War for the Union. A History of the part borne by Maine troops in the suppression of the Rebellion. *Fine portraits, 8vo. new hf. morocco, gilt top.* Lewiston, Me., 1865.

1406 Maintenon, Madame de. Life, Memoirs, and Letters. Translated from the French (by Mrs. Lennox), together 8 *vols.* 12*mo. new hf. cf. extra.* London, 1753–57.
A fine series, *scarce.*

1407 MAINTENON, MME. SECRET CORRESPONDENCE with the Princess des Ursins; from the original MSS. in the possession of the Duke de Choiseul. *Portraits, 3 vols. 8vo. boards, uncut.* London, 1827.

1408 MAITLAND, C. THE CHURCH IN THE CATACOMBS; a Description of the Primitive Church of Rome, illustrated by its Sepulchral Remains, *numerous woodcuts and inscriptions, 8vo. new hf. morocco, extra, very scarce.* London, 1847.

1409 MAITLAND CLUB BOOK. Sir BEEVES OF HAMTOWN; A Metrical Romance. Now first printed from the Auchinleck MS. *Frontispiece. 4to. elegantly bound in crimson morocco, extra, gilt edges.*
Maitland Club, Edinburgh, 1838.
100 COPIES PRINTED ON THE CLUB PAPER presented by W. B. D. D. Turnbull. E. V. Utterson's copy with his book-plate.

1410 MAITLAND, REV. S. R. List of Early Printed Books in the Archiepiscopal Library at Lambeth. *8vo. dark maroon morocco, extra, gilt leaves.* London, 1843
PRIVATELY PRINTED by the Archbishop of Canterbury for presents.

1411 MAJOR, RICHARD HENRY. LIFE OF PRINCE HENRY OF PORTUGAL, surnamed the Navigator, and its results; comprising the discovery, within one century, of half the world, with new facts in the Discovery of the Atlantic Islands; History of the Naming of America, &c., &c. *Handsomely printed; with fine portraits, maps, charts, &c. Thick imperial 8vo. hf. rox. morocco, uncut.* London, 1868.
LARGE PAPER, *few printed.*

1412 MALET, H. P. CIRCLE OF LIGHT, or Dhawalegeri. *Frontispiece.* Post 8vo. *new cloth.* London, 1869.

1413 MALIBRAN, MME. MEMOIRS OF, by the Countess de Merlin, with a selection from her correspondence. *Portrait, 2 vols. post 8vo. cloth.* London, 1844.

1414 MALLET, M. NORTHERN ANTIQUITIES; or, a Description of the Manners, Customs, Religion, and Laws of the Ancient Danes, and other northern nations, with notes, &c. by the Translator. 2 vols. 8vo. cf. gilt. London, 1770.
⁎ Edited by Bp. Percy.

1415 MALTHUS, R. T. Essay on the Principle of Population, or, a view of its past and present effects on human happiness. 3 vols. 8vo. *calf, extra, scarce.* London, 1817.
LIBRARY EDITION.

1416 MAN, THOMAS. A Picture of Woonsocket, or Truth in its Nudity, &c. *Woodcuts, 12mo. bds.*
(*Providence ?*), *Printed for the Author,* 1835.
1416* —————— Picture of a Factory Village, 12mo. bds.
Printed for the Author, 1833.

1417 Manati ore Long Ile, the Commodities of, &c. *8vo. uncut.*
J. G. Shea, N. Y., N.D.

1418 MANCHESTER ART CATALOGUE. CATALOGUE OF THE ART TREASURES OF THE UNITED KINGDOM collected at Manchester, 1857. 8vo. the text neatly inlaid in a *4to. page within ruled borders; with extra title-pages, &c., &c.* ILLUSTRATED *with an*

immense collection of Fine Portraits, including many fine ones of prominent artists, Views, Engravings after the most celebrated Paintings by Ancient and Modern masters. MANY BEAUTIFULLY COLORED, *also a fine series of Photographs from the more noticeable pictures exhibited.* 2 vols. roy. 4to. hf. morocco, gilt.
Manchester, 1857.

Collected by T. Purland, Esq.
An elegant memorial of one of the most interesting exhibitions of Art Treasures ever attempted.

1419 (MANDEVILLE). THE WORLD UNMASK'D; or, the Philosopher the Greatest Cheat, with Introduction, &c. 2 *vols.* 12mo. *new hf. vellum, extra.* London, 1743.

1420 MANLEY, MRS. NOVELS. The Power of Love, &c. in seven Novels. 8vo. *calf, gilt, very scarce.* London, 1720.

1421 MANN, HORACE. Inauguration of the Statue of. *Photograph.* Roy. 4to. uncut. Boston, 1865.
Only 50 *copies.*

1422 MANNING, MRS. ANCIENT and MEDIÆVAL INDIA. 2 *vols.* 8vo. *new cloth.* London, 1869.

1423 MANON LESCAUT; translated from the French of the Abbé Provost. PICTORIAL EDITION, with numerous spirited engravings by Tony Johannot. *Roy.* 8vo. *new hf. morocco, gilt top.* London, 1841.
The most attractive edition of this remarkable, powerfully written, and singularly touching tale.

1424 MANTELL, GIDEON A. Medals of Creation; or first lessons in Geology. *Illustrated,* 2 vols. 12mo. *cloth.* London, 1854.

1425 MANTELL, GIDEON A. Wonders of Geology; or a familiar exposition of Geological Phenomena. *Illustrated,* 2 vols. 12mo. *cloth.*
London, 1857.

1426 MANUEL. The Authentic History of Captain Castagnette, nephew of the "Man with the wooden head," translated from the French. *With* 43 *cuts from designs by* GUSTAVE DORÉ. 4to. *new cloth.* London, N D.

1427 MANUEL, PRINCE DON JUAN. Count Lucanor; or, the fifty pleasant stories of Patronio, 1335–1347, translated by James York. 12mo. *cloth, uncut.* Pickering, London, 1868.
" In one of them the reader will find the source of Shakespeare's ' Taming the Shrew,' and in others he will recognize the original of modern stories by Herder, Andersen, and others."

1428 MANUEL des SORCIERS, ou cours de récréations Physiques, Mathematiques, &c. *Front. Very curious.* 12mo. *hf. cf.*
Paris, 1820.

1429 MANUSCRIPT on VELLUM. *A beautifully written MS. on* 18 *pages.* ILLUMINATED with *gold and colors, two full-page miniatures, coats of arms, &c., &c.* 8vo. *old cf. gilt.* Venetiis, 1730.

1430 MANUSCRIPT ON VELLUM. MAMMOTRACTUS (or Mamotrepton) written by one Marchesimus of Regiolepidi, a town of Modena, by a monk of the Minorite Order. *Very neatly written on* 200 *leaves of vellum, in an old gothic hand, with rubricated initial letters, &c., &c.* Sm. 4to. *original calf binding, German silver mountings, &c.* Circa 1470.
The author flourished in the early part of the XVth Century, but from the MS. it appears that the work was not finished until the latter part of the century.

1431 [MARANA, PAUL JEAN.] THE JEWISH SPY; being Philosophical, Historical and Critical Correspondences which passed between certain Jews in Turkey, Italy, France, &c., translated from the originals by the Marquis D'Argens. *Portrait.* 5 vols. 12mo. *tree cf. extra, fine copy.* London, 1739.
" A most delightful work."—*D'Israeli.*

1432 MARCENAY DE GHUY (Peintre et Graveur). ŒUVRE DE, contenant differens morceaux d'Histoires, Portraits, Paysages, Batailles, &c. 55 remarkably fine engravings and etchings by this eminent artist, after paintings by POUSSIN, VANDYCK, REMBRANDT, and others. *Fine impressions.* Impl. 4to. hf. mor.
Paris, 1763–78.

Recueil de 55 planches très remarquables. Parmi les portraits : Henri IV, Charles I, le Prince Eugene, Sully, Surrenne, Villars, L'Hospital, De Thou, Bayard, La Pucelle d'Orleans, Rembrandt, Mirabeau, &c.

1433 MARCHMONT PAPERS ; a Selection from the Papers of the Earl of Marchmont, illustrative of events from 1685 to 1750. 3 *vols. 8vo. green calf, gilt.* London, 1830.
" A mine of instruction and amusement. This important and valuable work will stand forever on the same shelf with Evelyn, Pepys, and the Letters of Horace Walpole. It includes many curious letters, never before published, of Bolingbroke, Swift, Pope, Lord Cobham, the Great Duke of Marlborough, Sarah his Duchess, and others."

1434 MARGUERITE DE NAVARRE. L'HEPTAMERON FRAN-ÇOIS DE. *Profusely illustrated with engravings, by Longueil, after designs by Freudenberg.* PROOFS BEFORE LETTERS. *3 vols. 8vo. magnificently bound in crimson morocco, full gilt backs, with the Monogram and Arms of Margaret beautifully impressed on the sides ; heavy inside borders of gold, gilt edges, etc., by* CAPÉ. *Scarce.* Berne, 1780-81.

SPLENDID COPY, *Large Paper.*
" Jolie édition, publiée sous la direction de J. Rodolphe de Sinner, Les Estampes, fleurons et vignettes (ces derniers grav. par Dunker) sont d'une fort belle exécution."—*Brunet.*
" Les nouvelles publiées sous le nom de Marguerite de Valois sont l'ouvrage d'une Société qui se réunissait chez cette princesse : il est probable que Bonaventure Des Periers n'a pas été étranger à leur composition, et Marguerite elle-même a y avoir une grande part."

1435 MARKHAM, G. A WAY to get WEALTH ; containing six principal Vocations, or Callings, in which every good Husband or House-wife may lawfully employ themselves. Sm. 4to. *antique calf, red edges, fine copy.* London, 1695.

1436 MARMONTEL, MEMOIRS of, by himself, including anecdotes of the most distinguished Political and Literary characters of France. 4 *vols. post 8vo. new hf. vellum, extra, uncut.* Edinburgh, 1808.

1437 MARMONTEL, M. MORAL TALES. *Illustrated.* 3 vols. 12mo. *hf. vellum, gilt tops.* London, 1800.

1438 MARRIAGE of WIT and WISDOM, an ancient Interlude, with Illustrations of Shakespeare and the Early English Drama, by J. O. Halliwell. 8vo. *hf. cf. antique.*
Shakespeare Society, London, 1846.

1439 MARTIN, HENRI. THE HISTORY OF FRANCE from the Earliest Period to 1789. Translated from the 4th Paris edition. By

18

Mary L. Booth. *Portraits. 4 vols. imperial 8vo. boards, uncut.*
Boston, 1864–66.

LARGE PAPER, *only 75 copies printed.*
Comprises Age of Louis XIII, 1661–1715, and Decline of the Monarchy, 1715–1789.

1440 MARTINEAU, HARRIET. HISTORY OF THE PEACE, being a History of England from 1816–1854, with an Introduction, 1800–15. 4 vols. *roy. 8vo. cloth, uncut.* Boston, 1864.
LARGE PAPER: 75 *copies printed.*

1441 MARYLAND. Papers relating chiefly to The Maryland Line during the Revolution. Edited by Thomas Balch. One Hundred and Fifty Copies Printed. *8vo. boards.*
Philadelphia, Seventy-Six Society, 1857.

1442 MARY POWELL, afterward Mistress Milton. The Maiden and Married Life of. *Elegantly printed with antique type, on heavy toned paper. Sm. 4to. hf. crimson morocco, extra, uncut edges.*
New York, 1868.

LARGE PAPER, *only 100 copies.*

1443 MASCOU, JNO. J. HISTORY of the ANCIENT GERMANS; including that of the Cimbri, Suevi, Alemanni, Franks, Saxons, Goths, Vandals, and other Northern Nations. Translated from the Dutch by Thomas Lediard. 2 vols. roy. 4to. calf, gilt.
London, 1738.

1444 MASSACHUSETTS. Collections of the Massachusetts Historical Society. From 1792 to 1867. 38 vols. 8vo. bds. uncut. (The last 6 vols. in cloth, trimmed.) Boston, [v. d.]
A *fine copy,* very seldom found complete. A most important collection, containing the only reprints of many of the earliest and most rare tracts and books relating to the history of this country. Vol. IV. 3d series, is cut.

1445 MASSACHUSETTS. PROCEEDINGS of the Massachusetts Historical Society, 1855–65. Selected from the Records. 8 vols. 8vo. cloth, *uncut.* Boston, 1859–69.

1446 MASSACHUSETTS. Records of the Governor and Company of the Massachusetts Bay in New England. 1628–86. Printed by Order of the Legislature. Edited by Nathaniel B. Shurtleff, M.D. 6 vols. 4to. *cloth, gilt tops.* Boston, 1853–4.

1447 MASSACHUSETTS CONVENTION. Debates and Proceedings in the State Convention, May 4, 1853, to amend and revise the Constitution of the State. 3 thick vols. roy. 8vo. *cloth.*
Boston, 1853.

1448 MASSACHUSETTS. Lectures delivered in a course before the Lowell Institute, in Boston, by members of the Massachusetts Historical Society, on subjects relating to the early History of Massachusetts. Thick 8vo. *new cloth.* Boston, 1869.

1449 MASSILLON, J. B. SERMONS. 15 vols. 12mo, french cf. gilt.
Paris, 1774.

1450 MASTERS, MARTIN K. Progress of Love, a Poem. 12mo. hf. cf. *scarce.* Boston, 1808.

1451 MATHER, INCREASE. EARLY HISTORY OF NEW ENGLAND; being a Relation of Hostile Passages between the Indians and European Voyagers and First Settlers: By Increase Mather.

With an Introduction and Notes. By Samuel G. Drake. Sm. 4to. *cloth, uncut.* Boston, 1864.
Only 250 copies printed this size.

2 —————— Another copy. LARGE PAPER. Roy. 4to. *boards, uncut.* Boston, 1864.

3 MATHER, INCREASE. An Historical Discourse concerning the Prevalency of Prayer. Roy. 4*to. bds. uncut.* Boston, 1677.
LARGE PAPER. *Reprinted*, Albany, (1867) ?

4 MATHER, INCREASE AND COTTON. HISTORY OF KING PHILLIP'S WARS, with an Introduction and Notes by Saml. G. Drake. *Map and portraits of Increase and Cotton Mather, and Dr. Winslow Lewis, on India paper. Small 4to. hf. mor. antique, gilt edges.* Boston, 1862.

55 MATHER, COTTON. ORIGINAL AUTOGRAPH MANUSCRIPT. 𝔓𝔄𝔗𝔈𝔯𝔑𝔄. A volume of 355 pages, 8vo., closely written in the characteristic autograph of this widely known and justly celebrated New England Divine—"the bright, consummate flower" and fruit of the orthodox civilization of Massachusetts in the seventeenth century.

THE work is addressed to his Son, SAMUEL MATHER, whose autograph, with the date 1727, appears on the first leaf. It is an illustration of the beginnings and advances of a spiritual life, derived from the passages of his own career, which he had recorded from time to time, as they occurred, in his diaries and other "reserved Memorials," which it was his intention to leave behind him. He declares his purpose to be strictly anonymous, and his desire to discover himself to nobody but his son, whom he wished to endow with all the benefits of "a Father's life." He restricted himself to write no more of his own than might just serve as a direction to that of his son. It was mainly drawn from his diaries, and furnished a great portion of the material afterwards (in 1729) published by SAMUEL MATHER in the Life of his Father. A passage from the preface of that volume very well describes the work now offered in this catalogue.

"The following draughts will give the Publick an entertaining Specimen of his wonderful Improvement of Time, and the various and surprising Methods he invented and pursued for the Advancement of vital Piety, both in himself and Others. Tho' deliberate in Speech, yet expeditious in Inditing; and having the Pen of a ready Writer, that knew not how to faulter in its swift career; He continually preserved Records of the several Rules and Schemes He formed for his own Direction, and of his diurnal Prosecutions of them. He has by this means left a great Abundance of excellent Materials for his more private History: And the Accounts that follow being chiefly extracted from them, are also agreeable to that Part of his Life which fell under the Observation of those who were acquainted with Him; and so nearly answered to these latent Rules now published, that we could not but conclude He had them always in his eye, tho' we had never seen them."

In any point of view, this MS. cannot fail to be regarded as one of the most curious, interesting and valuable memorials of "THIS EXTRAORDINARY PERSON," as his Son very justly describes him. J. W. B.

456 MATHER, COTTON. MAGNALIA CHRISTI AMERICANA; or, the Ecclesiastical History of New England, from Its First Planting in the Year 1620, unto the Year of our Lord, 1698.

In Seven Books. *By the Reverend and Learned* Cotton Mather, Pastor of the North Church in Boston, N. E. *Folio, calf, neat.*
London, 1702.

A tall, clean copy, with the map.

1457 Mather, Cotton. Magnalia Christi Americana; or, The Ecclesiastical History of New England; from its first Planting, in the year 1620, unto the year of Our Lord 1698. With Introduction and Notes by the Rev. Thomas Robbins, D.D. and a Memoir of the author by Saml. G. Drake. *Portrait.* 2 vols. 8vo, hf. mor. Hartford, 1855.

1458 MATHIAS, T. J. PURSUITS OF LITERATURE. A Satirical Poem in four dialogues, with Notes, an Appendix; the citations translated, and a complete index. 16th Edition. *Thick folio, new hf. morocco, extra, gilt edges.* Largest Paper, *illustrated by the insertion of nearly one hundred fine portraits, all in the finest condition, autograph letter, &c.* London, 1812.

Fine Copy. Extra Illustrated. *Very few printed, expressly for illustration.*

1459 Matthias, Thomas James. Lyrick Poetry. *A new Edition,* Printed Privately. 12mo. *pp.* 40, *bds. uncut.* Naples, 1832.

Very Scarce. *Presentation copy from the author.*

1460 Matthias, T. J. Pursuits of Literature. A satirical Poem in four Dialogues. Also, Translations of the Greek, Latin, and Italian Passages quoted in the Prefaces and Notes to the Pursuits of Literature. 2 *vols. 8vo. hf. russia.* London, 1798.

These volumes have numerous curious portraits and newspaper-cuttings inserted.

1461 Matthews, Charles. Memoirs of, by Mrs. Matthews. *Numerous fine portraits.* 4 vols. 8vo. *new hf. green morocco, extra, uncut edges.* London, 1838.

A choice copy, with several extra plates inserted, and two autograph letters, referring to his professional engagements, also an autograph letter of Mrs. Matthews.

1462 Maudsley, Dr. Henry. Physiology and Pathology of the Mind. 8vo. *new cloth.* New York, 1867.

1463 Maurice, Thomas. History of Hindostan; its Arts and its Sciences, as connected with the History of the other great Empires of Asia during the most ancient periods of the World. *Profusely illustrated with plates of Antiquities, Heathen Gods, &c.* 4 *vols. roy. 4to. hf. russia, uncut.* London, 1795.

Fine, clean copy.
A highly important work; including dissertations on the Indian Cosmogony; The four Yugs, or grand Astronomical Periods; Longevity of the Primitive Races; Indian and other Oriental accounts of the Deluge; The Exaggerated Chronology of Eastern Empires; Astronomy; the Origin of the Sphere; and the formations of the Solar and Lunar Zodiacs of Asia, &c., &c.

1464 Maurice, Thomas. Indian Antiquities; or Dissertations relative to the Antient Geographical Divisions, the Pure System of primeval Theology, Grand Code of Civil Laws, the Literature, &c. &c. of Hindostan. *Numerous plates, chiefly illustrating the Ancient Worship of India.* 7 vols. 8vo. *boards.* London, 1806.

A very curious work.
" I beg to recommend the ingenious Mr. Maurice's History of Hindostan, and his Indian Antiquities. Such erudition, ingenuity, and unremitting dilligence, should not fail of an honourable reward."—*Pursuits of Literature.*

1465 Maury, Lieut. M. F. Physical Geography of the Sea, and its Meteorology. *8th edition, maps, &c. 8vo. cloth.*

New York, 1861.

1466 MAXIMILIAN. TRAVELS in the INTERIOR of NORTH AMERICA, by Maximilian, Prince of Wied. *4to. volume of letter-press, translated by N. E. Lloyd, Esq. with map and numerous cuts,* also, a folio Atlas *of 80 plates, beautifully tinted* after the Original Drawings, *new half green morocco, neat.*

London, 1843.

It may be safely asserted that this surpasses all other works dedicated to the delineation of the scenery, the manners, portraits of the aboriginal tribes, the Natural History, etc. of America. The drawings were made by an artist who accompanied the Prince in his travels, and are exactly reproduced in the beautiful plates of the work. A small edition only was printed of the text in English, which has long been exhausted, and copies are now quite rare.

1467 Maxwell, W. H. Life of the Duke of Wellington, *with numerous highly finished engravings after Cooper and others, also portraits, plans of battles, &c.* 3 *vols. 8vo. new cloth.* London, 1839.

"Mr. Maxwell's Life of the Iron Duke has no rival. It is free from flattery and bombast, succinct and masterly."—*Times.*

1468 May, Thomas. History of the Parliament of England, which began November 3, 1640; with a short and necessary view of some precedent years, also, Maj. Gen. Ludlow's letter to Sir Edward Seymour, pp. 150, (Amsterdam, 1691). *Portrait. 4to. calf, gilt.* London, 1812.

Robert Southey's copy, *with his autograph.*

The great Lord Chatham calls May's " a much honester and more instructive book of the same period of history than Lord Clarendon's."

" *No man could be fool enough to say this honestly if he had read them both.*"— R. S. (Southey's comment on the above note).

1469 Mayer, Brantz. Tah-Gah-Jute: or Logan and Cresap, an Historical Essay. *8vo. uncut.* *Munsell, Albany,* 1867.

1469* —— Another copy. Printed on India Paper. 8vo. *new hf. red morocco, gilt top,* by Bradstreet. *Albany,* 1867.

**** *One of 3 copies.*

1470 —— Another copy. Impl. 8vo. uncut. *Albany,* 1867.

Large Paper.

1471 Mayhew, H. London Labour and London Poor, including the Extra Volume relating to Prostitution, and those who will not work. *With numerous portraits and street scenes, from daguerreotypes.* 4 *vols. 8vo. new cloth, gilt.* London, 1861–62.

1472 Mayhew, Augustus. Paved with Gold, or the Romance and Reality of London Streets. *An unfashionable novel, with characteristic etchings by Phiz. 8vo. new cloth.* London, 1858.

1473 Mayhew, Henry. German Life and Manners as seen in Saxony at the Present day; with an account of Village, Town, Domestic, Married, and University Life of Germany. *Illustrated.* 2 *thick vols. 8vo. hf. cf. neat.* London, 1864.

1474 Melvin, J. A Journal of the Expedition to Quebec, in the year 1775, under the command of Colonel Benedict Arnold, by James Melvin, a Private in Captain Dearborn's Company. 8vo. *hf. green morocco, uncut. Franklin Club; Philadelphia,* 1864.

100 *copies printed.*

1475 ———— Another copy. LARGE PAPER. Roy. 4*to.* cloth, uncut.
Philadelphia, 1864.

*** *Only* 20 *copies.*

1476 MEMOIRS OF HARRIETTE WILSON (courtezan of London), and Prominent Persons of her Time, including the Trial of Stockdale, the publisher of the work. *Numerous plates.* 4 vols. 12mo. *new half morocco, gilt.* *London,* 1825.
FINE COPY.
These celebrated memoirs give a detailed account of her introduction to high life as the kept mistress of Lord Craven, her intrigues with the Hon. Fred. Lamb, Duke of Argyle, Duke of Wellington, Beau Brummel, &c. &c.

1477 MEMOIRS of QUEEN HORTENSE, mother of Napoleon III. compiled by L. Wraxall and Robert Wehrhan. *Portrait.* 2 *vols. post* 8*vo. new hf. cf. extra.* *London,* 1862.

1478 MEMOIRS of the COUNTESS BERCI, a Romance, translated from the French (by Mrs. Lenox). 2 *vols.* 12*mo. new hf. cf. gilt.* *London,* 1756.

1479 MEMORABLES of the Montgomeries. 8*vo. uncut.* *New York : Printed for the King of Clubs,* 1866.

1480 ———— Another copy, LARGE PAPER; 40 copies printed. *Roy.* 4*to. uncut.* *New York,* 1866.

1481 MENDELSSOHN, MOSES (*grandfather of the celebrated composer*). JERUSALEM; A Treatise on Ecclesiastical Authority and Judaism, translated by M. Samuels. 2 *vols.* 8*vo. hf. cf. gilt.* *London,* 1838.

1482 MENDELSSOHN, F. LETTERS from 1833–'47, with a Catalogue of his musical compositions. 16mo. hf. cf. extra. *New York,* 1868.

1483 MENZIES, SUTHERLAND. ROYAL FAVORITES. 2 thick vols. 8*vo. new hf. calf, extra.* *London,* 1865.

1484 MERCATOR'S ATLAS. Containing his Cosmographical Description of the Fabricke and Figure of the World, enlarged, &c. by L. Hondy. Englished by W(ye) S(altonstall). *Numerous fine old maps,* &c. *Folio, calf, neat.* *London,* 1635.
FINE COPY.

1485 MERIVALE, CHARLES. HISTORY of the ROMANS under the Empire, with a copious analytical Index, *Map,* &c. 7 *vols. fcap.* 8*vo. new hf. morocco, neat.* *New York,* 1863.

1486 MERIVALE, CHARLES. The Conversion of the Northern Nations. (Boyle Lecture, 1865). Post 8vo. *new cloth.* *New York,* 1866.

1487 MERVIN, JOSEPH. BUTTERFLYING with the POETS; a picture of the Poetical Aspect of Butterfly Life, *with nature-printed illustrations,* (the *real insects*). 8*vo. crimson morocco, extra.* London, 1864.
Only a limited edition.

1488 MESMERISM, CLAIRVOYANCE, &c. &c. containing MESMERISM and its OPPONENTS, by George Sandby. 8vo. the text neatly inlaid in a 4to. page, within ruled borders, *and most profusely illustrated with autograph letters of the author* and *prominent physicians*, &c. *several hundred fine portraits, views, newspaper cuttings*, &c. &c. also 2 VOLS. OF APPENDIX, comprising Reports from various Hospitals, Articles from Medical Journals, autograph letters, Pencil Drawings, &c. &c. *together 4 vols. 4to. uniformly bound in hf. morocco, neat.* London.

UNIQUE COLLECTION, *compiled* by Dr. Thos. Purland, and forming a complete history of the Rise, progress and practice of Mesmerism, Clairvoyance, &c. &c.

1489 MESSINGER FAMILY. Genealogy of, by the Hon. Geo. W. Messinger. *8vo. pp. 14, paper.* Albany, 1863.

1490 METASTASIO, ABBÉ PIETRO. DRAMAS and other POEMS of, translated from the Italian by John Hoole. *Fine plates after* STOTHARD. 3 vols. roy. 8vo. hf. cf. extra. London, 1800.
LARGE PAPER.

1491 METEYARD, ELIZA. LIFE OF JOSIAH WEDGWOOD, from his Private Correspondence and Family Papers, with an Introductory sketch of the Art of Pottery in England. *Fine portrait and several hundred beautifully executed engravings on wood.* 2 vols. *thick 8vo. new cloth.* London, 1865.

1492 Mexico. Report of the Secretary of State—W. H. Seward—on the present condition of, (1862.) 8vo. hf. roan.
Ex. Doc. Washington, 1862.

1493 MICHAUX AND NUTTALL. NORTH AMERICAN SYLVA; or, Description of the Forest Trees of the United States, Canada, and Nova Scotia, with a description of the most useful of the European Forest Trees. *Nearly 300 magnificently colored engravings.* BEST EDITION. *5 vols. imp. 8vo. morocco antique, gilt edges.* Phila., 1859.
FINE COPY.

1494 MICHELET, JULES. THE BIRD, translated from the French, *with upwards of* 200 *beautifully executed engravings on wood from designs by* GIACOMELLI. *8vo. new cloth, gilt.* London, 1869.

1495 MICHELET, M. J. L'Amour, translated by J. W. Palmer. 12mo. cloth. New York, 1860.

1496 MICHELET, J. LA SORCIÈRE; The Witch of the Middle Ages, trans. by L. J. Trotter. *12mo. new cloth.* London, 1863.

1497 MICHIAVEL, NICHOLAS. WORKS, translated from the Originals, and illustrated with Notes, Anecdotes, and a Life of the Author by Ellis Farneworth. *2 vols. 4to. calf, extra, fine copy, scarce.*
London, 1762.

MILITARY OPERATIONS OF THE REVOLUTION, see Orderly Books.

1498 MILL, JAMES. ANALYSIS of the PHENOMENA of the HUMAN MIND. *New Edition*, with Notes by Bain, Grote and John Stuart Mill. 2 vols. 8vo. new cloth. London, 1869.

1499 MILL, JAMES. ELEMENTS of POLITICAL ECONOMY. *2d Edition.* 8vo. calf, neat, very scarce. London, 1824.

1500 MILL, JNO. STUART. On Liberty. 12mo. cloth.
Boston, 1864.

1501 MILL, JOHN STUART. PRINCIPLES of POLITICAL ECONOMY, with some of their applications to Social Philosophy. *2 vols. 8vo. new hf. cf. extra.* New York. 1864

502 MILLER, JOHN. DESCRIPTION OF THE PROVINCE AND CITY OF NEW YORK, With Plans of the City and several Forts as they existed in the year 1695, Edited with an Introduction and Notes by John Gilmary Shea. *4to. cloth, uncut.* New York, 1862.
LARGE PAPER. Gowan's Bib. Americana, No. 3.

1503 MILLS, CHARLES. WORKS. HISTORY OF CHIVALRY, 2 *vols.*; HISTORY OF THE CRUSADES, 2 *vols.*; and HISTORY OF MUHAMMEDANISM, comprising the Life and Character of the Arabian Prophet, 1 *vol. Together 5 vols. 8vo. hf. calf, extra.* London, 1818–22.
FINE UNIFORM SET.

1504 MILLS, CHARLES. TRAVELS OF THEODORE DUCAS, in various countries in Europe, at the Revival of Letters and Art. 2 vols. in one. *8vo. hf. morocco, uncut.* London, 1822.
" An amusing *voyage imaginaire* written with considerable spirit."

1505 MILMAN, HENRY HART. HISTORY OF CHRISTIANITY, including that of the Popes to the Pontificate of Nicholas Vth. 8 *vols. post 8vo. new cloth. Riverside Press,* New York, 1860.

1506 MILTON'S PARADISE LOST. A Poem in Ten Books. FIRST EDITION. *Sm. 4to. calf, gilt.*
London : Printed by S. Simmons, for T. Helder, 1669.
A perfect copy of the *first edition,* with what *Lowndes* terms a *Seventh Title-page ;* the address to the reader, arguments, and table of errata, etc., pp. 356. This copy formerly belonged to E. Blakeway, the Historian of Shrewsbury, England, and has his autograph.
" Milton's contract for the copyright of Paradise Lost with S. Simmons, the bookseller, is dated April 27, 1668 ; and in the course of that year, the first edition of this grand result of intellectual power was given to the world."—*Symmons' Life of Milton.*

1507 MILTON, JOHN. PARADISE LOST. A Poem in twelve books. 2ND EDITION, *revised and augmented by the same author, portrait by Dolle.* 12mo. (*8vo.*) *calf, antique, red edges, very scarce.*
London, 1674.

1508 MILTON, JOHN. PARADISE LOST. *Third Edition.* Revised and augmented by the same author. 12mo. (*8vo.*) *calf, antique, red edges.* London, 1678.
⁎ Bound with this volume, is the FIRST EDITION of PARADISE REGAINED, London, 1680.
The three preceding lots are all fine, clean copies, in perfect condition.

1509 MILTON. PARADISE LOST. TONSON'S EDITION, edited by R. Bentley. Roy. 4to. calf, neat, *scarce.* London, 1732.
LARGE PAPER COPY, but considerably cut down.
In this Edition Bentley amended (?) the text according to his " canons of criticism." It was severely attacked by Bp. Pearce and others. See *D'Israeli's* " *Curiosities of Literature.*"

1510 MILTON, JOHN. PARADISE LOST. Edited with Notes and a Life of Milton by Robert Vaughan, D.D. *Illustrated with 50 large and finely executed plates from the celebrated designs by* GUSTAVE DORÉ. *Roy. 4to. new cloth.* London, 1868.

1511 MILTON, JOHN. PROSE AND POETICAL WORKS. Complete, with Notes and Life of the Author by John Mitford. 4 *vols. impl. 8vo. new cloth. Philadelphia,* 1864.
LARGE PAPER.

1512 Milton. L'Allegro and Il Penseroso, *with 30 illustrations beautifully engraved on wood by celebrated artists,* for the Art Union of London. *4to. new hf. red morocco, scarce.* London, 1848.
Not printed for sale.

1513 MILTON'S PLAGIARISMS. A highly interesting volume: containing Lauder's Two Tracts on Milton's Plagiarisms, 1750–1751; Dr. Douglass' Exposé of Lauder, 1756; Lauder's Recantation and Confession. 4to. (*This confession was drawn up by Dr. Johnson*). Also, Original Autograph Letter of Lauder to Dr. Mead (unpublished). Two Original Autograph Letters by Claude Saumaise (Salmasius, the Adversary of Milton). *Portraits, &c. Sm. 4to. hf. morocco, gilt.*
London, V. D.
An Interesting Collection. From Mr. Dillon's Library.
For an account of this controversy and Dr. Johnson's connection therewith, see Boswell's Life.

1514 Minutes of a Conspiracy against the Liberties of America. 4to. *boards.* *Philadelphia: John Campbell,* 1865.

1515 Mirabaud, M. System of Nature; or, the Laws of the Moral and Physical World; translated from the French. *Portrait.* 3 *vols. in one. 8vo. hf. mor. uncut.* London, 1820.

1516 Mirabeau, M. de. Nature, and her Laws; as applicable to the happiness of man, living in society, contrasted with Superstition and Imaginary Systems. 2 vols. thick 8vo. bds.
London, 1816.

1517 MIRROR for MAGISTRATES; edited, with Historical Notes, &c., by Haslewood. 3 vols. *4to. calf, gilt,* (only 150 copies printed). London, 1815.
The popularity of this work, and its influence on our National Poetry throughout the reigns of Elizabeth and James I. were very considerable. The excellent notes of the editor render this edition the most valuable and interesting.

1518 MISSAL ROMANUM. Ex decreto sacrosancti Concilii Tridentini restitutum S. Pii V. Pontificis Maximi Jussu editum Clementis VIII et Urbani VIII, &c., &c. *Elegantly printed, with rubricated text, the Missal notation, &c. Folio, handsomely bound in vellum, extra gilt, carmine edges.* Romæ, 1846.
Fine Copy, authorized version.

1519 Mitchell and Dickie. The Philosophy of Witchcraft. 12mo. Also, Beecher's Review of " Spiritual Manifestations." 2 vols. in one. 16mo. *hf. green morocco, uncut.* Paisley, 1839, &c.
A very curious and little known work; full of original narratives, documents, &c. Scarce.

1520 Mitford, William. History of Greece, from the earliest accounts to the end of the Trojan War. 8 *vols. 8vo. cf. gilt.*
London, 1814.

1521 Monstrelet's Chronicles of England and Wales, in continuation of Froissart's. Translated by Col. Johnes, with Notes. *Upwards of 100 wood-cuts. 2 vols. imp. 8vo. hf. morocco, gilt.*
London, 1840.
See Froissart.

19

1522 Montagu, Lady Mary Wortley. Letters and Works. Edited by Lord Wharncliffe. 3d Edition, with additions and a new Memoir, by W. Moy Thomas. *Portraits.* 2 vols. 8vo. *handsomely bound in tree-calf, extra.* London, 1861.
Fine Copy of the Best Edition.
"Lady Montagu's Letters are clever, spirited and easy, and invaluable for the traits of manner they have preserved of her own times."

1523 Montaigne, Michael de. Works of, comprising his Essays, Journey into Italy, and Letters, with Notes from all his Commentators, Biographical and Bibliographical Notices, by W. Hazlitt. New Edition, revised by O. W. Wight. *Portrait on India paper, Montaigne's Arms in gold and colors on the titles.* 4 vols. 8vo. *half morocco, uncut, by* Matthews.
Best Edition. *Riverside Press,* Cambridge, 1864.
Large Paper. *75 copies printed, 4 of which were destroyed by fire, at Richardson's.*
This copy has the extra illuminated title-pages.

1524 ——— Another Copy. 4 *vols. crown 8vo. calf, extra.*
New York, 1861.

1525 Montalembert, Count de. Monks of the West, from St. Benedict to St. Bernard. *Authorized translation.* 5 vols. 8vo. new cloth, *uncut.* Edinburgh, 1861.
Priced by Scribner & Co. at $40 in cloth.

1526 Montesquieu. Works (Spirit of Laws, &c.), complete, translated from the French, with Memoir, &c. 4 vols. *hf. green morocco, gilt, yellow edges.* London, 1794.

1527 MONTFAUCON'S Antiquities Explained, translated by Humphreys, with the Supplement, *upwards of 1000 engravings of antiquities,* 7 vols. *folio, calf, neat.* London, 1721–4.
Fine clean copy, from the library of Wm. Mitford, with his autograph, notes, &c.
"The great storehouse from which all succeeding writers on the subject have borrowed : no historical library should be without Montfaucon."

1528 Montpensier, Mademoiselle de. Memoirs of, written by herself. *Portrait.* 2 vols. *post 8vo. hf. vellum, gilt tops, uncut edges.*
London, 1848.

1529 MOOR, E. HINDU PANTHEON. Plates Illustrating the Hindu Pantheon. Edited, with brief descriptive Index, by the Rev. A. P. Moor. 104 *plates, roy. 4to. new cloth, gilt.*
London, 1861.
These plates form a valuable accompaniment to Wilson's Vishnu Purana, the Rig-Veda, and other Mythological Works of India.

1530 Moore, Frank. Diary of the American Revolution, from Newspapers and Original Documents. *Numerous portraits.* 2 *vols. 8vo. uncut.* New York, 1863.

1531 Moore, Frank. Heroes and Martyrs; Notable Men of the Time, Biographical Sketches of the Military and Naval Heroes, Statesmen, and Orators. *Numerous fine portraits on steel. Roy. 4to. new hf. morocco, extra, gilt top, uncut edges.*
New York, 1861.

1532 Moore, Geo. H. Historical Notes on the Employment of Negroes in the American Army of the Revolution. *8vo. pp. 24, paper.*
New York, 1862.

1533 MOORE, GEORGE H. Notes on the History of Slavery in Massachusetts. *8vo. new cloth.* New York, 1866.

1534 MOORE, GEORGE H. Treason of Major General Charles Lee, second in command in the American Army of the Revolution. *Portrait and fac-similes. 8vo. cloth, uncut.* New York, 1860.

1535 MOORE, THOMAS. The EPICUREAN; A Tale. *New Edition. 12mo. new cloth.* London, 1856.

1536 MOORE, THOMAS. THE FUDGER FUDGED; or, the Devil and T***y M***e, by the Editor of the New Whig Guide. (In Verse.) *Vignettes.* 12mo. bds. London, 1819.
A reply to the "Fudge Family in Paris."

1537 MOORE, THOMAS. LALLAH ROOKH. *With Illustrations from designs by Tenniel.* Post 8vo. hf. roxb. morocco, *uncut.*
New York, 1867.

1538 MOORE, THOMAS. Loves of the Angels; a Poem, with Notes. *8vo. calf, gilt.* London, 1823.
ORIGINAL EDITION. *Scarce.*

1539 MOORE, THOMAS. Memoirs of Richard Brinsley Sheridan. *Portrait.* 2 vols. 12mo. cloth. N. York, 1866.

1540 [MOORE, THOMAS.] Poetical Works of the late Thomas Little. [Amatory Poems.] *16mo. hf. cf. scarce.* 1803.

1541 MORGAN'S PHŒNIX BRITANNICUS, a miscellaneous Collection of Scarce and Curious Tracts in Prose and Verse, 4to. *calf, neat, scarce.* London, 1732.
Contains seventy-four most curious and rare pieces, Historical, Political, Biographical, Satirical, &c., many nowhere else published.

CHOICE ILLUSTRATED COPY.

1542 MORLAND, GEORGE. MEMOIRS of the LIFE of, with Descriptive and Critical Observations on the whole of his Works, by J. Hassell. *Having, in addition to the plates belonging to the works, upwards of 70 beautiful engravings inserted, comprising Portraits, Views, and specimens of his most celebrated pictures, including several brilliant proof plates, &c.* Roy. 4to. *handsomely bound in hf. crimson morocco, extra, gilt edges.* London, 1806.

1543 (MORLEY, H.) REALMAH. *2 vols. post 8vo. new cloth, uncut.*
London, 1868.

1544 MORRIS, R. R. BRITISH GAME BIRDS and WILD FOWL. 60 *large and very* BEAUTIFULLY COLORED plates *of Birds,* with descriptions. London, 1864.
A very beautiful Ornithological work, the plates of which are remarkable for the truthfulness of their drawing.

1545 MORRIS'S HISTORY OF BRITISH BIRDS; *containing upwards of* 350 *accurate and* BEAUTIFULLY COLORED PLATES *of Birds.* 6 *vols. roy. 8vo. new hf. morocco.* London, 1866.
"It is a work which every lover of nature, every one who wishes to become intimately acquainted with the feathered TRIBES of our land, ought by all means to possess himself of. The peculiar and happy manner in which each bird is introduced, its history given, its habits and peculiarities described, and the numerous anecdotes contained in each history, impart a charm of no ordinary kind to the work."—*Naturalist.*

1546 MORRIS'S NESTS AND EGGS OF BRITISH BIRDS, described, *with* 223 COLORED PLATES *of Nests and Eggs*. *3 vols. thick royal 8vo. new hf. morocco, gilt.* London, 1865.
This work is a fitting pendant to the preceding lot; all the nests and eggs were drawn from actual specimens, in most cases the name of the persons from whom the Author obtained these objects, being given.

1547 **MORRIS'S HISTORY OF BRITISH BUTTERFLIES;** *with* 70 EXQUISITELY COLORED PLATES, *containing several hundred figures of Butterflies in their various transformations. Royal 8vo. new hf. mor. extra.* London, 1865.

1548 MORT D'ARTHUR. History of King Arthur and the Knights of the Round Table, compiled by Sir Thomas Mallory, with Introduction and Notes by Thomas Wright. 4 vols. *post 8vo. cloth, uncut.* *Russell Smith*, London, 1858.
LARGE PAPER.

1549 MORTILLET, GABRIEL DE. LE SIGNE DE LA CROIX avant le Christianisme, *illustrated with* 117 *engravings on wood. Sml. 4to. paper, uncut.* Paris, 1866.
The author attempts to prove that the use of the cross as an emblem of Religion, was used prior to the time of Christ.

1550 MOSHEIM'S ECCLESIASTICAL HISTORY, ancient and modern, translated by Maclaine, continued to the present time by Coote. 2 *vols. 8vo. new hf. morocco, gilt.* London, 1838.

1551 MOTLEY, J. L. HISTORY of the UNITED NETHERLANDS, 4 vols., and RISE OF THE DUTCH REPUBLIC, 3 vols. *Maps and plates,* together 7 vols. 8vo. new hf. *blue cf. extra.* New York, 1868.
FINE COPY.

1552 MOTTEAUX, PETER. The Island Princess, or the Generous Portuguese, made into an Opera, &c. *sml. 4to. hf. vellum.*
London, 1699.

1553 MOURT'S RELATION, or Journal of the Plantation at Plymouth, with Introduction and Notes by Henry M. Dexter. *Maps, &c.* Roy. 4to. *uncut.* Boston, 1865.
LARGE PAPER. 35 *copies only.*

1554 MOZART, WOLFGANG AMADEUS. LETTERS, translated by Lady Wallace. *Portrait.* 2 vols. 12mo. new hf. cf. extra.
New York, 1866.

1554* ———— Letters from Switzerland. 16mo. new hf. cf. extra.
New York, 1865.

1555 MÜLLER, FRITZ. Facts and Arguments for Darwin, translated by W. S. Dallas. *Illustrations, crown 8vo. new cloth.* London, 1869.

1556 MULLER, J. Principles of Physics and Meteorology. *Colored front. and numerous woodcuts.* Thick 8vo. cloth. London, 1847.

1557 MÜLLER, MAX. CHIPS FROM A GERMAN WORKSHOP. 2 vols. 8vo. *new cloth, uncut.* London, 1868.

1558 MÜLLER, MAX. Lectures on the Science of Language, delivered at the Royal Institution of Great Britain. BOTH SERIES. 2 *vols. fcap. 8vo. new cloth.* New York, 1865.

1559 MÜLLER, MAX. On the Stratification of Language. Sir Robert Rede's Lecture. *P. 8vo. cloth.* London, 1868.

1560 MULLER, F. MAX. RIG-VEDA-SANHITA. The Sacred Hymns of the Brahmans, translated and explained. Vol. I. (all published). *8vo. new cloth, uncut.* London, 1869.

1561 MUNSELL'S HISTORICAL SERIES, complete.
    I. COMMISSARY WILSON'S ORDERLY BOOK. Expedition of the British and Provincial Army, under Major-General Jeffrey Amherst, against Ticonderoga and Crown Point, 1759. *Map.* 1857.
    II. NARRATIVE OF THE CAUSES WHICH LED TO PHILLIP'S INDIAN WAR OF 1675 and 1676, by Jno. Easton, &c. Edited by F. B. Hough. *Map.* 1858.
    III. ORDERLY BOOK OF THE NORTHERN ARMY, AT TICONDEROGA and Mt. Independence, from October 17, 1776 to January 8, 1776. With Biographical and Explanatory Notes, &c. *Portrait and Map.* 1859.
    IV. DIARY OF THE SIEGE OF DETROIT in the War with Pontiac. Also a Narrative of the Principal Events of the Siege, by Major Robert Rogers. Edited by Franklin B. Hough. *Facsimiles.* 1860.
    V. OBSTRUCTIONS TO THE NAVIGATION OF HUDSON'S RIVER; embracing the Minutes of the Secret Committee, appointed by the Provincial Convention of New York, July 16, 1776. *Map and cuts.* 1860.
    VI. THE LOYAL VERSES OF JOSEPH STANSBURY and Dr. JONATHAN ODELL, relating to the American Revolution. Edited by Winthrop Sargent. 1860.
    VII. ORDERLY BOOK OF LIEUT. GEN. JOHN BURGOYNE, from his entry into the State of New York, until his Surrender at Saratoga, October, 1777. Edited by Dr. E. B. O'Callaghan. *Map and plates.* 1860.
    VIII. EARLY VOYAGES UP AND DOWN THE MISSISSIPPI, by Cavilier, St. Cosme, Le Seur, Gravier, and Guignas. Edited with Notes, &c., by John Gilmary Shea. 1861.
    IX & X. PROCEEDINGS OF THE COMMISSIONERS OF INDIAN AFFAIRS, appointed by law for the Extinguishment of Indian Titles in the State of New York. Edited by F. B. Hough. 2 vols. 1861.
    Together 10 vols. small 4to. *uniformly bound in hf. olive morocco, gilt tops, uncut edges.* Albany, 1857–1861.
    A FINE SET. *The Maps are all mounted on linen.*

1562 MUNSELL'S COLLECTIONS ON THE HISTORY OF ALBANY from its Discovery to the Present Time. *Engravings, 2 thick vols. roy. 8vo. uncut.* Albany, 1865.

1563 MUNSELL. PROCEEDINGS OF A CONVENTION OF DELEGATES from several of the New England States held at Boston, August 3–9, 1780, to advise on affairs necessary to promote the most vigorous prosecution of the War, &c., &c. with Introduction and notes by Franklin B. Hough. *4to. bds. uncut.*
Munsell, Albany, 1867.
    Only 100 copies, uniform with Munsell's Historical Series.

1564 Murchison, Sir Roderick Impey. Siluria. The History of the Oldest Fossiliferous rocks and their foundations, with a brief sketch of the distribution of Gold over the earth. *Maps and numerous woodcuts, thick 8vo. new cloth.* London, 1859.
Third Edition, including the Silurian System.

1565 Murphy, Joseph J. Habit and Intelligence, in their connexion with the Laws of Matter and Force; a series of Scientific Essays. *2 vols. 8vo. new cloth.* London, 1869.

1566 MUSÉE FRANÇAIS, ou Collection Complette des Tableaux, Statues, et bas-reliefs, qui composent la collection Nationale, avec l'explications des sujets et des Discours sur la Peinture, la Sculpture, et la gravure par S. C. Croze, Magnan, Robillard, Peronville, Laurent, Visconti, et David. 343 *superb plates,* 4 vols. atlas folio. *hf. red morocco, uncut.* Paris, 1819.
L'un des plus beaux monumens élevés aux art est, contredit, cette vaste collection d'estampes, commencée en 1802, sous le nom de Musée Français, par MM. Laurent père et fils. A l'exposition de 1819, le medaille d'or fut decernée à Mr. Henri Laurent, jury considerant cet ouvrage comme le plus parfait qui ait eu lieu depuis l'existence de la gravure.
This very interesting publication is undoubtedly the most magnificent work that has issued from the Parisian Press; and will perpetuate the matchless collection which formerly graced the Louvre, combining as it did nearly all of the excellence of which the various countries on the Continent could boast of in painting and sculpture. And although a chain of wonderful events has restored many of the brightest gems of art to their rightful owners, so much of excellence still remains, that the gallery of the Louvre is yet, to the man of taste, the greatest attraction in Paris, and the very circumstance of the dispersion of so many wonderful productions gives additional value to the work which describes them in a collected state.
It is necessary to observe, that this work is not a mere collection of Prints, as it contains many luminous and masterly dissertations upon the state of the arts in different ages, observations upon the style, excellence, and defects of the various schools in painting; a minute description of every painting, &c., drawn with extreme care and correctness.

1567 MUSÉE ROYAL (*Secrete*) DE NAPLES. Peintures, Bronzes, et Statues Érotiques du Cabinet Secret. Avec leur explication par le Colonel Famin. Best Edition, *comprising 60 engraved plates, colored after the original examples. 4to. half red morocco, extra, edges uncut.* Paris, par l'Auteur, 1857.
A limited edition.
The only work in which the celebrated frescoes and ornaments are colored.

1568 Museum Florentinum, exhibens insigniora Vetustatis Monumenta quæ Florentiæ sunt in Thesauro Mediceo, studio Gorii. *Several hundred beautifully engraved plates of Gems, Medals, Coins, Statues, &c., &c. 6 vols. royal folio, elegantly bound in old crimson morocco, extra gilt backs and sides, and gilt leaves, with the name of its previous owner* (F. Morton, 1748) *impressed on the edges.*
Florent., 1731, &c.
This fine old copy comprises the Numismata, 3 vols. Gemmæ Antiqua, 2 vols., and Statues, 1 vol.
Complete sets of this "Collection très curieuse," were priced, 1821; Thorpe, £50; Bohn, £25; and the Marquis of Townshend's copy fetched £69. 6s.

1569 Museum of Painting and Sculpture, a Collection of the principal Pictures, Statues, &c. in the Galleries of Europe, 17 *vols. sm. 8vo. hf. crimson morocco, uncut,* (pub. £17. 17s.) Paris, 1829.
A choice copy.
This interesting work contains 1200 outline engravings, executed in a masterly style, and will be found extremely useful as a book of reference to the amateur and print collector. Annexed are descriptive notices.

1570 Musical Library. Vocal and Instrumental. English and Foreign, edited by W. Ayrton (of the Opera House), comprising upwards of 200 pieces of music by the most eminent composers. *4 vols. folio, hf. morocco.* London, 1843.

By far the best collection of music ever offered within the same compass, comprehending many of the most admired English Songs, Glees, Madrigals, &c.

1571 Muspratt, Dr. S. Chemistry, Theoretical, Practical, and Analytical, as applied to the Arts and Manufactures. *Illustrated with nearly 50 fine steel portraits, and numerous woodcuts. 2 vols. thick impl. 8vo. new hf. cf. antique.* London, 1860.

Best edition.

1572 Nantucket Papers, &c., edited by Franklin B. Hough. *Small 4to. hf. morocco.* Albany, 1856.

Privately printed, 150 *copies.*

1573 NAPIER. HISTORY of the WAR in the PENINSULA, and in the South of France, from 1807 to 1814. *Plans of battles,* etc. Best Library Edition. 6 *vols. 8vo. half calf, neat.* very scarce. London, 1832, etc.

Best edition; including the justificatory pieces in reply to Gurwood, Alison, Sir Walter Scott, Lord Beresford, and the Quarterly Review.

1574 Napoleon III. History of Julius Cæsar, with Atlas. 2 vols. 8vo. new cloth, and 4to. atlas. New York, 1865.

1575 Narraganset Club. Publications of the Narraganset Club. (First Series). 3 *vols. roy. 4to. sheets folded.* .
Providence, R. I., MDCCCLXVI–VII.

Large Paper; only 50 copies printed. Contents: Vol. 1. Williams' Key unto the Language of America. II. Cotton's Answer to Roger Williams, and Queries of Highest Consideration. III. The Bloudy Tenent of Persecution. Edited by S. L. Caldwell.

1576 Nason, Elias. Sir Charles Henry Frankland, Bart., or Boston in the Colonial Times. *8vo. uncut. Munsell,* Albany, 1865.
1577 ——— The Same. Impl. *8vo. uncut.* Albany, 1865.
Large paper.

1578 NATIONAL PORTRAIT GALLERY of DISTINGUISHED AMERICANS, conducted by James B. Longacre and James Herring. *Brilliant Impressions of the numerous Portraits. 4 vols. roy. 8vo. turkey morocco, antique, gilt edges.* Philadelphia, 1859.

1579 ——— Another copy. 4 vols. roy. 8vo. mor. antique.
Philadelphia, 1859.

1580 NEALE, J. P. MANSIONS of ENGLAND; or, Picturesque Delineations of the Seats of Noblemen and Gentlemen, arranged in counties. *Upwards of 400 fine engravings from drawings by J. P. Neale.* India proof impressions. *2 thick vols. roy. 4to. hf. olive morocco, extra, uncut.* London, 1847.

Fine early copy.

1581 Neill, E. D. The History of Minnesota; from the Earliest French Explorations to the Present Time. By Edward Duffield Neill. *Numerous fine steel plates on* India paper. *Roy. 4to. cloth. Philadelphia: J. B. Lippincott & Co.,* 1858.

Only 100 *copies printed.*

1582 NERE, PHILIP. Cursory Remarks on some of the Ancient English
Poets, particularly Milton. 8vo. *hf. morocco, uncut, scarce.*
Privately Printed, London, 1789.
Only 200 copies printed, for private distribution.
W. E. Burton's copy.

1583 NEW ENGLISH CYCLOPEDIA. A new Dictionary of Universal Knowledge, conducted by CHARLES KNIGHT, *with several
thousand engravings on wood.* 24 vols. 4to. *new cloth, gilt.*
London, 1854–66.
Comprises Geography, 5 vols. Arts and Sciences, 8 vols. Natural History,
4 vols. Biography, 6 vols., and Index, 1 vol.
The above is an entirely new edition of the celebrated *Penny Cyclopædia,* of
whose merits it is sufficient to say that no work of its class has enjoyed a
wider sale or more extended celebrity. Certainly none is better adapted for
general use.

1584 NEWGATE CALENDAR: Memoirs of the most notorious Characters,
Murderers, Traitors, Highwaymen and Thieves of every
Description, from the commencement of the 18th Century,
with their Speeches, Confessions, &c., by Knapp and Baldwin.
Engravings by Cruikshank. 4 vols. 8vo. *calf, neat, scarce.*
London, 1824.

1585 NEWMAN, FRANCIS W. THEISM, Doctrinal and Practical, or Di-
dactic Religious Utterances. *4to. cloth.* London, 1858.

1586 NEWMAN, REV. JOHN HENRY. PAROCHIAL and PLAIN SERMONS,
complete. *New Edition.* 8 vols. crown 8vo. *new cloth, uncut.*
London, 1868.

1587 NEWMARKET; or, an Essay on the Turf; a parallel between the
Newmarket races and the Olympic Games. 2 vols. in one, 12mo.
cf. London, 1771.

1588 NEWS FROM THE INVISIBLE WORLD; or, interesting anecdotes of
the Dead, containing a particular survey of the most remarkable and well authenticated Accounts of APPARITIONS, GHOSTS,
SPECTRES, DREAMS and VISIONS, &c. *Frontispiece.* 8vo. *calf,
gilt, scarce.* Leeds, 1815.
Very curious.

1589 NEWS from NEW ENGLAND, Being A True and last Account of the
present Bloody Wars carried on betwixt the Infidels, Natives,
and the English-Christians, and Converted Indians of New
England. *Roy. 4to. boards.* Boston, N. E., *Reprinted,* 1850.

1590 ——— Another copy. *Roy. 4to.* (fol.) *bds. uncut.* Boston, 1850.
LARGEST PAPER. *One of 4 copies on Drawing Paper.*

1591 NEWS from New England. [Another Edition.] *4to. half morocco,
gilt top, uncut, by Bradstreet.*
Albany: *Reprinted by Munsell for W. E. Woodward,* 1865.
LARGE PAPER; only 60 copies printed, on one side of the paper only.

1592 NEW TESTAMENT. ENGLISH HEXAPLA, exhibiting the Six important English translations of the New Testament Scriptures,
viz. Wicliff, 1380—Tyndale, 1534—Cranmer, 1539—Genevan, 1557—Anglo-Rhemish, 1582—Authorised, 1611. The
original Greek text after Scholz, &c., &c. *Thick roy. 4to. hf.
morocco, carmine edges.* *Bagster,* London, N. D.
The six principal English Versions of the New Testament are arranged in parallel columns, beneath the Greek Original Text. The meaning of the original is
reflected from the renderings of six independent Translations on the same
page.

1593 New Testament of our Lord and Saviour Jesus Christ. *A facsimile of the celebrated Genevan Testament,* 1557, with the marginal annotations and references, initial and other woodcuts, Prefaces, Indexes, &c. *Thick 12mo. sprinkled calf, extra, carmine edges.*
[Geneva, *Conrad Badius,* MDLVII.] London, *Bagster.*

1594 New York City During the Revolution. A Collection of Original Papers, published from the Original MSS. in the Possession of the Mercantile Library Association. *Map. 4to. boards, uncut.*
Privately Printed for the Association, New York, 1861.

1595 New York, College of. A Letter to the Governors of the College of New York, respecting the collection that was made in this kingdom in 1762–3 for the Colleges of Philadelphia and New York, with an Appendix, &c., by Sir James Jay. *8vo. (pp. 42), wholly uncut, hf. morocco.* London, 1771.

1596 New York Crystal Palace. Illustrated Description of the Building by G. Carstensen and C. Gildemeister, Architects. *Frontispiece in oil colors, and six large plates, comprising elevations, sections, &c. 4to. cloth.* New York, 1854.

1597 New York. Documents relative to the Colonial History of the State of New York, procured in Holland, England and France by J. R. Brodhead, Esq., edited by Dr. E. B. O'Callaghan. Numerous Maps, Charts, &c., *with an elaborate* Index. Together 11 thick vols. roy. 4to. cloth. Albany, 1856.
The Index is generally wanting in sets.

1598 New York. Documentary History of the State of New York, arranged under Direction of the Secretary of State. *Maps and plates.* 4 vols. 4to. cloth. Albany, 1850–51.

1599 NEW YORK HERALD. A File of, covering the entire period of the War of the Rebellion, from January, 1861, to June, 1865, with numerous cuttings, &c., comprising Reports of Battles, &c., from other papers, inserted. *11 vols. roy. folio, hf. sheep.* New York, 1861–65.
Formerly belonging to the late Fred. S. Cozzens, who contemplated compiling an account of the principal occurrences of the late war.

1600 NEW YORK. NATURAL HISTORY of the STATE, comprising: Zoology, 5 vols. [*Ornithology and Mollusca colored*]; Botany, 2 vols. *colored;* Mineralogy, 1 vol.; Geology, 4 vols. *some colored;* Agriculture, 5 vols. *colored;* Palæontology, 3 vols. in 4; and Introduction by W. H. Seward, 1 vol. Together 22 *vols. thick roy. 4to. cloth.* Albany, 1842–61.
Fine Copy, formerly belonging to the Hon. W. H. Seward, with his manuscript annotations and corrections to the Introduction, and including the two recently published volumes of Palæontology.
"The preparation of this splendid work by the ablest scientific men of the country has cost the State upwards of 200,000 dollars, and is a brilliant example of enlightened legislative liberality. As a work embracing every department of Natural History, it must find a place in the library of all scientific men, as well as of all persons of taste and refinement."

1601 New York Sanitary Fair. Spirit of the Fair, a complete set, 16 Nos.; also "Our Daily Fare," organ of the Philadelphia Fair, complete in 12 Nos. *In one vol. 4to. hf. morocco.*
Scarce. New York & Philadelphia, 1864.

1602 NICHOLS. LITERARY ANECDOTES of the Eighteenth Century, 9 vols.; and ILLUSTRATIONS of the LITERARY HISTORY of the Eighteenth Century, 8 vols. *Together* 17 *vols. 8vo. hf. morocco, neat.* London, 1812–59.

FINE CLEAN COPY, *from the Library of* THOMAS BUCKLE, *with his book-plate.*
It is impossible in a small space to give anything like an adequate idea of the vast amount of curious information which these volumes contain. The hundreds of literary celebrities who are brought forward, not merely by passing anecdotes, but by highly valuable memoirs and sketches, and the extensive bibliographical and literary matter which it contains, render it one of the most permanently interesting sets of books ever published.

1603 NICHOLLS, J. F. SEBASTIAN CABOT. The Remarkable Life, Adventures and Discoveries of. *Portrait, handsomely printed in antique style.* Sm. 4to. *new cloth.*

Chiswick Press, London, 1869.

For a very interesting notice of this book see Stevens' Bibliotheca Historica, Catalogue of the Library of Henry Stevens, sold in Boston, April, 1870.

1604 NICHOL, J. P. ARCHITECTURE of the HEAVENS. 9th Edition. *Profusely illustrated.* 8vo. *cloth.* London, 1851.

1605 NICHOL, J. P. CONTEMPLATIONS on the SOLAR SYSTEM. *Profusely illustrated with Diagrams, &c.,* post 8vo. *cloth, uncut, scarce.* Edinburgh, 1844.

1606 NICHOL, J. P. The Planet Neptune; an Exposition and History. Front. post 8vo. *cloth, scarce.* Edinburgh, 1848.

1607 NICHOL, J. P. The PLANETARY SYSTEM; its Order, and Physical Structure. *Illustrated with diagrams,* crown 8vo. *cloth.*

London, 1851.

1608 NICHOL, J. P. Thoughts on some Important Points relating to the System of the World. *Profusely illustrated,* post 8vo. *cloth, uncut.* Edinburgh, 1848

1609 ———— Another copy, post 8vo. *cloth.* Edinburgh, 1848.

1610 NICHOL, J. P. VIEWS of the ARCHITECTURE of the HEAVENS. *Profusely illustrated,* crown 8vo. *new cloth.* Edinburgh, 1845.

1611 NICHOLAS, SIR HARRIS. MEMOIRS and LITERARY REMAINS of LADY JANE GREY. LARGE and THICK PAPER, *portrait on India paper* and Genealogical table. 8vo. *dark maroon morocco, extra, gilt edges.* London, 1831.

VERY SCARCE. *Only few copies printed.* (?)
"This work contains every known production of Lady Jane Grey's pen, and the notes present an elaborate investigation of her claim to the throne."— *Lowndes.*

1612 NICHOLSON, WM. History of the Wars occasioned by the French Revolution, &c., &c., *profusely illustrated with colored portraits, folio, calf, gilt.* London, N. D.

1613 NIEBUHR, B. G. HISTORICAL WORKS, comprising Lectures on the History of Rome, 3 vols.; Lectures on Ancient History, 3 vols.; and History of Rome, 3 vols.; together 9 vols. 8vo. *new hf. calf, extra, marbled edges.* London, 1852, &c.

BEST LIBRARY EDITION.
"A thousand points in the history of Ancient Nations, which have hitherto been either overlooked or accepted without inquiry, are here treated with sound criticism and placed in their true light."

1614 NILES' WEEKLY REGISTER; containing Political, Historical, Geographical, Scientific, Statistical, Economical and Biographical Documents, Essays and Tracts; together with Notices of the Arts and Manufactures, and Record of the Events of the Times, by Hezekiah Niles. FIRST SERIES, *complete with Index and Supplements* to Vols. 5, 9, 15, 16, 23, 38 and 43. QUARTO SERIES, edited by W. Ogden Niles and Jeremiah Hughes. 23 vols. Together 74 vols. roy. 8vo. and 4to. *uniformly bound in hf. sheep.*
Baltimore, Philadelphia and Washington, 1811-49.
FINE COPY IN GOOD ORDER.
" Perfectly reliable and invaluble as a book of reference."

1615 NILES' WEEKLY REGISTER. Vols. 3–14, except vol. 8. FOURTH SERIES, 1830–36. 11 *vols. 8vo. hf. sheep.*
Baltimore, 1836, &c.

1616 NILSSON'S, SEVEN. Primitive Inhabitants of Scandinavia. An Essay on comparative Ethnography, and a contribution to the history of the development of mankind. Edited with an Introduction by Sir John Lubbock. *Numerous plates, 8vo. new cloth, uncut.* London, 1868.

1617 " NIMROD " (Charles James Apperly). LIFE OF A SPORTSMAN, *with* 36 *large* COLORED *illustrations from drawings by Alken.* Thick 8vo. *new cloth, gilt edges, scarce.* London, 1842.

1618 NINON DE LENCLOS. MEMOIRS OF, with her Letters to M. de St. Everemond and the Marquis de Sevigné, translated from the French. 2 vols. 12mo. hf. cf. *neat, scarce.* London, 1761.

1619 NIVELON, F. The Rudiments of Genteel Behavior. *A series of* 12 *copperplates by Boitard after Dandridge.* 4to. hf. cf. *neat.*
1737.

John Allan's copy.

1620 NOBLE, MARK. Memoirs of the Protectorate-House of Cromwell. *Portrait, Maps, &c.* 2 vols. 8vo. hf. calf, *neat.*
Birmingham, 1784.

1621 NORDHOFF, CHARLES. Cape Cod and All Along Shore; Stories. 12*mo. cloth.* New York, 1868.

1622 NORTH AMERICAN REVIEW and MISCELLANEOUS JOURNAL. A COMPLETE SET from its commencement in May, 1815, to and including Jan. 1870. 110 vols. 95 vols. *uniformly bound in hf. russia, neat, and Vols.* 3, 4, 62 *and* 98–110 *in numbers.* WITH THE SCARCE INDEX in bds. *Together* 111 *vols.*
Boston, 1815–70.

₊ COMPLETE SETS ARE VERY SCARCE.
" The *North American Review*, the oldest and most prosperous of the American reviews, was established in 1815, and writing its history is almost writing the history of the Literature of the United States. Its Founder was William Tudor, who, after the lapse of two years, relinquished his proprietorship to Wilhert Philips, or rather to the Anthologia Club, which had been reconstituted under the name of the North American Club, and the most active members of which were Sparks, Channing, and R. H. Dana. In 1820 the chief editorship devolved upon Mr. Edw. Everett, who, in the course of four years, contributed nearly 50 Articles; he resigned the editorship in 1823 to Jared Sparks, who was followed in 1829 by Alexander Everett (the elder brother of Edward Everett), who continued chief editor until 1835, when Dr. Palfrey undertook the management, which he continued until 1842, when it passed

into the hands of Mr. Francis Bowen; afterwards by the Rev. H. P. Peabody and Charles Eliot Norton, and more recently by Profs. James Russell Lowell and E. W. Gurney, its present editors. Besides Jared Sparks and the two Everetts, almost all the prominent writers of the United States have contributed to the *N. A. Review*, among them Joseph Story, Henry Wheaton, Daniel Webster, Prescott, Bancroft, W. C. Bryant (whose first poem, 'Thanatopsis,' appeared in its columns). Its literary criticisms emanated chiefly from the pens of R. H. Dana, Longfellow, Dr. Cheeve, and Whipple. Eminent service was rendered to philosophical studies by the pens of James Marsh, O. A. Brownson, Dr. Walker, Theodore Parker, W. R. Greene, and Francis Bowen."—*Clavigny*, "*Histoire de la Presse en Angleterre et aux États-Unis.*"

1623 NORTH BRITISH REVIEW, from its commencement in May 1844 to August 1852; also Numbers from Feb. '53 to August 1855. 17 vols. 8vo. new hf. calf, *neat*, and 6 vols. in Nos. Together 23 vols. 8vo. London, 1844–55.

1624 Norton, John Pitkin. Memorials of. *4to. sheets, folded.*
For Private Distribution, Albany, 1853.

1625 NOSTRADAMUS' True Prophecies and Prognostications. A work full of Curiosity and Learning, in French and English Verse, with Annotations by Garencieres. *Folio, calf, gilt.*
London, 1672.

"An amusing book, full of odd stories."

1626 NOTES and QUERIES. A Medium of Inter-Communication for Literary Men, General Readers, &c. A complete set from its commencement in November 1849 to December 1869, inclusive, with 3 Indexes. *The 1st and 2d series bound in hf. cf. antique, the remainder in new cloth, uncut.* Togther 42 vols. *sm. 4to.* London, 1849–69.

A fine, clean, and perfect set of this important periodical.

1627 Nott and Gliddon. Indigenous Races of the Earth; or, New Chapters of Ethnological Inquiry, including monographs on special departments of Philology, Iconography, Palæontology, &c., &c. *Large folding map, colored plates*, and *numerous woodcuts; thick imp. 8vo. morocco antique.* Philadelphia, 1857.
Subscription Edition.

1628 Nott and Gliddon. Types of Mankind; or Ethnological Researches, based upon the Ancient Monuments, Paintings, Sculptures, and Crania of Races. *Profusely illustrated. Thick 8vo. cloth.* Philadelphia, 1857.

1629 Novum Testamentum Græce. Augustus Hahn, *post 8vo. hf. mor.*
Lipsiæ, 1840.

1630 NUGENT, Maria, *Lady.* Journal of a Voyage to, and Residence in, the Island of Jamaica from 1801 to 1805, and of subsequent events in England from 1805–1811. *Portraits*, and *plates of Costumes.* 2 vols. Journal from the Year 1811 till the Year 1815, including a Voyage to and Residence in India, &c. *Together 4 vols. 8vo. dark-green morocco, extra, marbled-gilt edges.* Very Scarce. London, 1839.
Privately Printed.

From the Library of W. K. Eyton, who has inserted an autograph letter of Lord Nugent, and "Sonnet on Reading the Journals of Lady Nugent."

"Lady Nugent was the wife of Sir George Nugent, Bart., seventh daughter of Cortland Skinner, Esq., Attorney-General and Speaker of the House of Assembly of New Jersey, N. A." &c.

1631 O'CALLAGHAN, E. B. List of Editions of the Holy Scriptures and Parts thereof, printed in America Previous to 1860. With Introduction and Bibliographical Notes. *Fac-similes.* *Imperial 8vo. boards, uncut.* Munsell, Albany, 1861. ONLY 150 COPIES.

1632 O'CALLAGHAN, E. B. Brief and True Narrative of the Hostile Conduct of the Barbarous Natives towards the Dutch Nation. *Translated.* Impl. 8vo. hf. *red morocco, uncut, by Bradstreet.* Munsell, Albany, 1863. LARGE PAPER, *few printed.*

1633 O'CALLAGHAN, DR. E. B. The Register of New Netherland 1626 to 1674. *Roy. 8vo. boards, uncut.* Munsell, Albany, 1865. LARGE PAPER.

1634 OCELLUS, LUCANUS. On the Nature of the Universe; Taurus, on the Eternity of the World; Junius Firmicus, Maternus of the Thema Mundi, &c., translated by *Thomas Taylor. Post 8vo. bds.* Printed for the Translator, London, 1831.

1635 O'CONNOR. CHRONICLES OF ERI; being the History of the Gaal Sciot Iber; or, the Irish People. Translated from Original MSS. *Portrait. 2 vols. 8vo. hf. cf. neat, scarce.* London, 1822.

1636 O'DRISCOL, JOHN. HISTORY OF IRELAND. *2 vols. 8vo. boards.* London, 1827.

1637 ŒHLENSCHLÆGER, ADAM. THE GODS OF THE NORTH, an Epic Poem, translated from the Danish in Verse by Frye, roy. 8vo. *newly bound, calf, gilt, very scarce.* Pickering, London, 1845. A very interesting work, with copious notes and illustrations of Scandinavian Mythology.

1638 OGILBY, JOHN. GEOGRAPHICAL WORKS; A COMPLETE SERIES. Comprising:

BRITANNIA; or, an ILLUSTRATION OF THE KINGDOM OF ENGLAND and DOMINION OF WALES. *Profusely illustrated.* 1675.

AFRICA; being an accurate DESCRIPTION of the REGIONS of EGYPT, BARBARY, LYBIA, GUINEA, ETHIOPIA, ABYSSINIA, &c., *numerous fine engravings* by Hollar. 1670.

AMERICA; An ACCURATE DESCRIPTION OF THE NEW WORLD. The Conquest of Peru and Mexico, &c. *Numerous maps and plates.* (Original Edition.) 1671.

JAPAN; Containing a description of their several Territories, Cities, Fortresses, Temples, Customs, &c., &c. *Numerous plates.* 1670.

ASIA; Comprising China, Tartary, Persia, India, &c., &c., &c., with descriptions of their Laws, Customs, &c. *Profusely illustrated.* 3 vols. 1669–71–73.

Together 7 vols. folio, uniformly and neatly bound, pale russia, gilt, marbled edges, &c. London, 1669–75. AN ELEGANT COPY. Ogilby is called the English DeBry.

1639 OHIO HISTORICAL COLLECTIONS; containing a collection of the most interesting Facts, Traditions, Anecdotes, &c., relating to the General and Local History of Ohio. *Profusely illustrated, thick, roy. 8vo. new cloth.* Cincinnati, 1869.

1640 OLD GUARD. A Monthly Journal devoted to the principles of 1776 and 1787. Edited by C. Chauncey Burr. 1863–66, *numerous portraits on steel.* 4 *vols. 8vo. new cloth.*
New York, 1863, &c.

1641 OLDHAM, JOHN. Works, together with his Remains, 12mo. (8vo.) rough leather. London, 1686.
Includes the celebrated Satires on the Jesuits.
" Oldham is a very indelicate writer ; he has strong rage, but it is much like Billingsgate."—*Pope.*

1642 OLD MAIDS. A Philosophical, Historical, and Moral Essay on Old Maids, by a friend to the Sisterhood. 3 vols. 12mo. calf.
Dublin, 1786.

1643 OLDYS' BRITISH LIBRARIAN ; exhibiting a compendious review or abstract of our most Scarce, Useful, and Valuable Books in all Sciences as well in MSS. as in print. Index, &c. 8vo. old cf. *gilt.* London, 1738.
FINE LARGE COPY, *very scarce.*
From the Library of the Rev. John Mitford, (editor of the Aldine Poets,) with his Autograph and Manuscript Notes.
" Mr. Oldys, a man of eager curiosity, and indefatigable dilligence, who first exerted that spirit of inquiry into literature of the Old English Writers, by which the works of our great dramatic poet have of late been so signally illustrated. His bibliographical talents were not eclipsed by those of any contemporary."—*Boswell's Life of Johnson.*

1644 OLEARIUS, ADAM. VOYAGES AND TRAVELS of the Ambassadors, containing a complete History of Muscovy, Tartary, and Persia ; also Mandelslo's Travels in the East Indies, translated, *portraits and maps,* folio, *calf, neat.* London, 1669.

1645 OLIVE BRANCH (The) ; or Faults on both sides, Federal and Democratic. 2d Edition. 8vo. bds. *uncut.* Philadelphia, 1815.

1646 OLYMPIA MORATA ; her Times, Life, and Writings, arranged from contemporary and other writings by the author of " Selwyn." 12mo. *new hf. vellum, extra.* London, 1834.
" The famous Italian Lady, who embraced the faith of the Reformers."

1647 OPPIAN'S HALIEUTICKS of the Nature of FISHES and FISHING of the Ancients, in V Books. Translated from the Greek, with an account of the Life of the Author. 8vo. *hf. russia, gilt, edges uncut, scarce.* *At the Theatre,* Oxford, 1722.
The earliest known treatise on Fish and Fishing—the only English translation.

1648 **ORDERLY BOOKS of the REVOLUTION,** DIVISION AND REGIMENTAL. A remarkably complete and highly interesting series, covering the whole period of the War from the Occupation of Boston, June 10th, 1777, to the cessation of Hostilities in 1783, also 1784–1787. Together 44 *vols. oblong 4to. boards,* (*several unbound.*) Comprising :
 I. 1777–1779. Headquarters, Boston, June 11 to Sept. 30 ; Fishkill, Oct. 25–Nov. 2d ; White Marsh, Nov. 20–Dec. 2 ; Lancaster, Dec. 27, 1777, to March 5th, 1778 ; Valley Forge, April 1st, 1778. and Pawtucket, Jan. 24, 1779, &c.
 Includes the Trial of Major-General Stephens for unofficer-like behavior in the actions of Brandywine and Germantown.
 II. 1777–78. Headquarters, Boston, Lancaster, and Pawtucket, June 1st, 1777–78.
 The greater portion of this volume is occupied with Baron Steuben's Instructions for the Army.

Ʀrderly Books of the Revolution—

III. 1777–78. Headquarters, Boston and Providence, May 23, 1777—October 20, 1778.

Covers the period of Sullivan's campaign in Rhode Island, in which this regiment (Colonel Jackson's 9th Massachusetts) was engaged.

IV. 1778. Headquarters, Croton River, Wright's Mills, &c. April 10th–July 21st, 1778.

V. 1778. Headquarters, Providence, Pawtucket, &c. June 15th–August 16th, 1778. (Sullivan's operations on Rhode Island).

VI. 1778. Headquarters, Providence, Pawtucket, &c. September 5th–October 20th, 1778.

Contains Washington's General Order and Resolutions of Congress, complimenting the command, on their retreat from Rhode Island, August 30th, 1778.

VII. 1779. Adjutant Lovell's Orderly Book, Headquarters, Providence, July 8th to November 24th, and West Point, December 4th, 1779.

VIII. 1779. Adjutant Lovell's Orderly Book, Headquarters, Providence, May 15th–July 4th.

IX. 1779–80. Headquarters, Morristown, December 15th, 1779–March 21st, 1780.

X. 1780. Headquarters, Morristown, May 6th–21st, 1780. (Slightly imperfect at commencement.)

XI. 1780. Headquarters, Morristown, March 22d–June 7th, 1780.

Contains the Trial of General Arnold, with General Orders and Resolutions of Congress publicly reprimanding him.

XII. 1780. Headquarters, West Point, Tappan, &c. September 17th–November 19th, 1780.

*** This volume contains the account of the discovery of Arnold's Treason. (*Treason of the blackest dye, &c. &c.*), and the Trial and Execution of Major Andre.

XIII. 1780. Headquarters, Peekskill, Orangetown, and Ten Eyck, August 3d–September 20th, 1780.

XIV. 1780. Orderly Book of Major Nathan Rice, Headquarters at Peekskill, Orangetown, Ten Eyck, &c. August 1st–Sept. 17th, 1780.

XV. 1780. Headquarters, Chatham, Haverstraw, Springfield, Prianess, June 7th–August 8th, 1780.

XVI. 1780. Headquarters, Morristown, Brian's Tavern, and Prianess, May 23d–July 27th, 1780.

XVII. 1780. Headquarters, Morristown, February 21st–May 15th, 1780.

XVIII. 1780. Order Book of Adjutant Lovell, (16 Mass.) Headquarters, Tappan, Ten Eyck, Steenopia, &c. August 9th–September 20th, 1780.

XIX. 1780. Headquarters, Orangetown and West Point, September 21st–November 21st, 1780.

XX. 1780–81. Headquarters, West Point, (16 Mass.) November 19th, 1780–January 10th, 1781.

XXI. 1780–81. Orderly Book of Adjutant John Davis (4th Mass. Regt.) Headquarters, West Point, December 1st, 1780–February 7th, 1781.

XXII. 1781. Headquarters, West Point, January 15th–February 16th, 1781.

XXIII. 1781. Headquarters, Philipsburgh, and Dobbs' Ferry, July 4th, to August 10th, 1781.

XXIV. 1781. Headquarters, West Point, February 17th to April 10th, 1781.

XXV. 1781. Headquarters, West Point, April 26th to July 1st, 1781.

XXVI. 1781. Headquarters, Peekskill, Dobbs' Ferry, Williamsburgh, and before Yorktown, Va., June 7th to October 2d, 1781.

The Orderly Book of Adjutant Benjamin, 8th Mass. Regt.

In the General Order for September 27th, 1781, preparatory to advancing upon Yorktown, the following piece of advice was given. "The General particularly enjoins the Troops to place

ORDERLY BOOKS OF THE REVOLUTION—

their principle reliance on the bayonette, that they may prove the vanity of the boast which the British make of their peculiar prowess in deciding Battles with that weapon," &c. &c.

XXVII. 1781. Headquarters, Peekskill, August 22d–October 16th, 1781. 9th Mass. Regt. with Roster of Officers, &c.

XXVIII. 1781. Headquarters, Continental Village, Highlands, &c. October 18th–December 6th, 1781.

Includes General Order, announcing the surrender of Cornwallis at Yorktown, and ordering a celebration of the event.

XXIX. 1781–'82. Headquarters, Highlands, December 7th, 1781–January 20th, 1782.

(9th Mass. Regt. with Roster, &c.)

XXX. 1782. Headquarters, Newburgh and Highlands, March 24th–May 26th, 1782. (9th Mass. Regt.)

XXXI. 1782. Headquarters, Newburgh and Highlands, May 7th–June 12th, 1782. (Adjutant Chas. Selden, 9th Massachusetts Regt.)

XXXII. 1782. Headquarters, Newburgh and Highlands, June 14th to July 31st, 1782.

XXXIII. 1782. Headquarters, Newburgh and Highlands, July 24th–August 11th, 1782.

XXXIV. 1782. Headquarters, Verplanck's Point, September 30th–November 1st, 1782. (4th Mass. Regt. with Roster.)

XXXV. 1782–'83. Headquarters, Newburgh. Orderly Book of Adjutant J. Davis, 4th Mass. Regt., December 24th, 1782–January 7th, 1783, with Roster.
A large portion of this volume is occupied by the Rules and Regulations for the Army.

XXXVI. 1782. ORDERLY BOOK of Adjutant McKINNEY in GENERAL GIST'S CAMPAIGN in South Carolina, Headquarters, Pon Pon and Bacon's Bridge, March 13th–May 12th, 1782.

XXXVII. 1782. Headquarters, Newburgh and West Point, June 11th–August 12th, 1782.

XXXVIII. 1782. Headquarters, Dobbs' Ferry, Newburgh, and Verplanck's Point, August 3d to September 3d, 1782.

XXXIX. 1783. Headquarters, Newburgh, March 19th–May 7th, 1783.

Contains Washington's Order congratulating the Army on the prospect of Peace (March 28th); his address on the signing of the agreement for the cessation of hostilities (April 18th); and the Proclamation of Congress to the same effect, April 11th, 1783. " He cannot help wishing that all men (of whatever condition they may be) who have shared the toils and dangers of effecting this glorious revolution, of rescuing millions from the hand of oppression, of laying a foundation of a great empire, might be impressed with a proper idea of the dignified part they have been called upon to act, under the smiles of Providence, in this stage of human affairs—for happy—thrice happy shall they be pronounced hereafter, who have contributed anything, who have performed the meanest office in creating this stupendous fabric of Freedom and Empire," &c. &c.

XL. 1783. Headquarters, West Point, August 13th to September 27th, 1783.

XLI. 1783. Headquarters, Newburgh, January 8th–February 11th, 1783.

XLII. 1784. Headquarters, West Point, Adjutant Charles Selden, January 4th to May 10th, 1784.

XLIII. 1784. Headquarters, West Point, May 17th–June 17th, 1784.

XLIV. 1787. Headquarters, Boston, Castle Island, &c. Jan. 13th–April 20th, 1787.

THE MOST COMPLETE SERIES OF THESE IMPORTANT REVOLUTIONARY DOCUMENTS EVER OFFERED FOR PUBLIC SALE, AND PROBABLY A MORE INTERESTING SERIES DOES NOT EXIST OUTSIDE OF THE GOVERNMENT COLLECTION AT WASHINGTON. *It is also believed that the present comprise several of those known to be wanting in the Government series.*

From the above resumé it will be seen that they cover nearly the whole period of the active operations during the Revolutionary War, and with the exception of No. XXXVI. (Gen. Gist's campaign in South Carolina), relate exclusively to the Massachusetts forces, and particularly to those under the command of Col. afterwards Brig.-Gen. Jackson, of whose operations they form a remarkably complete record. As Historical Documents, these Orderly Books are often of the first importance; although, to the general reader, the details of the daily routine of Camps, orders incident to the Police and Discipline of Armies, &c., &c., may be devoid of interest, to the philosophical student of History they appear of heightened value as the key to events not otherwise understood.

*** For *thirteen* of the volumes in the above collection a former owner paid $1,000, at which price they have been twice sold.

1649 ORDERLY BOOK of the SIEGE of YORKTOWN, from September 26th, 1781, to November 20, 1781. Now first printed from the Original MSS. *Roy. 4to. uncut.* Philadelphia, 1865.
LARGE PAPER. 50 copies, printed on plate paper.

1650 ORPHEUS. MYSTICAL HYMNS, translated from the Greek by Thomas Taylor. 2d Edition, with additions, &c. *Post 8vo. bds. uncut, scarce.* Chiswick, *for the Author*, 1824.

1651 ORR'S CIRCLE of the SCIENCES, a Series of Treatises on the first principles of Science, with their Applications to practical Pursuits, complete in 9 vols. sm. 8vo. *new cloth.*
London, 1854–56.

Contains Treatises on Organic Nature by Professor Owen and Dr. Latham!; Mathematical Science by Twisden and Jardine—Elementary Chemistry by Dr. Scoffern; Inorganic Nature by Professor Ansted and others; Nautical Astronomy and Navigation by Professor Young: Practical Chemistry by Gore; Photography by Starling; Mechanical Philosophy by the Rev. M. Mitchell; Mechanical Drawings by Imray.

1652 OSGOOD, REV. SAMUEL. Discourse in Memory of Edward Everett. *Portrait. Impl. 8vo. uncut.* New York, 1865.

1653 OSSIAN'S POEMS, etc., including the Works of James Macpherson in *Prose and Verse,* with Notes and Illustrations. BEST EDITION. *2 vols. 8vo. calf, extra, marbled edges.* London, 1807.
BEST LARGE TYPE LIBRARY EDITION.

1654 OTTLEY, WM. YOUNG. FLORENTINE SCHOOL : a *Series of Plates engraved after the Paintings and Sculptures of the most eminent Masters of the Early Florentine School;* intended to illustrate the History of the Restoration of the Arts of Design in Italy. By William Young Ottley, F. A. S., *author of " An Inquiry into the Origin and Early History of Engraving."* 54 *superb plates, impl. folio, new hf. morocco, gilt.* London, 1826.

1655 OTTLEY'S INQUIRY CONCERNING THE INVENTION OF PRINTING, containing Notices of the early use of Wood Engraving in Europe, the Block Books, etc., with introduction by P. J. Berjeau, *with* 37 *plates and numerous wood cuts.* 4to. new half morocco, *uncut.* London, 1863.

This is one of the most important books ever produced on the vexed question of the Invention of Printing. The author reviews the systems of Meerman, Heinecken, Santander, and Koning, and has the courage to assert the claims of Holland to that honor.

1656 OTTLEY, WM. YOUNG. ITALIAN SCHOOL OF DESIGN. 84 *carefully engraved and tinted plates, being a series of Facsimiles of original* DRAWINGS *by the most eminent* PAINTERS *and* SCULPTORS *of Italy, with biographical notices,* [pub. at £12. 12s.] royal folio, *bds. uncut.* London, 1823.

21

1657 OUSLEY, SIR GEORGE. BIOGRAPHICAL NOTICES of PERSIAN POETS, with Critical and Explanatory Remarks, &c. . 8vo. *cloth, uncut.*
Oriental Society, London, 1846.

1658 OUTINIAN SOCIETY. Origin and Proceedings, founded for securing the Advantages of Benevolence and Justice, to lessen the Evils incident to the pursuit of Happiness by Marriage, &c. *Numerous portraits and woodcuts.* 4to. boards, RARE.
Privately Printed, 1822.

This Society was formed in the 100th year after the death of the celebrated Wm. Penn, of Pennsylvania, and their meetings held at the residence of his descendant, J. Penn, Esq., in New Street, Spring Gardens, London.

1659 OUVAROFF, M. Essay on the Mysteries of Eleusis, translated from the French by J. D. Price, with Observations by J. Christie. *Folding plates. 8vo. boards, scarce.* London, 1817.

1660 OVID'S ART OF LOVE, together with his REMEDY OF LOVE, translated into English Verse; also the Court of Love, from Chaucer, &c. *Copper plates, 12mo. cf. neat.* London, 1757.

1661 OVID'S METAMORPHOSES. En Latin, traduites en Anglais avec des Remarques et des Explications Historiques par M. l'Abbé Bannier. SPLENDID EDITION, *with superb impressions of the* 150 *large and beautiful engravings by* PICART, VAN GUNST, FOLKEMA, &c. 2 vols. roy. folio, new hf. russia, extra gilt.
Amsterdam, 1732.
FINE COPY.

1662 OWEN, DAVID DALE. REPORT of a GEOLOGICAL SURVEY of WISCONSIN, IOWA, and MINNESOTA, and a portion of Nebraska Territory, *numerous large folding maps and engravings on wood. Thick impl. 4to. cloth.* Philadelphia, 1852.

1663 OWEN, RICHARD. Comparative Anatomy and Physiology of Vertebrates, Fishes and Reptiles, Birds and Mammals. *Several hundred engravings on wood. 3 thick vols. 8vo. new cloth. (Vol. I has the edges cut.)* London, 1866–68.

1664 OWEN, ROBERT. Report to the County of Lanark, of a Plan for relieving Public Distress and removing discontent, &c. 4to. *calf, neat.* Glasgow, 1821.

1665 OXFORD SAUSAGE; or Select Poetical Pieces, written by the most celebrated Wits of the University of Oxford. *New Edition. Numerous engravings on wood, 12mo. sprinkled calf, extra, marbled edges.* Oxford, 1777.
FINE COPY; *scarce.*

1666 OXFORD SAUSAGE; or Select Poetical Pieces, written by the most celebrated Wits of the University of Oxford. CUTS BY THOMAS BEWICK. *Sml. folio, hf. morocco, uncut.* London, 1814.
LARGEST PAPER; *very scarce.*

1667 PAGE, DAVID. Advanced Text-Book of Physical Geography. 12mo. *new cloth.* Edinburgh, 1864.

1668 PAINE, ROBERT TREAT. WORKS in Prose and Verse, with Notes, Biographical Notice, &c. 8vo. sheep. Boston, 1812.

1669 PAINE, ROBERT TROUPE. MEMOIR OF, by his Parents. *Portrait. Roy. 4to. morocco, gilt leaves. Printed for Private Distribution.*
New York, 1852.
Presentation copy.

1670 PAINE, THOMAS. Political Works. *Portrait.* 12mo. *cloth.*
New York, 1860.

1671 PAINTING; THE PHILOSOPHY OF. A Theoretical and Practical
Treatise; comprising Æsthetics in reference to Art; Application of Rules to Painting, and General Considerations on Perspective. *Numerous illustrations. Impl. 8vo. new hf. morocco,
uncut, scarce.* London, 1849.

1672 PALFREY, JNO. GORHAM. HISTORY OF NEW ENGLAND during the
Stuart Dynasty. *Maps.* 3 *vols.* 8vo. *new hf. cf. extra.*
Boston, 1865.

1673 ―――― Another copy. 3 vols. *impl.* 8vo. *cloth, uncut.* Boston, 1865.
LARGE PAPER. 100 *copies.*

1674 PALGRAVE, SIR FRANCIS. HISTORY OF NORMANDY
AND OF ENGLAND. 4 *thick vols.* 8vo. *new calf, gilt, marbled
edges.* London, 1851–64.
FINE COPY.

1675 PALGRAVE, FRANCIS TURNER. Essays on Art. *Post 8vo. hf. rox.
morocco, uncut.* New York, 1867.

1676 PALLAS, COUNT. TRAVELS IN THE RUSSIAN EMPIRE, *with the* 120
*engravings of costumes, manners, and customs, buildings, scenery,
&c. finely colored,* 2 vols. 4to. *cloth, boards.* London, 1812.

1677 PALMER, PETER S. HISTORY OF LAKE CHAMPLAIN, from its first
Exploration by the French in 1609, to the close of the year
1814. 8vo. *uncut.* Albany, *J. Munsell,* 1866.
Large paper copy.

1678 PALMER, RAY. Hymns and Sacred Pieces, with Miscellaneous
Poems. 8vo. *uncut.* *Munsell,* Albany, 1865.

1679 PALMETTO DICTIONARY, wherein the true meaning of every word is
explained and the sound of every syllable distinctly shown, ex-
hibiting the principles of a pure and correct pronunciation.
Thick 16mo. cloth. Richmond, Va., 1864.
A new and carefully revised edition, the Advertisement to which, is dated
January, 1847.

1680 PAMPHLETEER, or Collection of the best Pamphlets of the
day, from its commencement in March, 1813, to December,
1826, 27 vols. in 26, 8vo. *half cf. gilt. Valpy,* London, 1813–28.
The pamphlets in this collection are, Theological, Historical, Political, and
Critical, selected with great judgment; many of them are here published for
the first time, and others are re-published, with additions by the authors.
Among the writers are Bishop Marsh, Lord Erskine, Canning, Wilberforce,
Sir T. Raffles, Bishop Milner, G. Chalmers, Bentham, Chas. Butler, Talfourd, &c., &c.

1681 PAPERS RELATING TO PUBLIC EVENTS IN MASSACHUSETTS preceding the American Revolution. 8vo. *boards, uncut.*
Seventy-Six Society, Philadelphia, 1856.

1682 PARADISE OF DAINTY Devises, edited with biographical and critical Notes by Sir Egerton Brydges. 2 vols. 4to. *hf. morocco,
edges untrimmed.* London, 1812.
LARGE PAPER. Only 150 copies of these curious old Elizabethan poems were
printed.

1683 PARALDI. Sūmariū Sūme virtutum et vitiorum per figura. *Printed with small type, in double columns, with rubricated initials, &c. sml. 4to. vellum.* *Impressa,* Basilea, *Joannī.*
Ammerbach, MCCCCXCVII.

1684 PARDOE, JULIA. BIOGRAPHICAL WORKS, comprising LOUIS XIVth and the COURT OF FRANCE, 3 vols. Life of MARIE DE MEDICIS, Queen of France, 3 vols. COURT AND REIGN OF FRANCIS I, 2 vols. *All profusely illustrated with portraits and engravings on steel.* Together 8 vols. 8vo. *new hf. calf, extra, marbled edges.*
London, 1849, &c.

Fine uniform set.
In these works Miss Pardoe has shown herself capable of charmingly lively, and, at times, gorgeously colored narrative, and of giving an attractive and novel exposition of history.—*Jeaffreson, " Novels and Novelists."*

1685 PARDOE, JULIA. COMPLETE WORKS. Comprising Confessions of a Pretty Woman, The Jealous Wife, Rival Beauties, The Wife's Trials, Romance of the Harem, &c. One vol. thick 8vo. *cloth.*
Philadelphia, N. D.

1686 PARDOE, JULIA. BEAUTIES OF THE BOSPHORUS, *with nearly 100 beautiful Views in Constantinople and its Environs, from original Drawings by Bartlett, 4to. new mor. gilt.* London, (1850).

1687 PARIS DANS SA SPLENDEUR. MONUMENTS, VUES, SCENES HISTORIQUES, Descriptions et Histoire, dessins et lithographs par MM. Philippe Benoist, Arnout, Ciceri, Mathieu, Sabatier, etc. Vignettes de Felix Benoist et Cattenacci, exécutées sur bois par les premiers Graveurs. Texte par MM. Audiganne, P. Merimée, Vinet, Voillet Le Duc, De Watteville, et autres. *With several hundred Large Plates of nearly every interesting building, principal street, square, church, etc. Also many plates of memorable events in the* history of Paris—" Prise de la Bastile," " Joan d'Arc," etc. *3 vols. folio, half crimson morocco, gilt, gilt tops, uncut edges.* Paris, 1861.

1688 PARIS AND ITS ENVIRONS. PICTURESQUE VIEWS OF THE CITY OF PARIS, consisting of Views on the Seine, Public Buildings, Characteristic Scenery, &c., from Drawings by Frederick Nash, with Descriptions by John Scott and M. De La Boissière. *65 large and highly finished Engravings by Cooke, Goodall, &c.* 2 *vols. folio, hf. morocco, uncut.* London, 1823.
PROOF IMPRESSIONS *of the Plates.*

1689 PARK, MUNGO. Journal of a Mission to the Interior of Africa in the year 1805, with an account of the Life of the Author. *Large Map, &c. 4to. hf. calf, neat.* London, 1815.

1690 PARK, MUNGO. TRAVELS in the Interior Districts of Africa, in 1795, '96, and '97, with Appendix, &c. *Map, Portrait,* and *numerous plates.* 4to. hf. cf. neat. London, 1799.

1691 PARKMAN, FRANCIS. FRANCE and ENGLAND in NORTH AMERICA. BOTH SERIES : Pioneers of France, and Jesuits in N. America. *Proof portraits. 2 vols. roy. 8vo. cloth, uncut.* Boston, 1866.
LARGE PAPER : *only 75 copies.*

1692 PARKMAN, FRANCIS. FRANCE and ENGLAND in NORTH AMERICA. A series of Historical Narratives. *8vo. new cloth.*
Boston, 1867.

93 Parkman, Francis. History of the Conspiracy of Pontiac, and the War of the North American Indians against the English Colonists after the Conquest of Canada. *Thick 8vo. cloth, uncut.*
Boston, 1866.
Large Paper; *only 75 copies printed.*

694 (Parr, Dr. Samuel.) Characters of the late Charles James Fox; selected and in part written by Philopatris Varricensis. *2 vols. 8vo. calf, gilt.* London, 1809.
Fine copy, from the Library of Dr. Disney, with MS. notes, &c.

695 Parry, William Edward. Voyages; Journal of a Voyage for the Discovery of a North-West Passage, in the Years 1819, '20. Second Voyage, 1821, '22, '23. Large *folding maps, and numerous fine steel engravings.* 2 vols. roy. 4to. hf. morocco, neat.
London, 1821.

696 Partenopex de Blois; a Romance, translated from the French of M. Le Grand, by W. Stewart Rose. *4to. hf. morocco, antique.*
London, 1807.

697 Parton, James. Life of Andrew Jackson. *Portraits.* 3 *vols.* 8vo. *cloth.* New York, 1861.

698 Parton, Jas. Life and Times of Benjamin Franklin. *Portraits on India paper, beautifully printed by Alvord.* 2 *vols. imp. 8vo. cloth, uncut.* New York, 1865.
Large Paper; *only 100 copies.*

699 Parton, James. General Butler in New Orleans; History of the Administration of the Department of the Gulf. *Portraits.* 8vo. new hf. cf. gilt. New York, 1864.

700 Pascal. Provincial Letters. Edited, with Introduction, &c., by O. W. Wight. *12mo. cloth.* New York, 1859.

701 Pasquin, Anthony (John Williams). Works: comprising, Poems, 1 vol. Children of Thespis, and Pin Basket, 2 vols. in 1 Eccentricities of J. Edwin, 2 vols. in 1. Together 6 vols. in 3. *12mo. new hf. cf. gilt.* London, 1789, &c.
Scarce.
Curious Theatrical History, Scandal and Anecdote.

1702 Patents. Recent Discussions on the Abolition of Patents for Inventions in the United Kingdom, France, Germany, &c., with suggestions as to International Copyrights, &c. *8vo. cloth.*
London, 1869.

1703 Patterson, R. H. The Science of Finance; a practical treatise. *Thick post 8vo. new cloth.* Edinburgh, 1868.

1704 Patterson, R. H. The Economy of Capital, or Gold and Trade. *Post 8vo. new cloth.* Edinburgh, 1865.

1705 Patterson, R. A Narrative of the Campaign in the Valley of the Shenandoah in 1861. *Imp. 8vo. half red morocco, gilt top,* by *Bradstreet.* Philadelphia, 1865.
Large Paper; 100 *copies printed.*

1706 Pattie, James O. Personal Narrative, during an Expedition from St. Louis to the Pacific, &c. *Plates, 8vo. sheep.*
Cincinnati, 1833.

1707 PAYNE'S Universum; or Pictorial World, with Descriptions, edited by Edwards, *nearly* 200 *highly finished and exceedingly beautiful engravings*, 3 vols. 4to. *cloth, gilt leaves.*

London (1852).

Comprises views in all countries, specimens of works of art of all ages and of every character, portraits of great men, &c.

1708 PEACHAM, HENRY. The WORTH of a PENNY; or a Caution to keep Money, with the causes of the scarcity and misery of the want thereof, in these hard and mercilesse Times. *4to. hf. morocco, uncut.* London, 1667.

(*Reprinted* by *E. Drewhirst*, Leeds).

LARGE PAPER; (*only 5 copies printed*).

1709 PEAKE, R. B. MEMOIRS of the COLMAN FAMILY, including their Correspondence. *Numerous fine dramatic portraits, newspaper cuttings, &c., &c.,* inserted. *2 vols. in one, 8vo. hf. cf. gilt.*

London, 1841.

1710 ——— Another copy. *2 vols. 8vo. bds.* London, 1841.

1711 PELLICO, SILVIO. My Prisons. *Engravings on wood.* 12mo. *new cloth, gilt.* Boston, 1868.

1712 PENHALLOW, SAMUEL. HISTORY of the WARS of NEW ENGLAND with the EASTERN INDIANS; or a Narrative of their continued Perfidy and Cruelty, from 10th of *August*, 1703, to the Peace renewed 13th *July*, 1713, &c., &c. 4to. cloth.

Boston, 1726; *reprinted*, Cincinnati, 1859.

PRIVATELY REPRINTED; 150 *copies*. Contains also "Lovewell's Fight," Gardener's Account of the "Pequot Warres," and "The Gospel in New England."

1713 PENLEY, A. ENGLISH SCHOOL of PAINTING in WATER-COLORS; its Theory and Practice, with the several Stages of Progression, accompanied with 74 *large and beautiful colored illustrations, in the first style of Chromo-lithography.* A *splendid vol. royal folio, handsomely bound in cloth.*

Day & Son, 1868.

1714 PENN, WILLIAM. WORKS; to which is prefixed, A Journal of his Life, with Correspondence, &c. *2 vols. folio, cf.*

London, 1726.

Only complete Edition.

1715 PENNSYLVANIA ARCHIVES; selected and arranged from Original Documents in the Office of the Secretary of the Commonwealth, &c., by Samuel Hazard. Commencing 1664 to 1790, with an APPENDIX. 11 *vols. 8vo. hf. sheep.* Philadelphia, 1852, &c.

1716 PENNSYLVANIA. A Brief State of the Province of, *Roy. 8vo. uncut.* London, 1755, *reprinted*, N. Y., 1865.

LARGE PAPER; *only 50 copies.* Sabin's Reports, No. 4.

1717 PENNSYLVANIA COLONIAL RECORDS. Minutes of the Provincial Council of Pennsylvania from the Organization to the Termination of the Proprietary Government, 1683–1789, inc. 16 *vols. 8vo. hf. sheep.* Harrisburgh & Philadelphia, 1852, &c.

PENNSYLVANIA, Geology of, see Rogers, Henry D.

1718 PEPYS, SAMUEL. MEMOIRS, DIARY and CORRESPONDENCE; edited by Richard, Lord Braybrooke. BEST EDITION, *with facsimiles, &c.* 5 *vols. 8vo. hf. calf, extra.* London, 1828.

EXTRA ILLUSTRATED COPY. *Richly illustrated by the insertion of several hundred fine and rare portraits, maps, views, &c., &c., a large portion being rare contemporary prints, all in fine condition, and, where necessary, neatly inlaid.*

"The ablest picture of the age in which the writer lived, and a work of standard importance in English Literature."—*Sir Walter Scott.*

PEPYS' DIARY, see Evelyn.

1719 PERCY ANECDOTES, Original and Select, by Sholto and Reuben Percy. *Portraits.* 41 *parts in 20 vols. 16mo. new hf. morocco, gilt.* London, 1820–26.

" No man that has any pretensions to figure in good society can fail to make himself familiar with the Percy Anecdotes."—*Lord Byron.*

1720 PERCY ANECDOTES. Chandos Edition. *Front.* 2 *vols. thick 12mo. new hf. cf. extra.* London, 1868.

1721 PERCY. FOLIO MANUSCRIPT. BALLADS and ROMANCES, LOOSE and HUMOROUS SONGS. Edited by J. W. Hales and F. J. Furnivall, assisted by Prof. Child and W. Chappell, &c. *Facsimiles.* 3 *thick vols. 8vo. new hf. morocco, extra, uncut, with the Loose Songs in paper.* London, 1867.

Only a limited edition printed for subscribers.

1722 PERCY FOLIO. ANOTHER COPY. LARGE and THICK PAPER. 3 *vols. 8vo. hf. morocco, uncut.* London, 1868.

FEW PRINTED.

1723 PERKINS, C. C. ITALIAN SCULPTORS; being a History of Sculpture in Northern, Southern, and Eastern Italy, *with Etchings by the Author, and Engravings on Wood from Original Drawings, &c.* 4*to. new cloth.* London, 1868.

This is an entirely new and carefully executed work, and has received universal commendation.

"Books upon Italian Painting abound; while the available works upon Italian *Sculpture,* including those which treat of it in conjunction with Painting, are few."

1724 PERKINS, C. C. TUSCAN SCULPTORS; their Lives, Works and Times, *with more than* 70 *engravings from original Drawings and Photographs.* 2 *vols.* 4*to. hf. brown morocco, extra, edges uncut.* London, 1864.

1725 PERRY. NARRATIVE of the Expedition of an American Squadron to the China Seas and Japan, performed in the years 1852, 1853, and 1854, under the command of Commodore M. C. Perry, United States Navy, by order of the Government of the United States. *Maps and numerous tinted plates.* 3 *vols.* 4*to. cloth.* Washington, 1856.

1726 PERRY'S JAPAN EXPEDITION. Graphic Scenes in the Japan Expedition, by William Heine. 10 *large chromo-lithographic plates in tints and colors. Folio, paper.* New York, 1856.

1727 PERRY, COM. NARRATIVE OF THE EXPEDITION OF AN AMERICAN SQUADRON TO THE CHINA SEAS AND JAPAN in the years 1852, '53, and '54, compiled from the original Notes and Journals, by Francis L. Hawks, D. D. *Maps and engravings. 8vo. cloth.* New York, 1856.

1728 PETER PINDAR [Dr. John Wolcott]. WORKS OF. BEST LIBRAR
EDITION. *Portrait.* 6 *vols. 8vo. new hf. calf, extra, fine copy.*
London, 1794

1729 PETITOT. ÉMAUX DE PETITOT, DU MUSÉE IMPÉRIAL DU LOUVRE
Portraits de Personnages Historiques et de Femmes Célèbre
du siècle de Louis XIV, *elegantly printed, and illustrated wit
the series of 52 portraits from the celebrated enamels of Petito
most exquisitely engraved by Ceroni.* 2 vols. 4to. cloth, gilt.
Paris, 1864

A most interesting, beautifully illustrated work. Petitot has been called th
inventor as well as the great master in the art of painting in enamel. Th
above series are exact copies of those in the Louvre, at Paris, and were painte
atter the flight of the family of Charles I to Paris, where he was retained b
Louis XIV.

1730 PETRONIUS ARBITER, TITUS. The Satyr, with its Fragments, re
covered at Belgrade, made English by Mr. Bunbury, &c
12mo. (8vo.) *crimson morocco, gilt.* London, 1694

"Scarce Edition, including matter not contained in any other."

1731 PFNOR, R. MONOGRAPH of the PALACE of FON
TAINEBLEAU, with a Historical Sketch by Champollior
Figeac [Librarian of the Imperial Palace]. 145 *very larg
and finely executed plates, 5 being colored.* 2 *vols. atlas folio, ne
hf. morocco, gilt. The plates mounted on guards.*
Paris, 1865

The first volume contains representations of the Oval Court, the Maintenc
Pavilion, La Cour des Fontaines, Henry IV's Court, the Stag Gallery, Lou
XIII's Baptistery, the White Horse Court, and the grand Vestibule an
Chapel of the Trinity. The second volume is specially devoted to the inte
nal decorations, containing detailed representations of François I's Galler
the Gallery of Henry II, the Salon Louis XIII, the State Rooms, and S
Saturnin's Chapel.
The historical and descriptive part, executed by Mr. Champollion-Figeac,
replete with interesting and hitherto unpublished information.

1732 PHANTOM FLOWERS; a treatise on the art of producing skeleto
leaves. *Illustrated.* 12mo. *new cloth.* Boston, 1864

1733 PHELPS, RICHARD H. HISTORY of NEWGATE, Conn., its Insurrec
tions and Massacres. *Portrait. Sml. 4to. uncut.*
Munsell, Albany, 1860

1734 PHILIP QUARLL the HERMIT; or, the unparalleled Sufferings an
Surprising Adventures of an Englishman upon an uninhabite
Island in the South Sea. *Front.* 8vo. *calf, neat.*
Westminster, 1727

Original Edition, very scarce.
This famous work was second only to Robinson Crusoe in popularity; th
author is unknown.

PHILLIPS, EDW. Theatrum Poetarum. See Brydges.

1735 PHILLIPS, HENRY, JR. Historical Sketches of the Paper Currenc
of the American Colonies. *Both Series.* 2 *vols. roy. 4to. uncu*
Roxbury, Mass., 1865
LARGE PAPER. *Only 50 copies.*

1736 ——— Another copy. *Small Paper.* 2 *vols. small 4to. uncut.*
Roxbury, 1865

1737 ——— Another copy. *Beautifully printed on* INDIA PAPER. (Onl
6 copies). 2 *vols. 8vo. hf. crimson morocco, gilt top, by Bradstree*
Roxbury, 1865

1738 Phillips, John. Vesuvius. *Maps, Plates, &c.* Crown 8vo. *new vellum cloth.* *Clarendon Press*, Oxford, 1869.

1739 Phillips, Theresa Constantia. Apology for the conduct of, *with her autograph attestation to each volume.* 3 vols. post 8vo. hf. cf. London, N.D.

1740 Phillips, Wendell. Speeches, Lectures, and Letters. *Portrait.* 12mo. *cloth.* Boston, 1863.

1741 Phillips, William. Mount Sinai; a Poem. *Fine plate by Martin, inserted. Roy. 8vo. hf. mor. uncut.* London, 1830.
Robert Southey's copy, with his autograph, dated Keswick, June 30, 1830.

1742 Philo Judæus (contemporary of Josephus). Works, translated from the Greek by C. D. Yonge. *4 vols. 12mo. cloth.* *Bohn*, London, 1854.

1743 Philobiblion (The). A Monthly Bibliographical Journal, containing Critical Notices of and Extracts from Rare, Curious, and valuable Old Books. *Printed on* India paper, *complete set.* 2 vols. small 4to. *sheets, stitched.* New York, 1862–63.

1744 ——— Another copy. 2 vols. small 4to. *numbers.* New York, 1862–63.

1745 PICART, Bernard. RELIGIOUS CEREMONIES, and CUSTOMS of the various nations of the World, translated into English. 200 *large and beautiful engravings by Picart.* Early Impressions. 7 *vols. in* 6, *folio, calf, neat.* London, 1731–33.
Fine clean and early copy.

1746 Pictures of Society, Grave and Gay, from the pencils of celebrated artists and the pens of popular authors. *Nearly* 100 *fine engravings on wood after Millais, Pickersgill, Cooper, Doyle, Corbould, Thomas, &c.* Roy. 8vo. hf. *morocco, uncut.* New York, 1866.

1747 𝕻𝖎𝖊𝖗𝖘 𝕻𝖑𝖔𝖚𝖒𝖆𝖓𝖘 𝖁𝖎𝖘𝖎𝖔𝖓. Visio Willi de Petro Plouhman, item Visiones ejusdem de Dowel, Dobet et Dobest, or The Vision of William concerning Piers Plouhman, and the Visions of the same concerning the Origin, Progress and Perfection of the Christian Life; together with an Introductory Discourse, a perpetual Commentary, Annotations, and a Glossary, by Thos. Dunham Whitaker, LL.D., also· Piers Plouhman's Creed. *Beautifully printed in large Gothic type, in red and black, with woodcuts.* Two parts *in one vol. roy.* 4to. hf. *olive morocco, gilt top, uncut edges.* London, 1813–14.
Fine copy, *scarce.*
"The Creed" is often wanting.
"A religious allegorical satire, in which the vices of almost every profession are attacked; generally attributed to Robert Langland or Longland—who flourished about the beginning of the XIVth century.

1748 Pierson, A. T. C. Traditions of Freemasonry and its coincidences with the ancient mysteries. *Front.* 12mo. *cloth.* N. Y., 1865.

1749 Pike, Luke Owen. The English and their Origin, a prologue to Authentic English History. 8vo. *cloth.* London, 1866.

1750 Pilkington. The Real Story of John Carteret Pilkington, written by himself. *Fine portrait of Mrs. Pilkington, the friend of Dean Swift. 4to. calf, neat, scarce.* London, 1760.
Includes the correspondence of Mrs. Pilkington with Lord Kingsborough.

1751 Pilpay's Fables, containing a number of excellent Rules for the conduct of persons of all ages, &c. *Numerous quaint old engravings on copper. 12mo. polished calf, extra, yellow edges, scarce.* London, 1747.
Fine copy.

1752 PINKERTON'S GENERAL COLLECTION of Voyages and Travels, from the Earliest Ages to the present time. *With nearly 200 engravings by Cooke. 17 vols. 4to. calf, gilt.* London, 1808–14.
Fine copy.
The most valuable collection of Voyages and Travels extant. The last volume contains a copious Index, and the bibliography of the subject.

1753 Pitt, William. Speeches in the House of Commons. 3 vols. 8vo. *elegantly bound in yellow calf, elaborately tooled sides and backs, marbled edges.* London, 1817.

1754 PLATO'S Works, translated from the Greek; Nine of the Dialogues by the late Floyer Sydenham, and the remainder by Thomas Taylor, with copious Notes by the latter, containing the substance of nearly all the existing Greed MS. commentaries on the Philosophy of Plato. 5 vols. roy. 4to. hf. *vellum gilt tops, uncut edges.* London, *printed for T. Taylor*, 1804.
Fine copy.
This work was printed at the expense of the Duke of Norfolk, who from some unaccountable whim locked up the whole edition in his house, where it remained until long after his decease.

1755 Plato. Commentaries of Proclus on the Timæus of Plato, in five books; containing a treasury of Pythagoric and Platonic Physiology, translated by Thomas Taylor. 2 vols. roy. 4to. hf. vellum, gilt top. *Printed for the Author*, London, 1820.

1756 Plato. Dialogues of, translated by Floyer Sydenham. *Portrait.* 3 vols. roy. 4to. hf. *vellum, gilt tops.* London, 1769.
Uniform with the preceding lot.
This copy has the autograph of Sydenham affixed to the dedication.
"How affecting is the death of Sydenham, who had devoted his life to a laborious version of Plato. He died in a spunging house, and it was his death which appears to have given rise to the Literary Fund 'for the relief of distressed authors.'"—*D'Israeli.*

1757 Plato. Six Books of Proclus on the Theology of Plato, also a translation of Proclus' Elements of Theology, &c., &c. by Thomas Taylor. 2 vols. roy. 4to. hf. *vellum, gilt tops.*
Printed for the Author, London, 1816.
Uniform with the preceding.

1758 Plato. Works. A new and literal version, chiefly from the text of Stallbaum, by Henry Cary. 6 *vols.* 12mo. *cloth.*
Bohn, London, 1858.

1759 Pliny's Letters, with occasional remarks, by William Melmoth. 2 *vols. 8vo. calf.* London, 1805.

1760 PLUTARCH'S LIVES. The Translation called Dryden's: Corrected from the Greek, and Revised by A. H. Clough. 5 *vols. royal 8vo. boards, uncut.* *Boston*, 1865.
Large Paper; *only* 100 *copies printed.*

1761 —————— Another copy. 5 vols. 8vo. cloth. Boston, 1865.

1762 PLUTARCH'S LIVES. Translated from the Greek, with Notes, Critical and Historical, and a New Life of Plutarch by J. & W. Langhorne. *Vignettes by Thomson. 6 vols. 12mo. calf, extra.*
London, 1826·

The Chiswick Edition.

1763 POLANO, PIETRO. HISTORIE of the COUNCEL of TRENT, translated into English by Nathaniel Brent. *2d Edition with additions,* folio, calf. London, 1629.

1764 POLI, MATHÆI. SYNOPSIS CRITICORUM aliorumque, SCRIPTURÆ Interpretum. *5 vols. folio, polished calf, extra, marbled edges.* Londini, 1669–78.
FINE COPY. "On this elaborate work the author spent ten years. It consolidates, with great skill and conciseness, all the Critici Sacri into one continued comment."—*Horne.*

1765 POLLARD, EDWARD A. LEE and his LIEUTENANTS; comprising the early Life, Public Services, and Campaigns of Gen. Robert E. Lee and his companions in Arms. *Numerous portraits, &c.,* thick 8vo. sheep. New York, 1867.

1766 POLLARD, E. A. The LOST CAUSE; A new Southern History of the War of the Confederates. *Map and numerous steel portraits,* thick roy. 8vo. sheep. New York, 1867.

1767 Polyanthea; or, A Collection of Interesting Fragments, in Prose and Verse, consisting of Original Anecdotes, Biographical Sketches, &c. *2 vols. 8vo. hf. morocco,* neat.
London, 1804.

Compiled by Charles Henry Wilson, Esq. These amusing volumes contain a Life of Captain John Smith, of Virginia, by Dr. Belknap; an abridged account of the Three Regicides, who at the Restoration fled to America, &c.

1768 POLYDORI VIRGILII de Rerum Inventoribus. Translated into English by John Langley; with an account of the author and his works. *8vo. hf. green morocco, uncut.*
Agathynian Club, New York, 1868.

Only 120 copies printed.

1769 POMPADOUR, MARCHIONESS of, (Mistress of Louis XV.) MEMOIRS of, written by herself, wherein are displayed The Motives of the Wars, Treatises, Embacies, and Negotiations, Cabals and Intrigues of Courtiers, &c., &c. *2 vols. 12mo. hf. cf. neat, very scarce.* London, 1766.

1770 POMPADOUR, MARCHIONESS. MEMOIRS, written by herself, translated from the French. *2 vols. in one. 12mo. new hf. vellum, extra, yellow edges, scarce.* London, 1766.

1771 POMPADOUR, MARCHIONESS. LETTERS of, from 1753 to 1762. *2 vols. in one. 16mo. hf. cf. extra.* London, 1771.

1772 POMPEII. ITS HISTORY, BUILDINGS, and ANTIQUITIES. An account of the destruction of the City, full descriptions of the remains, &c., edited by Thomas Dyer. *Illustrated with nearly 300 fine engravings on wood, maps, &c. Thick crown 8vo. new cloth.*
London, 1867.

1773 Pomponius Melæ. De Orbis situ, Libri tres accuratisme emendati, unà cū Commētariis Isacchimi Vadiani Heluetii, &c. *Curious Xylographic title and Initial letters. Folio, vellum.*
Basileæ, Anno. MDXVII.
Fine clean copy, from the Library of Whit. Kennett, with his Autograph.

1774 Poole, John. (*Author of ' Paul Pry.'*) Sketches and Recollections. *Portrait. 2 vols. post 8vo. hf. cf. extra, scarce.*
London, 1835.

1775 Pope, Alexander. Works. Additions to, together with many Original Poems and Letters of contemporary writers. *Vignette. 2 vols. in one, crown 8vo. polished calf, extra, yellow edges.*
London, 1776.
Very Scarce, edited by George Stevens, and containing most of Pope's writings suppressed for indelicacy, &c.
An interesting copy; with Autograph note of William Cooke, who says: "*These collections were made by me from the London Museum, &c., and the Preface written by me.*" Also Autograph notes by Joseph Hunter, the historian of South Yorkshire, who has added an Autograph letter from the Rev. Alex. Dyce, which contains the following: "*These pieces were collected by G. Stevens, Esq., from various quarters; and after being inserted in the St. James' Chronicle from time to time, were printed in the present form. Mr. William Cooke, the barrister, and author of an essay on Dramatic Criticism, &c., was employed—as he informed me—by Mr. Stevens to write the Preface.*"—A. C[halmers].

EXTRA ILLUSTRATED.

1776 POPISH PLOT. A compendious History of the most remarkable Passages of the last Fourteen Years, with an account of the Plot, as it was carried on both before and after the Fire in London to this present time.
8vo. the text neatly inlaid in folio, with ruled borders, and Illustrated with an Immense Assemblage of Rare and Curious Portraits, Views, Private Plates, Original Documents, &c., &c. (All contemporary.) Autographs of *Lord Southampton, Lord Shaftesbury,* Charles I, *Samuel Pepys,* James II, &c., &c. *folio, cloth.*
London, 1680.
UNIQUE! An unusually interesting and desirable volume.

1777 Pocket Magazine of Classic and Polite Literature. A complete set from its commencement, *profusely illustrated.* 28 vols. 16mo. *calf, gilt.*
London, 1818–26.
Complete sets are scarce.

1778 Poe, Edgar Allan. Complete Works. *Portrait.* 4 vols. crown 8vo. *hf. cf. extra.*
New York, 1867.

1779 POEMS relating to STATE AFFAIRS, from Oliver Cromwell to this present time; by the greatest wits of the age, the whole from their respective originals without castration. *Numerous caricature plates.* 4 vols. 8vo. *calf, rebacked, very scarce.*
London, 1705.
The 4th volume is generally wanting.
The most complete collection of Comic, Satirical and Facetious Poetry of the time of Charles II, by Lord Rochester, Tom Brown, Andrew Marvell, Duke of Buckingham, &c., &c.

1780 Porphyry. Select Works of, containing his Four Books on Abstinence from Animal Food; his treatise on the Homeric Cave of the Nymphs, &c., &c. Translated by Thomas Taylor. *8vo. bds. uncut, scarce.*
London, 1823.

1781 Porter, W. T.   Scenes in Arkansaw.   12mo. *cloth.*
Philadelphia, 1858.

1782 PORT-FOLIO ; A Collection of Engravings from *Antiquarian, Architectural and Topographical Subjects, Curious Works of Art, &c.,* by Storer.   200 *highly finished plates.*   Proofs on India Paper.   4 vols. roy. 8vo. *new hf. green morocco, gilt top, uncut edges.*
London, 1823.
Large Paper, *scarce.*

1783 PORTRAITS.   *A collection of over* 1000 *portraits, engraved in outline, comprising the most prominent celebrities of every age and nation,* all alphabetically arranged.   4 vols. 8vo. *new hf. calf, gilt.*
N. D.
Appropriate for illustrating a Biographical Dictionary.

1784 Portraits of the British Poets, from Chaucer to Cowper and Beattie, comprising 114 highly finished engravings, by Finden, Warren, Pye, Worthington, etc.   Brilliant Impressions.
London, 1824.
It is the only series, in an elegant form, and is adapted to illustrate all editions of the Poets' works from octavo size upwards.

1785 Portraits.   *A fine collection, comprising upwards of Three Hundred fine steel portraits, principally modern characters, all* Fine Impressions, *many* Proof; *and including a scarce series of the Chief Justices of England,* bound in 2 vols. impl. 8vo. *hf. morocco.*
London, V. D.
Worthy the attention of Collectors and Gentlemen engaged in illustrating.

1786 Portraits.   A scrap book, *containing* 100 *fine portraits, principally Literary Characters, and including a nearly complete series of the Fraser Portraits, and many that are scarce.   4to. hf. morocco, gilt.*
London, V. D.

1787 Portraits.   Beauties of the Court and Times of Queen Victoria, from drawings by eminent artists.   A series of 32 *fine steel plates by Chas. Heath.   Sm. folio, hf. morocco, gilt.*
London, 1857.
⁎⁎ Some of the plates loose.

1788 Portraits.   The Biographical Magazine, containing Portraits and Characters of Eminent and Ingenious Persons of Every Age and Nation.   *Upwards of* 200 *beautifully engraved portraits— vignette, by Audinet, Cromek, Storer, &c.*   Early Impressions.   2 vols. 8vo. *new hf. morocco, neat, scarce.*   London, 1794.

1789 Portrait Gallery of Distinguished Females, including Beauties of the Courts of George IV and William IV, with Memoirs by John Burke.   *A series of* 75 *beautifully engraved portraits.*   2 vols. impl. 8vo. *cloth, uncut.*   London, 1833.

1790 Portraits.   Galerie Française, ou Collection de Portraits des Hommes et des Femmes qui ont illustré la France, dans les XVIe, XVIIe, XVIIIe siècles.   *Several hundred beautifully executed portraits and fac-similes on stone, early impressions.*   3 vols. royal 4to. *hf. mor. uncut.*   Paris, 1821.

1791 Portraits.   Gallery of Portraits, British and Foreign, with memoirs by distinguished biographers.   168 *fine portraits beau-*

tifully engraved on steel, original impressions. 7 vols. impl.
8vo. *hf. calf, neat.* London, 1833–8

An interesting series, forming a desirable accompaniment to Lodge's Portraits.
The memoirs were written by Arthur Malkin, Henry Hallam, T. De Quincy,
&c.

1792 Portraits of the Generals of the Union and Rebel Armies. A
series of 94 portraits on steel. Proofs on India Paper, *many*
before the Letters, *on Large Paper.* 94 plates, 4to.

1793 Portraits of Illustrious Persons in English History, drawn by
G. P. Harding, from Original Pictures, with Biographical and
Historical Notices by Thomas Moule. 15 *large and finely exe-
cuted plates* Folio, *new cloth.* London, 1869.

1794 Portraits of the Most Eminent Painters and other famous Artists that have flourished in Europe. 100 *fine copper plates
engraved by Bouttats, P. De Jode, W. Hollar, P. Pontius, Voster-
man, from paintings by Van Dyck, Cocques, &c.* Beautiful
Impressions. *4to. calf, gilt.* London, 1739.

1795 Portraits. National Portrait Gallery of Illustrious and Eminent Persons of the XIXth Century, with Memoirs by Jerdan
and Stebbing. 184 *finely engraved portraits.* 61 *numbers complete, forming 5 vols. impl. 8vo.* (£12. 12s.) London, 1830–4.

Uniformly printed with, and forming a most desirable continuation to Lodge's
Portraits.

1796 Portraits. Physiognomical Portraits of Distinguished characters, with Memoirs. 100 *very highly finished portraits.* Proof
Impressions on India Paper. *2 vols. 4to. new hf. morocco, gilt,
fine copy.* London, 1822.
Large Paper.

This work, which has never been excelled in the beauty of its execution, contains the most authentic portraits, both English and Foreign, engraved by
the most eminent artists of the day.

1797 PORTRAITS of REMARKABLE CHARACTERS. An extraordinary collection of curious and Rare portraits of Robbers,
Prisoners, Murderers, Beggars, Prizefighters, Jockeys, Impostors, Courtesans, &c. &c. *including many curious old mezzotints,
some unique prints, &c. all in fine condition, and neatly mounted
in a folio scrap book, hf. bound in morocco.* London.

An interesting collection, nearly 200 in number.

1798 Portraits. Rodd's rare Portraits to Granger and Noble.
50 *fine and interesting portraits of famous or notorious personages,
from rare pictures and prints. 2 vols. in one. Roy. 4to. polished
calf, extra, marbled edges.* London, 1820.
Large Paper, *fine copy.*

A highly curious collection, forming an indispensable companion to Richardson's series, all the portraits being different and suitable for illustrating
Noble's continuation to Granger History.

Portraits, see Shakespeare, Boaden, &c.

Portraits, see Gallery, lot 889.

1799 Potter, George A. Instrument of Association ; a Manual of
Currency. 12mo. *cloth.* New York, 1868.

1800 Pouchot. Memoir upon the Late War in North America, between the French and English, 1755–60; followed by Observations upon the Theatre of Actual War, and by New Details concerning the Manners and Customs of the Indians; *with Topographical Maps.* Translated and Edited by Franklin B. Hough. *With notes, &c.* 2 *vols. imperial 4to. uncut.*

Roxbury, Mass., 1866.

Large Paper; *only 50 copies.*

1801 ——— Another copy. 2 vols. roy. 8vo. *uncut.* (150 *copies*).

Roxbury, Mass., 1866.

1802 ——— Another copy. *Beautifully* Printed on India Paper. 2 *vols. roy. 8vo. hf. crimson morocco, gilt top.* Roxb. 1866.

1803 Powers, Rev. G. Essay on the Influence of the Imagination on the Nervous System. 12mo. bds. Andover, Mass., 1828.

1804 Praed, W. M. Poems, with a Memoir by the Rev. Derwent Coleridge. *Portrait.* 2 vols. 12mo. *new cloth, uncut.*

New York, 1865.

1805 Prescott, Wm. H. Historical Works, complete; comprising Philip II, 2 vols.; Ferdinand and Isabella, 3 vols.; Conquest of Mexico, 3 vols.; Conquest of Peru, 2 vols.; Charles V, 3 vols.; and Literary Miscellanies, 1 vol.; together 14 *vols. 8vo. cloth, portraits,* &c. Boston, and Philadelphia, 1859.

1806 PREVOT D'EXILES, A. F. HISTOIRE GENERALE DES VOYAGES, ou nouvelle Collection de tous les Voyages par mer et par terre qui ont ete publies jusqu'a present. Avec la Continuation par MM. Querlon et De Leyre. *Several hundred maps and engravings.* 27 *vols. 4to. newly and uniformly bound in half calf, extra.* La Haye, 1747.

This edition of this great Work (a reprint of the Paris edition of 1746, with many additions) is celebrated for the beauty of the engravings, which were executed by the ablest artists from the designs of the famous Cochin.

1807 Price, Bonomy. Principles of Currency, with a Letter from Michael Chevalier, &c. 8vo. *new cloth.* London, 1869.

1808 Price, Major. Mahommedan History, compiled from original Persian authorities, *maps, etc.* 4 *vols. 4to. boards, uncut.*

London, 1811–20.

" This valuable work is the result of 24 years' research and study in the East; it may be said to be the only one faithfully representing Oriental records and traditions."

1809 Price, Sir Uvedale. Essay on the Picturesque as compared with the sublime and beautiful; also, A Letter to Sir Uvedale Price by H. Repton, and A Letter to H. Repton, Esq. by Uvedale Price, in *one vol. 8vo. red morocco, gilt.*

London, 1794–95.

A Repton's (the celebrated Landscape Gardener) copy, with his manuscript annotations, and autograph letters of Sir Uvedale Price, and Mr. Robson his Publisher, relating to the controversy between them on " The Picturesque."

1810 PRICHARD, Dr. RESEARCHES into the PHYSICAL HISTORY OF MANKIND, enlarged edition, *with numerous colored and other plates.* 5 vols. 8vo. *cloth.* London, 1851.

" This is one of the most interesting and learned works that has been printed in England for many years."—*Dub. Medical Journal.*

1811 PRICHARD, JAMES C. NATURAL HISTORY of MAN; comprising inquiries into the modifying influence of Physical and Moral Agencies of the different tribes of the Human family. 62 COLORED PLATES and 100 *woodcuts.* 2 vols. roy. 8vo. *new cloth.*
London, 1855.

1812 PRIESTLEY, JOSEPH. WORKS; Comprising, Notes on the Scriptures, 4 vols. Opinions Concerning Christ, 4 vols. History of the Christian Church, 6 vols. Theological Repository, 6 vols. Evidences of Revealed Religion, 3 vols. Corruptions of Chistianity, 2 vols. Institutions of Moses, 1 vol. Heathen Philosophy, 1 vol. Discussions, 1 vol. Letters to a Philosophical Unbeliever, 1 *vol.* Together 29 *vols. 8vo. uniformly bound in hf. cf. gilt.* London, V. D.

"His enlightened mind, his unwearied assiduity, the extent of his researches, the light he poured into almost every department of science, will be the admiration of that period when the greater part of those who have favored or those who have opposed him will be alike forgotten."—*Robert Hall.*

1813 PRINCE SOCIETY. Publications of the Prince Society. *Together 4 vols. small 4to. uncut.* Boston, 1865–67.

This Series consists of—
No. I. and II. the Hutchinson Papers. 2 vols. No. III. New England's Prospect. By William Wood. No. IV. Dunton's Letters ; Written from New England, A. D. 1686. In which are described his Voyages by Sea, His Travels on Land, etc. Now first published from the Original Manuscript.

1814 PRIOR'S POETICAL WORKS. Subscription Edition. *Frontispiece and Vignette.* Roy. folio, hf. russia, gilt.
Tonson, London, 1718.

The author is said to have cleared over £4,000 from this edition.

1815 PROCLAMATIONS FOR THANKSGIVING, issued by the Continental Congress, President Washington, by the National and State Governments on the Peace of 1815, and by the Governors of New York, &c. &c. with An Introduction and Notes (by F. B. Hough). *8vo. hf. dark blue morocco, gilt top.*
Albany, 1858.

Privately printed ; only 150 copies.

1816 PROCLAMATIONS of THANKSGIVING, issued by the Continental Congress, President Washington, and the National and State Governments, on the Peace of 1815. *Impl. 8vo. uncut.*
Munsell, Albany, 1858.

1817 PROCOPII GAZÆI in librorum regum, et paralipomenon, Scholia, Johannes Meursius, Nunc primus Græce edidit, et Latinam interpretationem adiecit. *Sml. 4to. vellum.*
Lugduni Bataviarum typis *Isaaci Elzeririi,* Anno
cIɔ Iɔ c XX. (1620).
Fine copy.

1818 PROSTITUTION in LONDON, with a comparative view of that of Paris and New York, by Dr. Ryan. *12mo. cloth.* London, 1839.

1819 PROTESTANT SISTERHOODS. Five Years in a Protestant Sisterhood, and Ten Years in a Catholic Convent. An Autobiography. *Crown 8vo. new cloth.* London, 1869.

820 PROVIDENCE. Report of the Centennial Celebration at Pautucket of the Incorporation of the Town of North Providence. *Roy. 4to. hf. mor. uncut.* Providence, 1865.
LARGE PAPER. *50 copies.*

821 PSALMS. The WHOLE BOOKE of PSALMES *faithfully* TRANSLATED *into* ENGLISH *Metre*, whereunto is prefixed a discourse declaring not only the lawfullnes, but also the necessity of the heavenly Ordinance of singing Scripture Psalmes in the Churches of God. *Imprinted* 1640. A *literal* reprint of the BAY PSALM BOOK ; being the earliest New England version of the Psalms, and the *first book* printed in America. *8vo. boards, uncut edges.*
Richardson, New York, 1862.
PRIVATELY PRINTED ; *and only* 50 *copies. Three were destroyed by fire at Richardson's.* EXCEEDINGLY SCARCE.
The copy of the *original* edition in the Crowninshield library was sold by its purchaser, Henry Stevens, of London, to the British Museum for *one hundred and fifty guineas.*
" In the reproduction of this quaint volume every *word*, every *letter*, and indeed every *point* has been sedulously collated with a perfect impression of the original work struck at Cambridge in the year 1640. Indeed, so exact and faithful has the compositor been in following the original copy, that the bad spacing, omission of spaces, irregular justification, bad divisions, broken type, letters inverted, mixed lower-case letters with italics, and typographical errors, are strictly reproductions of the printers' errors of the olden time."— *Preface.*

822 PUCKLE'S CLUB. A Dialogue between a Father and a Son. *Fine impressions of the numerous beautiful engravings on wood, from designs by Thurston.* Roy. 8vo. *hf. morocco, uncut.* London, 1817.
LARGE PAPER.

823 PUFFENDORF. LAW OF NATURE AND OF NATIONS. 4th Edition, with Notes by M. Barbeyrack, translated by Basil Kennett. *Folio, calf, neat.* London, 1729.

824 PUGIN, A. W. SKETCHES AND DRAWINGS; *a charming series of* 500 BEAUTIFUL PHOTOGRAPHS *by* S. AYLING, *from the originals, comprising curious and remarkable Buildings in various countries in Europe, Details from Cathedral and other Edifices, Reliquaries, Altars, Frescoes, Figures, Metal Work, Stained Glass Windows, and many other subjects, executed in his usual clear style by this great Architect and Draughtsman,* forming 2 large vols. imperial 8vo. *hf. bd. morocco,* (pub. £10 10s.) London, 1865.
Only 100 *copies executed.*
The Architectural Drawings of the late Mr. Pugin are unrivalled of their kind. The above two volumes contain a selection of his best productions, and preserve representations of many objects not to be found in other works.

825 PUGIN. PARIS AND ITS ENVIRONS, displayed in a series of Picturesque Views, *engraved under the superintendence of C. Heath.* INDIA PROOFS, with descriptive text. 2 *vols.* 4to. *cf. neat.*
London, 1829.

826 PUNCH. A Complete set of this famous Journal from its commencement to 1860. *With thousands of humorous engravings by Leach, Doyle, etc.* 39 vols. in 20, new cloth, gilt edge.
London, 1841–60.

827 PURCHAS, HIS PILGRIMAGE, or relations of the world and the religions observed in all ages and places discovered, from the
23

creation until this present, &c., by Samuel Purchas. Folio, old cf. gilt. *Fine copy.* London, 1617.

The synopsis and complement of the collection of voyages edited by the venerable author, of which it forms the 5th volume.

1828 PURSUITS OF LITERATURE. A Satyrical Poem, with Appendix, &c. *Best Edition.* Roy. 4to. hf. cf. neat. London, 1809.

1829 PUTNAM'S MONTHLY MAGAZINE of American Literature, Science, and Art, from its commencement in January, 1853 to July, 1857, inc. *Numerous fine portraits on steel, and many hundred engravings on wood.* 9 vols. thick 8vo. new hf. morocco, gilt. New York, 1853–57.

1830 PYNE'S HISTORY OF THE ROYAL RESIDENCES, *with* 100 RICHLY COLORED ENGRAVINGS, *facsimiles of original drawings, by C. Wild, Cattermole, Stephanoff, &c.* 3 vols. impl. 4to. new hf. morocco, gilt leaves, fine and original copy.
London, 1819.

This splendid work contains the following palaces :—Windsor Castle, St. James' Palace, Carlton House, Kensington Palace, Hampton Court, Buckingham House.

1831 QUARTERLY REVIEW. Complete from its commencement in 1809 to July, 1854, inc. With 3 Indexes. 94 vols. 8vo. hf. russia, gilt. London, 1809–54.
Fine, uniform set.

1832 QUEVEDO'S Works complete, translated from the Spanish, with Life, *curious engravings, best edition,* 3 vols. 8vo. calf, neat.
London, 1798.

1833 QUINCY, JOSIAH. Municipal History of the Town and City of Boston, during two centuries. *Plates, 8vo. new cloth.*
Boston, 1852.

1834 RABELAIS, FRANCIS. WORKS, Translated and Revised according to the Edition of M. Du Chat, by M. Ozell. *Portrait and numerous copper-plate engravings.* 5 vols. 12mo. old cf. neat.
London, 1738.

Fine copy. Best English Edition.

1835 RALEIGH, Sir W. HISTORY OF THE WORLD, with Life of the Author, by Oldys, including his Trial, *fine portrait by Vertue, and large maps,* 2 vols. folio, calf, gilt. London, 1736.

1836 RALEIGH, SIR WALTER. THE POEMS OF, nor first collected, with a Biographical and Critical Introduction, by Sir Egerton Brydges. *Roy. 4to. hf. morocco, uncut.*
Lee Priory Press, Kent, 1813.

PRIVATELY PRINTED. 100 *copies.*

1837 RAMSAY, ALLAN. THE GENTLE SHEPHERD ; a Pastoral Comedy; to which is prefixed a new Biographical Memoir, Glossary, &c. Portrait, and 12 plates in aqua-tints by David Allan, (the Scotch Hogarth). *4to. hf. green cf. neat. Scarce.*
Edinburgh, 1808.

1838 RAMESEY, WILLIAM. ASTROLOGIE RESTORED, an Introduction to the general and chief Part of the Language of the Stars, THE FOUR PARTS COMPLETE, folio, *hf. calf, gilt.* Scarce. London, 1653.
A very curious work. The author is alluded to in the Spectator, 582.

1839 RANDOLPH, T. J. MEMOIR, CORRESPONDENCE, and Miscellanies from the Papers of THOMAS JEFFERSON. *Portrait. 4 vols. 8vo. cf.* Charlottesville, Va., 1829.

1840 RANDOLPH, THOMAS. POEMS, with the Muses Looking-Glasse, and Amyntas. *Sml. 4to. hf. cf. gilt, red edges. Very scarce.* Oxford, *Printed by Francis Lichfield, printer for the University,* 1638.

Title-page repaired, otherwise in good order.
" First, and Mr. Heber says *most correct* edition."—*Lowndes.*

1841 RAPELJE, GEORGE. NARRATIVE OF EXCURSIONS, Voyages and Travels in America, Europe, Asia, and Africa. 8vo. cloth. New York, 1834.

Portrait by Durand.

1842 RAPHAEL'S FRESCOES IN THE VATICAN. Les Loges de Raphael gravees par Meulemeester, avec texte par le Baron de Reiffenberg. *The complete series of 52 large and most beautiful line engravings, comprising the whole of the famous paintings and frescoes by Raphael in the Vatican, fine early impressions on superior paper, atlas folio, half plain morocco, by Bedford.* Bruxelles, 1845–53.

One of the greatest Art works which has ever emanated from human genius. It is engraved in the same size and manner as the "Musée Français," to which it forms a most valuable accompaniment. The plates are by far the finest of any that have hitherto been executed to illustrate the great paintings and frescoes by Raphael, and will bear comparison with the best line engravings ever produced.

1843 RAPHAEL'S LOGGIES. ∫ ARCHITETTURA ed ORNATI DELLA LOGGIA del VATICANO. Opera del celebre Rafaele Sanzio de Urbino. *62 plates of the largest size, beautifully engraved on copper, depicting the Interior Decorations of the Vatican. Elephant folio, hf. morocco, uncut, scarce.* Venezia, 1783.

1844 RAPHALL, M. J. Past Biblical History of the Jews. *2 vols. 12mo. cloth.* New York, 1866.

1845 RAPIN de THOYRAS. HISTORY of ENGLAND, translated from the French, with Notes, &c., by N. Tindal. *Maps and Plates. 2 vols. folio, cf.* London, 1732.

1846 RASTELL, WILLIAM. OLD ENGLISH STATUTES. ORIGINAL EDITION. 𝕭𝕷𝕬𝕮𝕶 𝕷𝕰𝕿𝕿𝕰𝕽. *Folio, calf, neat, very scarce.* London, 1598.

Wants title (supplied in MS.) and Address to the Reader, two pages.
" A collection which well-read judges of this lore have pronounced to be essentially necessary to the library of an Antiquary as well as a Lawyer."—*Dibdin.*

1847 RAWLINSON, GEORGE. FIVE GREAT MONARCHIES of THE ANCIENT EASTERN WORLD ; or, the History, Geography, and Antiquities of Chaldea, Assyria, Babylon, Media, and Persia. *Maps and several hundred woodcuts. 4 vols. 8vo. handsomely bound in tree-marbled calf, extra, marbled leaves.* *Murray,* London, 1862–67.

Out of print, and *very scarce.*

1848 RAWLINSON, GEORGE. Historical Evidences of the Truth of the Scripture Records. *12mo. cloth.* Boston, 1860.

1849 RAY, JOHN. Three Physico-Theological Discourses concerning Primitive Chaos, the Deluge, and the Future Conflagration. *8vo. calf, neat.* London, 1713.

1850 RAYMOND, GEORGE. CHRONICLES of ENGLAND; a Metrical History. PROFUSELY ILLUSTRATED *by the insertion of Fine and Rare old Portraits of the Kings, monuments, &c., including a curious series of German portraits. Thick post 8vo. hf. morocco, uncut.*
London, 1842.

1851 READ, J. M., JR. HISTORICAL INQUIRY CONCERNING HENRY HUDSON, his Friends, Relatives and Early Life, his Connection with the Muscovy Company and Discovery of Delaware Bay. *Frontispiece. 8vo. new hf. green morocco, uncut.*
Munsell, Albany, 1866.

1852 ———— Another copy. LARGE PAPER. *Roy. 4to. uncut.*
Albany, 1866.
Only 40 copies printed for sale.

1853 REBELLION RECORD: A Diary of American Events, with Documents, Narratives, Illustrative Incidents, Poetry, etc. *A complete set.* Illustrated with Portraits on Steel, and *numerous fine steel Portraits, Maps and Diagrams, &c.* 12 vols. imp. 8vo. *sheets, folded.* New York, 1863–69.

1854 REBELLION RECORD. A complete series of the portraits for illustrating the Rebellion Record. BRILLIANT PROOF IMPRESSIONS on INDIA PAPER. 156 *portraits.* New York, 1863–69.

1855 RECONSTRUCTION LETTER. Reprinted from the "Tribune," Sept. 3d, 1866. *8vo. uncut. Privately Printed*, New York, 1866.
100 *copies.*

1856 **RECORD COMMISSION.** CHRONICLES AND MEMORIALS OF GREAT BRITAIN AND IRELAND DURING THE MIDDLE AGES. *The complete series as far as published*, embracing the period from the earliest time of British History down to the end of the Reign of Henry VII. *Numerous facsimiles and colored plates. Together* 100 *vols. roy. 8vo. hf. morocco, uncut.*
London, 1858–69.

A complete set of these important publications has never been offered for sale in this country.

On July 25, 1822, the House of Commons presented an address to the Crown, stating that the editions of the works of our ancient historians were inconvenient and defective; that many of their writings still remained in manuscript, and, in some cases, in a single copy only. They added, "that an uniform and convenient edition of the whole, published under His Majesty's royal sanction, would be an undertaking honorable to His Majesty's reign, and conducive to the advancement of historical and constitutional knowledge; that the House therefore humbly besought His Majesty, that He would be graciously pleased to give such directions as His Majesty, in His wisdom, might think fit, for the publication of a complete edition of the ancient historians of this realm, and assured His Majesty that whatever expense might be necessary for this purpose would be made good."

The Master of the Rolls, being very desirous that effect should be given to the resolution of the House of Commons, submitted to her Majesty's Treasury in 1857 a plan for the publication of the ancient chronicles and memorials of the United Kingdom, and it was adopted accordingly. In selecting these works, it was considered right, in the first instance, to give preference to those of which the manuscripts were unique, or the materials of which would help to fill up blanks in English history for which no satisfactory and authentic information hitherto existed in any accessible form. One great object the Master of the Rolls had in view was to form a *corpus historicum* within reasonable limits, and which should be as complete as possible.

Record Commission—

1 The Chronicle of England, by John Capgrave. *Edited by* the Rev. F. C. Hingeston, M.A. 1858.

Capgrave was prior of Lynn, in Norfolk, and provincial of the order of the Friars Hermits of England shortly before the year 1464. His Chronicle extends from the creation of the world to the year 1417. As a record of the language spoken in Norfolk (being written in English), it is of considerable value.

2 Chronicon Monasterii de Abingdon. Vols. I. and II. *Edited by* the Rev. Joseph Stevenson, M.A. 1858.

This Chronicle traces the history of the great Benedictine monastery of Abingdon in Berkshire, from its foundation by King Ina of Wessex, to the reign of Richard I. The author had access to the title-deeds of the house; and incorporates into his history various charters of the Saxon kings, of great importance as illustrating not only the history of the locality but that of the kingdom. The work is now printed for the first time.

3 Lives of Edward the Confessor. I.—La Estoire de Seint Aedward le Rei. II.—Vita Beati Edvardi Regis et Confessoris. III.—Vita Æduuardi Regis qui apud Westmonasterium requiescit. *Edited by* Henry Richards Luard, M.A. 1858.

The first is a poem in Norman French, addressed to Alianor, Queen of Henry III, and probably written in the year 1245. Nothing is known of the author. The second is an anonymous poem, written between the years 1440 and 1450, by command of Henry VI. The third, also by an anonymous author, was apparently written for Queen Edith, between the years 1066 and 1074, during the pressure of the suffering brought on the Saxons by the Norman conquest. It notices many facts not found in other writers, and some which differ considerably from the usual accounts.

4 Monumenta Franciscana ; scilicet, I.—Thomas de Eccleston de Adventu Fratrum Minorum in Angliam. II.—Adæ de Marisco Epistolæ. III.—Registrum Fratrum Minorum Londoniæ. *Edited by* J. S. Brewer, M.A. 1858.

This volume contains original materials for the history of the settlement of the order of Saint Francis in England, the letters of Adam de Marisco, and other papers connected with the foundation and diffusion of this great body. None of these have been before printed.

5 Fasciculi Zizaniorum Magistri Johannis Wyclif cum Tritico. Ascribed to Thomas Netter, of Walden, Provincial of the Carmelite Order in England, and Confessor to King Henry the Fifth. *Edited by* the Rev. W. W. Shirley, M.A. 1858.

This work derives its principal value from being the only contemporaneous account of the rise of the Lollards. Wycliff's little bundles of tares are not less metaphysical than theological, and the conflict between Nominalists and Realists rages side by side with the conflict between the different interpreters of Scripture. The work gives a good idea of the controversies at the end of the 14th and the beginning of the 15th centuries.

6 The Buik of the Croniclis of Scotland ; or, A Metrical Version of the History of Hector Boece; by William Stewart. Vols. I, II, and III. *Edited by* W. B. Turnbull, Esq. 1858.

This is a metrical translation of a Latin Prose Chronicle, and was written in the first half of the 16th century. The narrative begins with the earliest legends, and ends with the death of James I of Scotland, and the " evil ending of the traitors that slew him." The peculiarities of the Scottish dialect are well illustrated in this metrical version, and the student of language will find ample materials for comparison with the English dialects of the same period, and with modern lowland Scotch.

RECORD COMMISSION—

7 JOHANNIS CAPGRAVE LIBER DE ILLUSTRIBUS HENRICIS. *Edited by* the Rev. F. C. HINGESTON, M.A. 1858.

This work is dedicated to Henry VI of England, who appears to have been, in the author's estimation, the greatest of all the Henries. It is divided into three distinct parts, each having its own separate dedication.

8 HISTORIA MONASTERII S. AUGUSTINI CANTUARIENSIS, by THOMAS OF ELMHAM, formerly Monk and Treasurer of that Foundation. *Edited by* CHARLES HARDWICK, M.A. 1858.

This history extends from the arrival of St. Augustine in Kent until 1191. Prefixed is a chronology as far as 1418, which shows in outline what was to have been the character of the work when completed. The only copy known is in the possession of Trinity Hall, Cambridge.

9 EULOGIUM (HISTORIARUM SIVE TEMPORIS): Chronicon ab Orbe condito usque ad Annum Domini 1366; a Monacho quodam Malmesbiriensi exaratum. Vols. I, II, and III. *Edited by* F. S. HAYDON, Esq., B.A. 1858–63.

This is a Latin Chronicle extending from the Creation to the latter part of the reign of Edward III, and written by a monk of the Abbey of Malmesbury, in Wiltshire, about the year 1367. A continuation, carrying the history of England down to the year 1413, was added in the former half of the fifteenth century by an author whose name is not known. The Eulogium itself is chiefly valuable as containing a history, by a contemporary, of the period between 1356 and 1366. The notices of events appear to have been written very soon after their occurrence. Among other interesting matter, the Chronicle contains a diary of the Poitiers campaign, evidently furnished by some person who accompanied the army of the Black Prince.

10 MEMORIALS OF HENRY THE SEVENTH: Bernardi Andreæ Tholosatis Vita Regis Henrici Septimi; necnon alia quædam ad eundem Regem spectantia. *Edited by* JAMES GAIRDNER, Esq. 1858.

The contents of these volumes are—(1) a life of Henry VII, by his poet laureate and historiographer, Bernard André, of Toulouse; (2) the journals of Roger Machado during certain embassies on which he was sent by Henry VII to Spain and Brittany; (3) two curious reports by envoys sent to Spain in the year 1505 touching the succession to the Crown of Castile, and (4) an account of Philip of Castile's reception in England in 1506.

11 MEMORIALS OF HENRY THE FIFTH. I.—Vita Henrici Quinti, Roberto Redmanno auctore. II.—Versus Rhythmici in laudem Regis Henrici Quinti. III.—Elmhami Liber Metricus de Henrico V. *Edited by* CHARLES A. COLE, Esq. 1858.

This volume contains three treatises which more or less illustrate the history of the reign of Henry VI, viz. : A Life by Robert Redman; a Metrical Chronicle by Thomas Elmham, prior of Lenton, a contemporary author; Versus Rhythmici, written apparently by a monk of Westminster Abbey, who was also a contemporary of Henry V. These works are printed for the first time.

12 MUNIMENTA GILDHALLÆ LONDONIENSIS; Liber Albus, Liber Custumarum, et Liber Horn, in archivis Gildhallæ asservati. Vol. I, Liber Albus. Vol. II (in Two Parts), Liber Custumarum. Vol. III, Translation of the Anglo-Norman Passages in Liber Albus, Glossaries, Appendices, and Index. *Edited by* HENRY THOMAS RILEY, Esq., M.A. 1859–62.

The manuscript of the *Liber Albus*, compiled by John Carpenter, Common Clerk of the City of London in the year 1419, is preserved in the Record Room of the City of London. It gives an account of the laws, regulations, and institutions of that City in the twelfth, thirteenth, fourteenth, and early part of the fifteenth centuries.
The *Liber Custumarum* was compiled probably by various hands in the early part of the fourteenth century during the reign of Edward II. It

RECORD COMMISSION—

also gives an account of the laws, regulations, and institutions of the City of London in the twelfth, thirteenth, and early part of the fourteenth centuries.

13 CHRONICA JOHANNIS DE OXENEDES. *Edited by* Sir HENRY ELLIS, K.H. 1859.

Although this Chronicle tells of the arrival of Hengist and Horsa in England in the year 449, yet it substantially begins with the reign of King Alfred, and comes down to the year 1292, where it ends abruptly. The history is particularly valuable for notices of events in the eastern portions of the kingdom, which are not to be elsewhere obtained.

14 A COLLECTION OF POLITICAL POEMS AND SONGS RELATING TO ENGLISH HISTORY, FROM THE ACCESSION OF EDWARD III TO THE REIGN OF HENRY VIII. Vols I and II. *Edited by* THOMAS WRIGHT, Esq., M.A. 1859–61.

These Poems are perhaps the most interesting of all the historical writings of the period. They are various in character; some are upon religious subjects, some may be called satires, and some give no more than a court scandal; but as a whole they present a very fair picture of society, and of the relations of the different classes to one another.

15 The "OPUS TERTIUM," "OPUS MINUS," &c., of ROGER BACON. *Edited by* J. S. BREWER, M.A. 1859.

This is the celebrated treatise—never before printed—so frequently referred to by the great philosopher in his works. It contains the fullest details we possess of the life and labors of Roger Bacon: also a fragment by the same author, supposed to be unique, the "*Compendium Studii Theologiæ.*"

16 BARTHOLOMÆI DE COTTON, MONACHI NORWICENSIS, HISTORIA ANGLICANA; 449–1298 : necnon ejusdem Liber de Archiepiscopis et Episcopis Angliæ. *Edited by* HENRY RICHARDS LUARD, M.A. 1859.

The author, a monk of Norwich, has here given us a Chronicle of England from the arrival of the Saxons in 449 to the year 1298, in or about which year it appears that he died. The latter portion of this history (the whole of the reign of Edward I more especially) is of great value, as the writer was contemporary with the events which he records. An Appendix contains several illustrative documents connected with the previous narrative.

17 BRUT Y TYWYSOGION : or, The Chronicle of the Princes of Wales. *Edited by* the REV. JOHN WILLIAMS AB ITHEL, M.A. 1860.

This work, also known as "The Chronicle of the Princes of Wales," has been attributed to Caradoc of Llancarvan, who flourished about the middle of the twelfth century. It is written in the ancient Welsh language, begins with the abdication and death of Caedwala at Rome, in the year 681, and continues the history down to the subjugation of Wales by Edward I, about the year 1282.

18 A COLLECTION OF ROYAL AND HISTORICAL LETTERS DURING THE REIGN OF HENRY IV. 1399–1404. *Edited by* the Rev. F. C. HINGESTON, M.A. 1860.

This volume, like all the others in the series containing a miscellaneous selection of letters, is valuable on account of the light it throws upon biographical history, and the familiar view it presents of characters, manners, and events. The period requires much elucidation; to which it will materially contribute.

19 THE REPRESSOR OF OVER MUCH BLAMING OF THE CLERGY. By REGINALD PECOCK, sometime Bishop of Chichester. Vols. I and II. *Edited by* CHURCHILL BABINGTON, B.D. 1860.

The "Repressor" may be considered the earliest piece of good theological disquisition of which our English prose literature can boast. The author was born about the end of the fourteenth century, consecrated Bishop of St. Asaph in the year 1444, and translated to the see of Chichester in 1450. Apart from religious matters, the light thrown upon contemporaneous history is very small, but the "Repressor" has great value for the philologist, as it tells us what were the characteristics of the language in use among the cultivated Englishmen of the fifteenth century.

RECORD COMMISSION—

20 ANNALES CAMBRIÆ. *Edited by* the Rev. JOHN WILLIAMS AB ITHEL, M.A. 1860.

These annals, which are in Latin, commence in the year 447, and come down to the year 1288. The earlier portion appears to be taken from an Irish Chronicle, which was also used by Tigernach, and by the compiler of the Annals of Ulster. Its notices throughout, though brief, are valuable. The annals were probably written at St. Davids, by Blegewryd, Archdeacon of Llandaff, the most learned man in his day in all Cymru.

21 THE WORKS OF GIRALDUS CAMBRENSIS. Vols. I, II, and III. *Edited by* J. S. BREWER, M.A. Vol. V and VI. *Edited by* the Rev. JAMES F. DIMOCK, M.A., 5 vols. 1861–68.

The first three volumes contain the historical works of Gerald du Barry, who lived in the reigns of Henry II, Richard I, and John, and attempted to re-establish the independence of Wales by restoring the see of St. Davids to its ancient primacy. He is the only Welsh writer of any importance who has contributed so much to the mediæval literature of this country, or assumed, in consequence of his nationality, so free and independent a tone. Only extracts from these treatises have been printed before, and almost all of them are taken from unique manuscripts.
The Topographia Hibernica (in Vol. V) is the result of Giraldus' two visits to Ireland. The first in the year 1183, the second in 1185–6, when he accompanied Prince John into that country.

22 LETTERS AND PAPERS ILLUSTRATIVE OF THE WARS OF THE ENGLISH IN FRANCE DURING THE REIGN OF HENRY THE SIXTH, KING OF ENGLAND. Vol. I, and Vol. II (in Two Parts). *Edited by* the Rev. JOSEPH STEVENSON, M.A. 1861–64.

The letters and papers contained in these volumes are derived chiefly from originals or contemporary copies extant in the Bibliothèque Impérial, and the Dépôt des Archives, in Paris. We may here trace, step by step, the gradual declension of the English power, until we are prepared to read of its final overthrow.

23 THE ANGLO-SAXON CHRONICLE, ACCORDING TO THE SEVERAL ORIGINAL AUTHORITIES. Vol. I, Original Texts. Vol. II, Translation. *Edited and translated by* BENJAMIN THORPE, Esq. 1861.

This Chronicle, extending from the earliest history of Britain to the year 1154, is justly the boast of England; for no other nation can produce any history, written in its own vernacular, at all approaching it, either in antiquity, truthfulness, or extent, the historical books of the Bible alone excepted. There are at present six independent manuscripts of the Saxon Chronicle, ending in different years, and written in different parts of the country. In the present edition, the text of each manuscript is printed in columns on the same page, so that the student may see at a glance the various changes which occur in orthography, whether arising from locality or age.

24 LETTERS AND PAPERS ILLUSTRATIVE OF THE REIGNS OF RICHARD III AND HENRY VII. Vols. I and II. *Edited by* JAMES GAIRDNER, Esq. 1861–63.

The Papers are derived from MSS. in the Public Record Office, the British Museum, and other repositories. The period to which they refer is unusually destitute of chronicles and other sources of historical information, so that the light obtained from these documents is of special importance.

25 LETTERS OF BISHOP GROSSETESTE, illustrative of the Social Condition of his Time. *Edited by* HENRY RICHARDS LUARD, M.A. 1861.

The Letters of Robert Grosseteste (131 in number) are here collected from various sources, and a large portion of them is printed for the first time. They range in date from about 1210 to 1253.

26 DESCRIPTIVE CATALOGUE OF MANUSCRIPTS RELATING TO THE HISTORY OF GREAT BRITAIN AND IRELAND. Vol. I (in Two

Record Commission—

Parts); Anterior to the Norman Invasion. Vol. II, 1066–1200. *By* Thomas Duffus Hardy, Esq. 1862–65.

The object of this work is to publish notices of all known sources of British history, both printed and unprinted, in one continued sequence. The materials, when historical (as distinguished from biographical), are arranged under the year in which the latest event is recorded in the chronicle or history, and not under the period in which its author, real or supposed, flourished. Biographies are enumerated under the year in which the person commemorated died, and not under the year in which the life was written.

27 Royal and other Historical Letters illustrative of the Reign of Henry III. From the Originals in the Public Record Office. Vol. I, 1216–1235. Vol. II, 1236–1272. *Selected and edited by* the Rev. W. W. Shirley, D.D. 1862–66.

The letters contained in these volumes are derived chiefly from the ancient correspondence formerly in the Tower of London. They illustrate the political history of England during the growth of its liberties, and throw considerable light upon the personal history of Simon de Montfort. The entire collection consists of nearly 700 documents, the greater portion of which is printed for the first time.

28 Chronica Monasterii S. Albani.—1. Thomæ Walsingham Historia Anglicana; Vol. I, 1272–1381: Vol. II, 1381–1422. 2. Willelmi Rishanger Chronica et Annales, 1259–1307. 3. Johannis de Trokelowe et Henrici de Blaneforde Chronica et Annales, 1259–1296; 1307–1324; 1392–1406. 4. Gesta Abbatum Monasterii S. Albani, a Thoma Walsingham, regnante Ricardo Secundo, ejusdem Ecclesiæ Præcentore, compilata; Vol. I, 793–1290: Vol. II, 1290–1349; Vol. III, 1349–1411. *Edited by* Henry Thomas Riley, Esq., M.A. 7 vols. 1863–69.

In the first two volumes is a history of England, from the death of Henry III to the death of Henry V, written by Thomas Walsingham, precentor of St. Albans and prior of the Cell of Wymundham, belonging to that abbey. Walsingham's work is printed from MS. VII in the Arundel Collection in the College of Arms, London, a manuscript of the fifteenth century, collated with MS. 13 E. IX in the King's Library in the British Museum, and MS. VII in the Parker Collection of Manuscripts at Corpus Christi College, Cambridge.

29 Chronicon Abbatiæ Eveshamensis, Auctoribus Dominico Priore Eveshamiæ et Thoma de Marleberge Abbate, a Fundatione ad Annum 1213, una cum Continuatione ad Annum 1418. *Edited by* the Rev. W. D. Macray, M. A. 1863.

The Chronicle of Evesham illustrates the history of that important monastery from its foundation by Egwin, about 690, to the year 1418. Its chief feature is an autobiography, which makes us acquainted with the inner daily life of a great abbey, such as but rarely has been recorded. This work exists in a single MS., and is for the first time printed.

30 Ricardi de Cirencestria Speculum Historiale de Gestis Regum Angliæ. Vol. I, 447–871. Vol. II, 872–1066. *Edited by* John E. B. Mayor, M.A. 1863–69.

The compiler, Richard of Cirencester, was a monk of Westminster, 1355–1400. In the year 1391 he obtained a license to make a pilgrimage to Rome. His history, in four books, extends from 447 to 1066. He announces his intention of continuing it, but there is no evidence that he completed more than these four books.

31 Year Books of the Reign of Edward the First. Years 20–21, 30–31, and 32–33. *Edited and translated by* Alfred John Horwood, Esq. 1863–66.

The volumes known as the "Year Books" contain reports in Norman-French

RECORD COMMISSION—

of cases argued and decided in the Courts of Common Law. They may be considered to a great extent as the "lex non scripta" of England, and have been held in the highest veneration by the ancient sages of the law, and were received by them as the repositories of the first recorded judgments and dicta of the great legal luminaries of past ages.

32 NARRATIVES OF THE EXPULSION OF THE ENGLISH FROM NORMANDY; 1449–1450.—Robertus Blondelli de Reductione Normanniæ: Le Recouvrement de Normendie, par Berry, Hérault du Roy: Conferences between the Ambassadors of France and England. *Edited, from MSS. in the Imperial Library at Paris, by* the Rev. Jos. Stevenson. 1863.

This volume contains the narrative of an eye-witness who details with considerable power and minuteness the circumstances which attended the final expulsion of the English from Normandy in the year 1450. The history commences with the infringement of the truce by the capture of Fougères, and ends with the battle of Formigny and the embarkation of the Duke of Somerset.

33 HISTORIA ET CARTULARIUM MONASTERII S. PETRI GLOUCESTRIÆ. Vols. I, II, and III. *Edited by* W. H. HART, Esq., F.S.A. 1863–67.

This work consists of two parts, the History and the Cartulary of the Monastery of St. Peter, Gloucester. The history furnishes an account of the monastery from its foundation, in the year 681, to the early part of the reign of Richard II. Its authorship has generally been assigned to Walter Froucester, the twentieth abbot, but without any foundation.

34 ALEXANDRI NECKAM DE NATURIS RERUM LIBRO DUO; with NECKAM'S POEM, DE LAUDIBUS DIVINÆ SAPIENTIÆ. *Edited by* THOMAS WRIGHT, Esq., M. A. 1863.

Neckam was a man who devoted himself to science, such as it was in the twelfth century. In the "De Naturis Rerum" are to be found what may be called the rudiments of many sciences mixed up with much error and ignorance. Neckam was not thought infallible, even by his contemporaries, for Roger Bacon remarks of him, "this Alexander in many things wrote what was true and useful; but he neither can nor ought by just title to be reckoned among authorities." He had his own views in morals, and in giving us a glimpse of them, as well as of his other opinions, he throws much light upon the manners, customs, and general tone of thought prevalent in the twelfth century.

35 LEECHDOMS, WORTCUNNING, AND STARCRAFT OF EARLY ENGLAND; being a Collection of Documents illustrating the History of Science in this Country before the Norman Conquest. Vols. I, II, and III. *Collected and edited by* the Rev. T. OSWALD COCKAYNE, M.A. 1864–66.

This work illustrates not only the history of science, but the history of superstition. In addition to the information bearing directly upon the medical skill and medical faith of the times, there are many passages which incidentally throw light upon the general mode of life and ordinary diet. The volumes are interesting not only in their scientific, but also in their social aspect.

36 ANNALES MONASTICI. Vol. I:—Annales de Margan, 1066–1232; Annales de Theokesberia, 1066–1263; Annales de Burton, 1004–1263. Vol. II:—Annales Monasterii de Wintonia, 519–1277; Annales Monasterii de Waverleia, 1–1291. Vol. III:—Annales Prioratus de Dunstaplia, 1–1297; Annales Monasterii de Bermundeseia, 1042–1432. Vol. IV:—Annales Monasterii de Oseneia, 1016–1347; Chronicon vulgo dictum Chronicon Thomæ Wykes, 1066–1289; Annales Prioratus de Wigornia, 1–1377. Vol. V:—

Record Commission—

Index and Glossary. *Edited by* Henry Richards Luard, M.A. 1864–69.

The present collection of Monastic Annals embraces all the more important chronicles compiled in religious houses in England during the thirteenth century. These distinct works are ten in number. The extreme period which they embrace ranges from the year 1 to 1432.

37 Magna Vita S. Hugonis Episcopi Lincolniensis. From Manuscripts in the Bodleian Library, Oxford, and the Imperial Library, Paris. *Edited by* the Rev. James F. Dimock, M.A. 1864.

This work contains a number of very curious and interesting incidents, and, being the work of a contemporary, is very valuable, not only as a truthful biography of a celebrated ecclesiastic, but as the work of a man, who, from personal knowledge, gives notices of passing events, as well as of individuals who were then taking active part in public affairs. The author, in all probability, was Adam Abbot of Evesham.

38 Chronicles and Memorials of the Reign of Richard the First. Vol. I:—Itinerarium Peregrinorum et Gesta Regis Ricardi. Vol. II:—Epistolæ Cantuarienses; the Letters of the Prior and Convent of Christ Church, Canterbury; 1187 to 1199. *Edited by* William Stubbs, M.A. 1864–65.

The authorship of the Chronicle in Vol. I, hitherto ascribed to Geoffrey Vinesauf, is now more correctly ascribed to Richard, Canon of the Holy Trinity of London. The narrative extends from 1187 to 1199; but its chief interest consists in the minute and authentic narrative which it furnishes of the exploits of Richard I, from his departure from England in December, 1189, to his death in 1199. The author states in his prologue that he was an eye-witness of much that he records.
The letters in Vol. II, written between 1187 and 1199, are of value as furnishing authentic materials for the history of the ecclesiastical condition of England during the reign of Richard I.

39 Recueil des Croniques et anchiennes Istories de la Grant Bretaigne a present nomme Engleterre, par Jehan de Waurin. Vol. I:—Albina to 688. Vol. II:—1399–1422. *Edited by* William Hardy, Esq., F.S.A. 1864–68.

40 A Collection of the Chronicles and Ancient Histories of Great Britain, now called England, by John de Wavrin. Albina to 688. (Translation of the preceding Vol. I.) *Edited and translated by* William Hardy, Esq., F.S.A. 1864.

This curious chronicle extends from the fabulous period of history down to the return of Edward IV to England in the year 1471, after the second deposition of Henry VI. The manuscript from which the text of the work is taken is preserved in the Imperial Library at Paris, and is believed to be the only complete and nearly contemporary copy in existence. It was written towards the end of the fifteenth century, having been expressly executed for Louis de Bruges, Seigneur de la Gruthuyse and Earl of Winchester, from whose cabinet it passed into the library of Louis XII at Blois.

41 Polychronicon Ranulphi Higden, with Trevisa's Translation. Vols. I and II. *Edited by* Churchill Babington, B.D. 1865–69.

This is one of the many mediæval chronicles which assume the character of a history of the world. It begins with the creation, and is brought down to the author's own time, the reign of Edward III.
The two English translations, which are printed with the original Latin, afford interesting illustrations of the gradual change of our language, for one was made in the fourteenth century, the other in the fifteenth. The differences between Trevisa's version and that of the unknown writer are often considerable.

Record Commission—

42 Le Livere de Reis de Brittanie e Le Livere de Reis de Engletere. *Edited by* John Glover, M.A. 1865.

These two treatises, though they cannot rank as independent narratives, are nevertheless valuable as careful abstracts of previous historians, especially "Le Livere de Reis de Engletere." Some various readings are given which are interesting to the philologist as instances of semi-Saxonized French.

43 Chronica Monasterii de Melsa, ab Anno 1150 usque ad Annum 1406. Vols. I, II, and III. *Edited by* Edward Augustus Bond, Esq. 1866–68.

The Abbey of Meaux was a Cistercian house, and the work of its abbot is both curious and valuable. In addition to the private affairs of the monastery, some light is thrown upon the public events of the time, which are however kept distinct, and appear at the end of the history of each abbot's administration. The text has been printed from what is said to be the autograph of the original compiler, Thomas de Burton, the nineteenth abbot.

44 Matthæi Parisiensis Historia Anglorum, sive, ut vulgo dicitur, Historia Minor. Vols. I, II, and III. 1067–1245. *Edited by* Sir Frederic Madden, K.H. 1866–69.

The exact date at which this work was written is, according to the chronicler, 1250. The history is of considerable value as an illustration of the period during which the author lived, and contains a good summary of the events which followed the Conquest.

45 Liber Monasterii de Hyda : A Chronicle and Chartulary of Hyde Abbey, Winchester, 455–1023. *Edited, from a Manuscript in the Library of the Earl of Macclesfield, by* Edward Edwards, Esq. 1866.

The "Book of Hyde" is a compilation from much earlier sources, which are usually indicated with considerable care and precision.
There is to be found, in the "Book of Hyde," much information relating to the reign of King Alfred which is not known to exist elsewhere. The volume contains some curious specimens of Anglo-Saxon and Mediæval English.

46 Chronicon Scotorum : A Chronicle of Irish Affairs, from the Earliest Times to 1135 ; with a Supplement, containing the Events from 1141 to 1150. *Edited, with a Translation, by* William Maunsell Hennessy, Esq., M.R.I.A. 1866.

There is, in this volume, a legendary account of the peopling of Ireland and of the adventures which befell the various heroes who are said to have been connected with Irish history. The succession of events is marked, year by year, from A.M. 1599 to A.D. 1150. The principal events narrated in the later portion of the work are the invasions of foreigners and the wars of the Irish among themselves. The text has been printed from a MS. preserved in the library of Trinity College, Dublin, written partly in Latin, partly in Irish.

47 The Chronicle of Pierre de Langtoft, in French Verse, from the earliest Period to the Death of Edward I. Vols. I and II. *Edited by* Thomas Wright, Esq., M.A. 1866–68.

This chronicle is divided into three parts; in the first is an abridgment of Geoffrey of Monmouth's "Historia Britonum," in the second, a history of the Anglo-Saxon and Norman kings, down to the death of Henry III, and in the third a history of the reign of Edward I.

48 The War of the Gaedhil with the Gaill, or, The Invasions of Ireland by the Danes and other Norsemen. *Edited, with a Translation, by* James Henthorn Todd, D.D. 1867:

The work in its present form, in the editor's opinion, is a comparatively modern version of an undoubtedly ancient original. That it was compiled from

RECORD COMMISSION—

contemporary materials has been proved by curious incidental evidence. It is stated in the account given of the battle of Clontarf that the full tide in Dublin Bay on the day of the battle (23 April 1014) coincided with sunrise; and that the returning tide in the evening aided considerably in the defeat of the Danes. The fact has been verified by astronomical calculations, and the inference is that the author of the chronicle, if not himself an eye-witness, must have derived his information from those who were eye-witnesses.

49 GESTA REGIS HENRICI SECUNDI BENEDICTI ABBATIS. THE CHRONICLE OF THE REIGNS OF HENRY II AND RICHARD I, 1169–1192; known under the name of BENEDICT OF PETERBOROUGH. Vols. I and II. *Edited by* WILLIAM STUBBS, M.A. 1867.

This chronicle of the reigns of Henry II and Richard I, known commonly under the name of Benedict of Peterborough, is one of the best existing specimens of a class of historical compositions of the first importance to the student.

50 MUNIMENTA ACADEMICA, OR, DOCUMENTS ILLUSTRATIVE OF ACADEMICAL LIFE AND STUDIES AT OXFORD (in Two Parts). *Edited by* the Rev. HENRY ANSTEY, M.A. 2 vols. 1868.

This work will supply materials for a History of Academical Life and Studies in the University of Oxford during the 13th, 14th, and 15th centuries.

51 CHRONICA MAGISTRI ROGERI DE HOUEDENE. Vols. I and II. *Edited by* WILLIAM STUBBS, M.A. 1868–69.

This work has long been justly celebrated, but not thoroughly understood until Mr. Stubbs' edition. The earlier portion, extending from 732 to 1148, appears to be a copy of a compilation made in Northumbria about 1161, to which Hoveden added little. From 1148 to 1169—a very valuable portion of this work—the matter is derived from another source, to which Hoveden appears to have supplied little, and not always judiciously. From 1170 to 1192 is the portion which corresponds with the Chronicle known under the name of Benedict of Peterborough (*see* No. 49); but it is not a copy, being sometimes an abridgment, at others a paraphrase. From 1192 to 1201 may be said to be wholly Hoveden's work; it is extremely valuable, and an authority of the first importance.

52 ANCIENT LAWS OF IRELAND. Introduction to Senchus Mor; or, Law of Distress. 2 vols. 1865.

1857 REDFIELD, ISAAC F. The LAW of WILLS, embracing also the Jurisprudence of Insanity, &c., &c. *Thick 8vo. law sheep.*
Boston, 1864.

1858 REDPATH, JAMES. Public Life of Capt. John Brown. *Portrait.* *12mo. cloth.*
Boston, 1860.

1859 REED, ESTHER. Life of Esther de Berdt, afterwards Esther Reed. *12mo. cloth.*
Philadelphia, 1853.

PRIVATELY PRINTED.

1860 REED AND CADWALLADER Pamphlets, A Reprint Of, with An Appendix. *8vo. new hf. red morocco, uncut, by Bradstreet.*
(Philadelphia), 1863.

Privately Printed.

1861 REEVE AND MUGGLETON. A volume of Spiritual Epistles, being the copies of several letters written by the two last PROPHETS and MESSENGERS of God. Containing a variety of Spiritual Revelations, collected by Alexander Delmar. *Portrait. Thick sml. 4to. old calf, rare.*
London, 1755.

1862 REID, LIEUT. COL. Progress of the Development of the Law of Storms and of the Variable Winds. *Numerous charts, cuts, &c. Impl. 8vo. cloth.*
London, 1849.

1863 REIDESEL, MADAME DE. Letters and Memoirs, relating to the War of American Independence, and the Capture of the German Troops at Saratoga, translated from the Original German by W. L. Stone. *8vo. uncut.* *Munsell*, Albany, 1867.

1864 —— Another copy, LARGE PAPER. *Impl. 8vo. uncut.*
Munsell, Albany, 1867.

1865 REMARKABLE CHARACTERS. LIVES and PORTRAITS of, drawn from the most authentic sources. *Upwards of 60 fine and curious portraits. 2 vols. 8vo. hf. morocco, gilt, scarce.* London, 1819.

1866 REMY AND BRENCHLEY. JOURNEY TO GREAT SALT-LAKE CITY, with a sketch of the History, Religion, and Customs of the Mormons. *Portraits. 2 vols. thick impl. 8vo. cloth.* London, 1861.

1867 RENÉE OF FRANCE, *Duchess of Ferrara.* Memorials of. *Vignettes. 12mo. new hf. morocco.* London, 1859.

1868 REPORT of a FRENCH PROTESTANT Refugee in Boston, 1687 : Translated from the French. By E. T. Fisher. *8vo. new hf. crimson morocco.* *Privately Printed, Brooklyn,* N. Y. 1868.
UNIQUE. *The only copy printed on India Paper (?)*

1869 —— Another copy. *4to. uncut.* *Brooklyn,* N. Y. 1868.
Edition of 125 *copies.*

1870 REPTON, H. WORKS ON LANDSCAPE GARDENING, viz. OBSERVATIONS on the THEORY and PRACTICE of LANDSCAPE GARDENING, 1 vol. FRAGMENTS on the THEORY and PRACTICE of LANDSCAPE GARDENING, 1 vol. *With* 93 *large and finely* COLORED *plates, with movable slips showing the effect of the alterations, &c.* 2 vols. *Imperial 4to. hf. russia, extra,* edges un-trimmed. London, 1803–16.
SPLENDID COPIES OF THE BEST EDITIONS, *rare.*
Priced by Bohn 1845, £8. 10s.

1871 REPTON, HUMPHREY. ODD WHIMS and Miscellanies, *numerous fine tinted plates, from designs by the author.* 2 *vols. roy. 8vo. blue morocco, gilt edges.* London, 1804.
LARGE PAPER, *scarce.*
" An amusing and well written book, in which first occurs the Story of the Bashful Man."

1872 RERESBY, SIR JOHN. TRAVELS and MEMOIRS, exhibiting a View of the Governments and Society in the Principal States and Courts of Europe, and the Memoirs, containing Anecdotes and Secret History of the Courts of Charles II and James II. *Thick impl. 8vo. russia, extra, gilt edges.* London, 1813.
LARGE PAPER, *extra Illustrated with fine portraits and views.*
"Sir John Reresby was a staunch loyalist; his memoirs are written in a lively, pleasant style, but abound more in court anecdote than in political history."—*Censura Literaria.*

1873 RETROSPECTIVE REVIEW, AND HISTORICAL and ANTIQUARIAN MAGAZINE. Consisting of Criticisms upon, Analyses of, and Extracts from Curious, Valuable, and Scarce Old Books. *Both series complete.* 16 *vols.* in 15, 8vo. hf. cf. (*Vols.* 15 *and* 16 *not quite uniform.*) London, 1820–26, 1828.
" An excellent Review of early Eng'ish Literature. The Criticisms in the first series were written by George Robinson, Esq., W. Gray, Esq., Mr. Sergt. Talfourd, Joseph Parkes, Esq., etc., the whole being under the superintendence of H. Southern, Esq. The second series was edited by Henry Southern and Nicholas Harris Nicolas."—*Lowndes.*

1874 RETZSCH'S ILLUSTRATIONS to SHAKESPEARE complete, with Descriptions, Eng. and Ger. *upwards of* 100 *fine outline engravings, oblong 4to. hf. morocco, gilt top.* New York, 1849.

These beautiful plates illustrate Hamlet, Macbeth, Romeo and Juliet, King Lear, The Tempest, Othello, Merry Wives of Windsor, and King Henry IV.

REVOLUTIONARY WAR, see Orderly Books.

1875 REYNARD the Fox, translated from the German Version of Goethe by Thomas James Arnold, *with Illustrations from the designs by* KAULBACH. Sq. 8vo. *new cloth, gilt.* London, 1860.

1876 REYNARD the Fox, a renowned Apologue of the Middle Ages, reproduced in Rhyme, *elegantly printed on thick paper, with colored and floriated capitals. 8vo. hf. olive mor. gilt top.*
London, 1845.

1877 REYNARD the Fox. *A complete set of the celebrated engravings on steel of the designs of J. Wolf.* ARTIST'S PROOFS ON INDIA PAPER. 13 *plates, 8vo.*

1878 REYNOLDS, GEORGE W. M. NOVELS, a complete series. 27 vols. 8vo. cloth. Philadelphia, V. D.
Comprising :

Joseph Wilmot.	Queen Johanna.
Mary Stuart.	Isabella Vincent.
Young Duchess.	Mary Price.
Soldier's Wife.	Ruined Gamester.
Parracide.	Ciprina.
Agnes Evelyn.	Countess of Lascelles.
Gipsy Chief.	Eustace Quentin.
Massacre of Glencoe.	Life in Paris.
Lord Saxondale.	Rose Foster.
Rye House Plot.	Rosa Lambert.
Count Christoval.	Venetia Trelawney.
Banker's Daughter.	Kenneth, Earl of Glengyle.
Caroline of Brunswick.	Necromancer.

Mysteries of the Court of London.

1879 RHODE ISLAND. Official Record of, in the United States Army and Navy during the Rebellion of the Southern States. *Portrait. Thick impl. 8vo. boards, uncut.* Providence, 1866.

1880 RHODE ISLAND. RECORDS OF THE STATE AND COLONY OF, and of the Providence Plantations in New England, from 1636 to 1792. Edited by the Hon. Jno. R. Bartlett. *Numerous proof portraits inserted.* 10 vols. thick impl. 8vo. boards, uncut.
Providence, 1856–1865.

LARGE PAPER COPY.

1881 RICE, GEO. EDWARD. An Old Play in a New Garb; (Hamlet, Prince of Denmark), with *humorous etchings. 12mo. bds. uncut.*
Boston, 1853.

1882 RICHARDSON, ALBERT D. The Secret Service, the Field, the Dungeon, and Escape. *Portraits. 8vo. sheep.* Hartford, 1865.

1883 RICHARDSON, JONATHAN. WORKS. Theory of Painting, Essay on the Art of Criticism (in relation to painting), Science of a Connoisseur, New Edition with additions, &c. *with a fine series of etched portraits of celebrated painters by Worlidge. Sm. 4to. hf. russia, neat.* Strawberry-Hill (London), 1792.

FINE COPY, intended as a supplement to Walpole's Anecdotes of Painters and Engravers.

1884 RICHARDSON, SAMUEL. WORKS, comprising CLARISSA HARLOWE, 8 vols. SIR CHARLES GRANDISON, 7 vols. PAMELA, 4 vols. *Numerous illustrations, together 19 vols. 12mo. hf. cf. gilt.*
London, 1792.

"The power of Richardson's painting, in his deeper scenes of Tragedy, never has been, and probably never will be, excelled."—*Sir Walter Scott.*

1885 Ricraft, Josiah. A Survey of England's Champions and Truth's Faithfull Patriots; with the lively pourtraitures of the severall Commanders. *8vo. calf. Reprint from the edition of* 1647. 22 *Portraits.*
London, 1818.
LARGE PAPER.

1886 RIDPATH'S BORDER HISTORY of ENGLAND and SCOTLAND from the Earliest times to the Union. Last edition, revised by his Brother, *4to. hf. russia, gilt.*
Berwick, 1848.

An authentic, valuable, and highly interesting work, comprising the Transactions of the Two Nations with each other, Accounts of Remarkable Antiquities, Anecdotes of the most considerable Families and Distinguished Characters, &c.

1887 RILEY, JAMES. LOSS of the AMERICAN BRIG COMMERCE, wrecked on the coast of Africa, August, 1815, with an account of Timbuctoo and the hitherto undiscovered great city of Wassanah. *Map. 4to. cloth.*
London, 1817.

1888 ———— Another copy, *profusely illustrated. Thick 8vo. sheep.*
For the author, New York, 1817.

1889 RITSON, JOSEPH. ANTIQUARIAN AND POETICAL WORKS complete. BEST EDITIONS, with *engravings* by STOTHARD, BEWICK, &c. *Together* 27 *vols. crown* and *post 8vo. uniformly bound in bright calf, gilt, yellow edges.* London, *V. Y.*

FINE UNIFORM SET, *very scarce*, comprising the following works:

RITSON, JOSEPH. The English Anthology, *with Vignettes by Stothard.* 3 *vols. crown 8vo.*
T. & J. Egerton, London, 1793.

RITSON, JOSEPH. Scottish Song, with the Musick, (and an Historical Essay.) 2 *vols. crown 8vo.* VERY SCARCE.
J. Johnson & J. Egerton, Lond. 1794.

RITSON, JOSEPH. Ancient English Metrical Romancees, with a Dissertation on Romance and Minstrelsy. 3 *vols. crown 8vo.*
Bulmer, London, 1802.

RITSON, JOSEPH. Bibliographia Poetica; a Catalogue of English Poets, of the twelfth, thirteenth, fourteenth, fifteenth, and sixteenth Centuries, with a short Account of their Works. *Crown 8vo.*
G. & W. Nicol, London, 1802.

RITSON, JOSEPH. Northern Garlands. The *Bishopric Garland*, a choice Collection of Excellent Songs; The *Yorkshire Garland*, a Curious Collection of old and new Songs; The *Northumberland Garland*, or Newcastle Nightingale; The *North Country Chorister;* also *Gammer Gurton's Garland*, or the Nursery Parnassus. *Tree calf, gilt leaves, by Clarke and Bedford. Crown 8vo.* 5 *vols. in* 1. *The last one is very scarce. R. Triphook, London,* 1810.

RITSON, JOSEPH. Annals of the Caledonians, Picts, and Scots, and of Strathclyde, Cumberland, Galloway, and Murray. Introduction and Notes. 2 *vols. crown 8vo.*
Payne & Foss, London, 1828.

RITSON, JOSEPH. Ancient Songs and Ballads, from the Reign of King Henry the Second to the Revolution. 2d Edition. 2 vols. *crown 8vo. Payne & Foss*, London, 1829. (Reprint of the former edition (1790), corrected and enlarged by the author.)

RITSON, JOSEPH. Fairy Tales, to which are prefixed Dissertations on Pigmies and Fairies. Edited by Mr. Frank from a MS. copy. *Crown 8vo. W. Pickering*, London, 1831.

RITSON, JOSEPH. ROBIN HOOD: A Collection of All the Ancient Poems, Songs, and Ballads, relative to that celebrated outlaw, with Historical Anecdotes of his Life. Notes, &c. 2 vols. *crown 8vo.*
W. Pickering, London, 1832.
SECOND EDITION. This edition contains several additions made by Ritson in his own copy; and the editor (his nephew) has added in the Appendix the Tale of Robin Hood and the Monk. The woodcuts are better struck off, and clearer.—*Lowndes.*

RITSON, JOSEPH. Pieces of Ancient Popular Poetry, from Authentic MSS. and Old printed copies, with Preface and Notes. 2d edition, *with cuts by* BEWICK. *Crown 8vo.*
W. Pickering, London, 1833.

RITSON, JOSEPH. A Select Collection of English Songs ; with Preface and Historical Essay on the Origin and Progress of National Song. The second edition, with Additional Songs and Notes, by Thomas Park, F. S. A. *3 vols. crown 8vo.*
London, 1813.

RITSON, JOSEPH. The Caledonian Muse ; a Chronological Selection of Scottish Poetry from the earliest Times. *Portrait. Crown 8vo.*
London, 1785.

RITSON, JOSEPH. Poems written Anno MCCLII, by Laurence Minot ; with Introductory Dissertations on the Scottish Wars of Edward III on his Claim to the Throne of France, and Notes and Glossary. *Crown 8vo.*
J. H. Burn, London, 1825.

RITSON, JOSEPH. The Life of King Arthur ; from Ancient Historians and Authentic Documents. With Preface, Notes, and Appendix. *Crown 8vo.*
Payne & Foss, London, 1825.

RITSON, JOSEPH. Memoirs of the Celts or Gauls ; with an Appendix, in which will be found a Dictionary of Celtic Words and a Bibliotheca Celtica. *Crown 8vo.*
Payne & Foss, London, 1827.

RITSON, JOSEPH. The Letters of, Edited chiefly from Originals in the Possession of his Nephew, (Joseph Frank,) to which is prefixed a Memorial of the Author by Sir Harris Nicolas. *2 vols. crown 8vo.*
W. Pickering, London, 1833.

1890 ROBBINS, ARCHIBALD. Journal, comprising an account of the Loss of the Brig Commerce, of Hartford, upon the West Coast of Africa, &c. *Map, 12mo. sheep.* Hartford, (1821.)

1891 ROBERTSON, DR. J. On Diseases of the Generative System. *Plates. 8vo. boards.* London, 1812.

1892 ROBERTSON, DAVID. TOUR through the ISLE of MAN, to which is subjoined A Review of the Manks History. PROOF IMPRESSIONS *of the numerous aqua-tint plates.* Impl. 8vo. *russia, extra, marbled edges.* *For the Author*, London, 1794.

LARGE PAPER, containing the celebrated patriotic passage (p. 233) for which the author was imprisoned, and which was afterwards suppressed.

1893 ROBERTSON, JAMES A. GAELIC TOPOGRAPHY of SCOTLAND, and what it proves, explained ; with much Historical, Antiquarian, and Descriptive Information. *Map. Thick 12mo. new cloth.*
Edinburgh, 1869.

1894 ROBERTSON, WILLIAM. History of America. *12mo. sheep.*
Walpole, N. H., 1800.

A Scarce Imprint.

1895 ROBIN HOOD. Life and Adventures of, by John Marsh. *Profusely illustrated. 12mo. new cloth.* London, 1869.

1896 ROBINSON, HENRY CRABBE. DIARY, REMINISCENCES, and CORRESPONDENCE. Selected and edited by Thomas Sadler. *Fine portrait.* 3 thick vols. 8vo. *new cloth, uncut.* London, 1869.

One of the most interesting works issued within the last decade. Robinson was on the most intimate terms with Goethe, Coleridge, Lamb, Rogers, Wordsworth, and other prominent literary characters, whom he entertained at his famous breakfasts and dinners.

1897 ROBINSON, P. F. VITRUVIUS BRITANNICUS, complete, with *upwards of 50 large and fine engravings, by Le Keux, Shaw, Radcliffe, &c., from actual admeasurement, and illustrating the splendid interiors and decorations.* Impl. folio, *hf. red morocco.*
London, 1846.

Comprises the History and Views of Woburn Abbey, Seat of the Duke of Bedford, Hatfield House, Seat of Marq. of Salisbury, Hardwicke Hall, and Cassionbury Park.

1898 Robinson, W. Parks, Promenades and Gardens of Paris described and considered in relation to the wants of our own cities and Public and Private Gardens. *Elegantly illustrated with upwards of 400 fine engravings on wood.* Thick 8vo. *new cloth, extra.* *Murray,* London, 1869.

1899 Robson, G. F. Picturesque Views of English Cities, edited by J. Britton. *A series of 32 extremely beautiful engravings of English Cities, by Adlard, Barrenger, Barber, Higham, Le Keux, Jeavons, &c., &c.* Brilliant Proofs on India Paper, each plate *accompanied with the etching, also on India Paper.* Impl. 4to. *handsomely bound in crimson morocco, super-extra, gilt edges.* London, 1828.

Large Paper, with the Outline Etchings, *of which only 12 copies were issued.*

1900 Robson, John. Proofs of a Conspiracy against all the Religions and Governments of Europe, carried in the secret meetings of the Free-Masons, Illuminati, &c. 8vo. *cf. neat.* London, 1797.

1901 Rochefocault, Duke de. Maxims and Moral Reflections. 12*mo. paper.* Boston, by *I. Thomas and E. Andrews,* 1794.

1902 Rochefoucault, Liancourt. Travels through the United States of America, the Country of the Iroquois, and Upper Canada in 1795, '96, and '97. 4 vols. 8vo. *bds. edges untrimmed.* London, 1799.

1903 Rochester, John, *Earl of.* Poems, &c. with Valentinian, a Tragedy. 8vo. (12mo.) *calf, scarce.* London, 1696.

" Lord Rochester's Poems have much more obscenity than wit, more wit than poetry, and more poetry than politeness."—*Walpole.*

1904 Rockingham, Marquis of. Memoirs of, and his Contemporaries, with original Letters, &c., by George Thomas, Earl of Albemarle. *Portraits.* 2 vols. 8vo. *hf. morocco, neat.* London, 1852.

1905 Rodwell, G. Herbert. Memoirs of an Umbrella. *Illustrated with 68 humorous engravings on wood by Landell, after designs by* " *Phiz.*" 4vo. *hf. morocco, scarce.* London, 1846.

1906 Rogers, Henry D. Geology of Pennsylvania, Government Survey, with a general view of the Geology of the United States. *Numerous colored plates, woodcuts, &c.* 2 vols. royal 4to. *in three, with Atlas of Maps, &c.* 4 vols. *bds. uncut.* New York, 1868.

1907 Rogers, James E. T. History of Agriculture and Prices in England from the year after the Oxford Parliament (1259) to the commencement of the Continental War (1793), compiled from original sources. 2 vols. 8vo. *new cloth.* *Clarendon Press,* Oxford, 1866.

1908 Rogers, Samuel. Poems, *printed by Bensley, with woodcuts from drawings by Stothard. Title on India Paper.* 12*mo. maroon morocco, gilt.* London, 1816.

The Balmanno Copy.

1909 Rogers, Samuel. Pleasures of Memory, a Poem in two parts. *Original Edition.* 4*to. calf, extra.* London, 1792.

First Edition, *scarce.*

1910 ROLAND, MME. APPEAL TO AN IMPARTIAL Posterity, or a collection
of Tracts written by her during her confinement in Prison.
Also, MISCELLANEOUS WORKS. *Together* 3 *vols. 8vo. cf. Scarce.*
London, 1796, &c.

1911 ROMAN CATACOMBS. ROMA SOTTERRANEA; or some ac-
count of the Roman Catacombs, especially of the Cemetery of
San Callisto. Compiled from the works of Commendatore de
Rossi by the Rev. J. S. Northcote and Rev. W. R. Brownlow.
Large folding map, and numerous colored plates. 8vo. new
cloth. London, 1869.

1912 ROMERO, SEÑOR MATIAS. Account of the Complimentary Dinner
to. *4to. uncut.* *Privately Printed,* New York, 1866.

1913 RONALDS AND RICHARDSON. CHEMICAL TECHNOLOGY; or, Chemistry in its Applications to the Arts and Manufactures, with a
revision of Dr. Knapp's "Technology." *Upwards of* 1000 *illustrations.* 7 *vols. 8vo. new hf. olive morocco.* London, 1855.

1914 ROSCOE, HENRY. SPECTRUM ANALYSIS. Six Lectures delivered in
1868 before the Society of Apothecaries of London. *Profusely illustrated with* COLORED *plates, wood-cuts, &c. &c.* 8vo.
new cloth, gilt. London, (New York), 1869.

1915 ROSCOE'S SPANISH, ITALIAN, AND GERMAN NOVELISTS,
the THREE WORKS COMPLETE, 11 vols. post 8vo. *new hf. calf, extra,* (pub. in bds. £5. 15s. 6d.). London, 1826–36.
FINE, UNIFORM SET. *Scarce.*
The most interesting and valuable translations from the best authors, both
ancient and modern, accompanied by critical and biographical notices.

1916 ROSCOE, THOMAS. WANDERINGS AND EXCURSIONS IN NORTH AND
SOUTH WALES. *Profusely illustrated, upwards of* 100 *fine steel
plate engravings from drawings by Cattermole, Cox, and Creswick.
Maps, &c.* 2 *vols. 8vo. polished calf, extra, gilt edges.*
London, 1862.

1917 ROSCOE, WM. THE LIFE AND PONTIFICATE OF LEO THE TENTH.
Original Edition, *illustrated with portraits of Leo X, Luther,
Raffaello, also Manuzio, and a number of wood-cuts.* 4 vols. 4to.
calf. Liverpool, 1805.
Sir Francis Palgrave's copy, with his autograph.

1918 ROSS, ALEXANDER. HELENORE; or, The Fortunate Shepherdess;
a Poem in the broad Scotch Dialect. Edited, with Life of the
Author, &c., by John Longmuir. Sml. 4to. hf. mor. uncut.
Edinburgh, 1866.
LARGE PAPER, *few printed.*

1919 (ROSSET). L'AGRICULTURE, Poëme, avec une Discours sur la Poésie
Géorgique. *Vignettes by Marillier.* 4to. *french mottled cf. gilt.*
Scarce. *L'Imprimerie Royale,* Paris, 1774.

1920 ROSSETTI, D. G. EARLY ITALIAN POETS, from Ciullo D'Alcamo to
Dante Alighieri (1100, 1200, 1300) in the original metres, to-
gether with Dante's Vita Nuova. 12mo. *new cloth.*
London, 1861.

1921 ROUSSEAU, J. J. JULIE, ou la NOUVELLE HELOISE. ILLUSTRATED
EDITION, *numerous engravings by Tony Johannot, Wattier, Baron,
Girardet, Rogier, &c.* 2 *vols. thick impl. 8vo. new hf. mor. gilt.*
Paris, 1845.

1922 Rousseau, John James. Emilius; or, an Essay on Education, translated from the French by Mr. Nugent. *Front.* 2 *vols.* 8vo. *cf.*   London, 1763.

1923 Rousseau, Jean Jacques. Discourse upon the Origin and Foundation of the Inequality among Mankind. 8vo. new hf. morocco, uncut.   London, 1761.
Large Paper, *scarce.*

1924 Rowlands, Henry. Antiquities of the Isle of Anglesey, Natural and Historical, *engravings and map*, best edition, 4to. *calf, scarce.*   London, 1776.
This work contains many interesting particulars respecting the Aboriginal Britons, Druids, &c., comparative tables of the Celtic and other languages.

1925 ROYAL ENTERTAINMENT. Reports relating to the Entertainment of Her Majesty the Queen in the Guildhall of the City of London on Lord Mayor's Day. Unique copy, *with numerous large folding plates, Views, &c. &c. Autographs, &c.* Sml. folio, cloth, *uncut.*   London, 1838.

1926 Ruggles, Thomas. History of the Poor; their Rights, Duties, and the Laws respecting them. 2 *vols. 8vo. cf. gilt.*
                                                       London, 1793.

1927 Rushworth's Historical Collection of Private Passages of State, Weighty Matters in Law, and Remarkable Proceedings in Parliament. 7 *vols. folio, calf, neat.*   London, 1659.
" Vastly curious and valuable."—*Bp. Warburton.*

1928 RUSKIN, John. WORKS. Comprising Modern Painters, 84 *engravings on steel and* 216 *on wood,* 5 vols. Stones of Venice, 53 *engravings on steel,* 3 vols. Seven Lamps of Architecture, 14 *etchings by the author,* 1 vol. Elements of Drawing, Pre-Raphaeletism, *wood-cuts,* p. 8vo. 1 vol. Elements of Perspective, and the Two Paths, in 1 vol. p. 8vo. Lectures on Architecture and Painting, post 8vo. 1 vol. The Ethics of the Dust, p. 8vo. 1 vol. Political Economy of Art, p. 8vo. 1 vol. Sesame and Lilies and Crown of Wild Olives, 2 vols. p. 8vo. in 1 vol. Unto this Last and Time and Tide, in 1 vol. p. 8vo. Together 19 vols. *in* 16, *imperial and post* 8vo. *all uniformly bound, new hf. green calf, extra, marbled edges.*
                                                       London, 1850–67.
A very fine set, *all best English Editions.*

1929 Ruskin, John. Seven Lamps of Architecture, *with fine illustrations after drawings by the author.* Impl. 8vo. new cloth.
                                                       London, 1855.

1930 Russell, Lord John. Life of William, Lord Russell. *Portrait.* Crown 8vo. *crimson calf, extra.*   London, 1853.

1931 Russell, John, Earl. Life and Times of Charles James Fox. *Portrait.* 3 vols. *post 8vo. tree-calf, extra, by* Hayday.
                                                       London, 1866.

1932 Russell, Lord John. Memorials and Correspondence of Charles James Fox. 4 vols. 8vo. calf extra, marbled edges.
                                                       London, 1853.

1933 RUTGERS FEMALE COLLEGE. Proceedings of the Meeting held at the Inauguration of, April 25, 1867. *8vo. limp cloth.*
Agathynian Press, New York, 1867.

1934 RUTTENBER, E. M. Obstructions to the Navigation of Hudson's River, &c. *Sml. 4to. new hf. crimson morocco, gilt top, by Bradstreet.* *Munsell*, Albany, 1860.
One of 5 copies on INDIA PAPER.

1935 RYAN, MICHAEL, M.D. Prostitution in London, with a comparative view of that of Paris and New York. *Thick 12mo. cloth, scarce.* London, 1839.

1936 RYAN, RICHARD. BIOGRAPHIA HIBERNICA; a Biographical Dictionary of the Worthies of Ireland from the earliest period. 2 *vols. 8vo. boards, uncut.* London, 1822.

1937 RYCAUT, SIR P. HISTORY of the TURKISH EMPIRE, from 1623 to 1677, *fine portraits by Van Houe, folio, calf.* London, 1680.

1938 SABINE, LORENZO. BIOGRAPHICAL SKETCHES OF LOYALISTS of the American Revolution, with an Historical Essay. *Handsomely printed on toned paper.* 2 *vols. 8vo. new hf. cf. extra.*
Boston, 1864.

1938* SABIN, JOSEPH. A Dictionary of Books relating to America, from its discovery to the present time. 14 Parts. Roy. 8vo. *uncut.*
New York, 1867–69.
LARGE PAPER, *limited edition.*

1939 ——— Another copy. Small paper. 14 *parts, 8vo. uncut.*
New York, 1867–69.

1939* SABIN'S REPRINT OF RARE TRACTS RELATING TO AMERICA. QUARTO SERIES.

No. I. Byfield's Account of the Late Revolution in New England.
London, 1689.
II. Maryland. A Relation of, with Prefatory Notes, &c., by Rev. Dr. Hawks. 1635.
III. Whitfield's Farther Discovery of the Present State of the Indians in New England, &c. 1650.
IV. Certain Inducements to Well Minded People, &c. 1643.
V. Further Progress of the Gospel Among the Indians in New England. 1652.
VI. Progress of the Gospel Among the Indians in New England.
1659.
VII. New England's First Fruits, &c. 1643.
VIII. Further Queries upon the Present State of the New-English Affairs. 1689–90.
IX. Day Breaking if not the Sun Rising of the Gospel with the Indians in New England. 1648.
X. Clear Sunshine of the Gospel, &c. 1648.
Together 10 *parts, roy. 4to. uncut.* (Pt. I in boards.)
New York, 1865, &c.
LARGE PAPER, 50 *copies.*

1940 SADLER'S STATE PAPERS and LETTERS, edited by Clifford, with Memoir and Historical Notes by Sir Walter Scott, *portrait*, 3 vols. 4to. *new hf. russia.* London, 1809.
"This collection consists of four separate sets of Letters relating almost entirely to the affairs of Scotland; they throw a strong light on one of the most interesting periods in British History."—*Edin. Review.*

1941 Saint-Pierre. Paul and Virginia. Illustrated Edition, with *upwards of 300 beautiful engravings on wood. Roy. 8vo. new hf. morocco, gilt edges.* London, 1839.

1942 St. Pierre, J. H. Bernardin. Paul and Virginia, *with illustrations by Augustus Hoppin. Post 8vo. hf. roxburgh morocco, uncut.* New York, 1869.

1943 Saintine, X. B. Picciola. *Illustrated by Leopold Flameng. Handsomely printed, post 8vo. hf. morocco, uncut.* New York, 1867.

1944 Sakoontalá; or the Lost Ring, a free Translation, in prose and verse, of Kalidasa's Drama, by Monier Williams, *printed in the highest style of art, illustrated by original designs on wood, and enriched with head and tail pieces and borders in gold and colors* (pub. £2. 2s.). *Foolscap 4to. 300. pp. new cloth, gilt.* Hertford, 1855.

"The present translation of 'Sakoontalá,' by Professor Williams, is exceedingly creditable to his scholarship and taste, and is a great improvement upon the translation by Sir Wm. Jones. The manner in which it has been given to the public is well worthy of the merits of the original drama, which has been always held in the highest estimation by critics and scholars. The illustrations are of great beauty and of great accuracy, having been taken from illuminated MSS. in the Library at the East India House and that of the British Museum."—*H. H. Wilson.*

1945 Sale, Geo. Koran, commonly called the Alcoran of Mohammed, translated from the original Arabic, with explanatory notes, &c. 2 vols. 8vo. *hf. cf. neat.* London, 1825.

1946 Salem Witchcraft: Comprising Wonders of the Invisible World, Collected by Robert Calef; and Wonders of the Invisible World, by Cotton Mather; with Notes and Explanations by Sam'l P. Fowler. *Rubricated title pages, portrait, &c. 4to. cloth, uncut.* Boston, 1865.
Large Paper; *few printed.*

1947 Salem Witchcraft: Records of, copied from the Original Documents. *2 vols. small 4to. uncut.* *Munsell,* Albany, 1864.
Only 250 *copies printed.* Woodward's Historical Series, Nos. 1 and 2.

1948 Salmasius. Cl. Salmasii de Aunis Climactericis et Antiquis Astrologia Diatribæ. Thick 12mo. (8vo.) *elegantly bound in blue morocco, extra, full gilt sides, back and borders, with a ducal coronet impressed.*
Lugd Batavor. Ex Officina Elziriorum, CIↃIↃCXLVIII (1648).
A fine specimen of the Elzerir series.
A curious treatise on Astrology.

1949 Salverté, Eusebius. History of the Names of Men, Nations, and Places, in their connection with the progress of Civilization. Translated from the French by the Rev. L. Mordacque. 2 vols. 8vo. *new cloth.* London, 1862.

1950 Samson, G. W. Physical Media in Spiritual Manifestations. The phenomena of responding tables and Planchette. 16mo. *new cloth.* Philadelphia, 1869.

1951 Sand, George. Indiana, a Love Story. 12mo. *cloth.* Philadelphia, 1850.

1952 SANDERSON, JOHN. BIOGRAPHY of the SIGNERS of the Declaration of Independence. *Numerous fine portraits.* 9 vols. 8vo. *boards, uncut.* Philadelphia, 1820.

1953 SANDERSON, WILLIAM. A Compleate History of the Life and Raigne of King Charles from his Cradle to his Grave. *Portrait by Faithorne. Sml. folio, old cf. neat.* London, 1658.

1954 SANGER, Dr. W. W. History of Prostitution; its extent, causes, and effects, throughout the world. *Thick 8vo. new cloth.* New York, 1859.

1955 SARCASTIC NOTICES of the LONG PARLIAMENT, a list of the Members that held places, both civil and military, contrary to the self-denying ordinance of April 3, 1645, with the sums of money, &c., which they divided among themselves. *Reprinted from the original. Sml. 4to. hf. mor. uncut.* London, 1863.

1956 SARGENT, MAJ. WINTHROP. Journal of the General Meeting of the Cincinnati, 1784. *8vo. paper.* *Reprinted*, Philadelphia, 1859.
Only 39 copies.

1957 SARGENT, WINTHROP. LOYALIST POETRY OF THE REVOLUTION. With Preface and Notes. *Beautifully printed. Small 4to. hf. roxburgh morocco, uncut.* Philadelphia, 1857.
PRIVATELY PRINTED, and only 99 Copies.
This copy contains the suppressed stanza to "Hot Stuff," p. 124.

1958 SATURDAY MAGAZINE. Complete from its commencement in July, 1832. *Several thousand engravings on wood.* 25 vols. folio, *hf. calf, neat.* London, 1832–44.

1959 SATYRÆ SERIÆ; or, the Secrets of Things; written in Moral and Politicke Discourses. *32mo. calf, neat,* curious. London, 1640.

1960 SAVAGE, EDW. H. Chronological History of the Boston Watch and Police from 1631 to 1865, with recollections of a Boston Police Officer. *Portrait. 8vo. boards, uncut.* Boston, 1865.

1961 SAVAGE, JAMES. GENEALOGICAL DICTIONARY of the First Settlers of New England. *4 thick vols. 8vo. new cloth.* Boston, 1860.

1962 SAVAGE, JAMES. The LIBRARIAN, being an account of scarce, valuable, and useful books, Manuscripts, Public Records, &c. *3 vols. 8vo. new hf. green morocco, uncut.* London, 1808, &c.

1963 SAURIN, JACQUES. SERMONS sur divers textes de l'Ecriture Sainte. *Plates. 12 vols. 8vo. french cf. gilt.* Lausanne, 1759.
" Deservedly held in the highest esteem."—*Horne.*

1964 Saxon, Isabelle. Five Years within the Golden Gate. *Post 8vo. new cloth.* Philadelphia, 1868.

1965 SAY, THOMAS. AMERICAN ENTOMOLOGY, a Description of the Insects of North America. Edited by J. L. Le Conte, with a memoir by George Ord. *50 beautifully* COLORED *plates, comprising several hundred examples.* 2 vols. 8vo. *hf. calf, neat.* New York, 1869

1966 Scherzer, Dr. Karl. Narrative of the Circumnavigation of the Globe by the Austrian Frigate Novara, by order of the Imperial Government, in the years 1857–58, and 59. *Profusely illustrated. 3 vols. roy. 8vo. new cloth.*　　　　　London, 1861.

1967 SCHEUCHZERI. PHYSICA SACRA; or, Natural History of the Bible. (Text in Eng., Lat. and Germ.) Upwards of 750 *large and finely executed engravings on copper, including an immense number of scenes of prominent events, &c., &c. 2 thick vols. folio, polished calf, extra, gilt edges.*

Augusburg, 1731–32.

A fine series of Bible illustrations; the *plates* seldom occur separately, as in this instance.

1968 Schiller. Correspondence with Körner. Comprising Sketches and Anecdotes of Goethe, The Schlegels, Wieland, &c. *Portrait. 3 vols. post 8vo. cloth.*　　　　London, 1849.

1969 Schiller. The Knight of Toggenburg. Translated from the German. *Sml. 4to. handsomely bound in blue crimped morocco, full gilt.*　　　　*Privately printed,* for sale at the Shelford Bazaar, Oct. 27 & 27, 1842.

Unique Copy. Beautifully illuminated by hand in the Ancient Missal style, with floriated borders, &c., heightened with gold and silver.

1970 Schlegel, F. von. Philosophy of Life, and Philosophy of Language. 12mo. cloth.　　　　*Bohn,* London, 1847.

1971 SCHOOLCRAFT, HENRY R. INDIAN TRIBES of the United States. Historical and Statistical Information respecting the History, Condition, and Prospects of. *Profusely illustrated with upwards of* 300 *fine engravings on steel,* many colored, *and numerous woodcuts, maps, &c. 6 vols. in 12, roy. 4to. new hf. morocco, gilt edges.*　　　　Philadelphia, 1851, &c.

Collected and prepared under the direction of the U. S. Bureau of Indian Affairs.
The work comprises, the General History and Mental Type of the Indian Race; Antiquities of the United States; Physical Geography of the Indian Country; Tribal Organization; History and Government; Intellectual character and capacity of the Red Man; Population and Statistics, etc., etc. The information given is of the most reliable and interesting nature, having been prepared under the direction of the Bureau of Indian Affairs, and published by authority of Congress.

1972 Schoolcraft, Henry R. Notes on the Iroquois; or, Contributions to American History, Antiquities, and General Ethnology. *Portrait, &c. 8vo. cloth.*　　　　Albany, 1847.

1973 School for Wits; Containing a choice collection of Bons Mots, Anecdotes, Epigrams, and other poetical Jeux D'Esprits, &c., by celebrated wits, by Ralph Werwitzer. Post 8vo. hf. blue *morocco, extra, uncut edges, scarce.*　　　　London, 1815.

1974 Schrarcz, Julius. The Failure of Geological Attempts made by the Greeks from the earliest ages to the Epoch of Alexander. *4to. new cloth.*　　　　London, 1868.

1975 Schyn, Herman. Ontwerp tot vereeniging der Doopsgezinde Christenen Waar. 12*mo. vellum.*　　　　Amsterdam, 1723.

1976 SCOTT, SIR WALTER. COMPLETE WORKS. The
Splendid Abbotsford Edition, comprising the Waverley Novels, 12 vols. Poetical Works, 1 vol. Life of Napoleon,
1 vol. Tales of a Grandfather, 1 vol., and Biographical
Memoirs, 1 vol. *Upwards of two hundred highly finished engravings on steel and 2,000 beautifully executed woodcuts.* Together
17 vols. *thick roy. 8vo. half russia, extra, marbled edges.*
Edinburgh, 1842–52.
Fine Early Copy, *with brilliant impressions of the plates and cuts.*

1977 Scott, Sir Walter. Waverley Novels. Abbotsford Edition,
with 120 *highly finished engravings on steel and* 2,000 *fine woodcuts.* 12 vols. *in* 24, *royal 8vo. half morocco, gilt tops, uncut
edges.* *Edinburgh*, 1842.
Many of the *steel plates* in this copy are water-stained, but the text throughout is in perfect order.
It was the owner's intention to have illustrated it with extra plates.

1978 Scott, Sir Walter. Border Antiquities of England and
Scotland. 98 highly finished engravings of Old Castles, &c.
by *Le Keux, Turner, Finden, and others.* 2 vols. roy. 4to. *hf.
morocco, uncut.* London, 1814.
Large Paper, *fine copy.*

1979 Scott, Walter. Landscape and Portrait Illustrations of the
Prose and Poetical Works of, *upwards of* 100 *fine steel engravings.*
3 vols. sq. 12*mo. morocco, extra.* London, 1833.

1980 Scott, Sir Walter. Portraits of the Principal Female Characters in the Waverley Novels, with Landscape Illustrations
to the " Highland Widow," " Anne of Geirstein," " Fair Maid
of Perth," and " Castle Dangerous." 40 *fine plates. Earliest
impressions. Impl. 8vo. cloth.* London, 1834.

1981 Scott, Winfield. Memoirs of Lieutenant-General Winfield Scott,
LL. D. Written by himself. *Portraits. Royal 8vo. cloth,
uncut.* New York, 1864.
Large Paper.

1982 Scottish Ballads. Four Books of choice Old Scottish Ballads.
Comprises Ballad Book, edited by C. K. Sharpe, 1823, (30
copies). North Countrie Garland, edited by Maidment,
1824, (60 copies), Ballad Book, Edinburgh, edited by Geo.
R. Kinloch, (40 copies), and New Book of Old Ballads, edited by Maidment, (60 copies), in one vol. crown 8vo. *cloth
boards, uncut.*
Reprinted for Private Circulation, Edinburgh, 1868.
Only 155 Copies Printed.

1983 Scottish Ballads and Songs. Historical and Traditionary; edited by James Maidment. *Beautifully printed on heavy laid
paper.* 2 vols. post 8vo. cloth, uncut. Edinburgh, 1868.
Only a Limited Edition.

1984 Scott, John. Poetical Works, *numerous charming vignettes on
copper, after* Stothard, Blake, Heath, &c. Proof Impressions.
8vo. *tree-marbled calf, extra, yellow edges.* London, 1782.
Fine Copy, *very scarce.*

26

1985 Scottish Songs, Heroic Ballads, &c. Ancient and Modern, collected by David Herd, reprinted from the edition of 1776, with an appendix containing the pieces substituted in the edition of 1791, &c. *Beautifully printed.* 2 vols. 8vo. *vellum* cloth, *uncut.* Glasgow, 1869.

Large paper, *few printed.*

1986 Scrap Book. A collection of Poetical Scraps, Cuttings from American Newspapers, &c. 8vo hf. mor.

1987 [Scuderi]. Cassandra, a Romance, translated from the French by Sir Charles Cottrell, *copper-plate engravings* by Hogarth. 5 vols. 12mo. new hf. cf. extra. London, 1725.

1987* (Scuderi). The Famous History of Cassandra; containing many admirable Adventures of the most illustrious persons of either sex. *Frontispiece.* 8vo. old calf, neat. London, 1703.

1988 Seafield, Frank. Literature and Curiosities of Dreams. 2 vols. crown 8vo. new cloth. London, 1865.

1989 Sears, Robert. Pictorial History of China and India; comprising a description of those countries and their inhabitants, *maps and upwards* of 200 *woodcuts.* Roy. 8vo. cloth.

New York, 1855.

1990 Secret History of the Court of Berlin, or the character of the King of Prussia, his Ministers, Mistresses, Generals, &c. 2 vols. 8vo. calf, neat. London, 1789.

1991 Segur, *Count.* Memoirs and Recollections of, written by himself. *Portraits.* 3 vols. 8vo. hf. cf. gilt. London, 1825.

Serpent Worship, see Ferguson, J.

1992 Serviez, M. de. Roman Empresses; or the Lives and Secret Intrigues of the Wives of the Twelve Cæsars. Translated by Molesworth. 3 *vols. post 8vo. calf, scarce.* Dublin, 1752.

1993 Seward, William. Biographiana. Extra Illustrated Copy, *having an extensive collection of rare and curious illustrations, comprising Portraits, Views, &c. an Autograph Letter of the Author, and a beautiful* Drawing on vellum of Francis I. *inserted.* 2 thick vols. 8vo. hf. cf. uncut edges. London, 1799.

1994 Seymour, Rev. M. H. The Confessional; an appeal to the primitive and catholic forms of absolution, in the east and west. 12mo. new cloth. London, 1870.

1995 Shadwell, Thomas. Plays. Comprising Epsom-Wells, 1704. A True Widow, 1679. The Sullen Lovers, 1668. The Libertine, a Tragedy, 1676. The Squire of Alsatia, 1688. The Scowerers, 1691. The Humorists, 1670. *Together 7 plays.* Original 4to. Editions. Sml. 4to. hf. cf. neat.

London, 1688–1704.

Fine clean copies, scarce.
" Shadwell, and Etheridge, and the famous Aphra Behn, have endeavored to make the stage as grossly immoral as their talents permitted ; but the two former, especially Shadwell, are not destitute of humor."—*Hallam.*

1996 SHAKESPEARE, WILLIAM. The Works of. The Plays edited from the Folio of mdcxxiii, with various Readings from all the Editions and all the Commentators, Notes, Introductory

Remarks, a Historical Sketch of the Text, an Account of the Rise and Progress of the English Drama, a Memoir of the Poet, by Richard Grant White, Esq. *Portraits and woodcuts.* 12 vols. 8vo. *half olive morocco, gilt tops, red paper sides, edges uncut.*
Boston, 1857.

LARGE PAPER, *only 48 copies printed.*
" His notes prove him to be capable of profound as well as delicate and sympathetic exegesis, and we think that a careful collation justifies us in saying that in acute discrimination of æsthetic shades of expression, and often of textual niceties, Mr. White is superior to any previous editor."—*Lowell.*

997 SHAKESPEARE'S DRAMATIC WORKS, Poems, Doubtful Plays, and Biography. CHAS. KNIGHT'S ORIGINAL PICTORIAL EDITION, *with the most remarkably brilliant impressions of the many hundred beautiful engravings on wood, of Views, Costumes, Old Buildings, Antiquities, Portraits, etc. etc.* 8 vols. roy. 8vo. calf, extra, *marbled edges.* London, 1843.

998 SHAKESPEARE'S DRAMATIC WORKS, BOYDELL'S SPLENDID EDITION, *printed in exceedingly large and beautiful type by Bulmer, with the fine series of* 100 *highly finished engravings by the best Artists, from Paintings by* STOTHARD, WESTALL, SMIRKE, OPIE, NORTHCOTE, &c. 9 *vols. in* 6, *folio, handsomely bound in hf. dark-green levant morocco, extra, gilt tops, uncut edges.*
Bulmer, London, 1802.

A SPLENDID COPY, *scarce in uncut condition.*
This edition is one of the most finely printed books ever produced in any country.

999 SHAKESPEARE. WORKS. The Text Revised by the Rev. ALEXANDER DYCE. *Handsomely printed in large type.* Portrait. 2d edition. 9 *vols. 8vo. red cloth, uncut.* London, 1866.

" The present work is so far from being a reprint of the edition which appeared in 1857, that it exhibits a text altered and amended from beginning to end."—*Preface.*

2000 SHAKESPEARE. The Works of William Shakespeare. Edited with a Memoir of the Poet, and an Essay upon his Genius, by Richard Grant White. *Portrait.* 12 *vols. crown 8vo. new cloth.*
Boston, 1866.

2001 SHAKESPEARE'S WORKS. ORIGINAL EDITION of 1623. A reproduction in exact facsimile of the Famous First Folio, by the newly-discovered process of Photo-Lithography, at the suggestion and under the supervision of H. Staunton. *Folio, new cloth, uncut.* London, 1866.

This magnificent reprint (the only one which can justly claim to be an exact facsimile) was photographed by express permission of Lord Ellesmere and the Trustees of the British Museum, from the matchless copies in Bridgewater House and the National Library.

2002 SHAKESPEARE. PLAYS and POEMS, according to the improved text of Edmund Malone, including the latest revisions, with Life, Glossarial Notes, and Index, edited by A. J. Valpy. *One hundred and seventy illustrations from designs by English Artists.* 15 vols. 12mo. *white vellum cloth, uncut.* London, 1853.

2003 SHAKESPEARE. COMEDIES, HISTORIES, and TRAGEDIES, published according to the true originall copies. THE CELEBRATED FACSIMILE REPRINT of the RARE FIRST COLLECTED EDITION *with fine portrait after Droeshout, Verses, &c. Folio, boards, uncut.*
London, 1632. *Reprint,* 1808.

2004 SHAKESPEARE'S COMEDIES, publeshed according to the true originall copies. *Portrait.* *Sm. 4to. limp cloth.* London, 1862.
Booth's facsimile reprint.

2005 SHAKESPEARE. BOYDELL'S GRAPHIC ILLUSTRATIONS to, *consisting of a series of* 100 *fine plates after paintings by* NORTHCOTE, REYNOLDS, SMIRKE, OPIE, HAMILTON, &c., painted expressly for Alderman Boydell. FINE IMPRESSION. Folio, red morocco, gilt.
London, 1796.
A distinct series from that known as the "Shakespeare Gallery;" and presentation copy to the Duke de Hijar conde de Aranda, &c.

2006 SHAKESPEARE FORGERIES. Miscellaneous Papers and Legal Instruments under the Hand and Seal of Wm. Shakespeare, including the Tragedy of King Lear, and a Fragment of Hamlet. from the original MSS. in the possession of S. Ireland, *plates and facsimiles*, folio, *hf. morocco, uncut edges.* London, 1796.
CHOICE COPY, with several fine portraits, newspaper cuttings, &c. inserted, including an *unfinished proof* portrait of W. H. Ireland, Trotter's engravings of the Chandos Portrait in unfinished state, also a duplicate, finished impression, &c., &c.

2007 SHAKESPEARE'S JEST BOOK. A Hundred Mery Talys. with introduction and Notes by Dr. Herman Osterly. *12mo. hf. rox. morocco.* London, 1866.

2008 SHAKESPEARE NOVELS. Youth of Shakespeare; Shakespe re and his Friends; and Secret Passion. Thick roy. 8vo. cloth.
New York, 1848.

2009 SHAKESPEARE, WILLIAM. MEMOIRS OF THE LIFE OF, with an Essay toward the expression of his Genius, and an account of the Rise and Progress of the English Drama. *Portrait on India Paper. 8vo. hf. olive morocco, uncut.* Boston, 1866.
LARGE PAPER, *only* 100 *copies.*

2010 SHAKESPEARE HEROINES; comprising the principal female characters in the Plays of the great Poet. 45 *fine steel portraits by Heath.* Imp. 8vo. *morocco antique.* London, 1848.
ORIGINAL EDITION.

2011 SHAKESPEARE'S HOME at New Place, Stratford-upon-Avon. *Genealogical Tables, &c. Post 8vo. new cloth.* London, 1863.

2012 SHAKESPEARE ILLUSTRATED, in a series of Landscape and Architectural Designs, by G. F. Sargent, with notices of the several localities, by various authors. *A series of 45 finely engraved plates, early impressions. Imp. 8vo. new cloth, uncut.*
London, 1842.
Suitable for illustrating any of the 8vo. editions of Shakespeare.

2013 SHAKESPEARE ILLUSTRATIONS. *A series of* 20 *etchings, by* GEORGE CRUIKSHANK, *illustrating the Life of Sir John Falstaff.* 8vo. *paper.*

2014 SHAKESPEARE. HARDING'S SHAKESPEARE ILLUSTRATED by Portraits and Views, 147 *fine portraits and engravings of famous Buildings, Localities.* PROOF IMPRESSIONS. *Atlas folio, hf. morocco, uncut.* London, 1793.
LARGEST PAPER, *scarce.*
Includes the series of Portraits of the Editors of Shakespeare: and the scarce portrait of Jane Shaw bare-necked.

2015 SHAKESPEARE. Howard's (Frank) Spirit of Shakespeare, 483 *spirited outline plates, illustrative of the Dramas of our National Bard.* India proofs, large paper. *A complete set in the (24) original numbers forming 5 vols. 4to. original set* (pub. £25. 4s.). London, 1833.

The above are original impressions of these beautiful compositions, which are adapted for illustrating all octavo editions of Shakespeare.

2016 Shakespeare Gems. A series of Landscape illustrations of the most interesting localities of Shakespeare's Dramas. 50 *fine steel plates. 8vo. new cloth.* London, 1846.

2017 Shakespeare Portraits. Boaden, Jas. Inquiry into the Authenticity of various Pictures and Prints, which have been Offered as Portraits of Shakespeare. 5 *fine portraits. 8vo. bds. uncut.* London, 1824.

2018 Shakespeare. Tercentenary Celebration of the Birth of Shakespeare, by the New England Historic-Genealogical Society, at Boston, Mass., April 23, 1864. *Folio, boards, uncut.* *Privately Printed,* Boston, 1864.

Large paper (No. 3); *only 25 copies printed.*

2019 SHAKESPEARE SOCIETY'S PUBLICATIONS. Consisting of Works illustrative of Shakespeare, Old Plays, Poems, Curious Tracts, Memoirs, etc., either now Printed for the first time, or from their Rarity difficult to be procured. Edited by Eminent Literary Men. 48 *Parts. 8vo. new cloth.* London, 1841–53.

⁎ Includes part 48: Lodge's Defence of Poetry, Music, and Stage Plays, etc., etc., the last work issued by the society.

2020 SHAW, HENRY. DRESSES and DECORATIONS of the MIDDLE AGES, from the Seventh to the Seventeenth Centuries, with an Historical Introduction and Descriptive Letterpress. *Illustrated with Copperplates, numerous Woodcuts, and Initial Letters, every page being highly decorated.* 2 vols. impl. 8vo. *half olive morocco, red paper sides, edges uncut.* London, 1858.

With the plates highly illuminated, and the *whole* of the initial letters and *many* of the woodcuts finished in colors.

2021 Shelley, Percy Bysshe. QUEEN MAB. 8vo. *new hf. vellum, extra, gilt top, uncut edges.* London, 1829.

Very Scarce, containing much that was subsequently suppressed. This was a surreptitious issue, and was disavowed by Shelley in a letter to the "Examiner." "It is sufficient to say of 'Queen Mab,' that it is an effusion which no man should have written, no publisher should circulate, no family library should contain."—*Allibone.*

2022 Shepard, A. K. Papers on Spanish America. 8vo. *hf. crimson morocco, gilt top, by Bradstreet.* *Munsell,* Albany, 1868.

One of 5 copies on India Paper.

2023 Sheridan, Richard Brinsley. The Critic; or, A Tragedy Rehearsed. A Dramatic Piece in three Acts. 8vo. pp. 98, *elegantly bound in crimson morocco, extra, very scarce.* London, 1781.

Original Edition. *Presentation* copy *from the Author* (to Earl Spencer (?) see his book-plate, Wimbledon Park Library). The subsequent editions were all more or less altered.

2024 SHERIDAN, RICHARD BRINSLEY. SPEECHES, with a Sketch of his Life, edited by a Constitutional friend. *Portrait.* 3 vols. 8vo. *cloth.* London, 1842.

2025 SHERRING, REV. M. A. The SACRED CITY of the HINDUS; an account of Benares in ancient and modern times, with an Introduction by Fitzedward Hall. *Illustrated.* 8vo. *new cloth.* London, 1868.

2026 SHERLOCK, REV. WM. Discourse on Divine Providence. 12mo. *sheep.* Pittsburgh, 1847.

2027 SHERLOCK, REV. WM. Practical Discourse concerning Death. 8vo. *sheep.* London, 1776.

2028 SHIPLEY, REV. ORBY. The Church and the World; Essays on Questions of the Day in 1866, '67, and '68. 3 thick vols. 8vo. *new cloth.* London, 1867–68.

2029 SHIPLEY, REV. ORBY. TRACTS FOR THE DAY; Essays on Theological Subjects, by various Authors. 8vo. *new cloth.* London, 1868.

2030 SHIRLEY, JAMES. PLAYS. *Original 4to. Editions,* comprising The Young Admirall, (1637). The Duke's Mistris, 1638. Hide Parke, a Comedie, 1637. Love's Crueltie, 1640. The Wedding, 1633, (2d Edition). The Constant Maid, 1640. The Opportunitie, 1640. The Grateful Servant, (1655), together 8 plays, with one exception *Original editions,* in one vol. small 4to. hf. cf. neat. London, 1633–40.
A fine series, *all very scarce.*

2031 SHURTLEFF, N. B. A Decimal System for the Arrangement and Administration of Libraries. 4to. pp. 80. (Imperfect ?) *sheets folded.* *Privately Printed,* Boston, 1856.

2032 SHURTLEFF, NATHANIEL B. Thunder and Lightening; and Deaths at Mansfield in 1658 and 1666. 12*mo. bds.* Boston, *Privately Printed,* 1850.

2033 SIBLY, E. COMPLETE ILLUSTRATION of ASTROLOGY, or Art of Foretelling Future Events and Contingencies, *curious engravings of incantations, nativities, &c.* 2 vols. 4to. *in one,* hf. calf. VERY SCARCE. London, 1788.

2034 SIBLY, E. KEY TO PHYSIC and the OCCULT SCIENCES, opening to view the System and Order of the Interior and Exterior Heavens; The Analogy betwixt Angels and Saints, &c., &c. *Numerous curious colored plates. 4to. morocco, extra.* London, 1814.
FINE COPY, *scarce.*

2035 SIDDONS, MRS. LIFE OF by Thomas Campbell. BEAUTIFULLY ILLUSTRATED COPY, *with upwards of* 100 *fine portraits, including many of Mrs. Siddons in character, also numerous Views of Theatres, contemporary Play-Bills, &c., &c. All neatly arranged and where necessary inlaid.* 2 thick volumes, 8vo. *tree-marbled calf, extra, gilt tops, uncut edges.* London, 1834.
A VERY HANDSOME COPY.

2036 SIDNEY, Sir P. COUNTESS of PEMBROKE'S ARCADIA, to which is added Astrophel and Stella, Defence of Poesie, Sonnets, and Life, *portrait, folio, calf, gilt.* London, 1674.
"There is no work in the department of prose fiction which contains more apophthegamic wisdom than the Arcadia of Sidney."—*Drake.*

2037 SIGOURNEY, MRS. L. H. Poetry for Seamen, *with* MS. *alterations and corrections by the Author for a second edition.* 12mo. bds. Boston, 1845.

2038 SILIUS, ITALICUS. The Second Punick War between Hannibal and the Romans, with a continuation to the Death of Hannibal. Englished by Thomas Ross. *Handsomely printed, and illustrated with large engravings on copper, folio, calf, extra.* FINE COPY. London, 1661.

2039 SIMPSON, J. PALGRAVE. Pictures from Revolutionary Paris, sketched during the first Phases of the Revolution of 1848. 2 *vols. crown 8vo. hf. vellum extra.* Edinburgh, 1849.

2040 SIMS, C. S. Origin and Signification of Scottish Surnames, with a Vocabulary of Christian Names. *8vo. cloth, uncut.* *Munsell,* Albany, 1862.

2041 SIMMS, J. R. American Spy, or Freedom's Early Sacrifice ; A Tale of the Revolution, Founded on Fact. *Frontispiece. Roy. 8vo. boards, uncut.* *Munsell,* Albany, 1857.
LARGE PAPER ; *only 28 copies.*

2042 SIMSON, WALTER. History of the Gipsies, with specimens of the Gipsy language. 12mo. new cloth. New York, 1866.

2043 SINGER, SAMUEL W. The Text of Shakespeare vindicated from the corruptions and interpolations advocated by J. P. Collier, Esq. 8vo. cloth, *uncut.* *Pickering,* London, 1853.

2044 SITGREAVES, CAPT. L. Report of an Expedition down the Zuni and Colorado Rivers. *Numerous maps, and tinted plates.* 8vo. *boards, uncut.* Washington, 1853.

2045 SKENE, W. F. The Coronation Stone. *Photographic facsimile from an ancient* MS. Square 8vo. *new cloth.* Edinb., 1869.

2046 SLANG DICTIONARY ; or, The Vulgar words, street phrases, and "fast" expressions of high and low society, many with their etymology and a few with their history traced. *Handsomely printed on heavy toned paper. 4to. hf. mor. uncut.* London, 1869.
LARGE PAPER, *interleaved.* 100 *copies.*

2047 SLANG DICTIONARY ; or, the Vulgar Words, Street Phrases, and "Fast" expressions of high and low society. Post 8vo. *new cloth.* London, 1865.

2048 SLAVERY AND THE SLAVE-TRADE, Ancient and Modern ; History of, with the Political History of Slavery in the United States, compiled by W. O. Blake. *Numerous plates. Very thick impl.* 8vo. *embossed sheep.* Columbus, O., 1859.

2049 SLOAN, SAMUEL. The MODEL ARCHITECT. A series of Original Designs for Cottages, Villas, Suburban Residences, &c., with Specifications, Estimates, &c. *Upwards of 200 plates.* 2 vols. *impl. 4to. hf. morocco.* Philadelphia, 1865.

2050 Smedley, Frank. Harry Coverdale's Courtship and Marriage. *Illustrated,* 12mo. *cloth.* Philadelphia, (1859.)

2051 SMITH'S DICTIONARY OF GREEK AND ROMAN BIO-GRAPHY AND MYTHOLOGY. *Several hundred woodcut illustrations.* 3 vols. very thick 8vo. new hf. cf. neat. London, 1861.

2051* —————— DICTIONARY OF GREEK AND ROMAN ANTIQUITIES. Enlarged Edition. *Profusely illustrated.* 1 thick vol. 8vo. new hf. cf. neat. London, 1859.

2051** —————— DICTIONARY OF GREEK AND ROMAN GEOGRAPHY. *Numerous woodcuts.* 2 thick vols. 8vo. new hf. cf. neat. London, 1854.

2052 —————— DICTIONARY OF THE BIBLE; its Antiquities, Biography, Geography, and Natural History, by many distinguished scholars, *Woodcuts.* 3 thick vols. 8vo. new hf. cf. neat. London, 1863.
The above 4 lots are uniformly bound.

2052* SMITH, ADAM. COMPLETE WORKS, with an account of his Life and Writings, by Dugald Stewart. *Portrait.* 5 vols. 8vo. hf. cf. neat. London, 1812.

2053 SMITH, BUCKINGHAM. Rudo Ensayo, tentativa de una Prevencional Descripcion Geographica de la PROVINCIA DE SONORA, &c. Sm. 4to. *uncut.* (*Munsell,* Albany.)
San Augustine de la Florida, 1863.

2054 —————— Another copy. Impl. 4to. *bds. uncut.*
LARGE PAPER, *few printed.*

2055 SMITH, CAPT. JOHN. Advertisements for the Unexperienced Planters of New England, or Anywhere; or Pathway to erect a Plantation. *Fac-simile of Smith's Map of New England* (1635). *Royal 4to. uncut.* Boston, 1865.
LARGE PAPER, 25 *copies.*

2056 SMITH, CAPT. JOHN. DESCRIPTION OF NEW ENGLAND; Observations and Discoveries in the North of America-in the year of our Lord 1614. With the Success of six Ships that went the next year, 1615. *Map.* Royal 4to. *uncut.* Boston, 1865.
LARGE PAPER, 25 *copies.*

2057 SMITH, CAPT. JOHN. TRUE RELATION OF VIRGINIA, with an Introduction and Notes by Chas. Deane. *Map.* Sm. 4to. *uncut.*
Boston, 1866.
Only 250 *copies,* with the *new index,* wanting in many copies.

2058 SMITH. A TRUE RELATION OF VIRGINIA, by Captain John Smith, with Introduction and Notes by Charles Deane. *Maps.* Roy. 4to. *uncut.* Boston, 1866.
LARGE PAPER, *one of 4 copies on Drawing Paper.*

2059 SMITH. The True Travels, Adventures and Observations of Captaine John Smith, in Europe, Asia, Africke, and America: beginning about the yeere 1593, and continued to this present 1629. *Portraits and large folding Maps.* 2 vols. 8vo. *calf.*
Richmond, Va.,
Republished at the *Franklin Press,* 1819.

2060 SMITH, EDMUND. Phædra and Hippolitus; a Tragedy as it is acted at the Queen's Theatre. Sm. 4to. p. 64, *hf. vellum.*
London, N. D., (1709.)
The prologue was written by Joseph Addison, see *Baker's Biog. Dramatica.*

2061 SMITH, ELIZABETH. FRAGMENTS, in Prose and Verse, with an account of her Life. *Portrait, &c.* 2 vols. 8vo. *cf. neat.*
London, 1809.

"Tears have just been brought into my eyes by reading the Fragments of poor Miss Smith."—*Sir Jas. Mackintosh.*

2062 SMITH, GEORGE. The Gentile Nations ; or the History and Religion of the Egyptians, Assyrians, Babylonians, Persians, Greeks, &c. 8vo. *sheep.* New York, (1853).

2063 SMITH, GEORGE. The HEBREW PEOPLE ; or, the History and Religion of the Israelites from the origin of the nation to the time of Christ. 8vo. *sheep.* New York, (1850).

2064 SMITH, GEORGE. PATRIARCHAL AGE ; or, the History and Religion of Mankind from the Creation to the death of Isaac. 8vo. *sheep, scarce.* New York, 1848.

2065 SMITH, MATTHEW HALE. Sunshine and Shadow in New York. *Illustrated.* Thick 8vo. *sheep.* Hartford, 1868.

2066 SMITH, REV. WM. Recommendation of, to the University of Oxford. 4to. *sheets.* London, 1759. *Phila., reprinted,* N. D. *Only 50 copies.*

2067 SMITH, WILLIAM R. Uses of Solitude : a Poem (delivered before the Phi Beta Kappa Society of Tuskaloosa University). Impl. 8vo. *hf. red morocco.* *Printed for the Society,* 1860.

2068 SMITHSONIAN INSTITUTION. CONTRIBUTIONS TO KNOWLEDGE, a complete series to 1865, *containing a large number of plates, woodcuts and diagrams,* (pub. at £28.) 15 vols. roy. 4to. *cloth.* Washington, 1848–65.

Including, with many other valuable dissertations, the following : Squier's Aboriginal Monuments, Gray's Plantæ Texanæ, Whittlesea's Ancient Works in Ohio, Rees' Dakotah Grammar and Dictionary, Harvey's Nereis Boreali-Americana, Mayer's Mexican History and Archæology, Bowen's Yoruba Grammar and Dictionary, Leidy's Fauna of Nebraska, Coffin on Winds, Bailey's Miroscopical Organisms, Jones' North American Vertebrata, Brewer's North American Oology, Kane's Meteorological Observations in the Arctic Seas, etc.

2069 SMOLLETT, TOBIAS. MISCELLANEOUS WORKS, with Memoirs of his Life and Writings, by Robert Anderson. 6 vols. 8vo. *calf, neat.* Edinburgh, 1800.

LIBRARY EDITION.

2070 SMOLLETT, TOBIAS. MISCELLANEOUS WORKS, complete, with Memoir of the Author by Thomas Roscoe. *Portrait, and numerous etchings by George Cruikshank.* Thick royal 8vo. *green polished calf, extra.* London, 1866.

2071 SMYTH, C. PIAZZI. LIFE AND WORK AT THE GREAT PYRAMID during the months of Jan., Feb., March, and April, 1865 ; with a discussion of the Facts ascertained. *Profusely illustrated.* 3 vols. thick 8vo. *new cloth.* Edinburgh, 1867.

2072 SMYTH, C. PIAZZI. ANTIQUITY OF INTELLECTUAL MAN, from a Practical and Astronomical Point of View. *Front.* Crown 8vo. *new cloth.* Edinburgh, 1868.

2073 Smyth, Prof. Lectures on Modern History, from the Irruption of the Northern Nations, 2 vols.; and Lectures on the French Revolution, 3 vols. Together 5 vols. 8vo. *cloth, uncut.* *Pickering*, London, 1848.

> No historical works have ever given more enlightened and perspicuous views of the course of great events than these celebrated Lectures.

2074 Solon, L. Inventions Decoratives; choix de compositions et de motifs d'ornementation. *50 large and finely executed etchings on copper, comprising nearly 200 examples of ancient and modern ornament. Folio, new hf. red morocco, gilt.* Paris, 1866.

2075 Somerville, Mary. Molecular and Microscopic Science. *Profusely illustrated.* 2 vols. crown 8vo. *new vellum, cloth.* London, 1869.

2077 Sommers Tracts. A Collection of Scarce and Valuable Tracts on the most interesting subjects, Revised by eminent hands. 4 vols. sm. 4to. cf. *neat.* London, 1748.

> This valuable collection includes the most interesting and important Tracts in Print and MS. in the Royal, Cotton, Sion, and other public as well as private libraries.

2078 Songs in the Night; or Hymns for the Sick and Suffering, with Introduction by the Rev. A. C. Thompson. Sq. 8vo. *hf. cf. gilt.* Boston, 1863.

2079 SOTHEBY, S. Leigh. Ramblings in the Elucidation of the Autograph of Milton, *with 2 photographic Portraits of Milton, 27 finely executed plates of autographs, also some facsimiles of Sonnets, Inscriptions, &c. of surprising exactness.* Impl. 4to. *new hf. morocco.* London, 1861.

> This is a highly interesting and valuable accession to our knowledge of the writings of Milton. The plates are not confined to simple autographs, but comprehend complete Sonnets, MS. Poems, full pages of Prose Writings; Signatures of distinguished, literary, and scientific men; and curious Documents: also nearly 300 pages of text, comprising a fund of curious information and research.

2080 SOTHEBY, S. Leigh. The Typography of the Fifteenth Century: being specimens of the Productions of the Early Continental Printers, exemplified in a collection of facsimiles from 100 works, with their Water-marks. *Folio, hf. vellum, uncut edges.* London, 1849.

> Privately Printed; *and only* 100 *copies. Very Scarce.* Uniform with the "Principia Typographica."

2081 South, Robert. Sermons. Vols. 1 and 2. 8vo. *new cloth.* New York, 1866.

> The first installment of the projected "Library of Old English Divines." Edited by Dr. Shedd.

2082 Southey and Coleridge. Omniana, or Horæ Otiosiores. 2 vols. 12mo. *hf. morocco, gilt.* London, 1812.

2083 Southern History of the War (1861, '62, and '63.) Official Reports of Battles, as published by order of the Confederate Congress at Richmond. *Fine portrait.* 3 *vols.* 8vo. *cloth.* New York, 1863.

2084 SPALDING CLUB PUBLICATIONS : a complete set from the commencement to 1864, as follows :

Gordon (J.) History of Scots Affairs, 1637–1641, ed. Robertson and Grub, 3 vols. 1841.

Miscellany of the Club, ed. John Stuart, *facsimile of autographs,* 5 vols. 1841–52.

Gordon's Tounes of Aberdeene, ed. Cosmo Innes, *map and 4 plates.* 1842.

Extracts from the Presbytery Booke of Strathbogie, 1631–1654, ed. John Stuart. 1843.

Fragment of a Memoir of Field Mareschal Keith, 1714–34, written by himself. 1843.

Collections for a History of the Shires of Aberdeen and Banff, ed. Joseph Robertson, 4 vols. 1843–62.

Gordon (P.) Short Abridgement of Britane's Distemper from 1639 to 1649, ed. John Dunn. 1844.

Blakhal (G.) Breiffe Narration of the Services done to three noble Ladyes, 1631–49, ed. John Stuart. 1844.

Extracts from the Council Register of the Burgh of Aberdeen, 1398–1625, 2 vols. ed. John Stuart. 1844-48.

Registrum Episcopatus Aberdonensis, ed. Cosmo Innes, 2 vols. *illuminated plates and facsimiles.* 1845.

Selections from the Records of the Kirk-Session, Presbytery, and Synod of Aberdeen, 1562–1681, ed. John Stuart. 1846.

A Genealogical Deduction of the Family of Rose of Kilravock, ed. Cosmo Innes, *facsimiles and views.* 1848.

Spalding (John) Memorialls of the Trubles in Scotland and in England, 1624–1645, ed. John Stuart, 2 vols. 1850–51.

Letters Illustrative of Public Affairs in Scotland, addressed by contemporary Statesmen, to George, Earl of Aberdeen, 1681–84, ed. John Dunn. 1851.

Innes (T.) Civil and Ecclesiastical History of Scotland, 80–818, ed. Geor. Grub. 1853.

Fasti Aberdonenses; Selections from the Records of the University and King's College of Aberdeen, 1494–1854, ed. Cosmo Innes, *frontispiece.* 1854.

Sculptured Stones of Scotland, ed. John Stuart, 2 vols. folio, 306 *plates.* 1856–67.

After such an examination, we need scarcely say that these two volumes of Mr. Stuart are a noble monument of Scotch archæological zeal, the execution of the drawings, their transfer to the stone, and the whole " getting up " of the books leave nothing to be desired.— *Athenæum, Aug.* 17, 1867.

Barbour (Johne) The Brus ; from a Collation of the Cambridge and Edinburgh Manuscripts, ed. Cosmo Innes. 1856.

Book of the Thanes of Cawdor, 1236–1742, ed. Cosmo Innes, 2 *plates and facsimile.* Edinburgh, 1859.

Passages from the Diary of Genl. Patrick Gordon, 1635–1699, ed. Joseph Robertson. Aberdeen, 1859.

Diary of Alexr. Brodie of Brodie, and of his Son, 1652–1685, ed. David Laing. Ib. 1863.

Forbes (D.) Account of the Familie of Innes, 1698, ed. C. Innes. Ib. 1864.

Together 33 vols. 4to. and 2 vols. folio, cloth, uncut.

Aberdeen and Edinburgh, 1841-67.

2085 Spalding Club Miscellany. 2 vols. thick 4to. cloth, *uncut.*

Aberdeen, 1841.

2086 Sparks, Jared. In Memoriam. 8vo. pp. 32, *paper.* Boston, N. D.

Only 30 copies.

2087 Speeches of the Rt. Hon. the Earl of Chatham, Richard Brinsley Sheridan, Lord Erskine, and the Hon. Edmund Burke, with Biographical Memoirs, Introductions, &c. by a Barrister. *Portrait. Thick imp.* 8vo. *new hf. cf. gilt.* London, 1853.

2088 SPENCE'S Polymetis, or an Inquiry concerning the Agreement between the Works of the Roman Poets and the Remains of the Ancient Artists, *fine portrait by Vertue, and numerous fine gem-like engravings, original impressions,* folio, *calf, gilt.*

London, 1747.

A very fine copy of the First Edition, containing the *suppressed caricature portrait of Dr. Cooke,* Provost of Eton, as an Ass, teaching.

2089 SPENCER, JOHN. A DISCOURSE CONCERNING PRODIGIES. Wherein The Vanity of Presages by them is reprehended, and their true and proper Ends asserted and vindicated. *Sml. 4to. pp.* 110, *hf. cf.* London, 1663.
Rare and Curious.

2090 SPENCER, HERBERT. SOCIAL STATICS; or, the Conditions Essential to Human Happiness. *Portrait. 12mo. cloth.*
New York, 1865.

2091 SPENCER, HERBERT. Illustrations of Universal Progress; A series of Discussions. *12mo. cloth.* New York, 1864.

2092 SPOONER'S DICTIONARY. A BIOGRAPHICAL HISTORY OF THE FINE ARTS; or Memoirs of the Lives and Works of Eminent Painters, Engravers, Sculptors, and Architects, alphabetically arranged and condensed from the best authorities, including the works of Vasari, Lanzi, Kugler, Dr. Waagen, Bryan, Pilkington, Sir Chas. Eastlake, and Mrs. Jameson. With Chronological Tables of Artists and their Schools, Plates of Monograms, Dictionary of Terms, Essay on Engraving, etc., etc. *2 vols. 4to. with* 100 *photographic portraits.* *New York,* 1865.
LARGE PAPER.
Of this edition, only ninety copies were printed, for subscribers, for the purpose of illustration.

2093 ——— Another Copy. 2 vols. impl. 8vo. *new hf. morocco, extra.*
New York, 1867.

2094 Spooner, S. Anecdotes of Painters, Engravers, Sculptors, and Architects, and Curiosities of Art. *3 vols. crown 8vo. cloth, bds.*
New York, 1865.

2095 SPURIOUS REPRINTS of Early, Books by Delta. Reprinted from the Boston Advertiser, March 24, 1865. Sml. 4to. uncut. (75 copies.) *Privately Printed,* Boston, 1865.

2096 ——— Another Copy. LARGE PAPER, (30 copies.) *4to. uncut.*
Boston, 1865.

2097 SQUIER, E. G. Collection of Rare and Original Documents, and Relations, concerning The Discovery and Conquest of America. Chiefly from the Spanish Archives. *4to. uncut.*
Munsell, Albany, 1860.
LARGE PAPER.
CARTA DIRIJIDA AL REY DE ESPANA, PO EL LICENCIADO DR DON DIEGO GARCIA DE PALACIO, ANNO 1576. Published in the Original, with Translation, Illustrative Notes, Maps, and Biographical Sketches.

2098 SQUIER, E. G. Monograph of Authors who have written on the Languages of Central America, &c. *Roy. 4to. bds. uncut.*
Munsell, Albany, 1861.
LARGE PAPER.

2099 SQUIER, E. G. Rare and Original Documents and Relations concerning the Discovery and Conquest of America. *Sml. 4to. hf. morocco.* *Munsell,* Albany, 1860.
No. I, *Palacio.*

2100 STAFFORD, J. PACATA HIBERNIA; or, History of the Wars in Ireland during the Reign of Queen Elizabeth. *Portrait and numerous large folding maps.* 2 vols. sml. *folio, hf. morocco, uncut.*
Dublin, 1820.

2101 STAFFORD GALLERY. The Gallery of Pictures by Eminent Masters formed by the late Marquis of Stafford, *with descriptions by* W. Y. Ottley *and* P. W. Tomkins, *Esq.* 4 vols. atlas folio, *containing upwards of* 300 representations after very splendid and much admired pictures; *arranged according to Schools, and in Chronological order. Executed by Finden, Wright, Corbould, Fittler, Heath, &c.* Brilliant Proof Impressions on India Paper. *4 vols. atlas folio, hf. morocco.*
London, 1818.

Largest Paper.

2102 Stansbury, Howard. Report on the Exploration and Survey of the Valley of the Great Salt Lake of Utah. *Large folding maps and lithographic plates.* 2 vols. 8vo. cloth.
Washington, 1853.

2104 Stansbury and Odell. The Loyal Verses of, Relating to the American Revolution, Edited by Winthrop Sargent. *Small 4to. beautifully printed, hf. crimson morocco, gilt top, by Bradstreet.*
Munsell, Albany, 1860.

No. 6 of Munsell's Historical Series on India paper. *One of 5 copies.*

2105 STATE TRIALS. A Complete Collection of State Trials and Proceedings for High Treason, and other Crimes and Misdemeanors from the Reign of King Richard II. With both supplements. 10 *thick vols. folio, calf, gilt. 3d Edition.*
London, 1742.

Best Edition, *scarce.*

2106 State Trials. A Collection of. *Folio, old cf. scarce.*
London, 1678, &c.

2107 Statii, P. P. Opera. Edited by Gronovius, *engraved title.* 16mo. *vellum, gilt.* Amsterdami *Ludovici Elzevirii,* 1653.

Highly praised by Peinesius.

2108 Statutes of Illinois. Compilation of the Statutes of Illinois, of a general nature, in force Jan. 1, 1856, by N. H. Purple. 2 *vols.* 8vo. *law sheep.* Chicago, 1856.

2109 Stedman, C. History of the Origin, Progress, and Termination Of the American War. *Numerous large Maps and Plans.* 2 vols. 4to. *calf extra, yellow edges.*
London, *Printed for the Author,* 1794.

The Author's copy, with his book-plate.
"This work will always be valuable for the large and splendid Military Maps and Surveys, from the official originals by the British Engineering Staff, with which it is adorned."

2110 Steele, Arthur. The Law and Custom of Hindoo Castes, within the Dekhan Provinces subject to the Presidency of Bombay, chiefly affecting Civil Suits. *Roy. 8vo. new cloth.*
London, 1868.

2111 Steinmetz, Andrew. History of the Jesuits, from the foundation of the order, to its suppression by Pope Clement XIV. *Portraits. 3 vols. 8vo. hf. calf, gilt.* London, 1848.

2112 Steinmetz, Andrew. Romance of Duelling in all Times and Countries. 2 vols. *crown 8vo. new cloth.* London, 1868.

2113 STEPHENS, H. L. CARTOONS to Nursery Rhymes, comprising, " A Frog he would a wooing go," " Cock Robin," " Fox and Geese," " Mother Hubbard," " House that Jack Built," and " Five little Geese." *Nearly 100 plates*, proof impressions on India paper, mounted on card-board. 2 vols. roy. 4*to. morocco antique, gilt leaves.* New York, 1866.

Only 100 copies printed, Pub. at $75.

" Mr. Stephens has no superior in the peculiar style of illustration which is most effective in bringing out the spirit of these Rhymes."
" There is not one of these illustrations that does not exhibit genius of the highest order."—*Lond. Art Journal.*

2114 Sterne, Laurence. A Sentimental Journey through France and Italy. *Portrait and engravings by Bromley.* 16*mo. hf. morocco, gilt.* Scarce edition. London, 1794.

2115 Sterne, Laurence. Works, with Life of the Author. *Illustrated by Darley.* 8*vo. cloth.* Philadelphia, 1854.

2116 Stevens, Rev. A. History of the Methodist Episcopal Church in the United States of America. *Portraits and engravings on wood.* 3 vols. 8*vo. morocco, antique.* New York, 1864.

2117 Stevens, Rev. A. History of the Religious Movement of the XVIIIth century, called Methodism, to the Death of Whitfield. *Numerous fine portraits.* 2 *vols.* 8*vo. morocco, antique.*
New York, 1858.

Uniform with the preceding lot.

2118 Stevens, Henry. Historical Nuggets. Bibliotheca Americana or a Descriptive Account of my collection of Rare Books relating to America. 2 *vols. fcap.* 8*vo. cloth, uncut, elegantly printed.*
London, *Printed by Whittingham and Wilkins Tooks Court Chancery Lane,* MDCCCLXII

Contains the titles, at length, of three thousand books relating to America.

2119 Stevenson, Hall. Works, comprising Crazy Tales, Fables for Grown Gentlemen, Lyric Epistles, Pastoral Cordial, Pastoral Puke, Mackarony Fables, Moral Tales, and Monkish Epitaphs corrected and enlarged. 3 vols. *crown* 8*vo. hf. calf, neat, scarce.*
London, 1795.

" We can safely aver that they are full of obscenity, whether ' evidently designed ' or not ; and apparently calculated to inflame the passions."—*Monthly Review.*

Stevenson was a kinsman of Laurence Sterne.

2120 (Stewart, W. Grant.) Popular Superstitions and Festive Amusements of the Highlanders of Scotland. *Front.* 12*mo. boards.*
Edinburgh, 1823.

2121 Stiles, Henry R. Contributions towards a Genealogy of Family of Stiles, 1659–60. *Sml.* 4*to. uncut.* Albany, 1863.

2122 Stirling, James H. The Secret of Hegel ; being the Hegelian System in Origin, Principle, Form, and Matter. 2 *vols.* 8*vo. cloth, uncut.* London, 1865.

2123 Stith, William. History of the First Discovery and Settlement of Virginia. *Beautifully reprinted from the Williamsburgh Edition of* 1748. *Thick royal* 8*vo. hf. russet morocco, gilt top.*
Reprinted for Jos. Sabin, New York, 1865.

Large Paper ; 50 copies printed.

2124 STONE, EDWIN W. Rhode Island in the Rebellion. *Portraits on steel.* 8vo. cloth. Providence, 1864.

2125 STONE, WM. L. Life and Times of Joseph Brant [Thayendane-gea], including the Border Wars of the American Revolution, and Sketches of the Indian Campaigns of Generals Hormar, St. Clair, and Wayne, &c. *Portraits.* 2 vols. royal 8vo. *uncut, sheets.* Albany, 1864.
LARGE PAPER, *only 50 copies.*

2126 STONE, WM. L. Life and Times of Sir William Johnson, Bart. *Portraits.* 2 vols. royal 8vo. *sheets, stitched.* Albany, 1865.
LARGE PAPER.

2127 STONE, WM. L. Memoirs, Letters, and Journals of Major General Reidesel, during his Residence in America. *Portraits.* 2 vols. 8vo. uncut. *Munsell,* Albany, 1868.

2128 ———— Another copy. 2 vols. impl. 8vo. uncut. Albany, 1868.
LARGE PAPER; 30 *copies.*

2129 STONE, W. L. Poetry and History of Wyoming. 3d Edition. *Crown 8vo. new hf. morocco, gilt top.* Albany, 1864.

2130 STONE, W. L. Uncas and Miantonomoh; a Historical Discourse. 16mo. paper. New York, 1842.

2131 STORY, JOSEPH. Commentaries on the Constitution of the United States. 3d Edition. 2 vols. 8vo. *law sheep.* Boston, 1858.

2132 STORY, JOSEPH. Life and Letters, edited by his Son, Wm. W. Story. *Portrait.* 2 vols. 8vo. *new cloth.* Boston, 1851.

2133 STORY, JOSEPH. Miscellaneous Writings, edited by W. W. Story. 8vo. *new cloth.* Boston, 1852.

2134 STORY, W. W. Graffiti D'Italia. A Collection of Poems. *Sq.* 12mo. *new cloth.* Edinburgh, 1868.

2135 STOTHARD, THOMAS. Life of, with personal reminiscences by Mrs. Bray. EXTRA ILLUSTRATED COPY, *having nearly* 200 *fine engravings from the works of the artist, comprising many of his choicest designs, all in fine condition and neatly arranged.* Very thick sml. 4to. elegantly bound in crimson morocco, super-extra, gilt leaves, &c. London, 1851.
A beautiful copy.

2136 STOWE, PROF. C. E. ORIGIN and HISTORY of the BOOKS of the BIBLE. *Portraits, &c.* 8vo. *hf. cf. antique.* New York, 1868.

2137 STRAUSS, DR. D. F. Life of Jesus, critically examined, translated from the German by Marian Evans. *Portrait.* 2 vols. 8vo. cloth. New York, 1860.

2138 STRAWBERRY-HILL PUBLICATIONS. MORE, HANNAH. BISHOP BONNER'S GHOST. Vignette. 4to. pp. 4, *hf. morocco, gilt.* *Strawberry-Hill,* Printed by Thomas Kirgate, 1789.
ONLY 96 COPIES PRINTED; *very scarce.*
Written when on a visit to Beilby Porteus, Bishop of London, at his Palace, Fulham, 1789.

2139 STRAWBERRY-HILL. TRACTS, comprising Letters of Edward VIth to Barnaby Fitz-Patrick. Miscellaneous Antiquities No. 1, and Miscellaneous Antiquities No. 2 (Life of Sir Thomas Wyatt), *all published. Together 3 tracts in one vol. 4to. hf. green morocco, edges untrimmed, portrait inserted.* *Strawberry-Hill,* 1772. *Only 200 copies printed.*

2140 STRICKLAND, AGNES. LIVES OF THE QUEENS OF ENG-LAND, from the Norman Conquest. LARGE TYPE LIBRARY EDITION. *With portraits of every Queen.* 8 *vols.* 8*vo. beautifully bound in blue polished calf, extra, marbled leaves.*
London, 1866.
BEST EDITION.

2141 STRICKLAND'S LIVES OF THE QUEENS OF SCOTLAND and English Princesses connected with Regal Succession of Britain, complete. *Fine portraits.* 8 *vols. post* 8*vo. calf, extra, marbled edges.*
Edinburgh, 1856–59.

2142 STRICKLAND, W. P. The Pioneer Bishop; or Life and Times of Francis Asbury. *Portrait.* 12*mo. cloth.*
New York, 1858.

2143 STRONG, REV. C. D. Sanctæ Vigiliæ; or Devoute Musings on the Heavens, in Verse. 12*mo. cloth.* *Pickering,* London, 1844.

2144 STRONG AND FREE; or, First Steps towards Social Science. By the author of " My Life, and what shall I do with it ? " 8*vo. new cloth.*
London, 1869.

2145 STRUTT, JOSEPH. A COMPLETE VIEW of the DRESS and HA-BITS of the PEOPLE of ENGLAND from the Establishment of the Saxons in Britain to the Present Time. Illustrated by engravings taken from the most Authentic Remains of Antiquity. With an Introduction, containing a general Description of the Ancient Habits in Use among Mankind, from the Earliest Period of Time to the conclusion of the Seventh Century. A new and improved edition, with Critical and Explanatory Notes, by J. R. Planché, Esq., F. S. A. 153 *plates, all* BEAU-TIFULLY COLORED. 2 *vols. royal* 4*to. half olive morocco, extra, gilt tops, edges uncut.* London, 1842.

2146 STRUTT, JOSEPH. REGAL AND ECCLESIASTICAL AN-TIQUITIES OF ENGLAND; containing the representations of all the English Monarchs from Edward the Confessor to Henry VIIIth, and of many persons that were eminent under their several Reigns. NEW EDITION, with Critical and Explanatory Notes by J. R. Planché. 72 *copper-plates beautifully colored after ancient illuminated manuscripts. Roy.* 4*to. new half morocco, uncut.* London, 1843.

2147 STRUTT, JOSEPH. SPORTS AND PASTIMES OF THE PEOPLE OF ENG-LAND from the earliest period, *with all the curious engravings of recreations, mummeries, pageants, processions, &c.* 4to. *dark maroon morocco, extra,* gilt edges. *Scarce.* London, 1810.
BEST EDITION.

2148 STRYPE, JOHN. Ecclesiastical Memorials, comprising, Religion and its Reformation in the reigns of Henry VIII, Edw. VI, and Q. Mary, with the Appendixes. 7 vols. 4to. *newly bound, hf. morocco.* London, 1816.
Large Paper.
Only 80 copies printed in this superior manner, and sold at £9 each.

2149 Strype, J. History of the Life and Acts of the Most Reverend Father in God, Edmund Grindal, Bishop of London and York. *Fine portrait by Vander Gucht. Folio, calf, neat.*
London, 1710.

2150 Stubbes, P. The Anatomie of Abuses. Reprinted from the third Edition of MDLXXXV, under the superintendence of William B. D. D. Turnbull, Esq. 8vo. hf. morocco, extra, uncut.
London, *Pickering,* 1836.
100 copies printed ; *scarce.*

2151 Suckley and Cooper. Natural History of Washington Territory and Oregon, with much relating to Minnesota, Nebraska, Kansas, Utah, and California. *58 large plates, the Ornithology beautifully* colored. *Roy. 4to. cloth.*
New York, 1860.

2152 Sue, Eugène. Mysteries of Paris. (Only authorized translation). Illustrated Edition, *with several hundred engravings. 3 vols. royal 8vo. new half morocco,* gilt. London, 1845.

2153 Sully. Memoirs of Maximilian de Bethune, Duke of Sully, Prime Minister to Henry the Great, with the Trial of Ravaillac, &c. *3 vols. 4to. cf. neat.* London, 1756.

2154 Sumner, George Henry. Principles at Stake. Essays on Church Questions of the Day. *8vo. new cloth.* London, 1868.

2155 Swallow, G. C. Reports on the Geological Survey of Missouri. (1st and 2d Annual Reports). *Numerous maps, plates, &c. 8vo. cloth, scarce.* Jefferson City, 1855.

2156 Swamp Doctor's Adventures in the South-West. *Illustrated. 12mo. cloth.* Philadelphia, (1843).

2157 Swedenborg, Emanuel. Delights of Wisdom concerning Conjugal Love, with the Pleasures of Insanity concerning Scortory Love. *2 vols. 8vo. hf. cf. gilt.* Manchester, 1811.

2158 Swift, Dean. Works, complete, containing interesting and valuable papers not hitherto published, with Memoir of the Author by Thomas Roscoe. *Portrait and facsimile.* 2 thick vols. 8vo. *green polished calf, extra.* London, 1864.

2159 Swinburne, Algernon Charles. William Blake. A Critical Essay. *Facsimile plates from the " Songs of Innocences," &c. 8vo. new cloth.* London, 1868.

2160 Swinton, Wm. Twelve Decisive Battles of the War; a History of the Eastern and Western Campaigns. *Numerous fine portraits. 8vo. new cloth.* New York, 1867.

2161 Symmes' Theory of Concentric Spheres, &c. 12mo. bds. *uncut.*
Cincinnati, 1826.

2162 Syntax, Dr. Three Tours in Search of the Picturesque, in search of Consolation, and in search of a Wife (in Hudibrastic verse, by William Combe). *Illustrated with 81 humorous colored engravings by Rowlandson. 3 vols. royal 8vo. hf. calf, extra.*
London, (1851).

2163 Tales of the Genii; or, The Delightful Lessons of Horam the Son of Asmar. Translated from the Persian by Sir Charles Morell. *2 vols. 8vo. hf. cf. gilt.* London, 1805.

2164 Tandon, M. The World of the Sea. Translated and enlarged by the Rev H. M. Hart. *Colored frontispiece and several hundred fine illustrations on wood.* Impl. 8vo. new cloth, gilt.
London, (1869).

2165 Tanner, John. Narrative of his captivity and adventures during 30 years' residence among the Indians. *Portrait. 8vo. sheep.*
New York, 1830.

2166 Tasso's Jerusalem Delivered, translated into Spenserian Verse, with a Life of the Author, by J. H. Wiffen. *Fine portrait, and numerous beautiful wood-cuts by Williams, and others. 2 vols. imp. 8vo. hf. crimson morocco, extra, gilt top, uncut edges. Fine copy.* London, 1824.
Best Edition, contains a list of English Crusaders.

2167 Tassoni, Alessandro. Memoirs of. Author of "La Secchia Rapita;" or, the Rape of the Bucket. Also, an Appendix, containing Biographical Sketches of Rinuccini, Galileo, Gabriello Chiabera, &c., &c., by Jas. Cooper Walker, and edited by Samuel Walker. *Fine portraits. Sq. p. 8vo. hf. morocco, uncut.*
London, 1815.
Large paper, *few printed.*

2168 TAYLOR, Isaac. Works, complete, comprising : Ancient Christianity, 2 vols. Spirit of Hebrew Poetry, 1 vol. Natural History of Enthusiasm, 1 vol. Spiritual Despotism, 1 vol. Physical Theory of Another Life, 1 vol. History of the Transmission of Ancient Books to modern Times, 1 vol. Fanaticism, 1 vol. Process of Historical Proof, 1 vol. Saturday Evening, 1 vol. Pausanias' Description of Greece, 3 vols. Herodotus, 1 vol. Home Education, and Considerations on the Pentateuch, 1 vol. Loyola, and Jesuitism in its Rudiments, 1 vol. Wesley, and Methodism, 1 vol. Restoration of Belief, 1 vol. Spiritual Christianity, 1 vol. Elements of Thought, 1 vol. Logic in Theology, &c., 1 vol. Ultimate Civilization, and other essays, 1 vol. *Together, 22 vols. 8vo. and 12mo., all uniformly bound in new hf. green morocco, gilt tops, uncut edges.* Very Scarce.
London, 1839, &c.
A remarkably Fine and complete Series, all best editions.
"The author is evidently a man of ardent piety, of a vivid imagination, and of a vigorous and excursive understanding, and has a vast command of diction and imagery. He is never dull. Dulness, indeed, is at the very antipodes of his manner. There is an intensity about the composition which keeps our faculties perpetually upon the stretch. The man, beyond all question, is a very distinguished writer."—*British Critic.*

2169 TAYLOR, REV. E. S. History of PLAYING-CARDS, with Anecdotes
of their use in Conjuring, Fortune-Telling, and Card-Sharping.
Front. and *numerous plates.* Thick 12mo. new cloth.
London, 1865.

2170 TAYLOR, JEREMY. WORKS, comprising: HOLY LIVING and DYING,
2 vols. LIFE of CHRIST, 2 vols. And DISCOURSES, 3 vols.
Together 7 *vols. 8vo. calf, gilt.*   London, 1811, &c.

2171 TAYLOR, THOMAS. TRANSLATIONS, an unusual collection.
All PRIVATELY PRINTED, *and in limited editions, comprising:*
POLITICAL FRAGMENTS of Archytas, Charondas, Zaleucus, and
other ancient Pythagoreans, &c., &c. *8vo. hf. mor. gilt, very
scarce.*   Chiswick, 1822.

OCELLUS LUCANUS, &c. *Post 8vo. bds. uncut.* London, 1831.

PLOTINUS. Five Books. *8vo. cf. gilt.* LARGE PAPER. *One of
the rarest of the author's Works.*   London, 1794.

FRAGMENTS of PROCLUS. *Post 8vo. hf. cf. gilt.* London, 1825.

PROCLUS; two TREATISES. *Post 8vo. hf. mor. uncut.*
London, 1823.

Presentation copy to E. H. Barker, Editor of Stephen's Thesaurus.
PHYSICAL and METAPHYSICAL INQUIRIES. *8v. cloth.*
London, 1806.

PORPHYRY; SELECT WORKS. *Thick 8vo. bds. uncut.*
London, 1823.

*** *One of 10 copies on thick paper.*
THEORETIC ARITHMETIC; containing the writings of Theo. of
Smyrna, Nichomachus, Bœotius, &c. *8vo. hf. cf.*
London, 1816.

PLATO; The CRATYTUS, PHŒDRO, PARMENIDES, and TIMÆUS of.
8vo. hf. cf. gilt, very scarce.   London, 1793.

PYTHAGORAS. Life of, by Iamblichus. *8vo. hf. cf. gilt.*
London, 1818.

IAMBLICHUS, on the MYSTERIES of the EGYPTIANS, &c. *8vo. hf.
cf. neat.*   Chiswick, 1821.

MYSTICAL HYMNS of ORPHEUS. *12mo. hf. cf. neat.*
Chiswick, 1824.

TAYLOR'S MISCELLANIES, in Prose and Verse. *Post 8vo. hf. cf.
rare.*   London, 1805.

ARGUMENTS of CELSUS, Porphyry, &c., against the Christians.
12mo. hf. cf. rare. suppressed.   London, 1830.

ELEMENTS of the TRUE ARITHMETIC of INFINITIES. *4to. paper.*
London, 1809.

Together 15 vols. 8vo. and 12mo. in various bindings.
London, V. D.

Nearly all the above-mentioned tracts were privately printed for the Translator, and many are very scarce. *So complete a series is seldom found.*
"It was by making friends chiefly that Mr. Taylor, who was as poor as Sydenham, contrived to print works that must have cost more than £10,000, that
were not of the most saleable description, and that upon the whole produced
no pecuniary profit. Mr. Meredith, a wealthy tradesman, retired from business * * * having read Plato, he wished also to read Aristotle in an English translation, and Mr. Taylor was ready to help him to it, upon no other

condition than his undertaking to print it, which he did; and though he made a losing speculation of it, by printing too few copies (50), he was so well satisfied with Mr. Taylor's exertions that he not only assisted him in bringing out some of his minor publications, but settled a pension of £100 a year upon him, which he enjoyed to his death. Among Mr. Taylor's minor works, some will be found dedicated to persons who printed them upon similar terms; and in a few cases gave him the benefit of the whole edition. He never exacted payment for his labor."—*New Eng. Cyclopedia.*

2172 TEGETMEIR, W. B. THE POULTRY BOOK; comprising the Breeding and Management of Profitable and Ornamental Poultry, their Qualities, &c. *Profusely illustrated with full-page illustrations in* COLORS *after drawings by Harrison Weir. Impl. 8vo. cloth, extra.* London, 1867.

2173 TEMPLE, SIR JOHN. IRISH REBELLION, or an History of the beginnings and first progress of the General Rebellion, &c. to which is added Tichborne's History of the Siege of Drogheda, in 1641. Sml. 4to. old calf, *scarce.* Dublin.

2174 TEMPLE, SIR WILLIAM. WORKS, complete. With a Memoir of the Life and Character of the Author. *Portrait. 4 vols. 8vo. cf.* London, 1757.

2175 TENNYSON, ALFRED. ELAINE. *Illustrated with a series of beautifully executed engravings on steel from the designs of* GUSTAVE DORÉ. *Folio, new cloth, gilt.* London, 1867.

2176 TEXAS. JOURNALS of the HOUSE of REPRESENTATIVES, LAWS, ACTS, STATE PAPERS, &c. &c. of the Independent Republic of Texas, previous to its annexation to the United States. 8 vols. 8vo. hf. calf, &c. Houston, 1838–41.

An important collection, illustrating an obscure period of History, and wanting in most of our great Public Libraries.

2177 THACKERAY, W. M. WORKS. NEW LIBRARY EDITION. *Elegantly printed on heavy paper, and profusely illustrated, including all of the author's original designs.* 22 vols. thick 8vo. new cloth, gilt, *uncut.* London, 1868–69.

Only complete Library Edition.

2178 THACKERAY, W. M. MISCELLANIES. 3 vols. *post 8vo. cloth.* (London) Philadelphia, 1866.

2179 THACKERAY, W. M. The Newcomes. *Post 8vo. cloth.* (London) Phil. 1866.

2180 THE BOOK! or the Proceedings and Correspondence upon the subject of the Inquiry into the conduct of the Princess of Wales, in 1806. 8vo. boards, uncut. London, 1813.

2181 THIERS, M. A. HISTORY OF THE CONSULATE AND THE EMPIRE OF FRANCE under Napoleon, forming a sequel to the "French Revolution." *Authorized Translation* by Dr. Forbes Campbell. *Portraits.* 20 vols. in 10, *handsomely bound in calf, extra, marbled edges.* Colburn, London, 1845, &c.

FINE COPY, BEST EDITION.

"This great work deserves to be ranked as the FOREMOST HISTORICAL PRODUCTION of the AGE. M. Thiers indeed throws a fascination over every subject he touches. The translation is a perfect reflex of the original, and rendered with fidelity and spirit."—*United Service Gaz.*

2182 THIERS' HISTORY OF THE FRENCH REVOLUTION, translated, with Notes and Illustrations, by Shoberl. *Numerous fine portraits and engravings.* 5 vols. 8vo. hf. calf, extra, gilt top. London, 1838.

2183 THIRLWALL, RIGHT REV. CONNOP. HISTORY OF GREECE. 2 *vols.* *roy. 8vo. hf. calf, antique.* New York, 1860.

2184 THOMAS, GABRIEL. An Historical and Geographical Account of the Province and Country of Pensilvania; and of West-New Jersey in America, &c. With a Map of both Countries. *Post 8vo. cloth, uncut.* London, 1698.
Reprinted in fac-simile for H. A. Brady, Esq.
New York, 1848.

2185 THOMAS, ISAIAH. THE HISTORY OF PRINTING in America. With a Biography of Printers, and an Account of Newspapers. To which is Prefixed a Concise View of the Discovery and Progress of the Art in other Parts of the World. *Facsimiles,* &c. 2 vols. *8vo. new hf. calf, neat.* Worcester, 1810.
FINE COPY. The Rice copy (uncut), sold for $60.

2186 Thomas, J. N. The Little Reformer, Temperance Tract No. I. *Post 8vo. uncut.* Providence, 1866.
Only 16 copies on heavy paper.

2187 THOMPSON, W. F. Practical Philosophy of the Muhammadan Empire, a translation of the Akhlak-i-Jalaly, the most esteemed Ethical work of middle Asia. *8vo. cloth, uncut.*
Oriental Society, Lond. 1839.

2188 THOMS, WILLIAM J. EARLY ENGLISH PROSE ROMANCES, with Bibliographical and Historical Introductions, second edition enlarged, 3 vols. post 8vo. *hf. bound, uncut.* London, 1858.

2189 THOMSON, JAMES. SEASONS. BENSLEY'S SPLENDID EDITION, *printed in exceedingly large and beautiful type, with exquisite engravings by* BARTOLOZZI *and* Tomkins, BRILLIANT IMPRESSIONS *(equal to Proofs), folio, marbled calf, extra.*
Bensley, London, 1707.
The most sumptuous edition of a Poet every issued, and one of Bensley's finest productions ; the pictures were painted expressly for the work by W. Hamilton.

2190 THOMSON, RICHD. HISTORICAL ESSAY ON THE MAGNA CHARTA OF KING JOHN, to which are added various Old Charters, with Translations and Notes. *Every page surrounded by an elegant and differently designed border.* ORIGINAL EDITION. *8vo. hf. morocco, gilt tops, uncut edges. Fine copy.* *Major,* London, 1829.

2191 THORNBURY, WALTER. HAUNTED LONDON. *Numerous illustrations on wood by Fairholt. Thick 8vo. new cloth.* London, 1865.

2192 Thornton, J. Wingate. First Records of Anglo-American Colonization, &c. 8vo. pp. 12, cloth. Boston, 1859.

2193 THORPE, BENJAMIN. NORTHERN MYTHOLOGY, comprising the Popular Traditions and Superstitions of Scandinavia, North Germany, and the Netherlands, 3 vols. post 8vo. *new cloth.*
London, 1851.

2194 THUANI, J. A. HISTORIA SUI TEMPORIS, CURA BUCKLEY, *fine portrait and vignettes. 7 vols. folio, calf.* London, 1733.
"Chancellor Hardwicke is said to have been so fond of this admirable work, as to have resigned his office, and the seals, on purpose to read it."—*Clarke.*

2195 THURLOE, JOHN. COLLECTION OF STATE PAPERS, containing Authentic Memorials of English affairs from 1638 to the Restoration of Charles II, with Life by Dr. Birch, *fine portrait by Vertue*, 7 vols. folio, *hf. calf, very neat, fine copy.*

London, 1742.

"These State Papers form an excellent History of Europe during this period, and are at once a proof of Thurloe's abilities as a statesman and his excellence as a writer."— GRANGER.

"That vast collection of State Papers of Thurloe's, the secretary of Cromwell, which formed about 170 volumes in the original MSS., accidentally fell out of the false ceiling of some chambers in Lincoln's Inn."— *Curiosities of Literature.*

2196 TICKNOR, GEO. LIFE OF WILLIAM HICKLING PRESCOTT. With a Prefatory Notice, Appendix and Index. *Fine Portrait, engraving of the Bust by Greenough, and numerous illustrations on wood.* 4to. *cloth, uncut.* Boston, 1864.

2197 TILLEMONT, LOUIS-SEBASTIAN. ECCLESIASTICAL MEMOIRS of the Six first Centuries, made good by citations from Original. Authors, Chronological Table, &c. *2 vols. folio, calf, rebacked* (Only English translation.) London, 1733.

FINE COPY. "Gibbon's obligations to him are constantly and gratefully expressed, and Jortin seems to have consulted *him* yet more than Fleury."— *Dibdin.*

2198 TILLEY, HENRY A. Eastern Europe and Western Asia, Political and Social Sketches. *Plates. Crown 8vo. cloth.*

London, 1864.

2199 TIMBS, JOHN. WORKS, comprising: CURIOSITIES of LONDON, thick 8vo. 1 v.—ROMANCE of LONDON, 3 v. post 8vo.—CLUB LIFE of LONDON, 2 v. post 8vo.—CENTURY of ANECDOTES, 2 v. post 8vo.—ENGLISH ECCENTRICS and ECCENTRICITIES, 2 v. post 8vo.—LONDON and WESTMINSTER, 2 v. post 8vo.—LADY BOUNTIFUL'S LEGACY, 1 vol. post 8vo.—ANECDOTE BIOGRAPHY, 1 v.—HISTORIC NINEPINS.—ECCENTRICITIES of the ANIMAL CREATION, 1 v.—CURIOSITIES of SCIENCE, 2 v. 12mo.—SCHOOL-DAYS of EMINENT MEN, 1 v. 12mo.—NOTABLE THINGS, 12mo.—CURIOSITIES of HISTORY, 12mo.—KNOWLEDGE for the TIME, 12mo.—THINGS NOT GENERALLY KNOWN, 12mo.—STORIES of INVENTORS and DISCOVERERS, 12mo. Together 24 vols. 12mo. post 8vo. and 8vo. *uniformly bound in new hf. blue calf, extra, marbled edges, contents lettered.* London, 1866, &c.

A very fine set.

2200 TIMBS, JOHN. Ancestral Stories, and Traditions of Great Families, illustrative of English History. *Frontispiece. Thick 12mo. new cloth.* London, 1869.

2201 TOCQUEVILLE, ALEXIS DE. American Institutions and their Influence. Notes, &c. by J. C. Spencer. *8vo. cloth.*

New York, 1851.

2202 TOHFUT-UL-MUJAHIDSEN, an Historical Work in the Arabic Language, translated in English by Lieut. M. J. Rowlandson. *8vo. cloth.* *Oriental Society,* London, 1833.

2203 TOMLINE, BP. Life of the Rt. Hon. William Pitt. 2 vols. 4to. hf. cf. extra. London, 1821.

2204 Towle, George Makepeace. History of Henry Vth, King of England, Lord of Ireland, and Heir of France, &c. *Fine portrait.* *8vo. new cloth.* New York, 1866.

2205 Townley Rev. James. Illustrations of Biblical Literature, exhibiting the History and Fate of the Sacred Writings, with Biographical Notices, &c. *2 vols. 8vo. cf. scarce.* New York, 1847.

2206 Tracts. A Collection of 30 Political Tracts, comprising: Character of a Trimmer, 1689.—Letter to King James, 1689.—Dialogue concerning the Posture of Affairs in England, 1688-9.—Justice of the Gentleman's Undertaking at York, 1688.—Reflections upon the Great Revolution, 1689.—The Case of Allegiance, 1689.—Considerations touching Success on and Allegiance, 1689.—On the Oath of Allegiance, 1689.—King William or King Lewis, 1689.—Dialogue occasioned by the late Revolution, 1689.—Letter from a French Lawyer on the present Revolution, 1689.—Lawfulness of the new Oath of Allegiance, 1689.—Obedience due to the present King, &c., 1689.—The Scrupler's Case Considered, 1691.—Character of a Jacobite, 1690.—Answer to King James' Declaration, 1689. Character of a Bigotted Prince, 1691; &c., &c., all in fine condition. *In one volume, sml. 4to. calf, neat.* London, V. D.
A highly interesting collection, formerly in the Library of the Hon. J. B. Clopton.

2207 Trade. The Antiquity, Honor, and Dignity of, particularly as connected with the City of London; written by a Peer of England, and addressed to his youngest son, as an inducement to follow a mercantile career. *Portraits.* *8vo. hf. morocco, uncut.* Westminster, 1813.
Only 150 Copies Printed.

2208 (Trapp, Dr. Joseph.) Abra-Mule; or, Love and Empire. A Tragedy. *Sml. 4to. pp. 72, hf. vellum.* London, 1704.

2209 Travis, Henry. Free-will and Law in perfect harmony. *8vo. cloth, pp. 67.* London, 1868.

2211 Tregelles, Dr. S. P. Greek New Testament. *4 parts, 4to. cloth, uncut.* London, 1860–69.
Published by subscription.

2212 Trenck, Frederick (*Baron*). Life, containing his Adventures, with Anecdotes, &c., trans. by Thomas Holcroft. *Portrait.* *4 vols. 12mo. cf. gilt.* London, 1789.

2213 TRÉSOR DE NUMISMATIQUE et de Glyptique, ou recueil général de Médailles, monnaies, pierres gravés et bas-reliefs, tant anciens que modernes, les plus interresants sous le rapport de l'art et de l'histoire, gravées d'après le procédé de M. Ach. Collas, sous la direction de MM. P. Delaroche et H. Dupont, avec un texte par M. Ch. Lenorment. *Upward of Five Hundred plates comprising several thousand examples.* *7 vols. folio hf. green morocco, gilt.* Paris, 1834, &c.
Comprises Rois Grecs, Galerie Mythologique, Empereurs Romains, des Papes, Médailles Allemandes, Sceaux Françaises, Bas-Reliefs, Sceaux d'Angleterre, Bas Reliefs et Ornements Médailles Françaises, Sceaux des Communantes Révolution Française, Médailles de l'Empire, et Monnaies Françaises.

2214 TRIAL of QUEEN CAROLINE. *A complete collection*, comprising "REPORT OF THE PROCEEDINGS," edited by J. Nightingale. BEST EDITION, with all the evidence. *Numerous portraits.* 3 vols. MEMOIRS OF THE PUBLIC and PRIVATE LIFE of QUEEN CAROLINE by Nightingale. *Portraits, &c.*, 1 vol. LAST DAYS of *Queen Caroline, plate,* 1 *vol.*, and HONE'S POLITICAL TRACT, relating to the Trial of the Queen, *with numerous etchings by* GEO. CRUIKSHANK, 1 vol. *with a representation on linen of her Majesties' entrance into Jerusalem;* together 6 vols. 8vo. *uniformly bound in hf. cf. extra.* London, 1822, &c.
A FINE SERIES.

2215 TRIAL of QUEEN CAROLINE, consort of George IV. for "Adulterous Intercourse" with Bartolomo Bergami. *Portrait, thick 8vo. new hf. morocco, uncut.* Fine copy. London, 1820.
Best Edition; with verbatim reprint of the evidence.

2216 TRIAL of Arthur Hodge, Esq. for the murder of his negro man-slave Prosper. *12mo. bds. uncut.* Middletown (Ct.), 1812.

2217 TRIAL. Methodist Church Property Case, Arguments, Decision, &c. 8vo. hf. sheep. Cincinnati, 1852.

2218 TRIALS. CASE OF IMPOTENCY as debated in England, in that remarkable Tryal An. 1613, between ROBERT EARL OF ESSEX, and the Lady FRANCIS HOWARD, who after eight years' marriage commenc'd a suit against her for Impotency. Containing the whole of the Proceedings, the Report of the Seven Matrons appointed to search the Countess, &c., &c. by George Abbot, *Archbishop of Canterbury. Rare front.* 2 vols. in one, 12mo. new cf. *neat.* London, 1715.
FINE COPY, *very rare.*

2219 TRIALS. THE CASE OF IMPOTENCY DEBATED, in the famous Tryal at Paris, between the Marquis de Gesvus and his Lady, Mlle. de Mascranny; with the Pleadings on both sides, Reports of the King's Physicians, &c., &c. 2 vols. in one. *12mo. calf, very neat.* London, 1715.
VERY SCARCE, uniform with the preceding.

2220 TRIALS. CAUSES AMUSANTES ET CONNUES. *Illustrated, 12mo. hf. cf. neat. Scarce.* Berlin, 1769.

2221 TRIALS. A collection of Remarkable Trials for Murder, Adultery, Breach of Promise, &c., &c. (12) in one vol. 8vo. *hf. cf. neat.* London, V. D.

2222 TRIALS. Engaging and Instructive Histories; with the Judicial Proceedings to which the remarkable Facts therein recorded gave occasion, &c. 2 *vols.* 12mo. *cf. neat.* London, 1750.
Translation of the famous French reports of Trials, "Les Causes Célèbres."

2223 TRIALS. FRENCH IMPOSTORS; or, An Historical Account of some very Extraordinary Criminal Cases, brought before the Parliament of France, &c., &c. 12mo. *calf, gilt.* London, 1737.
Very curious.

2224 TROLLOPE, FRANCES. The Mother's Manual; or, Illustrations of Matrimonial Economy, *with 20 outline etchings by A. Hervieu* (son-in-law of the author). *Roy. 8vo. hf. mor. uncut. Scarce.*
London, 1833

2225 TROWBRIDGE, J. T. The Vagabonds, *with illustrations* by F. O. C. Darley. *4to. cloth, gilt.* New York, 1868.

2226 TRUE INTEREST of GREAT BRITAIN with Respect to her American Colonies, stated and impartially considered, by a Merchant of London. 8vo. pp. 51, sheets, stitched. London, 1766.

2227 TRUMBULL, JOHN. McFINGAL: An Epic Poem. With Introduction and Notes by Benson J. Lossing. *Fine Portrait. Royal 8vo. paper, uncut.* New York, 1860.
LARGE PAPER; *only 100 copies.*

2228 TUCKER, GEO. LIFE OF THOMAS JEFFERSON, with selections from his Correspondence, &c., &c. 2 vols. 8vo. hf. cf. neat.
London, 1837.

2229 TUCKERMAN, HENRY T. BOOK OF THE ARTISTS. American Artist Life, comprising Biographical Sketches of American Artists, preceded by an Historical Account of the Rise and Progress of Art in America. With an Appendix containing an account of notable pictures and private collections. *Portraits.* Impl. 8vo. *new cloth, uncut.* *New York: Putnam,* 1867.

2230 TURNER, SHARON. HISTORY of the ANGLO-SAXONS from the earliest period to the Norman Conquest. BEST EDITION. 3 vols. 8vo. *elegantly bound by* RIVIERE, *in tree-calf, extra, marbled edges.*
London, 1852.
"For accurate and full information, no treatise on the more ancient history of England can be valuable that preceded the works of Sharon Turner and Sir Francis Palgrave."—*Courtenay's Life of Sir Wm. Temple.*

2231 TURNER'S SOUTHERN COAST OF ENGLAND, Picturesque Views of, 80 *very beautiful engravings by G. and W. B. Cooke, &c. fine impressions, the vignettes on India paper,* with Descriptions. *Roy.* 4to. *hf. mor. gilt leaves.* London, 1849.

2232 TWINING, HENRY. ELEMENTS of PICTURESQUE SCENERY, considered with Reference to Landscape Painting. *Numerous fine plates, some* COLORED. 2 vols. in one, *imperial 8vo. new hf. green morocco, uncut.* *Printed for Private Distribution,* London, 1846.
VERY SCARCE.

2233 TWINING, LOUISA. TYPES and FIGURES of the BIBLE, Illustrated by the Art of the Early and Middle Ages. 54 *plates, comprising upwards of* 300 *outline engravings from early missal paintings, &c.* 4vo. cloth. London, 1855.
Autograph note of the authoress inserted.
"The most complete Work on Christian Symbolic Art;" out of print and scarce.

2234 TYMME, THOMAS. A Dialogue Philosophicall. Where Natures secret closet is opened and the cause of all motion in nature shewed out of matter and forme, &c., together with the wittie inuention of an Artificiall Perpetuall Motion. Sm. 4to. pp. 72, old cf. neat. *Printed by T. S. for Clement Knight,* London, 1612.
VERY SCARCE, not mentioned by Lowndes or Watt.

2235 TYNDALL, JOHN. The GLACIERS of the ALPS, being excursions and Ascents, &c., &c. 12mo. *new cloth.* Boston, 1861.

29

2236 TYNDALL, JOHN. Heat considered as a Mode of Motion. *Illus*
trated. 12mo. *cloth.* New York, 1865

2237 TYNDALL, JOHN. Lectures on Sound, delivered at the Royal In
stitution of Great Britain. *Portrait and wood cuts.* Post 8vo
new cloth. London, 1867

2238 Tyndall, John. On Radiation. 12mo. *limp cloth.*
New York, 1865

2239 ULLOA, DON GEORGE and ANTONIO de. Voyage to South America
describing at large The Spanish Cities, Towns, Provinces, &c
on that extensive Continent. Maps, &c. 2 *vols.* 8vo. *new hf*
morocco, neat. London, 1760

2240 UNIVERSAL HISTORY, ANCIENT and MODERN; from the earliest re
cords of time to the general peace of 1801, by the Rev. Wil
liam Mavor. *Numerous Maps, &c.* 25 *vols.* 12mo. *hf. cf. neat*
London, 1802

2241 UPHAM, CHARLES W. SALEM WITCHCRAFT, with an Account o
Salem Witches, and a History of Opinions on Witchcraft an
Kindred subjects. 4 *vols. sml. 4to. uncut.* Boston, 1867

2242 ——— Another copy. 4 vols. in 2, *thick imp. 8vo. new cloth, uncut*
Boston, 1867
LARGE PAPER, *No.* 38, *of fifty copies.*

2243 URE, DR. DICTIONARY of ARTS, MANUFACTURES, and MINES. *New*
Edition, greatly enlarged, by R. Hunt, with nearly 2,000 *woodcuts*
3 *thick vols.* 8vo. *half morocco, neat.* New York, 1866

2244 U. S. ASTRONOMICAL EXPEDITION to the Southern Hemisphere
during the years 1849, '50, '51, '52, by Lieut. J. M. Gilliss
Vol. 1, Chile; Vol. 2, The Andes and Pampas, Antiquities
&c.; Vol. 3, Observations to determine the Solar Parallax
Vol. 6, Magnetical and Meteorological Observations. *Several*
Hundred maps and plates, including the Natural History, Antiqui
ties, Costume, &c., &c., many of which are BEAUTIFULLY COLORED
4 vols. roy. 4to. hf. cf. *neat.* Washington, 1855, &c

2245 ——— Another copy. THE NARRATIVE. *Many fine plates.* 2 vols
roy. 4to. cloth. Washington, 1855, &c

2246 UTTERSON, EDWARD VERNON. SELECT PIECES of EARLY
POPULAR POETRY, republished principally from early printed
copies in the Black Letter. *Woodcuts.* 2 *vols. crown* 8vo
polished calf, extra, uncut edges, by Bedford. London, 1817
SPLENDID COPY, VERY SCARCE; *only* 250 *copies printed.*
W. F. Fowle's copy of the *reprint by Pickering,* (1825,) brought $25.

2247 VALDÉS, JUAN DE. LIFE and WRITINGS of, by Benjamin B
Wiffen, with a Translation from the Italian of the CONSIDERA
TIONS. Thick 8vo. *new cloth.* London, 1865

2248 VALENTIA, Lord. VOYAGE and TRAVELS to India, Ceylon, the Red
Sea, Abyssinia, and Egypt, in 1802, '3, '4, '5, '6. *With* 69 *fin*
engravings by Angus, Landseer, &c. 3 *vols.* 4to. *calf, gilt.*
London, 1809

2249 VAMBÉRY, ARMINIUS. TRAVELS in CENTRAL ASIA in the year 1863
Frontispiece. Thick 8vo. *new cloth.* New York, 1865

2250 VANBRUGH, SIR JOHN. PLAYS. 2 vols. 12mo. calf, neat. *Scarce.*
London, 1776.

The edition of the " Provoked Wife," in these volumes gives the offensive
original scenes, and also the new ones substituted for them by Vanbrugh,
when the play (which came out in 1797) was revived in 1725." *Note on fly leaf.*

2251 VAN BRUNT FAMILY, Genealogy of, by Tunis G. Bergen. *8vo. cloth,
uncut.* *Munsell,* Albany, 1867.

2252 VAN CHOATE, S. F. Ocean-Telegraphing; Adaptation of new
principles for the successful working of submarine cables, &c.
Profusely illustrated. 4to. paper. Cambridge, Mass., 1865.

2253 VAN HELMONT, JOHN BAPTISTA. ORIATRIKE; or Physic Refined,
the common errors therein refuted, and the whole Art reformed
and rectified. *Frontispiece.* Thick folio, calf, *rare and curious.*
London, 1662.

One of the fathers of modern science; the above volume includes the
author's mystical writings.

2254 VANITY FAIR. A Weekly Show of Political, Social, and Literary
Wares. Vol. Oct. 1868—June, 1869, *with the celebrated series of
Cartoon portraits of England's Statesmen, in chromo-lithography.
Folio, green vellum, cloth.* London, 1868–69.

2255 VASARI, GIORGIO. Vite de Piu eccellenti Pittori, Scultori, e
Architetti, *with upwards of* 300 *fine portraits of Painters, Sculp-
tors, &c.* 3 *vols. thick* 4to. *mottled calf, extra.* Roma, 1759.
FINE COPY.
A extensive series of portraits, suitable for illustration.

2256 VEDUTE DI ROMA. RACCOLTA DELLE PRINCIPALI VEDUTE DI
ROMÆ suoi, conforni, designati dal vero ed incise de Gætano
Cottafari. *A series of* 48 *very large and beautifully engraved
plates of the most celebrated architectural remains of Rome. Oblong
4to. half red morocco.* Rome, 1843.

2257 VEGA (G. de la, *the Inca*). ROYAL COMMENTARIES of PERU, their
Incas or Kings, their Idolatry, Laws, and Government, the
Conquest by the Spaniards, transl. by Sir P. Rycaut.
Portrait by White, engravings, &c. 2 vols. in one, thick folio, *calf,
neat, scarce.* London, 1688.

Treating of the Incas or Kings, their Idolatry, Laws, and Government, the
Spanish Conquest, &c. and containing many curious facts taken from authors
whose works were never published and are now lost.

2258 VEITCH, JOHN. MEMOIR of SIR WILLIAM HAMILTON. *Portrait.*
8vo. *new cloth.* Edinburgh, 1869.

2259 VENERIS ET PRIAPI, Observantur in Gemnis Antiquis. *Both
parts complete,* with descriptive text in Eng. *Upwards of* 70
*plates illustrating the mystery of Priapus, and engraved titles,
from antique gems.* 2 vols. in one. *Post 8vo. bds.*
Lugd. Bataviorum, N. D.

" This singular collection may be considered as a masterpiece of the fancy of the
Ancients, and a remarkable monument of their talents and taste in design.
Several of the figures represent the Greek Courtesan Elephantis. Xeuxis,
Philoxene, and Apelles himself amused themselves by painting such subjects.
Probably some of these Gems were of their invention."

2260 VENEREAL DISEASES. Report of the Committee appointed to
inquire into the treatment and prevention of Venereal Diseases
in the Army and Navy. *Thick 8vo. paper, pp.* 584.
London, 1864.

2261 VESTIGES of CIVILIZATION; or the Ætiology of History, Religious, Æsthetical, Political, and Philosophical. (Robert H. Shannon?) 12*mo. cloth.* New York, 1850.

2262 VESTIGES of the NATURAL HISTORY of CREATION. 10th edition with extensive additions and emendations. *Numerous engravings on wood.* 8*vo. new half morocco, extra.* London, 1853.

2263 VIDA, M. J. (*Bishop of Alba.*) LUDUS SACCHIÆ; Chesse-Play. A Game, both pleasant, wittie, and politicke; with certain briefe instructions thereunto belonging, &c. 4to. pp. 16 and 31. hf. cf. neat. London, 1597, *reprinted*, 1813.
LARGE PAPER; *only 150 copies.*

2264 VIDAL'S PICTURESQUE ILLUSTRATIONS of BUENOS AYRES and Monte Video, with Descriptions, 24 *large finely* COLORED *engravings*, roy. 4to. *new hf. morocco.* London, 1820.

2265 VIEWS on the RIVER THAMES. An extensive collection of engraved Views of the Scenery, &c. of the River Thames from its source to the Sea, *comprising upwards of* THREE HUNDRED and FIFTY *engraved plates, including the large* COLORED SERIES by HOVELL, *all neatly inlaid and arranged. Impl. folio, hf. russia, extra, gilt edges.* London, V. D.
A UNIQUE and very interesting collection, including many plates of great rarity.

2266 VILLARS, MARQUIS DE. Mémoires de la cour d'Espagne, sous le Regne de Charles II, 1678—1862, *handsomely printed on heavy paper, photographic portrait, &c.* 8*vo. new cloth, uncut.*
London, 1861.
Only 100 *copies printed.*

2267 VIRGIL. WORKS, containing his Pastorals, Georgics and Œnis, translated into English verse by Mr. Dryden. *Portrait and one hundred copperplates by Vander-Gucht.* 3 *vols.* 8*vo. cf. extra.*
Tonson, London, 1719.
FINE COPY, *scarce.*

2268 VIRGILIUS. OPERA, Varietate Lectionis et perpetua Ad notatione illustrata, a CHR. G. HEYNE; accedit Index uberrimus, (recognovit R. Porson), *numerous elegant vignettes designed by Fiorillo from Antique monuments.* 4 vols. in 7, roy. 4to. hf. *green morocco, gilt top, uncut edges.* London, 1793.
LARGEST PAPER, *few printed,* (Published at £21.)
" The London edition of 1793, which is a re-impression of the Leipzic one, is the most popular one in this country. Some copies are struck off on Large Paper, in roy. 8vo. and 4to. ornamented with beautiful vignettes. *Of the quarto size only very few were printed, and they sell at a great price;* the splendor of the paper, and elegance of the execution, render it a truly interesting publication."—*Dibdin.*
Stevens, £16. 16s. Marquis of Townshend, £11. 5s.

2269 VIRGINIA. Acts of Assembly passed in the Colony of Virginia from 1622 to 1715. Folio, hf. cf. London, 1727.
Also, with the same volume, Acts of Assembly made and enacted to the Bermuda or Summer Islands, 1690-1714.
Acts of Assembly passed in the Charibbee or Leward Islands, 1690-1734.

2270 Virginia. Acts of the General Assembly of the State of Virginia passed in 1861, '62, '63 and '64. 3 vols. 8vo. *boards.*
Richmond, 1862, &c.

2271 Virginia. Acts of the General Assembly passed in 1861. 8vo. *hf. sheep.* Richmond, 1861.
Includes the ordinances of the Secret Session in April and May, 1861.

2272 Vision of Rubeta, an Epic Story of the Island of Manhattan, *with illustrations.* 8vo. *boards.* Boston, 1838.

Vitruvius Britannicus, see Robertson.

2273 Vizetelly, Henry. The Story of the Diamond Necklace, told in detail for the first time by the aid of original documents, &c. *Portraits.* 2 vols. crown 8vo. *hf. cf. extra.* London, 1867.

2274 Voiture. Works, translated from the French by Dryden, Dennis, Ozell, &c. &c. *Portrait.* 2 vols. 12mo. *cf. gilt.*
E. Curll, London, 1736.

2275 Volney, C. F. Works, comprising Researches in Ancient History, 2 vols. Travels, 2 vols. Ruins, or Revolutions of Empires, 1 vol. America, 1 vol. *Portraits and plates.* Together 6 *vols.* 8vo. *uniformly bound in new hf. calf, extra.* London, 1821.

2276 Voltaire. Works, translated from the French, with Notes, historical and critical by T. Smollett, T. Francklin, &c. 24 *vols.* 12mo. *cf.* Dublin, 1772.

2277 Voltaire. Philosophical Dictionary, translated from the French with additional Notes, critical and argumentative. Portrait. *Thick impl. 8vo. sheep.* Boston, 1856.

2278 Voltaire. The White Bull, an Oriental History, from an Ancient Syrian manuscript. 2 vols. in one. 16mo. *hf. cf. gilt. Scarce.* London, 1774.
Unknown to Lowndes.

2279 Voltairiana. Selected and translated from the French by Mary Julia Young. 4 *vols.* 16mo. *hf. morocco, neat.* London, 1805.

2280 Von Gerning, *Baron.* Picturesque Tour along the Rhine from Mentz to Cologne, with illustrations of the scenes of remarkable events, and of Popular Traditions. 24 *highly finished and* colored engravings from *drawings by M. Schurtz, Maps, &c. Roy. 4to. hf. russia, gilt, marbled edges.* London, 1820.

2281 Von Sybel, Henrich. History of the French Revolution, translated from the German by Walter C. Perry. 2 vols. 8vo. *new cloth.* Murray, London, 1867.
To be completed in four volumes, priced by S. W. & Co. $12.

2282 **Voraigne, Jacobus de. GOLDEN LEGEND.** Lombardica Historia que a plerisqz Aurea *legenda* sctoruz appelatur. *Printed with a gothic character, in double columns, with rubricated initial letters.* Folio, *original calf binding, with heavy brass mountings, bosses, &c.*
Colophon. Explicuit quorūdam sancto legīde a diūcte post Lombardicā, Historia *Impresse Argentine* Anno dñi, mccccxcii.
Fine specimen.
The author, James di Voraigne, a celebrated Dominican, so called from the place of his birth in the state of Genoa, was born about 1230. His most cele-

brated work is a collection of legends of the saints, known as the "Golden Legend," the first edition of which was printed at Cologna in 1470. This work contains so many puerile and ridiculous fables, that Melchior Cano said " the author had a mouth of iron, a heart of lead, and but little wisdom, or soundness of judgment."

2283 VOYAGES of the SLAVERS ST. JOHN and ARMS of Amsterdam, 1659. 1663; Edited with Notes, &c. by Dr. E. B. O'Callaghan. *Sml. 4to. uncut.* Albany, 1867.

100 *copies.* N. Y. Colonial Tracts, No. III.

2284 WAAGEN. TREASURES OF ART IN GREAT BRITAIN, *best Library Edition*, with the SUPPLEMENT containing the GALLERIES and CABINETS visited in 1854–56, 4 vols. 8vo. *handsomely bound in yellow calf, extra, marbled edges.* London, 1854–57.

2285 WALDENSES AND ALBIGENSES. Comprising, Faber's, Geo. S., Inquiry into the History and Theology of the Ancient Waldenses and Albigenses, 1 vol.; Gilly's Waldensian Researches, 1 vol.; Gilly's Excursion to the mountains of Piemont and researches among the Vaudois, 1 vol.; Authentic Details of the Waldenses in Piemont and other countries, 1 vol. *Numerous maps, engravings, etchings, &c. Together 4 vols. 8vo. elegantly bound in mottled calf, extra, yellow edges.* London, 1826.

A VERY FINE SERIES.

2286 WALKER, ALEXANDER. BEAUTY Illustrated by an ANALYSIS and CLASSIFICATION of BEAUTY in WOMEN, with a critical view of the hypothesis of Hume, Hogarth, Burke, Knight, Alison, &c. *Illustrated with a fine series of plates from life, by Henry Howard.* Roy. 8vo. *cloth, uncut.* London, 1852.

2287 WALKER, ALEXANDER. WOMAN physiologically considered as to Mind, Morals, Marriage, Matrimonial Slavery, Infidelity, and Divorce, *post 8vo. cloth, uncut.* London, 1840.

2288 WALKER, ALEX. WOMAN, Physiologically considered as to Mind, Morals and Marriage, &c. *8vo. cloth, scarce.* London, 1840.

2289 WALKER, C. M. HISTORY of ATHENS Co., OHIO, and incidentally of the Ohio Land Company and the First Settlement of the State at Marietta, with Personal and Biographical Sketches of Early Settlers, Narratives of Pioneer Adventures, etc. *Map and steel portraits.* 8vo. *cloth, uncut.* Cincinnati, 1869.

2290 —— Another copy. *Printed on heavy toned paper, with proof portraits, &c.* 2 vols. imperial 8vo. cloth, uncut.
Cincinnati, 1869.

LARGE PAPER, *few printed.*

2291 WALLABOUT PRISON-SHIP SERIES.
I. Letters from the Prisons and Prison-Ships of the Revolution. With Notes, &c.
II. Account of the Interment of the Remains of American Patriots who perished on board the British Prison-Ships during the American Revolution. With Notes and Appendix by Dr. Stiles. *2 vols. royal 4to. uncut.* New York, 1865.

LARGE PAPER, *only 35 copies.*

2292 WALLACE, J. W. An Address Delivered at the Celebration of the Two Hundredth Birth Day of William Bradford, who Introduced the Art of Printing into the Middle Colonies of British America. 8vo. *hf. morocco, gilt top.* Albany, *J. Munsell,* 1863.

2293 —————— Another copy. *8vo. uncut.* Albany, 1863.

2294 WALLACK, JAMES W. A Sketch of the Life of James William Wallack (Senior), Late Actor and Manager. *4to. paper, uncut.* New York, 1865.

LARGE PAPER. 50 copies printed.

2295 WALLER, EDMOND. Poems, &c., written upon several Occasions and to several Persons. 4th Edition, with Additions, to which is prefixed a Life of the Author. TONSON'S FINE EDITION, *with numerous fine portraits by Vertue, including two of the author. 8vo. crimped red morocco, extra, Roger Paine style.* London, 1711.

FINE COPY.
Contains, among others, Portraits of Lord Falkland, the Countesses of Carlisle and Sunderland, Ben Jonson, John Fletcher, Lady Morton, Earl of Sandwich, &c.

EXTRA ILLUSTRATED.

2296 WALPOLE, HORACE. CORRESPONDENCE, including numerous letters now first published from the original MSS., 1735 to 1797. EXTRA ILLUSTRATED, HAVING IN ADDITION TO THE PORTRAITS PUBLISHED WITH THE WORK, NEARLY FIVE HUNDRED extra plates inserted, COMPRISING PORTRAITS OF PROMINENT CELEBRITIES, VIEWS, &C., &C., *all in fine condition.* 6 thick vols. 8vo. new hf. calf, *extra, marbled edges.* London, 1840.

" ' Incomparable letters ! ' Lord Byron says, and incomparable indeed they are. Horace Walpole was a statesman, the courtier, the man of vertu, the glass of fashion, the very quintessence of wit, the most learned, polite, engaging, and cleverest *gentleman* that ever appeared."

2297 WALPOLE. ÆDES WALPOLIANÆ ; or, a Description of the Collection of Pictures at Houghton Hall in Norfolk, the Seat of Sir Robert Walpole, Earl of Orford. 2d Edition with additions (by Horace Walpole) *with 6 fine portraits and plans. 4to. bds. uncut.* London, Printed in the year 1752.

PRIVATELY PRINTED. The collection of Pictures here described was purchased by the Empress of Russia; some curious information respecting it will be found in Beloe's Anecdotes, vol. I. p. 58–61.

2298 WALPOLE, HORACE. WORKS, ORIGINAL EDITION, *with numerous fine portraits and engravings by Heath, &c.* 4 vols. royal 4to. *half russia, neat.* London, 1798.

Comprises Royal and Noble Authors, Anecdotes of Painting, Catalogue of Engravers, Castle of Otranto, Description of Strawberry Hill, Historic Doubts, Correspondence, Miscellanies, &c.

EXTRA ILLUSTRATED COPY.

2299 WALTON, ISAAC. LIVES; of Dr. Donne ; Sir Henry Wolton ; Richard Hooker ; George Herbert ; and Dr. Sanderson. BEST EDITION, with notes and Life of the Author by Thomas Zouch. *4to. elegantly bound, sprinkled calf, extra, gilt edges.* York, 1796.

ELEGANT COPY.
Extended and Illustrated by the insertion of numerous fine and rare Portraits, old Engravings, Views, &c., &c. Fine early Impressions, INDIA PROOFS, *&c., including a rare series of portraits by* MARSHALL.

2300 WALTON AND COTTON. The COMPLETE ANGLER, or the Contemplative Man's Recreation ; being a Discourse of Rivers, Fish Ponds, Fish, and Fishing ; written by Izaak Walton ; and Instructions how to Angle for a Trout or Grayling in a Clear

Stream, by Charles Cotton. With Original Memoirs and Notes by Sir Harris Nicolas. *Portraits. Views and portraits of Fish. Rubricated titles. 2 vols. imperial 8vo. handsomely bound in polished calf, extra, gilt edges.* *W. Pickering*, London, 1836.
A Fine, early copy.

2301 WALTON and COTTON. The Complete Angler, or the Contemplative Man's Recreation; being a Discourse of Rivers, Fish Ponds, Fish, and Fishing; written by Izaak Walton; and Instructions how to Angle for a Trout or Grayling in a Clear Stream, by Charles Cotton. With Original Memoirs and Notes by Sir Harris Nicolas. *Portraits. Views and plates of Fish.* 2 *vols. imperial 8vo. new hf. green morocco, gilt top, uncut edges.*
London, 1869.

2302 WALTON and COTTON'S ANGLER; a series of *fifty-four beautiful illustrations, after Stothard and Inskipp, on India Paper.* In folio, for illustration.
This is without doubt the most beautiful series of Illustrations to Walton's Angler ever published.

2303 Walton, Isaac. Complete Angler. Literal reprint of the original edition of 1653. Sq. 12mo. *cloth.*
Murray's Reprint, London, 1869.

2304 Walton and Cotton. Complete Angler, or the contemplative man's recreation. Edited by John Major. *Numerous plates on India paper, and beautifully executed engravings on wood.* Thick 8vo. *bds. uncut.* Boston, 1866.
Large Paper, 100 *copies.*

2305 Walton and Cotton's Complete Angler. *Pickering's Miniature Edition, beautifully printed in diamond type by Corrall.* 48mo. *Cloth.* London, *Pickering*, 1825.

2306 Walton and Cotton's Complete Angler, with Notes, &c. by Edward Jesse. *Bohn's beautifully illustrated Edition. Crown 8vo. new hf. morocco, uncut.* London, 1856.

2307 Walton, Angler. Index to the Original and Inserted Illustrations contained the 'Complete Angler.' *Roy. 4to. hf. mor. gilt.*
New York, *Bradstreet Press*, 1866.
Only 50 *copies printed* for private distribution.

2308 Wanley, N. Wonders of the Little World; or, a General History of Man, displaying the various Faculties, Capacities, Powers, and Defects of the Human Body and Mind, *numerous plates.* 2 *vols. roy. 8vo. cf. neat.* London, 1806.
A most extraordinary and amusing common-place book of thousands of marvellous stories of former times; extracted from the Greek and Latin Classics and middle-age writers, chronicles, travels and miscellanies of every age and nation.

2309 War Lyrics, *with illustrations on wood* by F. O. C. Darley. 4to. new cloth. New York, 1866.

2310 Warburton, Bp. Works, complete, edited, with Life, by Bp. Hurd, *portrait, and facsimiles of writing,* 12 vols. in 6, 8vo. *calf gilt, scarce.* London, 1811–41.

2311 (Warburton.) Eothen; or Travels in the East. *Colored illustrations.* 8vo. *tree-marbled calf, extra, scarce.* London, 1845.
Best edition.

2312 WARD, A. W. The House of Austria in the Thirty Years' War. Two Lectures. 12mo. *new cloth*. London, 1869.

2313 WARD, NED. WORKS, comprising, MISCELLANEOUS WRITINGS, including London Spy, &c., 6 vols. WOODEN-WORLD DISSECTED, 1 vol. CERVANTES' MISCELLANEOUS WORKS, 1 vol. WIG-UN-MASK'D or secret history of the Calf's Head Club, 1 vol. NUP-TIAL DIALOGUES, *Best edition*, 2 vols. VULGUS BRITANNICUS; or the British Hudibras, 1 vol. HUDIBRAS REDIVIVUS, 1 vol. 4to. DON QUIXOTE, trans. into Hudibrastick Verse, 2 vols. FEMALE POLICY DETECTED ; or the arts of a designing Woman laid open, 1 vol. 12mo., *together* 15 vols. 8vo. *and* 12mo. *old calf,* (various). London, 1718, &c.

An unusual collection, *many of which are very scarce*.

2314 WARD, NED. DANCING DEVILS; or, the Roaring Dragon, a Dumb Farce, as it was lately acted at both Houses, but particularly at one, with unaccountable success. 8vo. pp. 70, *paper, scarce*. London, 1724.

The author of this satirical piece was Edward Ward ; it is divided into three acts, ridiculing the town for the encouragement given to the pantomime Harlequin Doctor Faustus at the Theatres in Drury Lane and Lincoln's Inn Fields.—*Baker's Biographia Dramatica*.

2315 WARREN, DR. JOHN C. DESCRIPTION OF a SKELETON of the MAS-TODON GIGANTEUS of North America. *Large folding plate, and* 30 *lithographs,* roy. 4to. *cloth, uncut, scarce*. *Printed for the Author*, Boston, 1852.

2316 WARREN, SAMUEL. WORKS, comprising Diary of a Physician, Ten Thousand a Year, Now and Then, and Miscellanies, *vignettes,* 5 *vols. post* 8vo. *tree calf, extra, fine copy*. Edinburgh, 1855.

2317 WARTON, REV. JOHN. DEATH-BED SCENES, and Pastoral Conversations, edited by his sons. BEST EDITION. 4 *vols.* 8vo. *calf, neat*. London, 1827.

2318 WARTON, THOMAS. COMPLETE WORKS, viz., POEMS and LIFE, 2 vols. HISTORY of ENGLISH POETRY, *Best Edition*, 4 vols. LIFE of DR. BATHURST, 1 vol. LIFE of SIR THOMAS POPE, 1 vol. EDITION of MILTON, 1 vol. OBSERVATIONS on SPENSER, 2 vols. *portraits, together* 10 *vols.* 8vo. *uniformly bound in new hf. russia, gilt tops*. London and Oxford, 1802, &c.

A FINE SET, *scarce*.

2319 WARTON, THOMAS. HISTORY of ENGLISH POETRY from the XIth to the XVIIIth Century, with Dissertations on the Origin of Romantic Fiction in Europe, &c. 3 vols. 4to. *hf. morocco*. London, 1774.

2320 WASHBURN, EMORY. Treatise on the Law of Real Property. 2 *vols.* 8vo. *law sheep*. Boston, 1864.

2321 WASHINGTON, GEORGE. THE WRITINGS OF, being his Correspondence, Addresses, Messages, and other Papers, Official and Private; selected and published from the original manuscripts; with Life of the Author; by Jared Sparks, LL. D. *Plates.* 12 *vols. imperial* 8vo. *half cf. neat*. Boston, 1837.

LARGE PAPER, uniform in size with the LARGE PAPER copies of *Franklin, Webster, Adams,* &c.

30

2322 Washington. Correspondence of the American Revolution; being Letters of Eminent Men to Washington, from the time of his taking Command of the Army to the end of his Presidency. Edited from the Original Manuscripts, by Jared Sparks, LL.D. *4 vols. imperial 8vo. cloth, uncut.* Boston, 1853.
Large Paper, uniform in size with the Large Paper copies of *Franklin, Washington's Writings, Webster, Adams, &c.*

2323 Washington. Irving's Life of George Washington. *With the Beautiful series of Portraits and Views. 5 vols. sml. 4to. handsomely bound in polished calf, extra, gilt edges.* New York, 1856.
Large Paper, uniform with the L. P. series of Irving's Works.

2324 Washington. Diary of Washington; from the First Day of October, 1789, to the Tenth Day of March 1790, from the Original Manuscript, with Introductory Remarks by B. J. Lossing. *Fac-simile, and a photograph from Mme. de Brienne's miniature, alluded to at page 12 of the Diary. Royal 8vo. full crimson morocco, extra, uncut edges, by Matthews.* New York, 1858.
Bradford Club. No. 2.
200 copies printed. No. 30.

2325 Washington. The Journal of Major George Washington sent by the Hon. Robert Dinwiddie to the Commandant of the French Forces in Ohio. *Map. Royal 8vo. uncut.* London, 1754.
New York, Reprinted for J. Sabin, 1865.
Large paper; only 50 copies.

2326 Washington. Letters from his Excellency General Washington to Arthur Young, Esq. containing an account of his Husbandry, *with a map of his Farm, &c., &c. 8vo. hf. mor. neat.*
London, 1801.

2327 Washington Memorial Medals, by W. E. Woodward. Impl. 8vo. *uncut.* *Privately Printed*, 1865.
50 copies.

2328 Washington. Vida de Jorge Washington, escrita por David Ramsay, y traducida al español. 2 vols. 16mo. sheep.
Nueva York, 1825.

2329 Washington. Kinlock, Francis. Eulogy on George Washington. *Impl. 8vo. uncut.* *Reprinted,* New York, 1867.
Only 60 copies.

2330 Washingtoniana; Or Memorials of the Death of George Washington, giving An Account of the Funeral Honors paid to his Memory, with a List of Tracts and Volumes printed upon the occasion, and A Catalogue of Medals concerning the Event, By Franklin B. Hough. *Map and Portraits. 2 vols. royal 4to. uncut.* Roxbury, Mass., 1865.
Large paper; *only 85 copies.*

2331 ———— Another Copy. 2 vols. *roy. 8vo. uncut.*
Roxbury, Mass., 1865.

2332 ———— Another Copy. Beautifully printed on India Paper. (*Only 6 copies.*) 2 vols. roy. 8vo. *hf. crimson morocco, gilt tops, by Bradstreet.* Roxbury, 1865.

2333 Washingtoniana (The); containing a Biographical Sketch of the late Gen. George Washington, with various outlines of his Character, From the pens of different eminent writers, both in Europe and America, &c., &c. *Portraits on India paper.* Roy. *4to. bds. uncut.* New York : *E. Dexter & Son,* 1865. Large paper. *50 copies printed.*

2334 Watkinson, John. Philosophical Survey of the South of Ireland, in a series of letters to. *Front. 8vo. hf. cf. rough edges.* London, 1777.

2335 Watson, W. C. Pioneer History of the Champlain Valley; being an Account of the Settlement of the Town of Willsborough, by William Gilliland, together with his Journal and other Papers, and a Memoir. *Royal 8vo. uncut.* Albany, 1863. Large paper. 50 copies printed.

2336 WATTS, Rev. George. A Sermon preached before the Trustees for establishing the Colony of Georgia in America; at their Anniversary meeting, Thursday, March 18, 1735. *4to. edges wholly untouched.* London, 1736. Remarkably fine copy, see also Francklin.

2337 Wayne. Journal of Wayne's Campaign against the North-western Indians, 1794. *4to. uncut.* Cincinnati, 1866.

2338 Wayne, Henry C. Report on the Purchase of Camels for the purposes of Military Transportation. *Illustrated. 8vo. new hf. morocco, gilt top.* Washington, 1857.

2339 Webb, William. An Analysis of the History and Antiquities of Ireland, prior to the XVth century, with a Review of the Celtic Nation. *8vo. hf. cf. neat, scarce.* Dublin, 1791.

2340 Weber, Henry. Metrical Romances of the Thirteenth, Fourteenth, and Fifteenth Centuries, from Ancient mss. *With Introduction, Notes, Glossary, &c. 3 vols. crown 8vo. hf. olive morocco, extra.* Edinburgh, 1810.

2341 Webber, Jos. Memoirs of Maria Antoinetta, Arch-duchess of Austria, Queen of France, &c., including several important periods of the French Revolution from its origin to October 16th, 1793, translated from the French by Joseph Dallas. *Numerous fine portraits. 3 vols. roy. 8vo. hf. cf. extra, scarce.* London, 1805.

Large paper.

2342 Webster, Daniel. Works and Correspondence, with a Biographical Memoir of his Public Life by Edward Everett. *Portraits, &c. 8 vols. 8vo. new cloth.* Boston, 1851–57.

2343 Webster, Daniel. Private Correspondence. Edited by Fletcher Webster. *Portrait. 2 vols. impl. 8vo. cloth.* Boston, 1857.

Large paper.

2344 WEBSTER, John. Displaying of supposed Witchcraft, also of the Existence of Angels and Spirits, the Truth of Apparitions, force of Charms, Philters, &c. folio, *calf, neat.* London, 1677

This curious and scarce work adduces many notable examples, and was written in opposition to the treatises of Glanvill and H. More the Platonist.

2345 WEBSTER, JOHN. DRAMATIC WORKS. Edited by W. C. Hazlitt. *Handsomely printed.* 4 vols. post 8vo. new cloth.
Russell Smith, London, 1857
LARGE PAPER.

2346 WEBSTER, NOAH. DICTIONARY of the ENGLISH LANGUAGE. Thoroughly Revised, and greatly Enlarged and Improved, by C. A. Goodrich, &c., &c. *Rubricated titles.* 2 *vols. folio, elegantly bound in crimson gros-grained levant morocco, extra, inside borders, gilt tops, uncut edges.* Cambridge, 1865.
LARGE PAPER; *only* 250 *copies.*

HISTORY OF BLOCK PRINTING AND ENGRAVING BEFORE DURER.

2347 WEIGEL, T. O. COLLECTIO WEIGELIANA : die Anfange der Druckerkunst in Bild und Schrift; an deren frühesten Erzeugnissen in der Weigel's schen Sammlung erläutert von T. O. WEIGEL und Dr. Ad. ZESTERMANN. 2 *vols. folio, with* 145 *fac-similes, and many woodcuts in the text.* Leipzig, 1866.

Only 325 copies were printed of this most important publication, the necessary companion to "SOTHEBY's Principia Typographica, 3 vols. folio, 1858," but executed with infinitely more critical sagacity and learning.

The text to this grand work was written by D. August Zestermann with the assistance of Mr. T. O. Weigel, and they have now placed before the world, in the above work, a complete HISTORY OF THE GRAPHIC ARTS, THEIR INVENTION AND CULTIVATION DURING THE FIFTEENTH CENTURY, illustrated throughout by the Art-Monuments of the Weigel collection, thus displaying a vivid picture of the thoughts, feelings, and superstitions of the Christian world previous to the Reformation, readily understood, and fully revealing the state of mind of Christian Europe during that period.

The artistic execution of the 145 fac-similes has been accomplished with marvellous fidelity,—and even the most rigid and fastidious critic would find himself compelled to acknowledge and extol their absolute correctness.

2348 WEISS, JOHN. LIFE AND CORRESPONDENCE of THEODORE PARKER. *Portrait, &c.* 2 vols. 8vo. new cloth. New York, 1864.

2349 WELLS, WM. V. LIFE AND PUBLIC SERVICES OF SAMUEL ADAMS, being a Narrative of his Acts and Opinions, and of his Agency in Producing and Forwarding the American Revolution, &c. *Portrait on India Paper.* 3 *vols. imperial 8vo. cloth, uncut.*
Boston, 1866.
LARGE PAPER; 100 *copies.*

2350 ——— ANOTHER COPY. Small paper. 2 vols. 8vo. new cloth.
Boston, 1866.

2351 WESLEY, REV. JOHN. JOURNAL, with corrections and additions; also, numerous translations and notes by John Emory. 2 *vols.* 8vo. sheep. New York, N. D.

2352 WESLEY, SAMUEL (Father of John Wesley). The LIFE of our Blessed Lord and Saviour JESUS CHRIST. An Heroic Poem in ten books. *With* 60 *large and finely executed portraits, and scenes from the life of our Saviour, by* FAITHORNE. *Fine impressions.* Folio, calf, gilt, nice copy. London, 1694.

2353 WEST, MRS. Poems and Plays. 2 vols. 12mo. *russia, gilt.*
Whittingham, London, 1799.

2354 WESTCOTT, THOMPSON. Names of Persons who took the Oath of Allegiance to the State of Pennsylvania between the years 1777 and 1789, with a History of the "Test Laws" of Pennsylvania. *Folio, uncut.* *J. Campbell*, Philadelphia, 1865.
LARGEST PAPER; *only* 25 *copies.*

2355 WESTERHOVIUS, ARN-HENR. HIEROGLYPHICA of MERKBOELDEN, der oude volkeren namentlyk Egyptenaren, Chaldeeuwen, Feniciers, Joden, Grieken, Romeynen, &c., (Holl.) *with 63 beautifully executed etchings on copper by* ROMEYN DE HOOGE. *Roy. 4to. hf. morocco, uncut.* Amsterdam, 1735.

2356 [WESTMACOTT, CHARLES MOLLOY.] ENGLISH SPY, an Original Work, Characteristic, Humorous, and Satirical, comprising Sketches of every rank of Society, *with numerous characteristic (colored) engravings by Cruikshank.* 2 *thick vols. roy. 8vo. hf. red morocco, uncut, very scarce.* London, 1826.
> This work was continued by the same editor, under the title of "The St. James Royal Magazine."

2357 WESTMINSTER REVIEW, complete from its commencement in January, 1824, to July, 1865, WITH 2 INDEXES. 58 vols. *8vo. neatly bound, maroon calf, very neat, and the balance in numbers, together 65 vols.* London, 1824–65.
> Wants Nos. for Jan. 1853 and Oct. 1855, otherwise perfect.

2358 WESTWOOD, T. CHRONICLE OF THE 'COMPLEAT ANGLER' of Izaak Walton and Charles Cotton, being a Bibliographical Record of its various Phases and Mutations, *elegantly printed in the old style, on toned paper, by Whittingham,* sm. 4to. *hf. bd. uncut.* London, 1864.

2359 WHARTON, GRACE and PHILIP. WITS and BEAUX of Society. *Illustrated.* 2 *vols. 8vo. new cloth.* London, 1867.

2360 WHEATLEY, PHILLIS. Letters. *8vo. hf. mor. uncut.* *Privately Printed,* Boston, 1864.
> 100 *copies.*

2361 WHEELER, J. TALBOYS. HISTORY OF INDIA from the earliest Ages. Maps, &c. 2 *thick vols. 8vo. new cloth.* London, 1867.

2362 WHISTON, WILLIAM. New Theory of the Earth, from its original to the consummation of all things. 6th Edition. *8vo. hf. calf, neat* London, 1755.

2363 WHITE, REV. GILBERT. NATURAL HISTORY and ANTIQUITIES of Selbourne, with the Naturalist's Calendar and miscellaneous observations extracted from his papers. Edited with notes by E. T. Bennett. BEST LIBRARY EDITION, *profusely illustrated with engravings on wood by Thompson, Nesbit, &c. 8vo. calf, extra, gilt edges.* London, 1837.

2364 WHITING, WILLIAM. War Powers under the Constitution of the United States. *8vo. cloth.* Boston, 1864.

2365 WHITMORE, W. H. HANDBOOK of AMERICAN GENEALOGY; or Catalogue of Family Histories, &c. *Roy. 4to. hf. green morocco, gilt top.* *Munsell,* Albany, 1862.
> LARGE PAPER, *few printed.*

2366 WHITMORE, WM. H. Handbook of American Genealogy; being A Catalogue of family Histories and Publications containing Genealogical Information, chronologically arranged. *Small 4to. hf. morocco, sprinkled edges.* *Munsell,* Albany, 1862.

2367 —— Another copy. *8vo. uncut.* Albany, 1863.

2368 WHITMORE, W. H. Brief Genealogy of the Descendants of William Hutchinson and Thomas Oliver. *4to. uncut.* Boston, 1865.

2369 WHITNEY, P. The HISTORY of the COUNTY of WORCESTER, in the Commonwealth of Massachusetts. With a Particular Account of every Town from its first Settlement to the Present Time; including its Ecclesiastical State, together with a Geographical Description of the same. *8vo. sheets, folded.*
Worcester: *Isaiah Thomas*, MDCCXCIII.

Very scarce.

2370 WHITTAKER, JOHN. MARY, QUEEN OF SCOTS, VINDICATED. 3 *vols. 8vo. cf. gilt.* London, 1790.

2371 WHITWORTH, CHARLES, *Lord.* An account of Russia as it was in the year 1700. *Vignette.* 12*mo. original tree-calf, gilt.*
Strawberry-Hill, 1758.

From the Catalogue of the Strawberry-Hill publications it appears that there were only 700 copies struck off.

2372 WHORES' RHETORICK, calculated to the Meridian of London. (London, 1683, 8vo.) *Vignette, and plate containing* 12 *portraits. Sml. 4to. hf. morocco, uncut.* *Reprinted,* Edinburgh, 1836.
VERY SCARCE; *only 50 copies printed.*

The daughter of a poor nobleman with a large family is instructed by a court-ezan (Mme. Creswell) who makes up to her, in the mysteries of her profession, and receives fifteen wholesome lectures in Rhetorick, to enable her to pursue successfully the calling she proposes to follow.

2373 WECKENDEN, J. FREDERICK. Seven Days in Attica in the Summer of 1852. ORIGINAL DRAWING, *and numerous plates inserted. Impl. 8vo. cloth, uncut.* London, 1857.

2374* WIELAND'S OBERON, a Poem. Translated from the German, in Verse, by W. Sotheby, with 12 *fine engravings from designs by Fuseli, inserted.* 2 *vols. in one,* 12*mo. half morocco, uncut.*
London, 1805.

2374 WIGGLESWORTH, MICHAEL. The Day of Doom; or, a description of the great and last Judgment. 12*mo. cloth.* London, 1715.
Reprinted, New York, 1867.

2375 WILKES CHARLES. NARRATIVE OF THE UNITED STATES EXPLORING EXPEDITION, during the years 1838, '39, '40, '41, '42. *Numerous fine engravings on steel, and several hundred woodcuts, Maps, &c.* 6 *vols. impl. 8vo. cloth, uncut.*
Philadelphia, 1845.

2376 WILKES. EXPLORING EXPEDITION. CASSIN'S MAMMALOGY and ORNITHOLOGY of the United States Exploring Expedition under Commodore Wilkes. 1 vol. 4to. with a folio *Atlas of over* 50 *beautiful colored steel engravings, executed under the superintendence of John Cassin,* Member of the Academy of Natural Sciences.
Philadelphia, 1858.

Only 150 copies published, at $50 each.

2377 WILKINS, J. MATHEMATICALL MAGICK, or the Wonders that may be performed by Mechanicall Geometry. 16*mo.* (8vo.) *calf, neat.*
London, 1648.

Curious and rare.

2378 WILKINSON, SIR G. ANCIENT EGYPTIANS, the Manners and Customs of. BOTH SERIES, *with numerous engravings, many of which are colored.* 6 *vols. 8vo. tree-calf, extra, gilt edges, scarce.*
London, 1837–41.

A BEAUTIFUL COPY. BEST EDITION.

2379 WILLIAMS, ELEAZER. Life of Te-ho-ra-gwa-ne-gen, alias Thomas Williams, a Chief of the Caughnawaga Tribe of Indians in Canada. *8vo. hf. morocco, gilt top.* Albany: *Munsell*, 1859. 200 *copies printed.*

2380 WILLIAMS, H. W. SELECT VIEWS IN GREECE, with Classical Illustrations. *Sixty-four fine views engraved in the best line-manner by eminent Artists. 2 vols. in 1. Imperial 8vo. richly bound by Wright in green morocco, extra gilt, gilt edges.* London, 1829.

2381 WILLIAMS' SELECTION of COMIC SONGS, *with a fine series of humorous etchings printed on tinted paper, the whole engraved on copper. Sq. 12mo. hf. mor.* London, N. D. Very scarce. At p. 72 will be found Matthews' song of " General Jackson."

2382 WILLIAMSON AND HOWITT. ORIENTAL FIELD SPORTS, being a complete, detailed, and accurate description of the Field Sports of the East, with Original, Authentic, and Curious Anecdotes. 50 *large and finely* COLORED *plates of the Wild Sports of the East. 2 vols. roy. 4to. citron morocco, extra, gilt edges.* London, 1819. FINE COPY.

2383 WILLIS, THOMAS. Two DISCOURSES concerning the SOUL of BRUTES, which is that of the Vital and Sensitive of Man. Physiological and Pathological. Translated by S. Pordage (the famous mystical writer). *Curious old copper plates, folio calf, very neat.* London, 1683.

2384 WILMOT, SIR JOHN EARDLEY. MEMOIRS OF THE LIFE OF, with selections from his Correspondence. *Brilliant Portrait, and two Autograph Letters, inserted. Roy. 4to. crimson morocco, gilt edges.* London, 1802. *Very scarce.*

2385 WILSON, DANIEL. PREHISTORIC MAN, researches into the Origin of Civilization in the Old and New World. *Colored front. and numerous engravings on wood, thick 8vo. new cloth.* ·London, 1865.

2386 WILSON, PROF. DANIEL. PREHISTORIC ANNALS of SCOTLAND. 2d *Edition, profusely illustrated. 2 vols. 8vo. new cloth, uncut.* Cambridge, 1863.

2387 WILSON, HORACE HAYMAN. WORKS, comprising: Essays on the Religion of the Hindus, 2 vols.—Essays on Sanskrit Literature, 3 vols.—Vishñu Paráña, 4 vols. *Together 9 vols. 8vo. new cloth, uncut,* SCARCE. London, 1862, &c. " Three works, which, for usefulness, depth of learning, and wide range of research, show him to have been the worthy successor of Sir Wm. Jones and H. T. Colebrooke."

2388 WILSON, H. H. RIG-VEDA SANLUTÁ. A collection of Antient Hindu Hymns, constituting the first Ashtaka or Book, of the Rig-Veda; the oldest authority for the Religious and Social Institutions of the Hindus. *8vo. cloth.* London, 1866.

2389 WILSON, JAMES. COMPLETE DICTIONARY OF ASTROLOGY, in which every technical and abstruse term is correctly explained, and the various systems of the most approved authors defined, &c., &c. *8vo. bds. scarce.* London, 1819.

2390 WILSON, JOHN. NOCTES AMBROSIANÆ. Revised edition, with Memoirs and Notes, by R. Shelton Mackenzie. *Portraits.* 5 *vols. imp. 8vo. cloth.* New York, 1863.
LARGE PAPER ; 100 *copies privately printed.*

2391 ———— Another copy. 5 vols. LARGE PAPER, *cloth.*
New York, 1863.

2392 WILSON, JOHN. RECREATIONS OF CHRISTOPHER NORTH. *Fine portraits.* 2 vols. *crown 8vo. hf. cf. extra.* Edinburgh, 1865.

2393 WILSON, J. PHRASES ; a Treatise on the History and Structure of the Different Languages of the World. *Portrait. Impl. 8vo. bds. uncut.* *Munsell*, Albany, 1864.
LARGE PAPER.

2394 WILSON, JOHN MACKAY. TALES OF THE BORDERS OF SCOTLAND, Historical, Traditionary, and Imaginative, with Illustrative Glossary by Capt. P. Brown. *Portrait.* 6 *vols. roy. 8vo. hf. cf. neat, uncut edges.* New York, 1848.

2395 **WILSON, BONAPARTE, AND JARDINE. AMERICAN ORNITHOLOGY,** or Natural History of the Birds of the United States. 97 *plates, comprising nearly* 400 BEAUTIFULLY COLORED *figures of birds.* 3 vols. 8vo. *new hf. green morocco, gilt tops, uncut edges.* Edinburgh, 1832.
FINE COPY, *scarce.*

2396 WINKLES' CATHEDRALS. ARCHITECTURAL and PICTURESQUE ILLUSTRATIONS of the Cathedral Churches of England and Wales. 181 *finely executed engravings, from drawings made expressly for the work, by Robert Garland,* with descriptions by Moule. 3 *vols. imp. 8vo. hf. morocco, gilt tops. Fine copy.*
London, 1836.

2397 WINKWORTH, CATHERINE. Christian Singers of Germany, *numerous fine portraits.* 12mo. *new hf. cf. extra.*
Philadelphia (London), 1869.

2398 WINSLOW, CHARLES FREDERICK. FORCE and NATURE, Attraction and Repulsion, &c., &c. 8vo. *new cloth.*
London [Philadelphia], 1869.

2399 WINTHROP, JNO. HISTORY of NEW ENGLAND from 1630 to 1649, from his Original Manuscripts, with Notes, &c. by James Savage. *Portraits, &c.* 2 *vols. 8vo. new hf. morocco, gilt top, uncut.* Boston, 1853.

2400 WINTHROP, R. C. LIFE and LETTERS of JOHN WINTHROP, Gov. of the Massachusetts Bay Company, at their emigration in 1630. *Beautifully printed. Portrait.* 8vo. *boards, uncut.*
Boston, 1864.

2401 WINWOOD, Sir R. MEMORIALS of AFFAIRS of STATE in the Reigns of Queen Elizabeth and King James I. *Fine portrait by Vertue.* 3 vols. folio, *calf, neat.* London, 1725
Most curious and valuable State Papers, including the Negotiations of Sir H. Neville, Sir C. Cornwallis, Sir D. Carleton, Sir T. Edmondes, &c. at the Courts of France, Spain, Holland, &c.

2402 WIRT, WILLIAM. Discourse on the Lives and Characters of Thomas Jefferson and John Adams. 8vo. pp. 69, *paper.*
Washington, 1826.

2403 WITCHCRAFT. A DISCOURSE of WITCHES, or Deceivers of Nine
Sortes; Idolaters, Divines, Astrologers, Conjecturers, Juglers,
Charmers, Oracle Givers, Soothsayers, and Necromancers, &c.
Sml. 4to. pp. 140, *paper. Wants Title.* London.

2404 WITCHCRAFT. TRIAL of JENNET PRESTON, of Gisborne in Craven,
at the York Assizes, July, 1612, for practising devilish and
wicked arts called Witchcraft. Vignette. PRINTED ON VELLUM, *on
one side only, post 8vo. cloth.* RARE. London, 1851.
UNIQUE, *the only copy printed on vellum,* and 60 copies on paper.

2405 WITCHCRAFT. MARY SCHWEIDLER, the Amber Witch, translated
from the German by Lady Duff Gordon. *12mo. boards.*
New York, 1845.
"The most interesting trial for witchcraft ever known, printed from an imperfect MS. by her father, Abraham Schweidler, Pastor of Coserow, in the island
of Usedom."

2406 WITCHCRAFT. A Tryal of Witches, at the Assizes held at Bury St.
Edmonds, March 10th, 1664, before Sir Matthew Hale. *8vo.
hf. crimson morocco,* scarce.
London, 1682, *Reprinted,* London, 1838.

2407 WITHER, GEORGE. FAIR VIRTUE, the Mistress of Philárete ————
The SHEPHERD'S HUNTING, reprinted from the edition of 1622.
Portrait. Post 8vo. half mor. Bristol, 1840.

2408 WITHER, GEORGE. HALLELUJAH, and HYMNS and SONGS, with
Introductions, &c. by Edward Farr. *Portraits.* 2 vols. 12mo.
tree-marbled calf, extra. Russell Smith, London, 1857.

2409 WRIGHT, THOMAS. ANECDOTA LITTERARIA; A Collection of
Short Poems in English, Latin, and French, illustrative of the
History and Literature of England in the XIIIth century. *8vo.
cloth, uncut.* London, 1844.
SCARCE, *only 250 copies printed.*

2410 WRIGHT, THOMAS. CARICATURE HISTORY of the GEORGES, or Annals
of the House of Hanover, compiled from the Squibs, Broad-
sides, Window Pictures, Lampoons, and Pictorial Caricatures
of the Time, *illustrated by nearly* 400 *engravings, frontispiece
colored, 4to. half morocco, roxburghe style, top edge gilt.* LARGE
PAPER. London, 1867.
Only 100 copies of this *large paper edition have been printed;* it contains two
portraits in addition to those in the small paper edition.

2411 WRIGHT, THOMAS. CARICATURE HISTORY of the GEORGES; or
Annals of the House of Hanover, &c. *Colored front. and
numerous engravings on wood, thick post 8vo. new cloth.*
London, 1867.

2412 WRIGHT, THOMAS. The CELT, the ROMAN, and the SAXON; a history of the Early Inhabitants of Britain, down to the conversion of the Anglo-Saxons to Christianity, *engravings on wood.*
Crown 8vo. *cloth, uncut.* O. P. London, 1861.

2413 WRIGHT, THOMAS. Essays on Subjects connected with the Literature, Popular Superstitions, and History of England in the
Middle Ages. *2 vols. crown 8vo. new cloth.* London, 1846.

31

2414 WRIGHT, THOMAS. LOUTHIANA; or, an Introduction to the ANTI-QUITIES of IRELAND, in upwards of 90 views, plans, &c., repre-senting the principal Ruins, Curiosities, Ancient Dwellings, &c. 3 *parts complete.* Royal 4to. cf. *neat, scarce.* London, 1748.

2415 WOLLSTONCRAFT, MARY. VINDICATION of the RIGHTS of WOMAN, with Strictures on Moral and Political Subjects. Vol. I. (all published). *8vo. calf, scarce.* London, 1796.

2416 WOMAN'S WORK in the CIVIL WAR. A Record of Heroism, Patriotism, and Patience, by L. P. Brockett, D.D. *Portraits.* Thick 8vo. cloth. Philadelphia, 1867.

2417 Woman in Black. *12mo. cloth.* Philadelphia.

2418 WOOD'S ARCHITECTURAL ANTIQUITIES and RUINS of PALMYRA and BALBEC, *upwards of 100 fine engravings, some very large and folding.* FINE EARLY IMPRESSIONS, 2 *vols. imp. folio in one, hf. calf gilt, fine copy.* *Pickering,* London, 1827.

One of the most splendid works ever published, and its accuracy is equal to its beauty. Succeeding travelers are all indebted more or less to Wood's de-lineations and descriptions.

2419 (WOOD, MRS.) AUTHENTIC RECORDS of the COURT of ENGLAND for the last Seventy years. *Colored front. 8vo. boards, uncut.* London, 1832.

VERY SCARCE, suppressed.
"The whole history of England does not present two reigns of equal enormi-ty to those of Queen Charlotte and her equally infamous son, George IV. *Baseness* of every kind was practised, and *murder became an every day occur-rence. Deception and villany* were esteemed *virtues ;* while *incest and adultery* proved passports to *court favor and promotion."—Preface.*

2420 WOOD, THOMAS. An Inquiry concerning the Primitive Inhabitants of Ireland. *8vo. boards, uncut. Very scarce.* London, 1821.

2421 WOOD, WILLIAM. NEW ENGLAND'S PROSPECT. Roy. 4to. *uncut.* *Prince Society,* Boston, 1865.

LARGE PAPER; 20 *copies printed* (17).

2422 WOODWARD'S HISTORICAL SERIES, complete, com-prising: RECORDS of SALEM WITCHCRAFT, 1691–92, 2 vols. HUBARD'S INDIAN WARS, 2 vols. DRAKE'S WITCHCRAFT DE-LUSION in NEW ENGLAND, 3 vols. HISTORICAL ACCOUNT of AMERICAN PAPER CURRENCY, 2 vols. *All beautifully printed by Munsell on heavy paper.* 9 vols. roy. 4to. *uncut.* Roxbury, Mass., 1864, &c.

LARGE PAPER; *only 20 copies printed.*

2423 WOODWARD'S HISTORY of WALES from the earliest time to its final Incorporation with England. *Numerous highly finished steel en-gravings.* 2 vols. TOURIST in WALES, comprising: *Picturesque Scenery, Towns, Castles, Antiquities, Seats of the Nobility,* &c. 50 fine engravings. 1 vol. Together 3 vols. roy. 8vo. hf. red calf, extra. London, (1850).

2424 WOODWARD, GEO. E. and F. W. COUNTRY HOMES. *Profusely illus-trated. 12mo. new cloth.* New York, 1865.

2425 WOODWORTH, JOHN. REMINISCENCES of TROY, from its Settlement in 1790 to 1807. Second Edition, with Notes. *Sm. 4to. cloth, uncut.* *Albany, 1860.*

2426 WOOLNOTH, THOMAS. STUDY of the HUMAN FACE. *Illustrated by twenty-six full-page engravings on steel.* 8vo. new cloth.
London, 1865.

2427 WOOLRYCH, H. W. Lives of Eminent [Serjeants-at-Law of the English Bar. 2 *vols.* 8vo. *new cloth.* London, 1869.

2428 WORLD'S DOOM, or the Cabinet of Fate unlocked; containing all the ancient and modern prophecies relative to the present and nearly approaching times. 2 *vols.* 12mo. *hf. cf. Curious.*
London, 1795.

2429 WORLD of WONDERS; a Record of Things wonderful in Nature, Science, and Art. *Several hundred engravings on wood. Imp.* 8vo. *new cloth, extra gilt.* London, N. D.

2430 WORCESTER, MARQUIS OF. CENTURY of INVENTIONS; the Life, Times, and Scientific Labors of the Second Marquis of Worcester. To which is added a Reprint of the Century of Inventions, 1863, with a Commentary thereon, by HENRY DIRCKS, C. E. *Portraits and wood-cuts.* 8vo. *new cloth.*
London, 1865.

2431 WORTH, GORHAM A. RANDOM RECOLLECTIONS of ALBANY, from 1800 to 1808. *3d edition,* with Notes by J. Munsell. *Imp.* 8vo. *uncut.* Albany, 1866.
LARGE PAPER.

2432 WORSDALE, JOHN. CELESTIAL PHILOSOPHY, or Genethliacal Astronomy; containing the only true method of calculating Nativitis, &c. 8vo. *hf. cf. neat, scarce.* London, (1819).

2433 WYATT, D. INDUSTRIAL ARTS of the NINETEENTH CENTURY; a *Series of Illustrations of the choicest specimens produced by every Nation* at the GREAT EXHIBITION of WORKS of INDUSTRY, 1851. 2 vols. roy. folio, *with 158 elaborate plates, executed in the exact* COLORS *of the originals,* SCULPTURES, METAL-WORK, TEXTILE FABRICS, LACE and EMBROIDERY, PORCELAIN, WOOD and IVORY CARVING, etc. (pub. £17. 17*s.* in bds.) *hf. bd. morocco, gilt edges, an original copy.* 1851.
This beautiful work forms in itself a perfect cyclopædia of Design in all branches of Art. The plates have the appearance of original paintings, and have never been surpassed in gorgeousness of coloring.

2434 WYCHERLY, WILLIAM. The WORKS of the ingenious Mr. Wm. Wycherly, collected into one volume. Containing the Plain Dealer, Country Wife, Gentleman Dancing-Master, Love in a Wood. 8vo. *polished calf, super-extra, yellow edges.* London, 1713.
SPLENDID COPY. Best Edition.
"Wycherly was a writer of infinite spirit, satire, and wit."—*Pope.*

2435 WYNNE, JAMES, M.D. PRIVATE LIBRARIES OF NEW YORK. *Imperial* 8vo. *hf. cf. extra, gilt top, uncut edges. Contains a duplicate impression, on India paper, of the plate representing the interior of Mr. Noyes' library.* New York, 1860.
LARGE PAPER; *only 100 copies.* Among the principal libraries mentioned in this work, are those of John Allan, George Bancroft, Thomas P. Barton, J. Carson Brevoort, Rev. Dr. Chapin, Almon W. Griswold, William Menzies, William Curtis Noyes, Dr. Purple, Geo. T. Strong, R. L. Stuart, and Richard Grant White.

2436 Wynter, Andrew. Curiosities of Civilization. A Series of Essays. 12mo. new cloth. London, (1868.)

2437 YALE COLLEGE. Catalogue of Books in the Library of Yale College in New Haven. *12mo.* (*pp.* 44), *hf. morocco, uncut.*
New Haven, 1755.

Very Rare.

2438 Youmans, E. L. Correlation and Conservation of Forces, a series of compositions by Profs. Grove, Helmholtz, Faraday, Liebig, &c. 12*mo. new cloth.* New York, 1865.

2439 Young, Archibald. Historical Sketch of the French Bar, from its origin to the present day, &c. *8vo. new cloth.*
Edinburgh, 1869.

2440 Young, Alex. Chronicles of the first Planters of the Colony of Massachusetts Bay from 1623 to 1636, from Original sources. *Portraits. 8vo. cloth, uncut.* Boston, 1846.

2441 Yonge, Charles Duke. Life and Administration of Robert Banks, second Earl of Liverpool. *Fine portrait.* Compiled from original documents. 3 vols. 8*vo. new cloth.*
London, 1868.

2442 [Yonge, Miss.] History of Christian Names. 2 thick volumes. 12*mo. new hf. morocco, uncut.* London, 1863.

2443 Zimmerman, J. Geo. Essay on National Pride, also Observations on Religious, Republican, and Monarchical Pride. *Beautiful plates, after Uwins. Post 8vo. cf. neat.* London, 1805.

INDEX.

THE TROW & SMITH BOOK MANUFACTURING COMPANY,
205-213 E. 12TH STREET, NEW YORK.

Printed in Dunstable, United Kingdom